Black Huntington

Black Huntington

An Appalachian Story

CICERO M. FAIN III

UNIVERSITY OF ILLINOIS PRESS
Urbana, Chicago, and Springfield

© 2019 by the Board of Trustees
of the University of Illinois
All rights reserved
1 2 3 4 5 C P 5 4 3 2 1
♾ This book is printed on acid-free paper.

Library of Congress Cataloging-in-Publication Data
Names: Fain, Cicero M. III, 1958– author.
Title: Black Huntington: an Appalachian story / Cicero M. Fain III.
Description: Urbana: University of Illinois Press, [2019] | Significant
 revision of author's thesis (doctoral)—Ohio State University, 2009,
 titled Race, river, and the railroad: Black Huntington, West Virginia,
 1871–1929. | Includes bibliographical references and index. |
Identifiers: LCCN 2019001712 (print) | LCCN 2019005745 (ebook) | ISBN
 9780252051432 (ebook) | ISBN 9780252042591 (cloth : alk. paper) |
 ISBN 9780252084423 (pbk. : alk. paper)
Subjects: LCSH: African Americans—West Virginia—Huntington—
 History—19th century. | African Americans—West Virginia—
 Huntington—History—20th century. | African Americans—West
 Virginia—Huntington—Social conditions—19th century. | African
 Americans—West Virginia—Huntington—Social conditions—20th
 century. | African Americans—Migrations—History—19th century.
 | African Americans—Migrations—History—20th century. |
 Migration, Internal—United States—History—19th century. |
 Migration, Internal—United States—History—20th century.
Classification: LCC F249.H95 (ebook) | LCC F249.H95 F35 2019 (print) |
 DDC 975.4/0496073—dc23
LC record available at https://lccn.loc.gov/2019001712

Cover illustration: First Taxi in Huntington, W.Va., Dan Hill and his horse drawn
wagon, circa 1873. Source: West Virginia History On View, West Virginia &
Regional History Center, WVU Libraries.

To Black Huntingtonians, past, present, and future.

Contents

Preface ix

Acknowledgments xv

Chapter 1. The African American Experience in Cabell County, Virginia / West Virginia, 1825–1870 1

Chapter 2. The "Grapevine Telegraph": Post-Emancipation Black Community and Early Black Migrant Influx, 1865–1871 22

Chapter 3. Into the Crucible: The Chesapeake and Ohio Railroad and the Black Industrial Worker, 1870–1900 45

Chapter 4. Community, Race, and Class: Black Settlement Patterns, 1871–Early 1900s 70

Chapter 5. Institutional Development, Public Space, and Political Aspiration in Early Huntington, 1870–Early 1900s 93

Chapter 6. Spreading Our Wings: Afro-Huntingtonian Progress during the Era of "Benevolent Segregation" 117

Appendix A. Virginia Slave Totals, 1860 147

Appendix B. Occupational Statistics for Huntington's African American Population 149

Notes 157

Bibliography 215

Index 237

Preface

On a pristine Saturday in early May 2009, I drove to Indianapolis, Indiana, to attend the fiftieth birthday party of Billy "Doc" Garrett, a lifelong friend of mine. Among the other partygoers that night were other long-time friends, including one whose association with me dates back to serving on the safety patrol in grade school. The next afternoon, five of us gathered on the back deck of Billy's house and reminisced about growing up in Huntington. Over the next few hours, we ate party leftovers, drank beer, and warmly (and, not infrequently, loudly) discussed, laughed, needled, lamented, and commemorated our experiences in black Huntington. Through the rose-tinted glasses of nostalgia, we remembered baskets made, footballs caught, girls courted (and lost), front-porch visits, stupid things done, church trips taken, and friends and family who had passed on. Interestingly, to a man, we recalled our formative years in the city fondly, with one stating, "I wouldn't have traded it for anything." It occurred to me then, that for many of us the years in Huntington had been the best years of our lives.

Unlike so many, to us, community was no notion; it was a foundational force in our lives, demonstrated in the intergenerational, interclass alliances and associations linking and binding us. It existed in the lives and deeds of African American teachers, postal workers, lawyers, factory laborers, preachers and parishioners, hustlers, and "players" who shaped our lives in subtle and explicit ways. It existed on the playgrounds, sports fields, churches, street corners, schools, basements, pool halls, and front porches of our neighborhoods where we played, congregated, learned, partied, and worshipped. At that time we didn't know that the experiences of our formative years would be, well, formative. That the lessons of our youth—to develop character, to be goal-oriented, to rely on faith, to demonstrate resiliency, to be good-humored, and to be compassionate—would provide the key elements needed to be productive, self-reliant, moral adults. Three generations of my family grew up in Huntington, with each generation building upon the labor and sacrifice of the previous. Before becoming a factory laborer at the now-defunct International Nickle Company, my grandfather worked as a butler. Before becoming a regional human resources manager for BASF, my father was a factory laborer. Before obtaining my PhD in history, I worked as a paperboy and then as a salesman at Sears and, later, at Keen Jewelers. None of these accomplishments would have occurred without the sacrifice, support, and strength of many women who also labored, in a variety of ways, to move the family forward. My family story, like so many of yours, is a quintessential American story.

Certainly, this ethos extends and compels many black Huntingtonians to return to the Douglass High School Black Alumni Reunion, which, since 1973, has been held every two years in the city. Yet, as more and more Douglassites die, the abiding intergenerational ties and enduring collective impulse linking black Huntingtonians wane. In response to this reality and in an effort to recognize and reify the social and familiar connections, a combined Douglass-Huntington High School Black Alumni Reunion was held for the first time in August 2009.[1] Since then, alumni, their children (and grandchildren), and extended family members have met every two years to commemorate the history and legacy of the two schools, to party and fellowship, and to commune and celebrate. It is a remarkable thing, this pilgrimage! Indeed, so important was it for my mom, severely weakened by cancer, to attend the 2007 reunion that she ignored doctor's orders against travel. Through sheer force of will, she basked in the well-wishes, hugs, compliments, and laughter of the weekend. By Sunday, though, she was too weak to make the return trip home. Within eight days she was dead.

At one point during the course of the afternoon birthday party I stepped into the kitchen and began chatting with Billy's father, a long-time Huntingtonian, and, for the first time during our acquaintanceship, with Billy's wife. It was a warm, intimate conversation, flavored with abiding affection for the elder, who worked long hours for many years in Huntington's factory economy to raise his family. While filling my plate with the leftover chicken, greens, and dirty rice, and probing as historians do, I discovered to my great surprise that Billy's wife and mother of their three children is the daughter of Susan Spencer and thus a descendant of the "Burlington 37." How remarkable! I thought. To be face to face with a descendant of that pioneering group of black migrants who settled into Burlington, Ohio, in 1849, across the river from Huntington, many of whom shaped black Huntington's metamorphosis.

Driving down I-70 to Columbus Sunday evening, radio off and window down, I savored the profundity of the day's event, of the synchronicity and serendipity between my (our) personal history and my professional interests. Though bemused (and a little dismayed) over my inability to retain the same level of recall of the people and places informing the old neighborhood and community as my friends, the trip had been gratifying, nourishing, and edifying. It had presented an opportunity to discover through the communion with lifelong friends the richness and uniqueness of our black experience in Huntington. It had reminded me that, at my core, I am a black Huntingtonian.

The trip also reaffirmed to me the importance of asking questions. It was this impulse that compelled me to ask, Why hasn't anyone done a scholarly study on black Huntington? Here, I thought, was a story waiting to be told! Why, given the history, vibrancy, and resonance of the experience, given the stories I've heard, the names spoken, the faces remembered, and the experiences recounted, had no one gathered the various threads and patches of fabric to construct the quilt of historic memory? Some years later I posed a similar question to Mrs. Edna Duckworth, the last of the black community historians, as we sat in her small senior-citizen apartment. Her response was to hand me a short, unpublished manuscript, "A Black History of Huntington." I departed her company with a conviction to build upon her research. With equal parts pride, impulsivity, and naivety, I started the process to put to pen to paper, flesh to bone, so to speak. Its culmination is this study. Needless to say, as a third-generation black Huntingtonian, attempting to separate myth from reality and reconcile sentiment with evidence wasn't an easy process, but it has been a deeply satisfying one. Thus, this is a personal and scholarly mission to chronicle and to better understand the seminal period of a black past heretofore available in bits and pieces, in front-porch conversations and street-corner rhetoric, photo albums and barber shops, school and church anniversary programs, biographies and local histories, dining-room recollections and newspaper articles, court records and census data, manuscript collections and slave testimonies, but not previously rendered in a comprehensive scholarly examination.

The story of black Huntington is a story of agency. From its formation as the transshipment hub of the Chesapeake and Ohio Railroad, Huntington experienced remarkable growth between 1871 and 1930. Drawn by the promise of jobs, opportunity, and self-determination, hundreds, then thousands flowed into the burgeoning village. Huntington's development proved a magnet for black migrants seeking jobs, improved housing, and social linkages. Looking for alternatives to sharecropping, tenant farming, and patronage, and utilizing kin and social networks, black migrants traveled long distances—not infrequently hundreds of miles over the central Appalachian Mountains to reach the town. There, they navigated an even harsher terrain: the forces of segregation, racism, industrialization, and urbanization. The genesis of the black Huntington's working class was a complicated and contested process encompassing differing oppositional strategies that produced varying degrees and interpretations of success. Lacking formal education, job mobility, and political representation, the first generation of black migrants faced formidable impediments and challenges to the achievement of its aspirations. Yet Huntington also offered liberating forces—a racial climate infused with tolerance, if not respect, proximity and sociocultural connections to historically black enclaves, opportunities for gainful employment, vibrant black institutions, the ability to purchase property, the potential of political action, and other benefits of urban circumstance—each playing a role in ensuring the black southern migrant remained.

Black Huntington's accomplishments are impressive and important. Black labor helped build the city and make it prosperous. Their labor also helped initiate the industrialization of southern West Virginia and link the town to regional and national markets, fueling impressive economic and population growth in it throughout the late-nineteenth and early-twentieth century. Within months of settlement, illiterate black migrants initiated the foundational process of institution building necessary for the formation of black Huntington, a process that continues to shape, albeit in a different and diminished manner, contemporary black Huntington. From the humble beginnings of Mt. Olive Baptist Church, situated in a log cabin, to the eventual establishment of Douglass High School, the city's first black high school, Huntington's black residents agitated for change. Property acquisition was one avenue they used. Throughout the Jim Crow era, savvy and ambitious black residents acquired property—so much so, that by 1924 black Huntingtonians owned a higher percentage of property than any other black residential population in the state. Further, in the black population's quest to live where they wanted, the local chapter of the National Association of the Advancement of Colored People (NAACP) initiated the 1929 legal challenge to restrictive covenants within the city. The victory in *White v. White* struck down the legality of such restrictions throughout the state. In truth, black Huntingtonians shaped greater Huntington's economic, political, social, and cultural development.

Forced to respond to the diverse strivings and successes of black Huntingtonians, white Huntingtonians embraced the tenets and manifestations of Jim Crowism as ways to constrict and constrain black agency and autonomy. Yet evidence indicates that black Huntingtonians abided rather than succumbed to life in a segregated, constraining environment. Their victories may have been small, but they were not inconsequential. In this manner, their story articulates and embodies the American ideal. Though compromised by southern ideologies, attitudes, and practices of race, black Huntingtons made the kind of progress that suggests a distinctiveness not merely regional but national in scope. Examination of black Huntingtonians' struggles provides insights into the multifaceted and nuanced character of African American resistance during the late nineteenth and early twentieth century, offering opportunities to interrogate the complicated operations of race, class, and gender within the fluid dynamics of social and power relationships. It is my sincere hope that this study does justice to their sacrifices, strivings, and successes.

Acknowledgments

This book is the culmination of a concerted, on-again, off-again, five-year distillation of my graduate research at The Ohio State University. Any acknowledgement therefore must start with the foundational assistance, counsel, and guidance of Stephanie Shaw, Kenneth Goings, and Stephen Hall. As this study was completed while I was employed as a Carter G. Woodson Fellow at Marshall University, I wish to thank the Office of the Provost, Division of Multicultural Affairs, Marshall University Graduate College, Center of African American Student Programs, my former students, and my former colleagues in the History Department for their assistance, encouragement, and enthusiasm. I would be remiss if I failed to mention the guys of the NBA (the Noon Basketball Association) at Marshall and my fellow "baller" grad students at OSU, who, week in, week out, provided me the best stress reliever I could have asked for. I also thank the staffs of Marshall University's Morrow Library, Boyd County (Kentucky) Library, Chesapeake and Ohio Historical Society, Cabell County Public Library, Huntington Herald-Dispatch, KYOWVA Genealogical Society, Briggs-Lawrence County (Ohio) Library, State Library of Ohio, Ohio Historical Society, Gallia County (Ohio) Public Library, Gallia County (Ohio) Historical Society, John Gee Black Historical Society (Gallipolis, Ohio), Nelsonville (Ohio) Public Library, Summers County (West Virginia) Public Library, Virginia Historical Society, State Library of Virginia, West Virginia University Library, State Library of West Virginia, and West Virginia Humanities Council. The initial research was supported by grants from the Marshall University Division of Multicultural Affairs, Marshall University Graduate College, and West Virginia Humanities Council.

This book is designed to appeal to a broader general audience, so I have excised academic language, concepts, and, in some instances, content in order to tell a *story*. I attribute whatever success I have achieved to that end in significant measure to the insightful, instructive, and cogent critiques of Ron Eller and Bill Turner, my illustrious friend and mentor, who graciously reviewed the prospectus twice. Their enthusiastic support of this study reaffirmed my belief in its importance. Likewise, I extend my deep appreciation to the staff of the University of Illinois Press, especially James Engelhardt, whose professionalism and friendship shepherded me throughout the process. I am also grateful to the assistance of Robert S. Conte and the kind folks at Greenbrier County (West Virginia) Public Library and the Greenbrier Historical Society, whose assistance contributed mightily to the construction of chapter 2. Thank you to the Division of Academic Affairs at the College of Southern Maryland for its support.

I am eternally grateful to my parents, Cicero M. Fain Jr. and Anna M. Fain; my siblings, Darren Fain, Patrick Fain, and Andrea Carelli; my ex-wife, Amina I. Fain; my grandmother, Mrs. Nellie Snow; and local historian Mrs. Edna Duckworth; they have all contributed materially and spiritually to my success. Other key contributors include Betty Cleckley (who was previously vice president of multicultural affairs at Marshall), Captain Nelson Barnett Jr., Phil Carter, Carrie Eldridge, Karen Nance, George Goode, John Moorhead, Owen and Imogene Pleasant, Miya Hunter-Willis, Barbara Brandau, Sandra Clements, Randy Spotts, Delores Johnson, and Wilma Fox.

I am also indebted to the loving support of my family, especially my children, Anas and Aanisah, and my wife, Helen Zublic-Fain, who patiently endured the fits and starts attendant to the challenging and frequently competing priorities of family, academia, and scholarship.

And last, all scholars know that the completion of any substantive historical work is dependent on a number of factors, both concrete and amorphous. I am keenly aware of the awesome serendipity encompassing and informing this book. My deep gratitude extends to the citizens of Huntington and the tri-state region for the numerous ways they demonstrated their faith in me and this project. The unique and collective contributions of all above were critical to the completion of this study. I sincerely hope this book honors your trust and serves as a fitting tribute to the legacy of Black Huntington.

Black Huntington

CHAPTER 1

The African American Experience in Cabell County, Virginia / West Virginia, 1825–1870

In 1865 former slave Mary Lacy faced a range of choices. At the end of the Civil War, after a lifetime of service to various members of the influential Jenkins family of Cabell County, she was free but uncertain. After surviving the nearly quarter-century reign of family patriarch Captain William Jenkins, who in 1825 purchased the immense Greenbottom Plantation from William A. Cabell, former governor of Virginia, and assumed ownership of her and approximately two dozen other slaves, she was *free*. She had survived rape by the lecherous overseer Jenkins hired that had produced George, her son who was now ten years old. She had also survived the five-year rule of Jenkins's

Mary, slave and "nanny" for Jenkins children

Figure 1.1. Mary Lacy, slave and caretaker for the children of Captain William A. and Thomas Jenkins, Cabell County, Va./ W.V. Source: Jenkins Family Collection, courtesy of Victor "Jenkins" Wilson.

son, Confederate Brigadier General Albert G. Jenkins. It was he who, upon the death of his father in 1859, had inherited Mary and her son. Now, having suffered a mortal wound at the Battle of Cloyd's Mountain, Albert Jenkins lay cold in the earth. Now, at age thirty and a single mother, she, along with the remaining residential slave population of Greenbottom, faced the very real prospect of leaving their home, her home since birth, and never looking back.

But history lay heavily upon her, a weight that could not be lifted by decree, victory, or freedom. *Thirty years . . .*

Over the years she had seen the increasing influx of slaveholders drawn by the county's cheap, arable land and strategic location adjacent to the Ohio River near the tri-state area that included southeastern Ohio and eastern Kentucky (see map 1.1).[1] She had also seen their slaves, most of whom accompanied their masters to the dozens of small farms that dotted the region.[2] Unlike Kanawha County, Virginia, to the immediate northeast, from which Cabell County was formed in 1809, it lacked a foundation of industrial slavery. Unlike Jefferson County in the far northeastern panhandle, it lacked the numbers to support plantation slavery.[3] Thus, Cabell County's residential slaves suffered the cruel paradox of slavery: the loneliness attendant to social and geographic isolation as well as the forced dependence and incapacity foundational to the personal relationship between the master and slave. In many cases, slaves separated by miles from the next slave-owning farm and thus unable to associate with other slaves developed attachments with the master's family and, in effect, became members of that family.[4] This was the conundrum Mary grappled with.

She had also seen the growth of Guyandotte, the town formed in 1810 downriver from Greenbottom at the confluence of the Guyandotte and Ohio Rivers. By the mid-1850s both Guyandotte and Barboursville, the county seat formed in 1813, were vibrant villages that linked the rural, undeveloped backcounties that comprised two-thirds of preindustrial West Virginia to Cabell County and, from there, to the regional and national marketplace.[5] Over the course of her years, she had seen how important slave labor was to this process. Both towns were beneficiaries of increasing river commerce and travel and the construction of a road that connected Guyandotte with the James River and Kanawha Turnpike at Barboursville.[6] The turnpike's importance as an east-west artery for all manner of travel and commerce was second only in use to the National Road and was a conduit for the transportation of slaves to the Deep South.[7] Occasionally, black migrants had traveled the road to safety.[8] In its sometimes difficult westerly course, it intersected and interconnected seven counties in the Virginia piedmont and four in West Virginia before encountering the eastern edge of Cabell

African American Experience in Cabell County 3

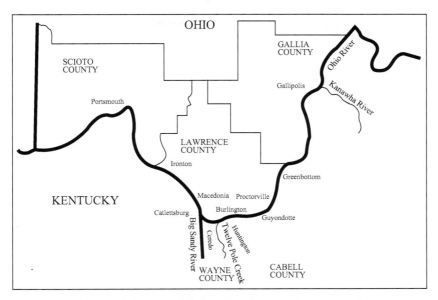

Map 1.1. Ohio River Underground Railroad stations in tri-state area. Source: "Underground Railroad Tri-State Area," tour brochure, Morrow Library, Special Collections, Marshall University, Huntington, W.V., 1.

County. At that point, the county was as far removed from Richmond and the Tidewater region of Virginia as any county in the state. Perhaps this would be the road she would take to start life anew.

More than anything, though, Mary had seen life at Greenbottom Plantation. Located adjacent to the Ohio River near the Mason County border, the plantation, home to more than 50 slaves in 1850, represented the least common form of slavery in the area and was the "social and economic centerpiece of the region."[9] It was also the locus of a historic presence of slaves possessing rudimentary literacy, which, at least through the mid-1800s, shaped the contours of social relations and power dynamics of the slave-master relationship within the county and, to some extent, within the region. As early as 1813, members of the slave community as well as the Greenbottom overseer knew that D'lea, a young female slave, possessed reading and rudimentary factoring skills, skills the overseer sometimes begrudgingly utilized. D'lea's abilities and her master's "unhappy dependence" on her reveal the complex interrelationship between slavery, spoken language, and functional literacy that existed in Cabell County and on the postrevolutionary western Virginia frontier.[10] The diversity of land, disorganized task delegation, dispersed population, lax and irregular supervision, and class and age variance of white laboring partners gave rise to a reluctant "multicultural" sharing of reading, writing, and factoring.[11] To help keep plantation records, a few of the slaves were trained to write, a skill that spread to other slaves during the unsupervised periods. Before long, many of the Greenbottom slaves could read and write and do simple math, a worrisome development for many slave owners.[12] Educated slaves were a threat to order, individually and collectively, because they were capable of communicating with other slaves to participate in surreptitious behavior, including escapes. In fact, by the late 1810s, slaves were escaping from the plantation with passes they had written for themselves.[13] Thus, as Marilyn Davis-DeEulis contends, "by the time William Jenkins and tanner John Hannah purchased Governor Cabell's land and many of his slaves in September 1825, they were buying into several generations of 'occupational literacy' forged in very confusing circumstances that were backbreaking, ruthless, yet often collaborative."[14]

While it is unclear as to what extent slave literacy impacted slave-labor relations for the betterment of the slave, it is difficult to believe that it did not shape, if only for a time, the movement and use of slaves through sale, importation, inheritance, or hire that increasingly became common practice within the county. Slaves were frequently rented out for labor in the county in addition to the labor they performed for the master. Naturally, slaves also had no say in their sale, transfer, or purchase. In effect, whatever the nature of personal relationships between the master and slave in the county's yeoman-based economy, it was not enough to overcome the recognition that the slave was seen as a unit of labor and vehicle of profit.[15] Mary knew this reality all too well. Upon his death in 1859, William Jenkins bequeathed "Mary and her issue" to his son Albert and instructed that slave Jacob be sold to the highest bidder among his three sons. Jenkins further stipulated "slave Mary and her sire to be similarly disposed of at the death of his sister."[16]

Intrinsic to the maintenance of the slaves' inferior status and abiding liquidity was the implied and/or actual threat or application of deprivation and violence. Notably, in its formative years Cabell County was what Ira Berlin labeled a "society with slaves"—a society in which slaves were never central to the economy or social structure. This distinguished the county from the rice- and cotton-growing regions of the deeper south—"slave societies"—where the political economy was inextricably woven into the fabric of the institution, and "the master-slave relationship provided the model for all social relations."[17] To what extent this dynamic contributed to or eased tension within the county, the harshest aspects of slavery associated with the Deep South are unknowable. What is known is that life on the plantation proved deadly for many, especially in its early years; that by the time of the

Civil War, many of Greenbottom's slaves had endured life on the plantation for nearly half a century; and that Mary's son had been produced through violence.[18]

Undeniably, this last fact must have complicated Mary's decision-making process on whether or not to leave Greenbottom. She could decide to leave, to proceed down the unexplored paths of future possibility that lay before her, paths fraught with peril and uncertainty but also with adventure. Or she could choose to stay with a Jenkins family member until she had time to think, strategize, and utilize the resources that had sustained and comforted her and her child though the most tumultuous episode in American history. Either choice carried risks. Each also promised profound change within her family and community.

This was as true for her as it had been for those county slaves previously manumitted. There were instances of the manumission of slaves, but rarely were more than one or two slaves freed at the same time. And, not infrequently, those freed were older slaves. For those fortunate to acquire their freedom, the State of Virginia, beginning in 1806, required them to leave the state within 12 months or face re-enslavement.[19] This law, and others that followed in 1816 and 1823, effectively acted as deterrents in cases of manumission within the state throughout the antebellum era.[20] Former slaves—free blacks—who remained in the county were required at all times to carry the legal document granting their freedom and apply to the county court annually for permission to remain in the county.[21]

The quest to remain in the county, or in close proximity, takes on added significance when we consider that Kentucky was a slave state and that Ohio, Indiana, and Illinois restricted or forbade free-black influx throughout the mid-1800s. In fact, in 1829, the Supreme Court of Ohio passed legislation requiring free blacks within the state to post a $500 bond within 30 days to remain in the state, a development that provoked 2,000 free blacks to petition the court to postpone implementation of the measure for three months.[22] The following year, in Portsmouth, Ohio, a key station on the Underground Railroad located 45 miles upriver from Cabell County, local whites fed up with the pace of enforcement of the law forced approximately 80 blacks to leave the town. Though not uniformly enforced, these laws were invoked by white citizens when they felt justified or threatened, a development that could include harassment, violence, and/or expulsion of free blacks.[23]

These developments (and others discussed herewith) help to reveal the peculiarities of the Ohio River valley and the contested nature of the borderland demarcated by the Ohio River during the era.[24] The fact that Virginia and Ohio shared access to a river that was a main artery of trade and commerce and that defined the border between slave and free states emphasizes the accommodations and discontinuities of the middle-river borderland during the antebellum era. Despite the fact that a border divided them, however, Americans on both sides of the Ohio River shared common social and cultural backgrounds, each bound by the contradictions and ambiguities of slavery and race. The centrality of fugitive slaves and free blacks to this dynamic and the fluidity of their presence further complicated the relationship. Thus, residents and settlers on both sides of the river sought either to utilize or to exploit opportunities mandated or proscribed by prevailing policies.[25]

The most notable case of manumission in the county occurred in 1849, when wealthy Cabell County slaveholder Sampson Sanders manumitted 51 slaves, nearly one-fourth of the 218 slaves freed that year in Virginia. Remarkably, Sanders, in his will, not only provided for his slaves (collectively) to receive $15,000 in cash, but he also encouraged them to take needed materials from his estate. In all, Sanders spent what one authority estimates was eventually more than $45,000. Sanders "also selected lawyers to go with the group [on their journey to their new home in Cass County, Michigan] to protect them in their travels, making sure everyone purchased good property, and ensuring they were fairly treated in all the legal dealings."[26] In all, the journey took three full days.[27] Upon their arrival into the "comparative wilderness of Cass County," where a residential free-black population of approximately 340 existed, each of the former slaves was given a tract of 18 acres of land, and a log cabin was constructed for each family. The aggregate acquisition of land approximated 700 contiguous acres.[28]

Coincidently, that same year, with $45,000 they'd received from their slavemaster James "Pap" Twyman, the "Burlington 37," led by former foreman Walker Fry, traveled by wagon train from Madison County, Virginia, across the Blue Ridge Mountains to Lawrence County, Ohio. "Their journey was made in fear and dread: fear that something might happen to prevent their reaching the haven of rest, dread that some shrewd lawyer might pick out some flaw in the papers and that they would be remanded back to await the tedious motions of the law's delay."[29] Susan Spencer, whose grandmother gave her a copper kettle used during the voyage, imagined that "they stopped and cooked beans or stopped to boil baby diapers in it."[30] Composed of four generations, including the youngest member, "Littler Traveler" (later called William "Traveler" Smith), born somewhere along the journey, they settled into Burlington, Ohio, four miles downriver from Guyandotte. There they undertook their first task: the acquisition of surnames.[31]

While it is impossible to know to what extent, if at all, Mary knew of the manumission of Sanders's slaves or the arrival of the Burlington 37, it is difficult to believe that she remained unaware of the two events for long. The fluidity of movement and influx within the county, the status of its owners, the primacy of Greenbottom to the county's slave economy, and her position within the Jenkins household would have afforded her opportunities to acquire, either directly or surreptitiously, knowledge of important developments within the county and the river borderland area.

Steamboats serving the rivers of the region from Gallipolis to Cincinnati, with the assistance of black labor, also deposited visitors and freight into the towns. One, the *R. H. Lindsey*, a double-decker boat, docked in early 1855 into Barboursville. "Black porters assisted the ladies off the deck and onto the Barboursville landing, as eager boys stood by to carry their luggage to one of the fine hotels."[32] Steamboats also offered autonomy not found on land. Sometime in the late 1820s or early 1830s, thirteen-year-old fugitive slave Joseph Jones obtained work as a "deck sweep" on a steamboat passing Point Pleasant, West Virginia, on its way to Cincinnati. By the end of his three-year term, during which he traveled frequently to Ohio towns such as Gallipolis, Point Pleasant, Ripley, and Burlington, which were home to small black populations, Jones had learned to read and write and had "advanced far enough in arithmetic to take care of his accounts, that is, he had mastered the ... fundamentals ... considered a good education in that day."[33]

Steamboats also offered slaves the opportunity to glean strategic information from fellow slaves, pioneers, and river boatmen, a potentially important development given the historical presence of slave literacy at Greenbottom. In his examination of slave labor at the Kanawha Salt Works, historian John E. Stealey noted the "corrosive influence on the institution" produced by slave employment aboard steamboats servicing the Kanawha Salines. "The steamboat," he related, "transported ideas as well as merchandise," providing opportunities to erode slave discipline, allow slaves to make contact with "liberated slaves," and offer a quicker mode of transportation for those seeking to flee rather than attempt overland flight.[34] A fascinating look into the antebellum African American experience on the steamboats that served the rivers of the region from Gallipolis to Cincinnati is relayed through the reminiscences of Hiram H. Swallow, a white resident of Point Pleasant, West Virginia.

> On the steamboats was depicted every phase of life. . . . The cabin boys were either all white or all black for no self respecting white boy at that time wanted to work with the slave boys employed on the boats. For while the blacks were always respectful to their superior officers nowhere in the south were relations [more] pleasant [than] when blacks and whites worked side by side on

an equal footing and the insults hurled from the blacks to the whites of "Poor White Trash," were more insulting and harder to bear than all the encomiums of "Nigger" that the whites could heap.... The chambermaid and her assistants were always black. There were enough of them that they were not only the laundresses of the boats, but were always ready to take turns as ladies' maids.[35]

To what extent these racial and social dynamics aboard the steamship existed in the small ports that dotted the Ohio River valley is speculative, yet, given the greater social fluidity and "openness" associated with commercial port towns, it seems plausible that African Americans in the region were able to carve out spaces of autonomy and humanity, as well as acquire knowledge, unavailable in a more closed society.[36] Certainly, given such developments, it would not be surprising for the county's slaves to have cast an expectant eye toward the passing river craft plying the waters while their owners simultaneously cast a wary eye at the same craft.

By the mid-nineteenth century the county increasingly operated as a nexus and flashpoint, located on the axis of North and South, slavery and freedom. On the one hand, fugitive slaves and, not infrequently, slave hunters in pursuit traversed the rolling hills, creek beds, and Indian trails to cross the Ohio River into Ohio. On the other hand, the county's diverse population—African American and white, free black and slave, slave and master, abolitionist and proslavery advocate—existed in an uneasy, unsteady dance, one that embodied the troubled posture of the nation. Emblematic of the tangled web of complex issues, actions, and thoughts related to the issue of slavery in the county and region were divisions over religious affiliation, political representation, and slavery.[37]

Limited but important evidence of black people's community and spirituality can be found in the diary, written between 1855 and 1871, of Cabell County businessman, dentist, and slave owner William F. Dusenberry. As early as 1850, Dusenberry attended a service by Uncle Tom, a slave and noted Baptist preacher in the area, who was held in such high regard by local whites that he made appointments to preach in various localities where he would address the gathered slaves.[38] Subsequent entries in 1855 and 1856 show his continuing high regard by area whites, though no improvement in his status.[39]

Indicative of the loose structure of the institution within the county, slaves were allowed to gather, observe cultural and religious practices, and have unsupervised travel. One local authority reports, "Sometimes the slave owners took slaves to preaching as both attended the same service. Other times the slaves borrowed a buggy and drove themselves to the religious meetings."[40] In 1856, Dusenberry notes that Judy, "hired for one year for $40," traveled frequently to "meetings, quilting, to help, [and] to church" in the course of her duties.[41] Slave owners also allowed their slaves to cross the Ohio River to attend church in the town of Burlington, then the county seat of Lawrence County, Ohio, where a substantial religious congregation of former slaves resided.[42] Situated across the Ohio from the mouth of Twelve Pole Creek and present-day Westmoreland in western Huntington, Burlington, from its earliest days of settlement, had been a major transshipment point and shelter for runaway slaves and those manumitted by their masters in Kentucky and Virginia. It is difficult to imagine why slave masters would have allowed such activities as it is to imagine what slaves thought as they attended church in a free state. While slaves' initiative, mobility, cultural activities, and communication provided opportunities to acquire knowledge, recreate, socialize, and perhaps, strategize, there is no doubt that the county's slaves, like those throughout the South, operated under a hegemonic slave system that greatly mitigated occurrences of slave runaways and/or threats of insurrection.[43]

Yet, the historical record shows some of the county's slaves openly resisting their enslavement from the 1820s forward.[44] In one incident in 1856, recounted in Dusenberry's diary, his wife and cousin "attempted to lick their nigger [and] she licked them," surely a mortifying affair for the family members: so much so, the slave woman was sold two days later in Kentucky.[45] Another entry relates the account of a group of slaves who "intended to meet with a lot of other niggers about three miles below Guyandotte and there cross the Ohio."[46]

Undoubtedly, many runaway slaves sought to connect to the Underground Railroad, the network composed of individuals and safe houses traversing the Ohio valley, including in Barboursville and Guyandotte, where hundreds, perhaps thousands, of escaping slaves crossed the "River Jordan" from then Virginia into the free territory of Ohio.[47] It is important that, while the network may have been less organized than previously thought and the linkages not explicitly revealed, throughout the Ohio River valley cross-community ties linked African American individuals and communities on both sides of the river.[48] From the earliest days of settlement, Lawrence County and Burlington, Ohio, had served as transit points. After leaving his job as a steamboat worker and settling in Gallipolis in the late-1840s with his new wife, Temperance Reed of South Point, Ohio (located just south of Burlington), Jones became the conductor for the Gallipolis station. As a family member noted, "The thirteen years that he lived in Virginia gave him a vague idea of slavery, and he was willing to sacrifice his life if need be for the cause of freedom."[49] He was known never to leave home "without his two ominous-looking guns about 18 inches long."[50] Both William Chavis and James Dicher (alternately spelled Ditcher) transported runaways from Greenup County, Kentucky, and Cabell County, Virginia. Chavis brought runaways to a remote pokeberry field in Poke Patch, Ohio.[51] Dicher, a free mulatto, was known as the "Red Fox of the Underground Railroad" because of the color of his skin, which resembled that of a Native American.[52] Once across the river, runaways surreptitiously traveled from farm to farm and town to town before settling in the north, with many traveling to the Great Lakes, and on to Canada.[53]

Interestingly, a significant number of these incidents and developments occurred prior to the arrival of a group of abolitionists into the area, led by Massachusetts congressman Eli Thayer. In 1857, after visits to Ashland and Catlettsburg, Kentucky, and Guyandotte, Thayer started a prolabor abolitionist community at Ceredo, Virginia, located just a few miles below nearby Barboursville and Guyandotte. The townspeople aided fugitive slaves across the river to Quaker Bottom (later Proctorville), Ohio, where they might find sanctuary and eventual safe passage on the Underground Railroad to Canada.[54]

Reflecting the growing national controversy over the institution, regional and local newspaper editorials relayed the conflicting attitudes held by locals up and down the river over the Thayer group.[55] Slaves did seek to capitalize on the presence of abolitionist sentiment in their midst by using information gained from ministers and gossip.[56] Open and covert resistance of enslaved people kept the controversy over slavery stirring. Runaway Asbury Parker crossed the Ohio River in 1857 to escape from Jim Rowe, his Greenup County (now Boyd County), Kentucky, master. Parker crossed the river near Guyandotte and traveled the "railroad," where he was "advised to act like a free man" before finally joining others from the same county in Canada. Another incident, recounted in a local newspaper article, notes the return to Cabell County of "a couple of old people . . . formerly slaves belonging to the Holderby estate," ages eighty-five and ninety, who had run away with their family in 1858. "They say they stole a skiff . . . and floated down to Burlington, O. where they got a wagon and went into the country."[57] In 1859, after hearing of John Brown's raid at Harper's Ferry, Virginia, Fred, a "mean" slave belonging to Conwelzie Simmons, ran away. Some weeks later, he returned to take the remaining six of Simmons's slaves to freedom, only to be captured. He, along with four other slaves implicated in the failed attempt, were sold away to southern buyers.[58] The slaves of Charles Morris represented such a threat that at the outset of Civil War hostilities, Morris moved his slaves to Wytheville, Virginia, to avoid additional runaway attempts.[59]

As throughout the South, whites attempted to use religion to placate and indoctrinate Cabell County slaves. Upon moving into Greenbottom in 1825, William Jenkins's young wife, Janetta, recognized the opportunity and

Figure 1.2. Asbury Parker, of Ironton, Ohio. A fugitive in his slave clothes, 1894. Source: Wilbur H. Siebert Underground Railroad Collection, Ohio History Connection, www.ohiomemory.org/siebert.

regularly discussed the Bible and other topics with the Greenbottom slaves to encourage their conversion to Christianity, even having weekly services for them. In 1835, the Greenbottom Baptist Church was founded near the Jenkins Plantation, and a few years later, black members were allowed to join. Both William and Janetta encouraged several slaves to join the church, issuing passes for them to attend services. Slaves from surrounding farms joined as well, making Greenbottom Baptist the most important church in the county for slaves. Some of the slaves even signed their names to the church books, thus publicizing the fact that they knew how to write, an illegal act.[60] Speaking of the county's slaves, one local resident related that

> religion was a great moral force among these people, and they were not only permitted to join the church, but were encouraged to do so. They sat on the back seats, or when the church had a balcony, as they had in some churches, they occupied it. The slaves were thoroughly indoctrinated with the teachings of the Bible regarding servants. One of these verses is found in Peter 2:18, "Servants, be subject to your masters with all fear; not only to the good and gentle, but

also to the froward." Titus 2:9 says: "Exhort servants to be obedient unto their own masters, and to please them well, in all things, not answering again."[61]

One way for a slave to escape punishment for a transgression was to abide by "The Church Covenant" and confess his or her sin. After being caught "trying to abscond" together, "a willful violation of the scriptural injunction," Charlotte and her husband, Isaac, were presented with the option of confessing before their captors. While Charlotte did so, Isaac refused. Charlotte would be granted a reprieve, while Isaac, "who didn't know much about the Scriptures, but knew all about slavery, and had a good idea of the blessedness of freedom," was sold down south.[62]

The evolution of black life on the early Ohio valley/Virginia frontier and its complex relationship to local church and plantation literacy demographics in the mid-1800s help us understand why this region assumed its particular cultural, social, and labor structure. The dynamics of this connection also suggest the forces that shaped attitudes about reading and writing among enslaved blacks, which white settlers encountered when they moved into the smaller farms of the Ohio and Virginia frontier. These dynamics also help account for the literate sophistication of antislavery enclaves on opposite sides of the Ohio River during the late antebellum period. Ohio communities such as Burlington have a longer and more functionally complex literacy history than what is generally presupposed.

In truth, though, one's loyalty, occupation, or professed faith afforded little protection from the whim of a master. After helping raise twenty children for their master Martin Moore, preacher "Uncle Tom" and "Aunt Dinah," referred to as "splendid negroes" by one white contemporary, had to endure the loss of two sons, sold at the cost of $1,000 each to help Moore stave off foreclosure proceedings.[63] Just before the Civil War, as a young slave girl, Mrs. Emma ("Auntie Em") Anderson Layne remembered seeing her parents, brothers, and sisters sold at the old Buffington Street landing in Guyandotte and put on a steamboat. As she watched the crew ready the boat for departure, she spied her mother and father on deck chained to other slaves. She watched from the river bank as the boat pulled away from the landing and began its journey down the Ohio to the Deep South. She never saw any of her family again.[64] Such examples as these refute the romanticized notions, held by many area whites and perpetuated in family and community histories, that slavery in the county and region was somehow more benign and paternalistic than in the Chesapeake Bay region or the Deep South.[65]

Throughout the mid-1800s the mechanics and mechanism of migration into the region differed. Between 1840 and 1860 increasing numbers of white settlers arrived from eastern Virginia accompanied by their slaves. In 1850,

Figure 1.3. Stagecoach on the James River and Kanawha Turnpike, 1846. Courtesy of *West Virginia History on View*, West Virginia and Regional History Center, WVU Libraries.

out of a total population of 304,000 for the area of what is now West Virginia, there were 3,820 slaveholders owning an average of six slaves each (22,920 total). Many of these were slaveholders came from adjoining states.[66] In 1860 Virginia's slave population totaled 498,887, with only 12,771 found in the 48 counties originally constituting the state of West Virginia.[67]

In 1860, out of an aggregate population of 8,020,329 African Americans, representing 4.1 percent of the total, resided within Cabell County. Fully 305 of the 329 lived in bondage among the county's 84 yeoman slaveholders, an average of slightly more than 3.6 persons per slaveholder (see appendix 1). Guyandotte possessed the largest number of slaveholders and slaves, with 27 and 101, respectively, an average of 3.7 slaves per household. With 17 slaves, Guyandotte resident Susan Holderby was the single largest slaveholder of the district. The district of Cabell Court House contained the second-largest total, with 22 slaveholders and 88 slaves, an average of four slaves per household. The district contained the county's second- and third-largest slaveholders, William Williams and John Morris, who held 14 and 12 slaves, respectively. Of the seven remaining county districts, only Mud Bridge possessed similar slaveholder numbers and slave household averages as that of Guyandotte and Cabell Court House.[68]

Examination of Greenbottom, "with 4,444 acres, the largest slave plantation in Cabell, Wayne and Mason counties in 1850 and 1860," allows further entry into the black circumstance in antebellum as well as immediate postbellum Cabell County.⁶⁹ As has been discussed, throughout the mid-1800s Greenbottom was owned and operated by various members of the influential Jenkins family, including entrepreneur and businessman Captain William A. Jenkins and later his son, "Harvard graduate, congressman, and future confederate general Albert Gallatin Jenkins," who in 1860 was "probably the richest man in western Virginia."⁷⁰ One reason the youngest slaves made up the largest cohort of the county's slave population in 1860 is that the county's owners regularly sold off their young adult males. After visiting Greenbottom, prominent Mason County businessman Charles Cameron Lewis noted, "The father owned a large number of Negro slaves, which he kept in order by selling the young men, and tilling his crops with the labor of the old men, boys, and women."⁷¹ In 1850, the Jenkins family owned 58 slaves, 23 males and 35 females—with 88 percent (91 percent of males and 83 percent of females) of the slave population aged thirty-five or younger. Fully 65 percent of the males and 54 percent of the female slaves were fifteen or younger. In effect, the Jenkins family engaged in the practice of regularly selling off their young adult males to achieve maximum return on their investment. The practice also ensured that a significant number of the Jenkins's slave population would be entering adulthood as well as their prime labor and reproductive periods as the decade progressed, while simultaneously reducing the number of those most likely to challenge the status quo.⁷²

Certainly, at an early age Greenbottom slaves knew that their bodies determined their value. The realization that they were living property, commodities to be deposed at the discretion of the master at any time, without warning, or perhaps worse, with prior notice, permeated their existence. The specter of being sold, of being physically and psychically removed from loved ones, determined every slave's actions and responses. Yet, unlike the menace of physical punishment that encompassed every slave's existence, the potential relocation and atomization of one's social identity threatened an unfortunate select few. Their value, not their humanity or affiliation, determined their worth. This knowledge, that one of them, no matter his or her station or affiliation, had a price, pervaded every slave, their family, and their community who well knew the ramifications of a sale upon the collective. Whether sold from a good master to a bad one, from the worst to the best, locally or down south, every slave was subject to the "chattel principle," in which the master, trader, and buyer undergirding the slave system valued their bodies over their humanity. Notably, the county's slave population, assisted by manumission, sell-offs, and runaways, decreased by 180 (31 percent) between 1840 and 1850.⁷³ As historian Walter Johnson notes, "Of the two-thirds of a million interstate sales made by the traders in the decades before the Civil

War, twenty-five percent involved the destruction of a first marriage and fifty percent destroyed a nuclear family—many of these separating children under the age of thirteen from their parents. Nearly all of them involved the dissolution of a previously existing community."[74] In effect, regardless of how the slave viewed him/herself, or whether the Jenkins family or other county slave owners were good or bad masters, each abided by and embraced the mechanisms and dictates of the chattel principle.

In 1850 Captain Jenkins valued the plantation at $80,000, with 1,500 acres improved for use out of a total 2,395 acres. Upon his death in 1859, his three sons (William, Thomas, and Albert) took over, expanding the total acreage improved to 1,700 acres by 1860; by this time, the three sons were quite wealthy. The aggregate land value owned by the three was $195,000 ($65,000 each) with the next-highest value in the county owned by John Morris ($105,000) followed by Peter Buffington ($50,000), who had two farms. Slave labor on the Jenkins plantation revolved primarily around the myriad tasks associated with field work, tending livestock, and raising horses. In 1860 the Jenkins sons possessed the highest value of farm implements and equipment and produced the highest crop yields in the county. The Jenkins's slaves produced the highest yield in wheat (2,200 bushels) and Indian corn (7,000 bushels) and produced the second-highest yield in potatoes (300 bushels) and butter (1,300). The slaves tended to the largest number of cattle (425—compared with the second-largest of 150), the largest number of swine (300) (compared with the second-largest of 200), the largest number of horses on one plantation (46) (compared with 16 on the second-largest plantation), and the second-largest number of both milk cows (34) and oxen (19).[75] Slave production and oversight enabled the plantation to have the county's highest value of livestock at $12,300, compared with $6,000 for the second-ranked plantation.[76]

Slaves at Greenbottom did suffer maltreatment, physical violence, and sexual coercion. Though Captain Jenkins was known to be "somewhat cruel," his "overseers were particularly so." To punish or coerce the plantation's slaves, overseer D. B. Scott regularly employed a sycamore log with large "staples" in it. After tying a slave to the staples, Scott whipped and then salted them. After Scott's departure, the next overseer employed by Captain Jenkins, Lewis (John) Page, regularly raped the slave women. In at least one instance, his rape of slave "Mary" produced a son.[77]

In 1850 free blacks in the county faced renewed threats to their status from a Virginia law that "required an owner to provide for any freed slave for the rest of the slave's natural life [a potentially expensive proposition]. Any former slave who remained in the state could be returned to servitude for failure to pay taxes, failing to show an acceptable means of support, forgetting to present himself before the county justices each year, or simply by someone['s] claiming that he was an escaped slave." Between 1850 and 1860, those free blacks who registered with the court were invariably granted approval to remain in the county.[78] In 1861 a Cabell County ruling reaffirmed the necessity for free Negroes to petition the court annually.[79]

In 1860 a smattering of free blacks lived in the county. As the head of household of a family of eight, including her six daughters and her sixty-five-year-old mother, Delphia, thirty-eight-year-old Mary Haley was unique. The Guyandotte resident was one of only 24 free people residing within the county, one of only two women (along with twenty-year-old laundry woman Nancy Anderson) who was head of a household, one of only three black heads of a household (along with Isham Sanders and Lewis Fullerton), and head of the largest all-black household and family in the county. Moreover, behind farmer Stephen Witcher and Fullerton, who possessed $150 and $100, respectively, in personal property, her $40 in personal property made her the wealthiest freewoman and the third-wealthiest free person (along with Sanders, who also possessed $40 in property) in the county.

Although the number of free black females, like slave females, was greater than free black males, the division was greater than that reflected in the slave population. Compared with the 1860 female slave population, which represented 55.4 percent of the general slave population, free black females, including the eight females of the Haley family, made up 62.5 percent (15/24) of the county's free-black population. These fifteen were found in seven households, averaging 2.1 per household. However, removal of the Haley family from the equation shows an average of slightly more than one black female per household. Study of the age ratios within the county's free black population shows it was disproportionally older than the slave population. Forty-two percent (10/24) were fifty-five or older, 17 percent (4/24) were ages thirty to

Table 1.1 Antebellum Population in Cabell County, Virginia, 1810-1860

	1810	1820	1830	1840	1850	1860
Slave	221	392	561	567	389	305
Free Black	1*	9	60	64†	29	24
White	2,717	4,388	5,263	7,532	5,881	7,691
Total	2,963	4,789	5,884	8,163	6,299	8,020

Source: U.S. Census Bureau, Third Census (1810), Fourth Census (1820), Fifth Census (1830), Sixth Census (1840), Seventh Census (1850), Eighth Census (1860).
* 1815 Tax List of Cabell County, Virginia
† Includes fifty-one manumitted by Sampson Sanders

Table 1.2 Antebellum African American Population for Cabell County, Virginia, 1810–1860

	1810	1820		1830		1840		1850		1860	
		Male	Female	Male	Female	Male	Female	Male	Female	Male	Female
Slave	221	206	186	289	272	273	294	190	198	136	169
Free	1	2	7	2	3	33	23	15	14	9	15
Total	222	208	193	291	275	306	317	205	212	145	184

Source: U.S. Census Bureau, Third Census (1810), Fourth Census (1820), Fifth Census (1830), Sixth Census (1840), Seventh Census (1850), Eighth Census (1860).

fifty-four, while 42 percent (10/24) were ages one to twenty-nine. Thus, 59 percent of the free-black population was age thirty and older.[80]

During the Civil War, the county, rent by the divided allegiances of its populace, was a microcosm of the protracted and fractious nature of the sectional schism that produced the natural resource–rich thirty-fifth state. In direct contrast to the State of Virginia, whose people voted to secede from the Union, Cabell County's citizens voted to remain in it. However, the town of Guyandotte voted to secede. Thus, within the county, families and clans split, literally brother against brother, cousin against cousin. In 1861 the first battle of the war within the county occurred in Barboursville on Fortification Hill. Later that year, the town of Guyandotte, by now a small, bustling river port, was nearly burnt to the ground by Union forces retaliating against a Confederate raid.[81] For many, the issue of slavery was not nearly as important as the threat of Northerners to their way of life, and the social, economic, and political dominance exerted by slave holders in the Chesapeake Bay area. However, for significant numbers of western Virginians, sentiments situating black people as inferior remained conspicuous.[82]

Slaves within the county, like those within the region, took advantage of the fluid state of affairs during the Civil War. Historian Forrest Talbott argues that the state's black population declined 13.5 percent during the decade of the war, while the number of whites entering the state during the same period grew by 25 per cent.[83] The number of slaves fleeing the region "to make their war-born freedom secure in a free state" help explain the drop in the county's African American population during the decade from 329 to 123.[84]

Slaves in Cabell County as well as throughout West Virginia were not freed by the Emancipation Proclamation but by an act of the state legislature in February 1865. Thus, the state's black residents were forced to wait another two years after the proclamation for their freedom, certainly an exceedingly difficult proposition for many seeking to "seize the moment" and flee or leave the county. Indeed, white residents were sharply divided over the status of slavery in the new state constitution but had no issue with agreeing to a Negro exclusion policy that would ban either slave importation or free-black migration into the state.[85] Consequently, the question of immediate or gradual emancipation for the state's slaves had embroiled the Constitutional Convention of 1863 in contentious debate. Refuting arguments (while simultaneously denigrating Negroes) by those fearful that the state would soon be overrun by free Negroes, Senator Waitman T. Willey stated in the state Constitutional Convention of 1863, "There is nothing in the soil or climate of West Virginia to attract a free negro, but much to repel him. Besides, the kind of labor which will be required here, will not be of a character to induce his employment."[86] Ultimately, Lincoln's prerequisite for statehood forced the hand of state legislators who passed the Thirteenth Amendment in 1865.

The end of the Civil War only amplified apprehension within the state over the nature and extent of black citizenship. In truth, many white residents (like whites throughout the South) feared that every gain achieved by freedmen and women after the Civil War would result in a loss of white stature and authority, a difficult prospect for many trapped in the past.[87] Despite these sentiments, however, the state legislature's gradualist approach to recognizing black citizenship rights produced results. In 1866 the state legislature in Charleston took steps addressing African American citizenship, the same year legal marriages between Negroes as well as others were first recognized.[88] In due time, blacks were allowed to act as witnesses in the courts, and the Fourteenth Amendment was ratified. Yet, in 1868 West Virginia's African American residents could not vote, hold office, or serve on juries, and while the state provided and supported education, blacks were segregated in schools.[89] Intense debate over how to incorporate the substantial number of Confederates who were barred from voting by test oaths ignited passions that endangered the passage of the Fifteenth Amendment. After another two years of legislative and gubernatorial debate, some highly charged and inflammatory, the question of black suffrage was finally settled. In 1870, with the passage of the hard-fought Flick Amendment, the test oaths were finally repealed and the Fifteenth Amendment passed.[90]

These measures did little to stem the tide of black out-migration from the state. Affiliated with out-migration during the war years, black population throughout the region declined between 1860 and 1870. Confederate sentiment and limited economic opportunities in the immediate postwar years compelled out-migration.[91] There were some who freed their slaves after the Civil War.[92] In fact, 20 percent of southern West Virginia black residents moved out of the state after emancipation.[93] For example, although the black

Table 1.3 Slave Population for Select Virginia Counties, 1860

	Total pop.	Slave	% Slave	Region
Jefferson	14,535	3,960	27.2	Ridge and Valley
Kanawha	16,150	2,184	13.5	Appalachian Plateau
Berkeley	12,525	1,650	13.2	Ridge and Valley
Greenbrier	12,211	1,525	12.5	Appalachian Plateau
Monroe	10,757	1,114	10.4	Cumberland Plateau
Putnam	6,301	580	9.2	Ohio Valley
Fayette	5,997	271	4.5	Appalachian Plateau
Mason	9,173	376	4.1	Ohio Valley
Cabell	8,020	305	3.8	Ohio Valley
Wayne	6,747	143	2.1	Ohio Valley
McDowell	1,535	0	0	Cumberland Plateau

Source: Inter-university Consortium for Political and Social Research, Historical, Demographic, Economic and Social Data: The United States, 1790–1970, https://www.icpsr.umich.edu/icpsrweb/ICPSR/studies/3.

population of Mercer County increased slightly from 391 to 394 in the decade from 1860 to 1870, it decreased 5.4 percent in Kanawha County, home to Charleston, 18 percent in Monroe, 22 percent in Jefferson, and 36 percent in Greenbrier.[94] In 1860, each of these three counties had a Negro population exceeding 10 percent, in contrast to Cabell County's 4.1 percent.[95]

With black travel and out-migration came increasing numbers of whites into the region. By 1860 the Virginia counties composing current West Virginia contained the largest percentage of whites of several southern slave states. That year, the black population found in the Virginia counties in the current state of West Virginia totaled only 5.9 percent of the general population, with most found in the western Virginia mountain region.[96] Concurrently, by 1860 Cabell County possessed the largest percentage of whites in its history, exceeding that found throughout the soon-to-be state of West Virginia. Certainly, many white migrants arriving into the county, exemplary of Dusenberry, who was northern-born and a Unionist, remained unreformed racists. The "whitening" of the region and county would complicate the quest for black suffrage during the state's formative years and contribute to the hardening of race relations throughout the Jim Crow era.

Though it is impossible to ascertain the reason or reasons why, or how "faithful and kindly" their former masters were, a few blacks did remain with their former masters (or their kin) after emancipation.[97] For most slaves,

Table 1.4 Racial Composition of Southern Appalachians, 1790–1860

Appalachian Counties of:	% White 1790	% White 1820	% White 1860	%African-American 1790	%African-American 1820	%African-American 1860	% Cherokee 1790	% Cherokee 1820	% Cherokee 1860
Alabama	B	83.8	77.6	B	9.8	22.0	95.0	6.4	0.4
Georgia	B	84.5	82.7	B	8.3	16.8	92.0	7.2	0.5
Kentucky	88.3	86.4	91.5	11.7	13.6	8.5	B	B	—
Maryland	89.3	80.6	87.6	10.7	19.4	12.4	B	B	—
North Carolina	78.1	79.1	84.8	8.1	14.1	13.8	14.8	6.8	1.4
South Carolina	91.3	76.6	78.0	8.7	23.4	22.0	B	B	—
Tennessee	84.1	88.9	87.5	7.9	9.9	12.2	8.0	1.2	0.3
Virginia	81.5	69.7	71.6	18.5	30.3	28.4	B	B	—
West Virginia	90.5	87.8	93.8	9.5	12.2	6.2	B	B	B
Region	85.0	79.0	84.0	10.6	19.3	15.7	4.4	1.7	0.3
Cabell County	B	91.6	95.9	B	8.4	4.1	B	1.0	—

B: *not* tabulated
Source: U.S. Census Bureau, First Census; U.S. Census Bureau, Census of 1820; U.S. Census Bureau, Population in 1860; Thornton, *Cherokees*, 43, 49–50; *Report of Indian Commissioner, 1884*, li–liii. State percentages obtained from electronic archive of Wilma A. Dunaway, *Southern Laboring Women: The Gendered Boundaries of Race, Ethnicity, and Class in Antebellum Appalachia, 1700–1860*, Virginia Tech Library.

severing established daily routines, cultural practices, and social linkages, and contemplation of the consequences (real or imagined) of such actions required remarkable psychological strength and a deep, abiding faith. Undoubtedly, each former slave (and free person) encountered a range of emotions, options, and thoughts regarding emancipation. For many freed persons, the rational assessment was to stay.

Yet what are we to make of Mary Lacy's decision to stay near her former masters, the Jenkinses, given that Captain Jenkins's will instructed that she and her son be sold to the highest bidder among his three sons and considering the alleged rape that presumably produced her youngest son? In 1860 the twenty-five-year-old slave and caretaker was the mother of a five-year-old son, George. By 1870, she and George, now a farm laborer, along with former slave Christine (twelve years old) and John Page, Mary's three-year old mulatto son, resided in the white household of James B. Bowlin (alternately spelled Burlin) where Mary served as caretaker of Albert G. Jenkins's children. They were joined in the household by Anderson Rose, a thirty-five-year-old farm laborer and former slave of Captain Jenkins's. Later, she served in the same position within the household of Thomas Jefferson Jenkins, son of the late Captain Jenkins, until his death in 1873. Only after Thomas Jenkins's passing did Mary leave the Jenkinses with her family, stating that "she had seen too much death," and settle elsewhere in the county.[98]

Presumably, Mary, like a number of slaves who called Greenbottom home during the mid-1800s, possessed some level of rudimentary literacy, which provided greater knowledge and insight, allowing her to see a greater range of possibilities as she surveyed the uncharted territory before her. Further, her aptitude would have made her more valuable as a resource to the now-decimated Jenkins family. Given that her occupational and social terrain operated within the interwoven contours of labor, family, and community, Mary's decision to stay with her former masters, like tens of thousands throughout the South, should not be viewed as unique or unexpected: remaining there provided some sense of stability, security, and perhaps even a sense of purpose.[99] But, it is important to note, when Mary felt it time to move on, she demonstrated she was capable of doing so.

The Civil War initiated a shift in the balance of power within Cabell County. What had been in 1860 was no more. By 1863 the former Cabell County, Virginia, was no longer a part of Virginia. It, along with a significant portion of the state's western expanse, was now firmly ensconced within the nascent state of West Virginia.[100] The county's former 305 slaves, 24 freepersons, and 84 slaveholders now faced profound choices. Now emancipated, many African Americans—male and female, black and mulatto, young and old, individual and family—across the county left to seek their future elsewhere, as did many of the county's free blacks. In their strivings and responses, African Americans would help define the nature of space, autonomy, and work within Huntington's postbellum urban-industrial economy. The tragedy of this process and transformation is that although slavery within Cabell County differed from that in other regions in Virginia and the South, in the postwar period the lives of the county's black residents became more like those of other African Americans in neighboring states and in the South generally as the county's white residents and leaders increasingly embraced the tenets and practices of Jim Crow.

CHAPTER 2

The "Grapevine Telegraph"

Post-Emancipation Black Community and Early Black Migrant Influx, 1865–1871

Anne Eliza Riddle was distraught. Her mother inconsolable. Somehow, while she labored in the fields, she had lost Robert, Anne's younger brother. After all the family had endured and sacrificed, it didn't make any sense. Her mother did not know how he had vanished, but the child was gone. Gone! Family members had searched far and wide for him but found no sign. And he had failed to respond to their increasingly desperate calls. Had someone taken him? But that didn't make sense. Although Buckingham County contained both Union and Confederate patrols, what would have prompted either to take him? And if either had, where would they have taken him? Hadn't they seen Anne's mother in the fields, mere yards away? Hadn't they heard the family's cries? That night Anne and other members of the search party returned empty handed—a process that would be repeated with the same result subsequent nights until the search would end, unfulfilled.

Even after the chaos and upheaval of the Civil War, Anne never forgot her brother. Even years later, on her migration journey from Buckingham County to White Sulphur Springs to Huntington, she, emblematic of the tens of thousands of other freedpersons searching for loved ones in post–Civil War America, listened for a wisp of gossip or a passing conversation, any snippet that might provide a clue to his whereabouts. Her eventual reunion with him would be a testament not only to her tenacity and devotion but also to the providence linked to the enduring grapevine telegraph utilized to find him.

In the quest to absorb the full measure of freedom, black agency throughout the South and West Virginia influenced white actions and attitudes in the immediate post–Civil War years. But it was a gradual, frequently contentious process. The severing of Virginia divided many groups in West Virginia. Grievances born of secession inflamed questions of taxation, political representation, and constitutional change greatly complicated black aspirations. It must be remembered that the black population in 1860 found in the Virginia counties composing the current state of West Virginia totaled only approximately 21,000, most found in the eastern part of the state. In contrast, the white population totaled 355,526.[1] Thus, long-standing attitudes on race and slavery held great sway throughout the region.

It is important to note that in southern West Virginia the state's largest contingent of black citizens resided among the state's largest contingent of former slave owners and Southern sympathizers. To meet the mandates for statehood recognition established by President Lincoln, the state's legislators were forced to rectify a particularly troublesome conundrum: how to grant citizenship to the state's black residents as well as to its former Confederates. While both populations eventually garnered the rights of citizenship, the fact that significant numbers of southern West Virginia's black residents departed the region (with many presumably departing the state) suggests that the political gains granted to them were not enough to stem the tide of out-migration during the state's formative years, from 1863 to 1870. This was especially true of the black residential population of Cabell County, West Virginia.

More than political gain, the impetus for black migrant influx into southern West Virginia and Cabell County was initiated by the construction of the Chesapeake and Ohio Railroad from Richmond, Virginia, to Huntington, West Virginia, through the New River valley. Attracted by the promise of wage-labor employment, thousands of workers, many of them black, poured into the valley, reversing the trend of black out-migration in the region between 1860 and 1870. Enduring great hardship while treading the well-worn pathways of their ancestors and peers and relying on the twin cornerstones of family and community, many of these black migrants settled in the villages and towns that sprung up adjacent to or near the railroad, including Huntington, West Virginia, located on the banks of the Ohio River in Cabell County. Attracted by the promise of jobs attendant to the town's founding as a western transshipment station for the railroad in 1871, the first wave of black migrants arrived into the county. Here, they settled among a small black residential population of farmers and agricultural workers who were facing their own particular but not dissimilar challenges and barriers in the quest to realize their dreams.

Visionary railroad magnate and itinerant migrant Collis P. Huntington arrived in Guyandotte early in 1869. There is no record that he spent much if any time among Cabell County's black residents during his sojourn. Brilliant, obstinate, and indefatigable, the six-foot four-inch former "peddler and storeowner" was a man unlike any other to visit the area. From humble beginnings he had built a fortune through his association with Leland Stanford's Central Pacific transcontinental railroad endeavor.[2] Now, far away from his California roots, Huntington was scheduled to survey personally the largely uninhabited southern shore of the Ohio River over the course of several days. His quest: to find the perfect site for the western terminus of his recently acquired railroad, the Chesapeake and Ohio, for which he had paid a purported $850,000. Only after a great deal of comprehensive, persuasive, and in some cases, forceful legal maneuvers and financial negotiations did Huntington acquire control of the C&O. Availing himself of his contacts, expertise, and stature, and aware of the vast potential wealth to be made, Huntington sought and gained financial backing from both sides of the Atlantic in his quest.[3] As one historian relays, "Huntington was accustomed to buying legislators, inspectors, even U.S. congressmen to get what he wanted. Only Virginia's western mountains stood in the way."[4] One biographer, more pointed in his commentary, referred to Huntington as "a hard and cheery old man with no more soul than a shark."[5]

After spending weeks scouting several sites on the Kanawha and Guyandotte Rivers for his transshipment beachhead, Huntington settled on four miles of river frontage west of the Guyandotte River and the town of Guyandotte.[6] Here, he decided, would be the western terminus of his railroad, linking Richmond, Virginia, to the Ohio River, a dream dating back to men like George Washington, who as a surveyor saw the potential of the C&O Canal connecting the Virginia Tidewater ports with the Ohio valley.[7] Like Washington, Huntington envisioned America's future in western expansion—with him at the corporate helm of his transcontinental railroad. The future West Virginia town figured mightily in his plans: its close proximity to timber, coal fields, iron mines, oil, and natural gas furnished advantages as a manufacturing center. Additionally, and of great import, it offered favorable opportunities for connections with steamboat lines to Cincinnati.[8]

Thus, through the auspices of his Central Land Company, Huntington purchased some 5,000 acres of property, including sufficient ground for the uses of the railroad, rights of way, extensive machine and car shops, engine houses, depots, and accessory buildings for various purposes, and land on the north side of the Ohio for the site of a planned future bridge. On February 27, 1871, the town of Huntington, West Virginia, was incorporated. The U.S. Post Office officially recognized the new town the following May.[9] After clearing off four miles of riverfront property, crews began construction of "a round-house, a brass and iron foundry, a blacksmith and boiler shop, a shop to build passenger cars, a large building to manufacture and repair freight cars, and a drying house for lumber."[10]

Against the backdrop of postwar sociopolitical, cultural, and economic transition, black migrants arrived in the region, Cabell County, and Huntington. Migration, by its very nature, frequently left migrants exposed and vulnerable. As the state with the highest average elevation of any state east of the Mississippi River, navigation through West Virginia was difficult, with the New River valley especially hazardous terrain. On his journey west, Booker T. Washington noted, "One of the most hazardous parts of the journey was crossing the New River gorge, descending from the spectacular towering cliffs on one side, crossing a shallow mountain river, then up again by another winding narrow road to the top of the cliffs on the other side."[11] Washington further reflected on the arduous nature of such ventures:

> All of our household and other goods were packed into a small wagon drawn by two horses or mules. I cannot recall how many days it took us to make this trip, but it seems to me, as I recall it now, that we were at least ten days. Of course, we had to sleep in the wagon, or what was more often true, on the ground. The children walked a great portion of the distance.
>
> One night we camped near an abandoned log cabin, and my mother decided that, instead of cooking our frugal meal in the open air, as she had been accustomed to do on the trip, she would build a fire in this cabin and we should both cook and sleep in it during the night. When we had gotten the fire well started, to the consternation of all of us, a large and frightful looking snake came down the chimney. This, of course, did away with the idea of our sheltering ourselves in the cabin for the night, and we slept out in the open air, as we had done on previous occasions.[12]

Even after completing the journey, some experienced the harsh reality of racism. Remarking on the experiences, African American John Williams Matheus relates, "But after the surrender some of the people in Ohio were not so good to the colored people. The old folks told me they were stoned when they came across the river to Ohio after the surrender and that the colored people were treated like cats and dogs."[13]

Yet blacks were not unfamiliar with the territory, having inhabited and traversed the region as freedman and slaves from the opening up of the western frontier. As early as 1753, Edward Tarr, "a skilled, literate, bilingual, free black man" had settled west of the Blue Ridge Mountains in Augusta County, Virginia.[14] Like Tarr, a few blacks arrived on the frontier of their own volition;

the rest, however, arrived as chattel. Beginning with the War of 1812 to the eve of the Civil War, the salt mines of the Great Kanawah valley in western Virginia had utilized slaves leased and/or rented from their eastern Virginia owners. In 1832 the completion of the James River and Kanawah Turnpike allowed blacks to transport goods and/or accompany their masters overland from the James River to the Ohio and into Barboursville and Guyandotte. Skilled slave boatmen were common sights on Appalachia's waterways, with many transporting goods without white supervision. Once one crossed over the Appalachian Mountains, slaves could be found in the farms and small towns that dotted the region, and that formed an almost continuous link into the Kanawha and Ohio valleys. Moreover, they could be found working in Virginia's springs and spas, which used and housed large numbers of slaves during the antebellum era. By 1860, historian Wilma Dunaway notes, more than 8 percent of Appalachian slaves worked in the transportation systems that moved traded goods into and out of the region and more than one-fifth of the region's slave hires were contracted with companies that operated, maintained, or constructed transportation systems. Between 1850 and 1860, Appalachian masters were probably leasing out more than 11,000 slaves per year to water and overland transportation companies.[15] In effect, the region offered slaves unique opportunities for travel, education, autonomy, fraternization, and cross-fertilization with other slaves and their communities. This process surely provided a number of slaves and free blacks valuable information and insight into the region's physical, racial, and social geography.

Examination of White Sulphur Springs, "the most fashionable of all Virginia spas during antebellum times," allows entry into the ubiquitous presence of slaves at the resort, the unique nature of its slave community, and the construction of a counter-hegemonic culture.[16] Named after the white deposits left by sulfur water on the surrounding rocks during the late eighteenth century, the resort entered its first era of prominence during the 1830s as merchants, lawyers, judges, politicians, ministers, and diplomats, primarily from the South, congregated at the preeminent Southern summer destination. Between 1831 and 1860, the resort served as the de facto summer capital of the Old South. In fact, five sitting presidents from Andrew Jackson forward visited, savoring the pristine surroundings, the trappings of high society, and its cosmopolitan ambience.[17]

By 1860, White Sulphur Springs "was the largest resort in the area and perhaps the nation" and served as the commercial engine and social nexus for the area.[18] Like other places associated with Virginia's springs, the resort's importance as a central meeting place for Southern elite men grew as tensions between the North and South increased. Unquestionably, many a night was

Figure 2.1. "Hotel and Grounds," White Sulphur Springs. Source: *Harper's New Monthly Magazine* 57 (June–November 1878), 337.

highlighted by animated dinner conversation among guests and patrons over the issues of the day, none more central than slavery and slaves.

Besides serving as the mecca for Southern men of ample means and political sway, the resort also served as the economic and social locus of the area's slave-labor force. Not unlike the Southern elites they catered to, the black community housed at White Sulphur Springs was very different from that of the surrounding plantations, farms, or towns. Several sources have documented the historical presence of slaves at Virginia springs and spas, in general, and the resort, specifically, and the unique nature of its slave community. They reveal a particularized culture there, one in which black workers and visitors experienced greater autonomy and freedom. Not only did a web of intimate social relations connect resort slaves with slave and free black visitors, but the resort's blacks also established sociocultural links with those outside of the locality. The acquisition of knowledge and education attendant to their interactions with each other and Southern whites helped resort and area blacks to subvert, if only for a time, their subordinate status.[19]

Each summer throughout the middle decades of the century, the resort utilized dozens of slaves who worked there for a variety of motives. Clearly, the promise of joining or reconnecting to a spouse, family member, or friend, and/or the opportunity to earn money incentivized many, as did the prospects for adventure, a temporary break from their master and the arduous/mundane workload, and/or unwilling sexual advances or coercion. Recalling the plantation workday recollections of her great-great-grandmother Mary Charlott Perkins Rose, former Greenbrier County resident Edith E. Perkins Matthews explains:

> All able-bodied slaves were up by four o'clock in the morning: Eggs to be gathered, cows to be milked, stir up the fire to begin breakfast for a large family. ... The "house girl" gets the children up, dressed and to breakfast—probably with the mistress also. There is bed-making, scrubbing, cleaning and nursemaid for the children and the sick; help in the kitchen; spin, weave, and sew; serve mid-day meal—clean-up afterwards. Laundry is an all day affair. Lye soap—linens—clothing—in turn—are pumped, pummeled, with a laundry stick, and scrubbed clean ...
>
> The slave house required the same labor as the 'Big House.' The only time slaves could do for themselves was at night. Occasionally Charlot and Eliza were "loaned out" to the households of the brother or sisters or married children of the owner.[20]

Given the nature of the workday and the intrinsic threats Charlot and Eliza faced during their working lives in the county's plantation-based economy, White Sulphur Springs may have represented the closest thing to sanctuary a Greenup County female slave might experience in her lifetime.

The growing importance of slave labor to the resort throughout the mid-1800s is seen as early as 1831 when the value of the resort's real estate holdings totaled $100,000 and $56,000 for its slaves.[21] The resort's growth during the middle decades of the century coincided with the continuing importance of slavery in the county. In 1850 the county contained 1,317 slaves, 13.1 percent of the total population of 10,022. In 1860 slaves numbered 1,525 out of a total population of 12,211, or 12.5 percent.[22] By late 1850 White Sulphur could accommodate 1,500 visitors and employed and utilized a small army of black and white workers, locals and outsiders, seasonal and year-round, to meet every whim of its patrons.[23] That year, related to cost-cutting measures, the resort dramatically shifted the composition of its labor pool and began leasing slaves, paying nearly $17,000, 10 percent of the total hotel department expenses for the season, for slave-servant hire. An additional $1,217 for slave artisans and repairmen came under "Improvements" expenses.[24]

Work at Virginia's springs, generally, and at White Sulphur Springs, specifically, where, at any given time, dozens of black men, women, and children from across the South intermingled, resulted in a distinct work culture from the prevailing regional slave society. Operating within the circle of the service-oriented economy, resort slaves working as servants, waiters, bartenders, chambermaids, cleaners, and cooks recognized their labor offered opportunities to gain compensatory rewards, and they engaged in activities to exploit them. All front-line resort slaves—even the youngest—expected and pursued tips from patrons, ingratiating themselves as thoroughly as they could through flattery, good humor, exemplary and enthusiastic service, professional demeanor, fawning attention, and deference, each providing evidence of his or her subordinate status. Yet flattery also created the conditions that compelled whites to give money to the slave, thus undermining one important foundational aspect of slavery.[25] This ethos differentiated the resort slave from the agricultural slave who operated within a system of coercion not directly linked to monetary rewards for work performed.

Resort blacks met, worked, and socialized with a variety of blacks from outside of their locality, including slave and free-black musicians from Richmond, Baltimore, and Washington. Moreover, resort and visiting slaves enjoyed leisure activities, frequently outside the prying eyes of disapproving white patrons or managers. In the process of working and recreating with others, they exchanged knowledge and culture, helping to create a distinct communal ethos that shaped and molded the actions and responses of resort workers as well as free and visiting blacks. Christian Friedrich Mayr's remarkable 1838 painting, *Kitchen Ball at White Sulphur Springs, Virginia*, vividly illustrates the exceptional nature of African American life there.

Depicting a black wedding celebration, the painting portrays black cultural interaction by privileged household servants of various pigmentations who had accompanied their plantation masters to the springs. Void of the crude caricatures so commonly rendered during the era by American artists, the recently arrived German immigrant instead illustrated the insular nature of black cultural cross-fertilization while elevating black individuality and humanity in his depiction of slaves at play. Not only does Mayr portray "all the well-known coloured people in the place," including "the band of musicians," but, significantly, he illuminates the hierarchy of slavery that existed at the springs. Like their masters, blacks at the resort mimicked and embraced the trappings of fashionable society, leisure activities, and mutual competition, vying with one another in courting, dressing, and dancing, in the quest for status and acclaim. In effect, the black community at the springs engaged in behavior and attitudes that helped to construct their own signs of status, fashion, and identity.[26]

Figure 2.2. *Kitchen Ball at White Sulphur Springs, Virginia*, Christian Friedrich Mayr, 1838. North Carolina Museum of Art, Raleigh. Purchased with funds from the State of North Carolina.

While not totally dismissing the occasional reprimand, verbal spat, or even fistfight attendant to the acquisition of a prized cut of meat, a special dish, or other privilege for a select patron, or even those associated with tensions related to social stratification within the black resort community, resort life fostered mutual cooperation, assistance, and black solidarity. At White Sulphur Springs, emblematic of community formation on the plantation discussed by historian John Blassingame, "the socialization process, shared expectations, ideals, and enclosed status system of the slave's culture promoted group identification and a positive self-concept."[27] This ethos is readily discernible when one considers that black workers were expected to maintain a certain level of etiquette, deference, and professionalism in discharging their duties. Any leased slave who failed to adhere to societal expectations and resort standards faced the real prospect of contract termination, return to their master, and probable punishment. Thus, resort life mitigated, even if irregularly, incrementally, and temporarily, the corrosive

Figure 2.3. Nostalgic portrayal of black waiter at White Sulphur Springs. The caption reads, "'Haven't I Waited on you Befo', Suh?'" Source: *Harper's New Monthly Magazine* 73 (June–November 1886), 428.

and coercive measures of subjugation. Recognizing the exceptionality of resort life and labor, resort slaves preserved resort as well as black communal ethical standards. One patron, noting the uncommon level of honesty and professionalism demonstrated at White Sulphur, remarked,

> Nobody ever locked a door or closed a window. Cottages most remote were left open and without guard, miscellaneous articles of the toilet were left about, trunks were not locked, waiters, chambermaids, porters, washerwomen, were constantly coming and going, having access to the rooms at all hours, and yet no guest ever lost so much as a hairpin or a cigar. This fashion of trust and of honesty so impressed the artist that he said he should make an attempt to have it introduced elsewhere. This sort of esprit de corps among the colored people was unexpected.[28]

Further evidence of black cultural ethos is relayed by another patron, who described her view behind the scenes at the Old White: "In the various departments we found admirable system, healthy, likely slaves all employed;

yet evidently not overworked or oppressed—a corps of subordinates having their duties so arranged, that they relieved each other in quick succession whenever the work was severe. Whether the perfection of the management arises from perseverance in method, or efficient servants, the result is certainly admirable."[29] In effect, black resort workers, incentivized by the positive outcomes of their labor and community allegiance, in contrast to their agriculture-centered and oppressed lives outside the grounds, worked not only because of their status; they also worked because they recognized the real and potential benefits of their labor to their spiritual, psychic, communal, and, occasionally, material well-being.

The social organization of resort life helped transmit a degree of self-awareness and empowerment, creating what historian Wilma Dunaway calls "subcultures of resistance."[30] Resort slaves exercised an uncommon degree of

Figure 2.4. An example of the unique racial and social environment contributing to the cross-fertilization process found at the White Sulphur Springs. Source: *Harper's New Monthly Magazine* 57 (June–November 1878), 342.

power over the delivery of service, so much so that whites frequently found it expedient to negotiate with individual slaves to achieve their wishes. Because frontline workers could *choose* to serve or ignore patrons, bribes and tips were common. As one astute patron remarked, "Bribery furnishes you with the best to be got."[31] This was especially true in the huge dining rooms where slaves could frustrate a large number of wealthy men and women by the pace and quality of their response.[32]

For many, the necessity for negotiation must have been a mortifying affair. Arriving to the resort after traveling upriver from Natchez, Mississippi, to Guyandotte, before connecting to an overland stage, "Miss Matilda Jane Routh, daughter of John Routh, and granddaughter of Job Routh" faced this prospect. Commenting on her dilemma, one observer noted, "Miss Matilda will have to bribe the slaves at this place to get proper service (bribing slaves will give a young lady from the Deep South something of a jolt) and tipping will set her back, say $3.50 a week, though there were those who figured it twice as much."[33] Ironically, those Southerners who sought special accommodation undercut the social and racial distinctions so intrinsic to their elevated sense of self. Addressing the unique circumstances at Virginia springs, historian Charlene M. Boyers Lewis notes, "Around their duties, free and slave blacks, whether visitors or workers, created their own community at the resorts. They had their own leisure experiences and sometimes claimed the same spaces as whites. They even shaped their own version of fashionable society, with its own rules and competition for status."[34] Slaves recognized the implicit power given to them by paternalistic white resort managers and patrons and exploited it as best they could. In effect, as Eugene D. Genovese noted, in contrast to the master's notions of paternalism being confined only to reciprocal duties, slaves "added their own doctrine of reciprocal rights."[35]

Another way slaves acted on their perceived rights was through the appropriation of public space normally reserved for whites. Whether "promenading" on the only walks attached to the spring, relaxing at scenic and/or leisure sites, or filling the air with the "fumes of bad segars," black waiters and maids challenged prevailing norms. Further evidence of this dynamic is seen in a letter published in July 1858 in the *Charleston Daily Courier*, in which "A CAROLINIAN" protested "negro waiters being allowed to *ride within* and upon the stage occupied by ladies and gentle" and urged the proprietors of White Sulphur to use their influence with stage companies to prevent such affronts to the racial order. "You may imagine my horror," he continued, "when, on starting the stage, the driver was stopped by the agent, and two black waiters were put *inside*, in close proximity with the ladies." After stepping out of the stage for a moment and losing his seat to a white man, one of the slave waiters demanded it back and, to the Carolinian's mortification, received it."[36] Clearly, the behavior and attitudes of resort slaves demonstrate that they believed they possessed an equal right to these spaces, no matter the wealth, status, or chagrin of white guests.

Travel also opened up opportunities for resort slaves to carve out spaces of autonomy. Leased and visiting slaves often traveled back and forth between their home plantations and the Virginia springs on public stages by themselves, some carrying money for their expenses. Occasionally, one or more slaves drove a carriage alone to either retrieve or transport their master, mistress, or other family member. Travel afforded slaves the opportunity to establish informational, social, and cultural ties with local, visiting, and hired slaves as well as with slave invalids, servants, and free blacks from across the region.[37] Resort workers interacted not only with a variety of black people but also with a diverse collection of white staff, management, and patrons, receiving and passing on gossip, news, stories, and personal and family histories. These encounters provided opportunities for the resort blacks to gain solace, insight, and information from multiple sources, knowledge that could be used for their betterment.[38] Discussing the "grapevine telegraph" linking slave to slave and plantation to plantation during the Civil War, Booker T. Washington commented, "While there was not a single slave on our plantation that could read a line, in some way we were kept informed of the progress of the war almost as accurately as the most intelligent person. . . . When Lee surrendered, all of the plantation people knew it, although all of them acted as if they were ignorant of the fact that anything unusual had taken place."[39]

The remarkable arrival of sixty-three free African American males—37 black and 26 mulatto employees, from Washington, D.C., to work as "servants" in the main dining room of "the Old White" during the summer of 1860 further attests to the potential ways the unique cultural, social, and economic conditions existing at the spa might have contributed to the grapevine telegraph. Ranging from ages fourteen to fifty-six, with Reason Blow, the youngest, and Daniel Blow, presumably his father, the eldest, the employment of free blacks into the preeminent Southern resort on the eve of the Civil War raises numerous questions. For example, what rationale drove the decision to use such a labor force? What were the logistics and challenges of recruiting and then transporting dozens of free blacks and mulattoes through the heart of Virginia slave country? And what of the nature of their sojourn at the resort?

One can only imagine the curiosity, incredulity, and perhaps outrage of whites and blacks at the arrival and use of such a population. Undoubtedly, the prospect of employment, recreation, and adventure at a summer resort provided great incentive for prospective hires to leave Washington's summer heat and humidity and competitive environment. Yet the utilization of the assemblage, instead of locally leased slaves, in the hotel's largest and most complex dining room reveals the contradictions and fault lines attendant to White Sulphur Springs's service-based economy situated within the region's slave-based society.[40] On the one hand, the use of free blacks to provide a premier level of service reinforced the fundamental aspects of white superiority: class standing, paternalism, and racial subordination. On the other hand, the *employment* of free blacks subverted the very quintessence of the spa and the fundamental principles undergirding the Southern slave system: the inferiority and incapability of blacks.[41] Additionally, while employment by its very nature differentiated wage earner from slave, presenting conditions conducive to producing class fissures and thus undermining black cultural development and community solidarity, employment at the resort also produced the conditions most feared by the planter: free blacks and slaves in direct, unsupervised contact with each other, as they both traveled to and from the spa and region.

The exceptionality of black resort life at the spa was noted by local owners, who frequently found themselves conflicted by the monetary gain derived from hiring out their slaves and the discomforting influence of the resort environment upon their property. The corrupting influence of White Sulphur Springs on locally leased slaves was noted by manager and slave owner Jeremiah Morton, who cautioned his sister-in-law against hiring out a female slave who wished to join her husband at the resort. "My advice," he advised, "is, never to permit a servant to be hired at Springs, especially at the White Sulphur" for "few are well satisfied afterwards" to resume their plantation duties. He explained, "I shall never permit Chapman or any of my young servants to come here again if I have my way."[42] Even more worrisome for local whites was the threat that the resort's toxic slave culture might spread beyond its walls and infect the area's slave and free-black population. So palpable was this threat that Greenbrier County authorities petitioned the Virginia Legislature to change the law to limit the stay of free blacks in the county to only one month after their manumission. In this way, the county authorities believed that they freedpersons would have less time to "spread discord and disaffection" or to map the mountain roads that could be used to "purloin off [their] slaves and reach a free state."[43]

Trapped at the bottom of Southern society, resort blacks at White Sulphur Springs were still subject to the insults and indignities, terror and brutalities so common to the era and region. Women were subject to unwanted sexual advances or sexual coercion by white patrons and possibly black co-workers.

Table 2.1. Slave Population for Greenbrier County, Virginia, 1850 and 1860

	1850	% of total population	1860	% of total population
Slave	1,317	13.1	1,525	12.5
Free			198	1.6
White	8,705	86.9	10,488	85.9
Total	10,022	100	12,211	100

Source: U.S. Census Bureau, Fifth Census (1850), Sixth Census (1860)

And, while they were barred from entering the resort to conduct business, slave traders did ply their trade in the area, endangering individuals and families. In fact, the owner of hired slave Israel attempted to sell him after Israel's tenure at the resort.[44] Ultimately, no matter the benefits of resort labor and the development of antebellum black culture, community, and education, one must remember that Greenbrier County was firmly proslavery and pro-Confederacy throughout the Civil War era. Consequently, it, like the rest of slaveholding Virginia, was inextricably linked to the dictates of the master class and thus strongly against the formation of West Virginia. Yet blacks housed at the spa achieved small, daily victories denied them outside its confines. In truth, over the course of its antebellum history White Sulphur Springs served as a unique enclave of refuge, regeneration, and reconnaissance for hundreds of local and visiting slaves, poor whites, and free blacks.

Even during the Civil War, while the resort suffered near devastation, the town of White Sulphur Springs served as a sanctuary for blacks who benefited from the regional grapevine telegraph. After enduring slavery, her near-sale by her owner to pay off debts, and the separation from her family, Anne Eliza Riddle, the mother of Carter G. Woodson, suffered the additional heartbreak of her younger brother's disappearance while she worked in the fields. Unaware that Union soldiers had taken him with them as they moved through the area and unable to find him, Riddle presumed him lost forever. Ultimately, the boy was left with a family in the town who did not know his origins, and he was too young to tell them. Several years later, while living in Huntington in the early 1870s, a worker from the town overheard the now Mrs. Woodson speak of her lost brother and remembered a man from his hometown who had heard the name that she used. Shortly afterward, the man returned home and made inquiries of her brother. And, through his efforts, she was reunited with Robert D. Riddle, who lived his entire adult life a few miles outside of White Sulphur Springs in the Ronceverte area of West Virginia, as a teacher and farmer.[45] Given the primacy of family in her life, one can only imagine her joy at their reunion.

Both the Civil War and West Virginia's formation irrevocably changed the fate of the spa. The former devastated it, leaving it nearly beyond repair, while the creation of West Virginia in 1863 removed it from Confederate Virginia and relocated it, along with a number of other counties, to the nascent pro-union state. The war also changed the fortune of thousands of the area's blacks. In its aftermath, Greenbrier County experienced significant black out-migration. The county's black population decreased by 36 percent from 1860 to 1870, the largest drop of any county in West Virginia. Certainly, despite the state's elevated ideological stance, harsh memories, ongoing racism, the quest for loved ones, and opportunities elsewhere compelled large numbers of blacks to leave. Many were undoubtedly aided in their exertions and aspirations by money and information gained from their labor at White Sulphur Springs.

Although the *specifics* of the migrant experience in the post–Civil War era might have differed, the general conditions of the aggregate did not. Black agency (as well as social interactions between blacks and whites) in postbellum Greenbrier and/or Cabell County, as in the rest of the South, was constrained for years by paternalistic attitudes. In fact, many whites never adapted to the changes emancipation wrought. Certainly, this was as true throughout southern West Virginia as it was throughout the shattered South. Black migrants challenged the historical status quo in their quest to build lives. With their worldly possessions tightly secured, tens of thousands, many composite families, embarked, in wagons and on foot, to distant destinations, frequently outside of their native state.[46] Like other mass migrations, this stream was predictable.[47] Recalling conversations with the descendants of early Huntington's black migrants, local black historian Edna Duckworth recalls that many times she heard, "'My family came over the Blue Ridge in a wagon.' I heard it so often until I wondered, was it a wagon train?"[48]

Even if calibrated by purpose and order, for significant numbers of black migrants traveling from central Virginia into southeast West Virginia (and onto Cabell County) the journey must have been an emotional and uncertain experience, one intensified by travel though White Sulphur Springs, the most visible and important expression of slaveocracy (and its demise) in the region. Notably, as illuminated here, for decades the springs had served as the epicenter of the black historical experience in the county, if not the region. Thus, black migrant interaction with Greenbrier County's black residential population, the first sizable black population in the state along the James River and Kanawha Turnpike, would have produced ample opportunities for socializing, collaboration, and strategizing, abetting the cross-fertilization process. Unquestionably, for many black migrants, successful and safe migration and navigation through southern West Virginia's resistant racial and social environment was linked to the intelligence culled from their interactions with the county's residential blacks, fellow migrants, and, perhaps, sympathetic whites. There is little doubt, then, that a large percentage of the black influx into Cabell County, and throughout the region, was linked to the web of information generated and/ or encountered at the springs via the grapevine telegraph.

Common features of early black migration included the initial exploratory trip performed solo by a young black male on foot or horseback; evaluation, sometimes over extended periods, of prospective locale; a return trip to retrieve family and/or friends, or the relaying of word through a third party for them to come; preparation for the move; and, finally, migration. Extended periods of isolation or separation compelled mindfulness of one's place, geographically and socially. In his study on black migration to McDowell County, West Virginia, Howard P. Wade notes, "Since strange blacks were suspect once they left the community in which they were known, it was a dangerous undertaking."[49]

The vast majority of black migrants engaged in purposeful, frequently informed journeys, yet many newly freed blacks, lacking a clear destination or perceived to lack one, were seen as threats to civil society. We should remember that freedom had different meanings for different people and populations. Frequently, whites conflated unstructured and seemingly recreational movement of the newly emancipated with aimlessness.[50] Carter G. Woodson challenged the portrayal of newly emancipated black men as wayward, hedonistic, and corruptible, as well as the rationale behind it. In the aftermath of the demise of the "peculiar institution," unfettered travel and joyful expression, he argued, was merely the natural articulation of emancipation by the Negro "to put his freedom to a test." Thus, it is understandable that for a time, the profundity and intensity of liberation was interpreted by black people "not only as freedom from slavery but freedom from responsibility."[51] Any understanding of the county's (and Huntington's) nascent black migrant population lies in examining how it interpreted and acted on the contours of newfound freedom.[52]

What is clear is that on the heels of the Civil War and emancipation, blacks and whites, for reasons both linked and separate, departed Virginia (and West Virginia). Emancipation precipitated significant change throughout Cabell County as well. After the war, the county's total population declined from 8,020 in 1860 to 6,429 in 1870. Yet due to increasing land values associated with the established territory, and because the county had remained largely untouched by the war, the value of its 160,500 acres fell only slightly, from $1.68 million in 1860 to $1.55 million in 1870, a negligible drop compared to the Virginia counties under discussion.[53]

Yet the value of personal assets per white household in the district of Guyandotte dipped from $1,192 to $503, a fact partially attributable to the damage inflicted to the town during the war, white out-migration, and the loss of the town's 101 slaves. This loss mirrored the dramatic drop in the county's black residential population, from 329 in 1860, including 24 free blacks, to 123 by 1870.[54] Interestingly, tobacco production nearly doubled during the decade as more people, eyeing increased profits, shifted to the crop and away from corn and wheat.[55] In truth, in 1870 Cabell County's economic foundation was still firmly entrenched in agriculture.[56]

In spring of 1871, just months after the incorporation of Huntington, West Virginia, a group of black migrants arrived in the village. Like so many before them, this group had traveled the James River and Kanawha Turnpike to traverse the Appalachia Mountains before arriving at their destination. They were led by thirty-one-year-old itinerant preacher Nelson Barnett, who, after spending some time preaching at churches throughout the Ohio valley, acquired a job on an upstart railroad and then walked back to his homeland in Buckingham County, Virginia. There, he spread the word to friends and family of "honest work to be had" on the railroad. Soon, he explained, Huntington would be a key station of the Chesapeake and Ohio Railroad, and jobs and other blacks would surely follow.[57]

Although the primacy of economic opportunity is clearly stated as a "pull" factor for black migration to Huntington, some discussion on the possible "push" factors is warranted. In 1870, Buckingham County contained 6,411 black residents, a drop of 2,400 over the preceding decade, a fact that impacted yeoman and planter alike.[58] Deprived of their enslaved workers who, through the sweat of their daily labor, primed, topped, and sorted more than 4.75 million pounds of tobacco in 1860, the county's tobacco production collapsed to a mere 890,000 pounds in 1870, a total lower than each of its neighboring counties save for Appomattox. The assessed value of the county's real estate also fell precipitously to $1.85 million, nearly half its 1860 total, a development mirrored throughout the South. As one authority notes, "The value of land in Buckingham, which had increased by approximately 15% from 1850–1860 plunged to levels below the 1820 values after the war."[59] Discussing the county's economic demise, the U.S. Bureau of the Census noted of tobacco production, "Tenants, the majority of who[m] are negroes, raise, as a rule, an inferior grade, which is forced into the market through local dealers in an unfit condition."[60] Addressing the economic realities of Buckingham County African Americans, Dianne Swann-Wright states, "The reality of freedom challenged the notion that the bottom rail could ever be on the top. In this community, economic realities and necessities made for unmet needs and unobtainable wishes in many instances."[61] Thus, the logical choice for many of Buckingham County's freedpersons was migration.

Given Nelson Barnett's calling, native intelligence, and persuasive powers, it is easy to imagine his group seeking guidance and counsel through prayer before making their decision. Eventually, James Henry Woodson, Barnett's brother-in-law, agreed to join him. Other able-bodied men joined in, and eventually, after packing their belongings and as many people as they could onto Woodson's horse drawn wagon, the "family" began the journey west from the farmlands of New Canton, Virginia. Six years after the end of the Civil War and eight years after West Virginia obtained statehood, the assembly, composed of Barnett, his twenty-five-year-old wife, the former Betty Woodson, and their children—Carter, age five, McClinton, age five, and, George, age one—James Henry Woodson, and family friend Anderson Radford (and perhaps others) arrived in the town. There, they, like thousands of other black migrants in immediate postbellum America, built a life.[62] In their efforts, they were unremarkable, merely participants in the long-standing historical process of movement and migration. Yet in no small way they were pioneers, perhaps even heroes.

A few months before the end of the Civil War, James Woodson was a slave in Fluvanna County, Virginia, when he learned that Abraham Lincoln had issued the Emancipation Proclamation. Woodson fled his master and later came under the protection of Union soldiers; he then assisted in raids upon Confederate soldiers and storage facilities. After the war, Woodson returned to Fluvanna County and shortly thereafter married former slave Anne Eliza Riddle of New Canton, Buckingham County, Virginia. (During the war, Riddle had watched over her mother and siblings. Her efforts ensured the family remained intact and safe during the transition from slaves to freedpeople.) The couple moved to New Canton and eventually became the parents of nine children, the youngest of whom was Carter G. Woodson.[63]

After her marriage to James Woodson in 1869, the couple and relatives traveled to White Sulphur Springs as they moved west across the Appalachians. There they camped with other families whose men, like Woodson, all hoped to gain employment with the Chesapeake and Ohio Railroad or in the coal mines. Woodson acquired work at a railroad construction site on the western section of the railroad close to where Huntington would eventually rise. In 1870 the family moved back to Buckingham County, where they resided before deciding to migrate to Huntington in 1871.[64] Surely, the travails and successes of the past informed, guided, and fortified their efforts as they traveled west to the dusty hamlet located on the Ohio River.

Despite the impediments, political agitation, while muted, was one method the state's early black residents used to address the complexity of the new era. Stephen D. Engle states, "Politics became the chief instrument by which freedom could be realized, since it served to bring local mandates in line with national legislation."[65] In the fall of 1870, black men voted for the first time in Cabell County, when fourteen—26 percent of the total black voting population—cast their ballots in the state election of 1870.[66]

That year, only a small and dispersed black residential population resided in the county. A few still possessed the surnames of prominent Cabell County white families: Black, Kilgore, Jenkins, and, most prominently, Morris. Scattered throughout the county's five districts of Barboursville, Guyandotte, Union, Grant, and McComas were 70 black adult females and fifty-three adult males, including 25 mulattoes (20 percent of the population altogether), and 66 children under age eighteen (see map 4). The 112 African American pioneers residing within the county represented 1.9 percent of the general population. Fifty-eight were West Virginia natives, forty Virginians, six from North Carolina, three from Ohio, two from Kentucky, and one person each from Tennessee, South Carolina and Louisiana. Unfortunately, the 1870 federal census fails to cite familial or household relationships.[67]

Examination of the black residential population within the various districts provides insight into the economic status of early black settlers in the county. In 1870 the district of Barboursville, the county seat and most affluent white district, encompassed territory that abutted the other four, stretching from the Cabell-Wayne County line in the west to the Union district line in the east. Combined black wealth, comprising real estate and personal assets and excluding income, totaled $415. No black person owned real estate, and personal assets averaged $46 per black household. Average white household real estate value in Barboursville was $2,439 and personal assets averaged $610 per household. Average white household size was 5.7 persons while average black household size was five, with the households of Benjamin and Mandalay Morris, and Patsey Dean with seven individuals each, comprising the largest. The district included 45 nonwhites in 1870 (23 blacks and 22 mulattoes) out of a total population of 1,228. (Within the town of Barboursville resided 14 blacks and 371 whites.) Nine African American households are listed, including two sets of Morrises, the only familial (along with the George Morris household in McComas) relationship listed in the 1870 census. Eighty-five-year-old Virginia-born farm worker Samuel Morris possessed a personal estate valued at $200. His household included Louisa; a twenty-eight-year-old housekeeper, Ester, age thirty; and Henry, twenty-two, the only West Virginian. Not far away lived his mulatto sister, Eliza Morris, a sixteen-year-old live-in domestic servant. The thirty-two-year-old West Virginian Benjamin, a farm worker, headed the other Morris household with Mahala, his wife, who was a housekeeper and native to the state. Together,

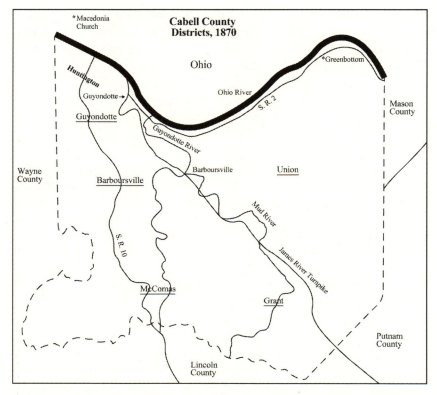

Map 2.1. Five districts of Cabell County, 1870. Source: Eldridge, *Cemeteries of Cabell County, West Virginia*, vol. 2.

the two had a personal estate listed at $140; two daughters, Ann and Mary, ages eight and two, respectively; and sons, Moses (six), Charles (four), and William (three months).[68]

Located at the junction of the Ohio and Guyandotte Rivers south of Greenbottom, the district of Guyandotte encompassed the oldest part of Cabell County and contained its second-most-affluent population. Out of a population of 2,095, the district (not surprisingly) also housed the largest number of nonwhites within the county—30 blacks and 24 mulattoes. Here resided the county's most affluent black residential population. Combined black wealth totaled $1,128, with blacks possessing $645 in real estate and personal wealth and the mulatto population holding $483. Interestingly, $375 of real estate (inheritance?) was owned by sixteen-year-old farm worker and student Richard David.[69] All six of the black children attending school in the county were from Guyandotte.[70]

Total real estate holdings for the 365 white households in Guyandotte totaled nearly $817,000 and more than $183,400 in personal assets. The average household real estate holding for whites was $2,238; personal assets averaged $503 per household, totals slightly below those of Barboursville's white population. Nine black households, the same number as in Barboursville, resided within the district. However, the size of nonwhite households was greater than those found in the remaining districts. The average nonwhite household size in Guyandotte was six (compared to 6.2 persons per white household). Six of the nine black households in Guyandotte consisted of five individuals. Three held more than six persons. Two households held more than eight persons—the largest nonwhite households in the county, that of Elijah and Virginia Tucker, with eight, and James and Julia Farrist, with 10.[71]

The largest district, Union, was in the northwest, lying east and west of County Road leading from Greenbottom on the Ohio River to Mud River. It possessed only one black household, that of previously mentioned former Cabell County slave and current farm worker Anderson Ross (Rose) and his longtime companion, former Jenkins family slave and servant Mary Lacy, both age thirty-five and West Virginia born, and three children, fifteen-year-old farm worker George, twelve-year-old Christina, and three-year-old mulatto John P. Although schools were in the area, neither George nor Christina attended, suggesting that either their value to household maintenance precluded school or the racial dynamics of the area precluded the possibility. The state did not pass any provision addressing the funding, appropriation, and enumeration of Negro schools until 1872. These five lived among 972 whites in a rural, predominately agricultural area, a situation rendering unlikely a separate school for black people. A similar geographic, demographic, and social circumstance existed in Grant Township, in the northeast corner of the county, adjacent to Lincoln County, where two nonwhite, native-born households resided. Like Union, the township possessed five blacks in a township of 980 whites.[72]

McComas, located in the southern part of the county and straddling the Guyandotte River, was home to ten nonwhites—nine blacks and one mulatto, eleven-year-old Henry Smith. These ten resided within a total population of 1,149. George and Nancy Morris, ages fifty-two and fifty-five, respectively, maintained a household consisting of four children. George, an illiterate farm worker and Nancy, a housekeeper, possessed a personal estate valued at a remarkable $1,215, a sum nearly four times higher than for any other black household in the county and greater than the total reported wealth of county's remaining black population.

The large size of some households, the age differences among members, and the various surnames within them were typical for black (and even white) households of the era and provide evidence of the power of kinship and social networks in 1870 Cabell County. Black households comprised diverse kin, generational, and racial configurations influencing economic status for better and worse. The three Morris households, containing 17 individuals (nine adults and eight children), controlled personal estates worth an extraordinary $1,555 a sum exceeding the $1,203 amassed by the county's remaining 17 African American households. None of the five school-age children within the Morris households attended school. The household of thirty-three-year-old West Virginian and Barboursville resident Patsey Dean included Frederick (sixteen) and Henry Wheatfield (seven), Marcellis (thirteen), Susan (eight), and Charles Mills (five), and Anabelle Price (two), all from West Virginia. None of the school-age children attended school. The household of Virginia-born Elijah and Virginia Tucker included the following family members: Virginians Jupiter and Virginia Vivey (ages fifty and fifty-one), Lupita Vivey (sixteen, from West Virginia) and Leah Vivey (eleven, from Virginia), Rose (twelve, from West Virginia), and Henry Blake (eleven, from Virginia). Leah, Rose, and Henry attended school.

Though the county's black residents were no longer shackled to the institution, work and land still bound them to a particular lifestyle, which, when combined with their low numbers and dispersed population, largely precluded school attendance. Moreover, the lack of interest by the state legislature did not help matters, yet it is important to note that given their economic realities, they did not confront patronage or tenancy as a transitional economic system, as African Americans did in Virginia and throughout the South. Thus, it is probable that the absence of racially based economic systems helped to facilitate the development and institutionalization of wage-labor capitalism in Huntington.

As it was for African Americans throughout the South, the immediate postemancipation period for black West Virginian's was pregnant with possibilities. Collis P. Huntington's decision to establish the western transshipment terminal in the county for the Chesapeake and Ohio Railroad that would connect Richmond, Virginia, to the Ohio River valley compelled black migration into the region and county, continuing the multitiered transition in the journey of the county's black population. The actual founding of Huntington, West Virginia, in 1871 encompassed the first phase of industrial capitalism that would transform Cabell County, Appalachia, and America and would fundamentally alter the lives of black migrants who arrived in the region seeking gainful employment, which is the subject of chapter 3. But, at this point, the black population in the county was too small, too dispersed, and too poor to witness much change in their lives beyond the fact that they were all now free.

CHAPTER 3

Into the Crucible

The Chesapeake and Ohio Railroad and the Black Industrial Worker, 1870–1900

The men were tired and cranky. This was the fifth consecutive day the temperature had reached the eighties by noon. High on the side of a mountain, deep within the primeval forest of the New River valley, black, Italian, and Irish sweated, groaned, bled, and cussed. By now, three weeks into blasting the tunnel, they had learned to ignore the shouts of encouragement and recriminations from the foremen, most much more concerned about the schedule and deadlines than their safety and security. They knew the routine. But the workload and heat took their tool. It was hard, physically exhausting, and mentally draining work. Like ants, they roamed the tunnel, lifting, laying, driving, carrying, digging, clearing, cutting, shoveling, grading, pounding, and blasting. One misstep, one mistake, and you could find yourself cold in the ground. Some had already lost their lives. The previous week, one blasting accident killed six. Their mangled bodies had been dumped unceremoniously in a makeshift mass grave about halfway down the mountain.

Unable to unleash their animus toward their bosses, workers instead had to direct their frustration and animosity toward each other. Heat, fatigue, and anxiety could get the best of any man; on occasion, tensions had flared, personal, racial, and cultural alliances had frayed, and blows were exchanged. Yet after the eruption, tempers subsided, relations normalized, and the work proceeded. Track was laid, spikes driven, and bit by bit, the railroad advanced. By sunset, muscles aching, many workers were so drained by the exertions that they had trouble walking upright as they trudged down the mountain to the chuckwagon. Most were too tired and too hungry to engage in extended conversation during or after the meal. Instead, their bellies full, they drifted off to sleep, knowing that at the crack of sun-up, day six would begin. And, it was going to be another hot one.

From the early to mid-1800s forward, the presence of African American laborers in western Virginia and West Virginia helped bind the area to a broader regional commercial network. Slaves helped make the antebellum Kanawha valley salt mines productive and profitable.[1] As early as 1852 the value of black labor to the construction of railroads in the region was well known. Indeed, the construction of four tunnels in the Blue Ridge Mountains for the Virginia Central Railroad Company had been accomplished "with pick and shovel, the brawn of negro laborers and the hauling power of mules. The construction gangs had no dump carts, steam drills, or modern blasting powder."[2] After the Civil War an influx of black laborers, including a young Booker T. Washington, arrived to work the area's coal mines.[3] Craftsmen and artisans also arrived into the region.[4]

After the war, Collis P. Huntington, along with his army of workers, initiated the industrialization of southern West Virginia through the construction of the Chesapeake and Ohio Railroad. More than a dozen tunnels were projected, aggregating some 24,000 linear feet, more than four and half miles. Enormous amounts of dirt and stone required removal. Miles of roadbeds adjacent to West Virginia's rivers had to be raised above flood level. To carry out his plans, Huntington needed millions of dollars and thousands of laborers to cross to the rugged mountains of the southern part of the state. Black southerners played an integral and vital role felling forests, raising roads, driving spikes, and blasting tunnels. In fact, not more than 125 miles southeast of the town, in the primeval wilderness of the New River valley, a stout and skilled John Henry, along with nearly 1,000 men, most of them African American, constructed the mile-long Big Bend Tunnel, which, when completed, was the longest tunnel in America.[5]

Given their number, efficacy, and cost, there is little doubt that African American laborers were the *preferred* labor force on the Chesapeake and Ohio. Contributing to this development was the known quality of black labor and the unknown worthiness of the European immigrant.[6] As a white boy of fourteen, A. W. (Alex) Hamilton worked in early 1870 on the construction of the West Virginia extension between White Sulphur Springs and Hawk's Nest (near Charleston). Born and raised near the James River and Kanawha Turnpike, Hamilton noted the importance of black labor from Virginia and North Carolina "brought in on trains from White Sulphur Springs where they began the long trek on foot over the James River and Kanawha turnpike (now Midland Trail) to the point or points where they were to work. These gangs would run from one to three hundred, accompanied by 'chuck-wagon' and the boss or bosses in charge."[7]

Overwhelmingly composed of single men, work gangs frequently existed on the frontier in isolated work camps. Notably, though, some of these camps grew into enclaves, boomtowns, and even permanent communities, with many named after railroad officials—Alderson, Crozet, Talcott, Thurmond, Huntington, and Parsons, to name a few.[8] Life in the work camps provided opportunity; as well, extended periods of isolation afforded time to save substantial sums of money. Many black laborers acquired enough money to purchase farms when the road they were working on was completed. Many also acquired skills and took great pride in blacksmithing, masonry, tunneling, and mining.

Significantly, there seems to have been little racial strife in the construction of the railroad. Perhaps part of the reason is that white observers were overwhelmingly the ones providing accounts of the construction of the line. While acknowledging the color line in living accommodations, these accounts depicted harmonious relations on the line. New York writer Charles Nordhoff, who toured the line in 1871, noted: "Wherever we rode, I saw whites and Negroes working together, pushing at the same car, shoveling at the same dirt heap, lifting together at one rock. In the work there is absolutely no distinction of color; nor did I in any case see any dislike, or bullying of a colored man by a white man."[9] Another reason is that there existed little wage discrimination between the races, with skilled African American laborers earning proportionally more than their unskilled white counterparts. Certainly, another factor to consider is that black laborers were aware of the constraints affecting their employment. While white accounts of black laborers by engineers and contractors celebrated their industriousness, aptitude, and equanimity, it is important to note, as historian Ronald Eller does, that "in order to maintain his position, the Negro laborer had to be sober, hardworking, and well disciplined."[10] This is important when one considers that to attract laborers to Big Bend, ex-Confederate Army captain John Johnson recruited, among his pool, ex-slaves to the precarious worksite.[11] Johnson was just one of many ex-Confederates employed by the railroad in positions of authority in the New River valley, including Claiborne R. Mason.[12] One historian relates that "Mason's long experience controlling men and recapturing runaways made him an able if brutal boss for the C&O. Many Southerners already hated and feared Mason for what he had done to stop Confederate desertions."[13]

There is, however, evidence of resistance by black laborers to the dictates of industrial-capitalism. On at least one occasion white engineers and contractors supervising construction of the line through the New River valley complained that many of the Negroes "would go home to Virginia during harvest and at Christmastime, thus delaying the progress of the road."[14] In

Figure 3.1. *Driving Steel* [photograph]. Blacks from rural areas of the Upper South helped lay track for the Chesapeake and Ohio Railroad through the New River valley, connecting Richmond, Virginia, to Huntington, West Virginia. Courtesy of C&O Historical Society, Clifton, Va.

1870 black and white "workers all down the line" from Guyandotte to Charleston struck when they were denied a pay increase from $1.50 to $1.75 per day.[15] The fact that black workers felt empowered enough to resist the pressures and mandates imposed by the railroad and, by extension, the wage-capitalistic system suggests that they recognized their value as workers.

Work on the tunnel was dangerous, arduous, and backbreaking for all involved. "Six hammer men working 12-hour shifts needed a full day to bore enough holes for just one blast, which advanced the heading by only ten feet."[16] Fatalities among the tunnel workers are believed to be incredibly high. Many died of tunnel fever (later known as silicosis), caused by the fetid stone dust generated by nitroglycerin explosives and the smothering heat they encountered in the poorly ventilated cavern. In total, 83,000 pounds of explosives were used for tunnel construction: so dangerous was nitroglycerin during the period that the Nitroglycerin Act was passed in 1869, forbidding its use without the permission of the U.S. Secretary of State; so widespread was such concern that in 1871 the editors of *Scientific American* argued against the general and indiscriminate use of the explosive. Normally, nitroglycerin was transported delivered frozen (a stabilizing practice) in order to reduce accidents; however, as Louis Chappell reports, "such precautions . . . taken against the dangers of nitroglycerin in the hands of Negroes in the Big Bend Tunnel and elsewhere in the C&O Railroad seems to lack support in the records."[17] Accidents resulting from bungled blasting and falling rocks were widespread. One historian "estimates that hundreds of laborers, men and boys, of African and Irish descent, perished during the three-year construction of the tunnel. The dead were buried quickly and unceremoniously in makeshift pits near the portals at both ends and covered with rocks."[18] Another authority argues it was in the best interests of the C&O contractors to keep their workers' origins obscure. "Negroes who died at Big Bend hailed from nowhere and had not been christened," he observed, and "it was easy not to notice when such men were used up and cast aside."[19] Freedman James Henry Yancey noted that "no one knows how many men or mules died" in the deadly construction of Big Bend Tunnel, an area he worked laying railroad from 1870 to 1874 before acquiring employment in the Huntington C&O Shops.[20]

To what extent C. P. Huntington knew or cared about the day-to-day operations at Big Bend or the reputed death toll is speculative. However, beyond dispute are three facts: he needed to sell $10 million worth of bonds to New York investors; he promised the Virginia legislature that the tunneling would be complete by 1872; and he thought nitroglycerin was critical to achieving his plans.[21] It is difficult to imagine an overriding concern on his part for general labor or worksite issues: that was the job of his subordinates—the contractors, engineers, managers, directors, and superintendents. In fact, it is more likely that Huntington spent his time dealing with the company's substantial debt load, which increased dramatically during construction of the tunnel and railway to Huntington.[22] The deaths of hundreds (perhaps thousands) of free African American workers, as well as those of 380 African American convicts leased from the Virginia State Penitentiary to the railroad between September 1871 and September 1872 occurred during this period of construction.[23] On the lack of information on this latter development, one authority writes, "Aside from the stray mention in the penitentiary minutes, the event seemed elusive. No one mentioned the deaths in the local newspapers, company reports, the private letters of railroad builders, or even the proceedings of the Virginia Assembly, where the penitentiary board had presumably reported its findings."[24] These deaths probably raised no outcry because thousands of black migrant laborers in the New River valley were introduced to the machinations of industrial labor under the supervision of a number of ex-Confederates who were beholden to the dictates of capitalism and racism.

Black laborers also died after construction was complete and the railroad became operational. Newspaper articles report numerous occupational hazards that caused injury, loss of limb, and death. During the summer of 1875 two black laborers in the Huntington area were killed within a month of each other. One was Lewis Richardson, "a very good man ... who has worked on that train three years." Richardson's death, resulting from a fall between cars in which "the train ran over him and cut his head right in two, throwing teeth and brains off on one side of the track," illustrated the dangers of railroad employment for novice and experienced workers alike.[25] In fact, in 1880, the second-leading cause of accidental death for men between ages of twenty and sixty within the Ohio valley was railroad-related accidents.[26]

Despite the dangers, the railroads provided opportunity for black migrants seeking gainful employment. Though the number of whites and immigrant laborers far exceeded that of blacks in southern West Virginia during the 1870s, there is no doubt that black migrant laborers were sought after and valued by railroads. In 1871 the railroad employed 5,000 black laborers.[27] That year the Charlottesville *Chronicle* complained that the Chesapeake and Ohio was draining off all the Negro labor in Virginia, leaving many farms and plantations neglected. As the editor affirmed, "They will listen much more readily to the agents of the railroad companies than to the planter."[28] By fall 1871, Huntington served as the center of much of this activity, with more than a thousand men employed in various projects in the immediate proximity of the town.[29] Black workers undoubtedly worked on the completion of the line from Huntington to Charleston in December 1872; to Coalbury in March 1872; and to Kanawha Falls in June 1872.[30] Referring to migrant railroad laborers in West Virginia and Ohio, a correspondent for a Cincinnati newspaper wrote in 1872, "I am informed by the contractors that the negroes make the most faithful hands they can get."[31]

Despite this affirmation, it is not difficult to imagine many black migrant workers' ambivalence at their new status as wage laborers within the C&O: the arduous, dangerous, coercive, constraining, and potentially alienating nature of industrial work made for complex transitions, even when providing some solace. Early on in the construction of the line, the assistant engineer mandated that contractors pay no more than "a dollar and board per day for ordinary laborers" and set the hours of labor at "six o'clock AM till sunset allowing for one hour for dinner."[32] Additionally, for many, it must have been reminiscent of the immediate post-emancipation days, during which a gang of 40,000 black men known as trackliners built and rebuilt the railroads of the South after the Civil War.[33]

Arguably, John Henry, in his futile quest to outperform a machine, to leave behind his past, and prove his manhood and humanity while simultaneously grappling with the insistent dictates of wage employment, embodied the duality within black migrant struggles. As sociologist Guy Johnson illuminated in 1929, Henry's iconic life encapsulated a culture of enduring "myths, legends, sagas and traditions that contained the essential ingredients of memory, endurance and triumph which are necessary for the survival of a race or a nation." In essence, Henry spoke to a generation because he embodied black people's efforts to find their place in America.[34] It may be tempting to diminish the historical importance of John Henry, yet the fact remains that songs chronicling his exploits were already widespread by the 1880s, and that one-fifth of the nation's railroad mileage in 1939 was constructed between 1886 and 1893.[35] By the time Johnson initiated his study, Henry's legend had circulated throughout the country, making him perhaps "the most well known Negro personage" among black workers. He was a moral hero who demolished the stereotypes and expectations of society by playing *within the rules*.[36] McDowell County native and Huntington educator Memphis T. Garrison addresses the power of the myth in her memoir when she states that prior to his death, her father "had all of those John Henry things, ballads of all kinds and he would read them."[37] In the final analysis, history masks whether, and to what extent, black workers on the C&O sang John Henry's ballad. But given his origins and the dispersion of his legend, it is easy to believe that regardless of the version, his ballad was a work song that assisted black laborers in enduring harsh conditions both physically and psychically throughout the Central Appalachia region.[38]

If the C&O was the ignition, coal was the fuel, both for Huntington's dramatic economic expansion and black influx into the central Appalachian Plateau (see map 1). This expanse, comprising nine counties in central and southern West Virginia as well as parts of eastern Kentucky, southwestern Virginia, and northern Tennessee, lacked the required transportation networks prior to the completion of the C&O to move economically the more than fifty million acres of fossil fuel, the nation's largest supply. In 1871, though, coal was not yet "King" in the central Appalachian Plateau: West Virginia's topography and the sheer scope and volume of its southern coalfields initially slowed capital infusion and worker influx throughout the 1870s. However, the rate for both would substantially increase by the 1880s. Yet even with the retarded growth, substantial rewards awaited.[39] Historically, the five southern counties of West Virginia—Fayette, McDowell, Raleigh, Mercer, and Wyoming—and a bit of Tazewell County, Virginia, were collectively known as the Smokeless

Coalfields, home to the highest-quality coal, deemed, as Charles Kenneth Sullivan states, "literally too precious to burn in the ordinary sense."[40]

The opening up of nearly 420 miles of railway, through stretches of dense and difficult terrain, from the Ohio into Virginia, heralded a dramatic transformation of the central Appalachian Plateau and would not have occurred without substantial financial assistance from local and state authorities. The conclusion "marked an epoch of new growth for a vast area and opened a new channel of trade between the East and the West," an Ironton, Ohio, newspaper reported, before concluding, "The effect that the opening must have in development of West Virginia can hardly be over-estimated."[41] Thus, in 1873, when the first C&O train traveled west, down the iron rails from Charleston to Huntington, linking the Ohio valley with the Kanawha and New River Gorge, and Richmond farther east, it initiated the industrialization of the central Appalachian coalfields and the rise of an industrial city (see map 1). The region's political economy and cultural moorings were immediately and irrevocably changed in the process, altering "the fundamental patterns of mountain life."[42] Soon thereafter, as Cerinda Evans states, "a train load of coal arrived at Huntington every night about twelve o'clock. The coal was put on barges ready for the towboats to take down the Ohio next day. Sometimes as many as 10,000 bushels of coal were shipped in one day."[43]

The use of indigenous agents to administer, supervise, and construct the C&O helped transition the region from a preindustrial rural market to an industrialized urban one. Completion of the railroad linked the region to the world capitalistic system in which it operated within the web of assorted stages of incorporation: the "core" is the major metropoles of investment capital and commerce; the "semiperiphery" comprises highly developed commercial staging areas for capital and trade; and regions are "periphery" of the system, where raw materials are extracted to support more-developed spheres within the system. The infusion of capital from New York bankers, the establishment of Huntington as a transshipment station, and the penetration of the New River valley reconfigured and dramatically expanded the region's links to the world system through the transportation of goods and services and the extraction of timber, oil, gas, and coal. In effect, as Ronald Lewis writes, complicating the historical model of Appalachian economic development, "change is not simply an external imposition."[44]

Ironically, the completion of the line coincided with the nationwide depression of 1873, complicating Huntington's aspirations for his railroad and affecting his workers. As one local authority notes, "No pay car came to town for six months. Wage-earners were in near riot."[45] The depression exacerbated an already untenable financial situation for Huntington. That year, the average cost of the Chesapeake and Ohio Railroad was $88,000 per mile, nearly two and a half times the $36,000 average per mile of Southern railroads.[46] As one authority notes, "So deficient were the company's operating funds that for five months after the completion of the line to Huntington, the employees of the railroad received no pay."[47] In December 1873, with the depression deepening, C&O employees were paid in script "bearing the promise" to pay in thirty, sixty, or ninety days.[48] That winter, in Huntington, only the personal intervention of W. C. Wickham, then vice-president of the company, ensured the extension of further credit for a limited time to the company's laborers by the city's merchants.[49] Local employees continued to suffer from the railroad's financial difficulties until at least May 1874, when one local newspaper noted, "The pay car on the C.&O. R.R. visited Huntington on last Monday and payed [sic] the employe[e]s in thirty and sixty day 'scrip.'"[50] Scrip was utilized with great regularity in the isolated mining and logging towns of central Appalachia during the late-nineteenth and early-twentieth centuries. In effect, as substitute currency, scrip usually confined workers' purchasing power for meals and goods to the company-owned store or designated proxies. Forced to pay markups for meals and/or goods purchased, employees frequently were subject to the dictates of the company, reinforcing their dependency and powerlessness. Still, unlike in the Church Hill Tunnel incident in Richmond, in which striking black workers were replaced by 200 newly landed Italian immigrants, its utilization certainly demonstrates some sense of employer obligation and responsibility for the well-being of its employees.[51] Moreover, given that no other alternatives were presented, the use of scrip, in lieu of cash wages, was surely better than not receiving either.[52]

The effects of the depression lingered for fifteen years, impacting the industrial development of the entire state, with only two small railroad developments—a short line north of Wheeling and a narrow gauge from Weston to Clarksburg—completed between 1873 and 1881.[53] During the fifteen-year period, the Chesapeake and Ohio Railroad fell into the hands of receivers twice. Because of continuing financial difficulties, Huntington stopped his line at the Ohio River for some years, unable to connect to his western and midwestern holdings. In fact, "at the end of the fiscal year 1874–5, two years after the opening of the road to the Ohio River," the debt load had ballooned to more than $31 million and, by 1878, a debt load of more than $35 million.[54] That same year, the Chesapeake and Ohio Railroad went into receivership and was renamed the Chesapeake and Ohio Railway.[55] By then, the Huntington C&O Shops included "an engine house designed for 42 locomotives, a smith shop, four machine and car shops, a foundry, and a passenger house."[56] Throughout the late 1870s and early 1880s, construction of the railroad proceeded, albeit in fits and starts, until Huntington's luck ran out. In 1885, the C&O owed the state of West Virginia $193,000 in back taxes.[57] In 1888 Huntington lost control of the railroad to the J. P. Morgan and Cornelius Vanderbilt interests.[58]

Despite Huntington's ongoing difficulties with financial stability, of great import to black migrant influx were the prospects of regular wages, fringe benefits, and long-term employment the railroad offered. Stephen D. Engle notes, "The economic opportunities of working on the railroad, or in the salt or timber industry, was perhaps more important to blacks than taking an active political role."[59] A. A. Taylor noted in 1926, "Throughout the South, the wages offered able-bodied male 'cotton-hands' ranged from eighteen to twenty-five dollars a month, and the planters provided shelter and rations. At the same time, the wages paid railroad laborers ranged from $1.50 to $1.75 a day, and the contractors provided shelter. In addition, transportation was invariably advanced, and, in some instances, furnished free of charge."[60] Railroad laborers performed a number of tasks. Ben Brown, born a slave in Grayson County, Virginia, remarked, "After wanderin' about doin work where I could get it I got a job on the C an O Railroad workin' on de tracks."[61] Migrant Nelson Barnett was one of the first black men to acquire employment with the C&O Railroad, attaining a position of foreman in the section from White Sulphur Springs (West Virginia) to Huntington before he was ordained.[62] Nell Radford Francisco, a 1911 graduate of Huntington's black Douglass High, says of her father, William "Anderson" Radford, "I don't know about father driving spikes, or laying rails, but he sure cleared the bushes so the C&O shops could be built." Bessie Woodson Yancey, sister to Carter G. Woodson and a 1901 graduate of Douglass, wrote, "From 1870 to 1874... father worked as a laborer in constructing the Chesapeake and Ohio Railroad through the center of this state and served this company later as a worker in its shops in Huntington."[63] Not only did black men obtain jobs with the railroad, some obtained formal authority. After working for the C&O on the White Sulphur Springs extension connecting the Big Bend Tunnel near Talcott, West Virginia, transplanted Youngstown, Ohio, resident Charles H. Anderson recalled, "I worked on the railroad, bossin'. Always had men under me."[64] In truth, blacks served in various capacities, from laborers, to runners, to servers.[65]

In effect, black migrants seeking to improve their lives by negotiating and navigating through what Joe W. Trotter Jr. calls "the dynamics of industrial capitalism" transformed the industrial labor force of southern West Virginia.[66] Some of this transformation resulted from changes in the population itself. While the population of the state increased by the rate of 17 percent in the

1860s, in the decade of the 1870s the population rose by nearly 40 percent. In the six counties contiguous to the C&O line, the number of residents grew by more than 59 percent from 1870 to 1880. The increase of black residents in these counties rose by more than 89 percent in the decade.[67] In 1870, during the initial stages of construction in the New River valley, little opportunity related to industry existed in Cabell County, as evidenced by the fact that only two black residents were listed as railroad employees.[68]

Within a decade of completion of the C&O west to Cincinnati, the Norfolk and Western Railroad (N&W), with lines to the southwest of the C&O line, linked the fields of southern West Virginia and southwestern Virginia to Norfolk and eventually along the Guyandotte River valley to the Great Lakes. Many of the railroad workers were section hands who helped advance the railroad in sections through the wilderness by performing the needed manual labor. Because of the arduous and hazardous nature of their job, and their status as temporary laborers, many black workers chose to remain behind in the villages and towns that dotted the railroad lines instead of moving on. Migrants also traveled back and forth on the rail line, with many stopping at a particular location to inquire about employment opportunities, to start anew, to renew acquaintances, friendships, or romances, or just to shop or see the sights. Thus, these stations also served as hubs on the collective black migrant network. While some blacks settled down and became invested in their new community, a significant number decided to move on to seek opportunities that granted more permanent, expansive options. Many of them traveled to Huntington.

Assisted by a large number of black workers, the N&W later connected the important "Billion Dollar" Pocahontas Field to national markets. The two railroads, with their web of main lines, branch lines, and feeder lines, combined to connect the countless coal mines and coke ovens that began to dot the region. By the end of the nineteenth century, at least four major geographically interlocking coalfields had been discovered in West Virginia: the Kanawha and New River Field, the Winding Gulf Field, the Williamson-Logan Field, and the Pocahontas Field, which employed 100,000 miners by the early 1900s.[69] Associated with these developments was the formation of towns and cities along the rail lines, including Bramwell, Beckley, Keystone, Welch, Williamson, Kenova (located less than ten miles west of Huntington), and, most important, Bluefield, known as "gateway to the Pocahontas coal field," which mirrored Huntington's impressive growth during the late-nineteenth and early-twentieth centuries.[70] Before arriving in Huntington in 1895, brothers Carter and Robert Woodson worked on the railroad, then in the coal mines of Fayette County.[71]

Employment options in Huntington did not parallel, entirely, developments in the region. Notwithstanding the rise of the C&O and King Coal during the late nineteenth century, in the 1870s, agriculture still dominated Huntington's local economy, with the vast majority of black males within Cabell County employed on white-owned farms, as they had been in the 1860s. Eighteen black males (69 percent of black male workers) worked on farms. The balance of black Huntington's male employees comprised five farmers, two railroad laborers, two general laborers, one drayman, and one barber (see Appendix A). This represents the entirety of the occupational range for black males within the county in 1870.[72]

Given the era and place, mirroring the low level of gainfully employed women in the state, it is not surprising that the occupational range for the county's 34 black females in 1870 was even more limited.[73] Thirteen females (38 percent) were cited as domestics, five (15 percent) as remaining "at home," 16 (47 percent) as housekeepers (see Appendix table B.3). In 1880, of the city's 130 black female workers, 40 were domestics (31 percent), and 76 (58 percent—an increase of 11 percent over county totals) cite "keeping house" or "keeper of house."[74] Widow Millie Hopkins (from Virginia) and single, twenty-four-year-old Jane Kelly (from West Virginia) were employed as washerwomen.[75] Maggie Watson (daughter of a Virginia migrant), Caroline King (a widow), and Belle Perkins (age thirty-four from Ohio and wife of Virginian Robert Perkins) were listed as "laborers."[76]

The 1880 census cites no black female dressmakers, hairdressers, laundresses, cooks, or nurses. The lack of occupational diversity among these women only serves to highlight their importance in establishing and maintaining households in the preindustrial economy. With limited employment options, women supported themselves, their families, and communities in important and vital ways. Household duties and childrearing responsibilities provided the emotional, psychological, and social stability needed to sustain and maintain a fledging home. Sewing, cooking, cleaning, retrieving water, the rearing, supervision, and feeding of children, and shopping were some of the routine chores. In truth, women performed immense quantities of indispensable labor. In such an environment, household maintenance and family stability occupied much of their time and energy.

Huntington's African American women had few alternatives. Like many of the town's white women, a number of black women were illiterate, including three (save for Belle Perkins) of the four named above. Although 53 were illiterate, the proportion (40 percent) compared favorably to the white rate of 32 percent, a figure not including the considerable number of those deficient in either reading or writing. Moreover, mutual-aid organizations such as the

Daughters of Friendship, the Sisters of Love, or the Daughters of Liberty to assist and support had yet to be established even in 1880 in the city and in fact were years away. In the event of conflicts (disagreements over wages and length of work day were common for the era), there were no mechanisms in place to renegotiate terms or gain redress with an employer. Yet despite the barriers and constraints, employment within early Huntington offered a greater sense of control than that offered in rural areas with light industry, greater poverty, economic stratification, and little demand for agricultural labor.

Between the 1870s and 1880s, Huntington's economy broadened. Members of the Jasper family, who in the late 1870s traveled from Albemarle County, Virginia, where they had been owned by several aristocratic families, were involved in several ventures. The family patriarch, "Grandpa" Jackson Jasper, worked at the Eighth Street stables, where prominent Huntington doctors J. O. Wall and E. S. Buffington kept their horses. His son, the well-regarded James Murray Jasper, drove a dray, transporting freight from the Ohio River wharf to the C&O Railroad. Rev. A. D. Lewis, who drove the first express wagon in the city of Huntington for Adams Express, notes that "Christian washerwomen paid draymen 25¢ a barrel for Ohio river drinking water."[77]

While Huntington's economy produced jobs and optimism, it also shaped black response from those largely locked out of broader access to upward occupational mobility. Restricted to the bottom of the economic ladder and dependent on white patronage, black laborers' progress was largely dependent on effective and vigorous action that evolved and adapted to generate positive change. Dandridge Hill began his career as a railroad porter for the C&O before opening a grocery and restaurant business on Ninth Street. He also was one of the first to cart drinking water to Huntington residents prior to the installation of water works by the Huntington Water Company in 1887. William O. James was one of the first black residents and a prosperous agrarian who farmed a large tract of land south of the C&O tracks and west of Eighth Street. James possessed numerous skills and briefly served as teacher of the first black school. A cement contractor who laid many of the early sidewalks in Huntington, he assisted in the formation of the town's first Baptist church. From a downtown location, he operated a number of horse teams that saw continuous use due to the construction boom of the 1870s and 1880s.[78] In addition to his work as a laborer, Tom Wilkins ran a soup house at the C&O Shops "for the clerks, office force, and foreman." So popular was the restaurant it was said he "always had a waiting list."[79]

By 1880, there was still little occupational diversity, with 90 percent of Huntington workers employed in three categories: unskilled (77 percent), service

(17 percent), and semi-skilled (4 percent) (see Appendix table 5). Huntington's black male inhabitants worked on steamers, in kitchens, stores, hotels, and stables. Blacks, however, worked in 23 separate occupations, from laborer to cigar maker to hostler. These numbers reveal how important black laborers were to Huntington's development and illuminate the shift from agricultural occupations. In comparison to 1870, when 23 African Americans cited their occupation as farmer or farm worker, only six cited the same occupation in 1880, representing an even smaller proportion of the black population. Employed as a foundry worker, thirty-one-year-old William Black was emblematic of another profound shift experienced by many of the county's black residents: from slave to wage earner. By 1880 21 blacks (11 percent) were employed in the railroad industry, a substantive increase from the two employed in 1870. Expanding the base to include the county's 342 wage-earning African American males between ages fourteen and seventy-five shows fully 158 (46 percent) were employed as "railroad worker" or "works on railroad," further demonstrating the growing pull of railroad employment in the county.[80] Moreover, west of Cabell in adjacent Wayne County, forty-five black laborers, forty-three of them Virginia natives, worked on the railroad in 1880.[81] Out of a total population of 219 blacks and mulattoes, the 45 represented 21 percent of the county's total black population.[82]

No matter where they were employed on the C&O, Huntington's black laborers performed the most dangerous and arduous work. This was the same within the C&O Shops. Denied the more important positions of engineer, fireman, and conductor, African Americans worked as unskilled laborers, brakemen, switchmen (brakeman and switchman were frequently combined into a single job), or yardmen. Laborers performed the menial, labor-intensive, and physically exhausting jobs. From transporting timber to laying tracks to hammering railroad ties and clearing underbrush, laborers performed the thankless work necessary for railroad construction to advance and the railroad to operate. As brakemen, they manually operated the brake on a railcar before the advent of the airbrake. Each man used a brake club, similar to a small baseball bat, inserted into a brake staff, and then twisted it to make the hand brake stop the wheels through the friction created. It was a difficult, dangerous job made more so by the hills and valleys of the West Virginia countryside. As one authority noted, "The brakeman in those days, as the engine would push the cars, would insert this link. It fit into a slot which had two holes, top and bottom and as the link was inserted and the pin was dropped. That was one of the ways that the railroads hired their employees looking at their hands. So often many of the brakemen had fingers missing, parts of fingers missing from using this connection."[83] Switchmen were those workers responsible for assembling trains and switching railroad cars in a yard, a hazardous task given the size of some yards, the number of trains involved, and the time afforded to perform the job.

As yardmen, black laborers roamed the "yard," the area where trains were housed, switched, maintained, loaded, and off-loaded. Depending on the size of the yard, the number of men actually working it, and the extent of work to be done, a yardman's job could be exceedingly difficult and dangerous. Navigating the rails and ties, weaving between individual cars or trains, and lifting and/or carrying freight could prove draining for even the most physically fit, especially for those who had to cover for someone else who had called off (a chronic problem). It could also involve extended stretches of inactivity. Many injuries in the yard occurred because of worker's inattention during slow periods. While stretching the point a little, it might be difficult to say which state proved more dangerous to the worker: work or boredom.

As numerous scholars have illuminated, labor unrest within southern West Virginia during the early twentieth century was commonplace and frequently violent. While examples of biracial cooperation existed, black migrant influx contributed to ongoing racial and labor hostilities in the region. Arriving primarily from Virginia, Maryland, and Ohio, with smaller numbers from Kentucky, North Carolina, and South Carolina, the state's black population increased from almost 4,800 in 1880 in the southern counties to more than 40,000 in 1910. Increasing relocation from northern black migrants, mostly from the Pennsylvania coalfields, also contributed to the population increase in the southern counties.[84] Joe W. Trotter states, "Only about 21 percent of the state's blacks lived in the southern counties in 1880; by 1910, that figure had climbed to 63 percent."[85] Notably, "The increase [in black migration] in the southern counties and practically throughout the state was by in-migration" until significantly influenced by natural increase in the 1920s.[86] With 6 percent of the total in 1880, by 1910 black residents represented nearly 14 percent of the total population in the area, more than twice the number and percentage that were immigrants.[87]

In conjunction with black influx was the arrival of the thousands of native whites and European immigrants into southern West Virginia. The region's immigrant population, mostly from southern, central, and eastern Europe, grew from only 1,400 in 1880 to around 18,000 in 1910, increasing from less than 2 percent of the total population in 1880 to 6 percent in 1910. In total, southern West Virginia's population increased from about 80,000 in 1880 to nearly 300,000 in 1910. So extensive was migration into the coalfields that between 1890 and 1910 West Virginia was the only Southern state to increase in population. Drawn by favorable economic conditions, migrant influx transformed the southern coalfield region into a "contested zone" of social tension and labor strife as native whites, European immigrants, and African Americans competed for jobs, housing, and autonomy.[88]

As illustrated by the Haymarket Riot in 1886 Chicago and the Great Railroad Strike of 1877 (initiated in Martinsburg, West Virginia), the potential of violence related to social tensions and labor strife seemed ever present during the late nineteenth century. In fact, labor strife plagued West Virginia during the era.[89] Given this reality, it should not be surprising that local worker dissatisfaction existed even in Huntington. In 1886 and 1898, workers struck Ensign Manufacturing Car Works, one of Huntington's largest employers, in disputes over wages and contractual obligations.[90] Though the race of the participants is not identified, given blacks' status as common laborers, the lack of a formal black labor organization or leadership cadre, and the absence of white overtures for interracial labor reform, it is hard to imagine black involvement in the strike.

Black men were, however, involved in early black labor activism. In his quest to establish interracial trade unionism within the Hocking River valley, the Ohio valley, and the New River valley, black coal miner Richard L. Davis, who twice won election to the National Executive Board of the United Mine Workers in the mid-1890s, frequently experienced mistrust and hostility from black residents and fellow black coal miners. Interestingly, Davis's attempts to straddle the line of racial friction and ethnic mistrust in the Central Appalachia coalfields produced animosity from both whites and blacks. Negro critics in Rendville, Ohio, angry at his call for cooperation with local whites (a position they perceived antithetical to their best interests), called him a "traitor" and promised not to re-elect him to the local union office.[91] Traveling through the New River region in 1892, Davis wrote, "The whites say they are afraid of the colored men and the colored men say they are afraid of the whites."[92]

Herbert Gutman's explanation of the forces working against the formation of interracial labor organizations in the coalfields illuminates the nature of Huntington's labor situation in the mid-1890s.

> Widespread belief in Negro racial inferiority, itself the continuing influence of the historic master-slave relationship, together with the rapid general deterioration of the Negro's social and political status in the 1890s, explained some of the obstacles faced by white and Negro trade unionists. The Southern rural background of most Negroes laboring in the late nineteenth-century and mining complicated the difficulty. Education was limited for Negroes in the rural South, and deference and dependence more normal in the rural than urban environment. Although little is known of the early Negro miners, it is possible

that their aspirations differed from those of native white workers. They may have viewed their status as workers as a temporary one. In parts of West Virginia, for example, [and in] North Carolina, and Virginia, Negro farmers worked as miners only in the winter months to accrue income to pay farm mortgages. To such workers, unions often seemed unnecessary. Viewing their industrial work as a means to another way of life, they must have thought the danger of union affiliation unnecessarily risky.[93]

Although there are examples of racial animosities and violence between working-class blacks and whites in Huntington, none seems linked to the workplace. There is also no evidence of black-initiated strikes or work actions, or the development of a black working-class reform movement. This is especially important given the establishment of a local affiliate of the Locomotive Engineers in the city in 1878 and the Norfolk and Western Railroad's policy in Bluefield of offering blacks shop-level management positions, a practice not followed by the C&O in Huntington.[94] Unlike the formation of the Colored National Labor Union in Reconstruction Richmond, which sought labor reform as a hedge against growing dissatisfaction with the Republican Party, there was no such organization within Huntington. Further, there is no evidence of interracial working-class activism within the city that might have created an effective vehicle for change, as with the United Mine Workers in the southern West Virginia coalfields or the Noble and Holy Order of the Knights of Labor, which produced impressive though short-lived results in Richmond and in southeastern Ohio.[95]

That Huntington's white unskilled workers failed to act on the commonalities of their circumstance with black laborers is important. Discussing Huntington's white class structure, black Huntington resident Professor J. W. Scott illuminates the forces arrayed against black and interracial labor agitation:

> Roughly speaking, the whites may be divided into five classes: 1. The capital, or moneyed class. 2. The professional class. 3. The merchant class. 4. The skilled-labor class. 5. The common labor class. From the beginning the white population embraced all these classes and each class since then has been growing in power and influence. Labor has its unions, merchants have their Chamber of Commerce, the professions have their various associations, trusts, and banks. Thus the whole social structure of the white population stands like a pyramid—solid, compact, and self-sustaining.[96]

Scott's observations suggest that workplace constraints, exploitation, and instability never reached a level that compelled white workers to abandon the social hierarchy and their racial identification and to choose, on a large scale, "new relationships of equality with their black counterparts," as had been done successfully in Richmond.[97] In this manner, Huntington was symptomatic of a national reality.[98]

In truth, in Huntington, like elsewhere, we lack the internal transcripts to detail the life of urban working-class blacks and "their community life and collective aspirations as well as their interaction with white workers and employers."[99] If covered at all by local newspapers, coverage touted the benefits and promise of industry, not the plight of the worker—and certainly not that of the black worker. But it would be a mistake to presume that the lack of collective (union) activities by Huntington's black workers precluded individual acts of resistance. White settler Chas. R. Wilson's description of black migrant and river yard switchman "Jim Mangrum [sic]," who, "never went out of his way, other than he had outlined in the morning and if he was told to give you a switch, it was after Jim got good and ready illustrates this point." Further depicted by Wilson as "a good switchman and intelligent, but somewhat peculiar," Mangrum's stubbornness pointedly suggests his resistance to the prevailing status quo.[100]

Irrespective of the individual ways black workers resisted, analysis of Huntington's black workers suggests that some responsibility for the absence of working-class agitation or union formation, black or interracially led, belongs with them. By 1882, a branch of the Colored Masonry had existed for ten years in Portsmouth, Ohio, providing, at the least, a model to emulate, and at the best, a resource to call upon.[101] By 1898, a branch of the Colored Waiters' Alliance was in full swing in Cincinnati.[102] That no black labor leader emerged from Huntington's black working class during the city's early years is suggestive and calls into question the nature of black agency and "black community." Moreover, the city's black religious leaders demonstrated no articulated formal support on behalf of the black working class or any political action to address their conditions. This is noteworthy given that in 1890 the western division of Chesapeake and Ohio Railroad, based in Huntington, employed 1,109 employees in various capacities.[103] Some suggestion of the occupational constraints imposed on the company's black workers is illustrated by the fact that from 1871 to 1900 no African Americans are among the forty-two workers listed in the C&O's Engineers and Fireman's Age Roster of the Huntington Division.[104] Nor are any among the seven cited in the Conductors and Brakeman seniority list of the Huntington Division covering the same time period.[105]

There is little data to support the contention that black Huntington experienced a process of proletarianization during the late-nineteenth century. Earl Lewis's study of Norfolk, Virginia, is instructive. Lewis concluded the city's black workers largely failed to "manifest a semblance of worker consciousness" because their "consciousness was so embedded in the perspective of race that neither blacks nor whites saw themselves as equal partners in the same labor movement."[106] Estranged from white workers, blocked by white management, and disdained by a small but growing class of black leaders, black workers found no incentive to leave the psychic refuge of race as the prime modality of consciousness. In light of this development, largely reflected nationwide, one authority suggested, "Both the decline in the political fortunes and the failure to achieve unity with white working classes forced Negroes to turn their greatest efforts toward achieving wealth and middle-class respectability by their own efforts."[107]

There were other models for black workers to emulate to address their plight. Historian Stephen Brier's examination of the growth of the Knights of Labor and the early UMW between 1880 and 1894 in the state's southern coal mining region demonstrates how early interracial unionism could be achieved. "Perhaps the most striking aspect of this episode in American working class history," he contends, "is the fact that southern West Virginia black miners, many recently migrated from the cities and farms of eastern Virginia, came to view interracial trade union organization as the vehicle through which they could fight for their liberation both as workers and as black people."[108] Gutman's examination of the letters of black coal miner and UMW labor leader Richard L. Davis reveals an equally unusual dynamic for the time. Throughout the rural-industrial coal-mining region of southeastern Ohio, just across the Ohio River from West Virginia, Davis and other black miners compelled interracial agitation in local miners' unions, independent of or affiliated with the Knights of Labor, to achieve notable gains benefiting black workers.[109]

Despite the sustained growth of labor unions in the state during the late nineteenth century, the absence of interracial union agitation within Huntington is noteworthy.[110] For instance, six local unions were formed in the state in the 1870s, 26 in the 1880s, and 54 in the 1890s.[111] Comparing industrial and union development in Wheeling to that in Huntington helps provide context to this growth. In the quest to correct and improve working conditions and better organize the often diffused and confused nature of labor agitation by the Wheeling's unions and assemblies, a central labor union was created in the city. Formed in the early 1880s and called the Ohio Valley Trades and Labor Assembly, the organization contained female and black members; one, Gerald Jackson, was elected an officer in the assembly in 1893 and was still a member in 1910.[112] The assembly embraced various methodologies to address disputes between labor and management, including arbitration, demonstration, boycotts, and, when these failed, the strike.[113] At the end of the nineteenth century Wheeling was the state's largest manufacturing site, home to 400 manufacturing interests, employing more than 7,000 workers (in comparison, Huntington possessed 89 manufacturing interests, employing roughly 1,860 workers).[114] Comprising most of the state's 10,000 union members in 1902, Wheeling boasted 42 of the state's 52 locals, with 4,000 members, while Huntington, the state's second-largest labor center, possessed 14 locals and fewer than 700 wage earners.[115]

Gainful wage-labor employment, the solace of family, community, and social freedom, and the explicit threat of replacement labor sufficiently outweighed the negative aspects of constrained employment, thus providing a disincentive for militant labor agitation. Reverend Cecil Hill, a white man who had gone to work for the C&O as a boy of fifteen, noted, "We worked six days a week, 10 hours a day. I made $2.50 for 10 hours work."[116] Many of the shop's unskilled black workers garnered comparable or worse wages. Located at the bottom of the occupational ladder, these men remained vulnerable to the dictates of the marketplace and discrimination. In fact, one local authority reports that many of C&O's laid-off white skilled laborers were able to find work constructing the city's first underpass beneath the railroad tracks at Sixteenth Street, a job denied to blacks.[117] In another instance of employment rather than dismissal, blacks fared only marginally better when all the white workers from "the yard," one of the most grueling and dangerous areas in the railroad industry, were replaced by black laborers.[118]

Another perspective is provided by the constricted nature of urban-industrial work offered by the C&O Shops and Ensign Manufacturing, Huntington's largest employers of black workers during the late nineteenth century. While supplying decent wages and stable working conditions for its black employees, the city lacked a variety of large employers who might have, through competitive forces, provided opportunities for blacks to exploit. Further, alternative employment options in government, trade unions, or business were blocked. Commenting on black job availability within the city, Nell Radford Francisco notes of the C&O Shops, "It was the only job."[119] Speaking on black Appalachian workers, one scholar provides important perspective by noting, "Most, if not all blacks, probably agreed with [Booker T.] Washington's assertion that the true friends of black workers were the capitalists who supplied them with jobs, rather than the unions which excluded them."[120] Thus, prevailing economic realities within the city cannot be ruled out as a contributing, perhaps even primary, reason for the absence of concerted black worker activism.

Some evidence for this contention is supported by the longevity of some workers and the intergenerational quality of black employment with the

C&O. Marcellus Turner migrated from the Charlottesville, Virginia, area at age thirteen and obtained a position as water boy in the Huntington division in 1880. He served the railroad in various capacities and locales for more than fifty years.[121] John Henry Banks, or "Banks," as he was known to all those in the Huntington and Hinton division, migrated in 1889 at age sixteen from Charlottesville and served many years with the railroad as a section laborer and, later, train porter in Huntington. One writer commented on his dependability: "So seldom is he absent from duty, he is known better for his steady, attentive and dependable service."[122] Yet neither of these men, or many others for that matter, could top the legacy of Pat Jackson. Born in 1849, Jackson initially obtained employment with the railroad in Clifton Forge, Virginia, as a laborer in 1869 before transferring to Huntington in 1880 for a short stint. The next year he transferred to Ashland, Kentucky, serving as a laborer in various departments there for the remainder of his employment. Upon being "presented his fifty-year service pin, and on receiving notice of his pension, his eyes sparkled with happiness. A loyal and faithful worker was receiving his notification." By the time he retired in 1930, at age eighty-one, Jackson had served sixty years with the railroad.[123] Before migrating to Huntington, Rev. Albert D. Lewis "followed construction and railroad work, first laboring out of Baltimore building a tunnel and then working for the C&O at Richmond for about six years." He "went to Kentucky to do grading for the L. & N. [Louisville and Northern] Railroad and then back to Richmond with the C. & O."[124]

Examination of the Barnes's family history reveals that after migrating from Alabama, U. L. Barnes Sr. started employment with the C & O in the late 1890s. By the time his grandson, U. L. Barnes III, "Bud," retired in 1998, the three generations of Barneses compiled a remarkable 117 years of employment with the C & O Shops.[125] By 1900, William "Anderson" Radford was a twenty-year veteran with the C&O and had assumed a supervisory position of "odds and ends" about the C&O Shops. Each of his three sons also worked there.[126] While it is difficult to imagine any family bettering these examples, surely many sons (and perhaps, sons of sons) followed their fathers into the crucible of urban-industrial employment, mindful that their working lives, no matter how difficult, were an improvement over those of the previous generation.

Prevailing circumstances compelled a level of thoughtfulness and appraisal among black common laborers, ostracized and trapped at the bottom of the occupational ladder as they were, understandably producing a heightened level of conservatism among the black masses. As Scott accurately noted of the city's black laborers, "They could do no skilled work, and they had no knowledge of business."[127] Thus, black migrants' ability to address workplace constraints and formulate effective strategies and/or tactics was severely limited. Nevertheless, the economic gains were made.

The employment of black people from across the river in Huntington, which probably contributed to a larger black workforce than cited in census figures, reflected this reality. Blacks living in Proctorville, Burlington, South Point, and Buffalo Creek, Ohio, among other towns, traveled to Huntington to work. William Radford traveled back and forth to his job from Proctorville in a skiff he had made with fellow workers and bosses at the C&O Shops.[128] Mrs. Beatrice Vinson Connally of Buffalo Creek indicated that her father, Frank Vinson, who died in 1917, "carried hod" to Huntington during its early years. Likewise, noted local black historian Mrs. Edna Duckworth stated that her father, Rush Smith, followed the same routine before eventually moving to Huntington. By 1910, both William Radford and his thirty-one-year-old first-born son, James, worked as urban-industrial workers, William as a carpenter and James as laborer. Teacher Theodore Wilson, son of former Cabell County slave George Wilson, relocated numerous times from Ohio to Huntington and back again throughout his working life, a story more fully examined in chapter 4.[129] These examples illustrate the draw of Huntington's industrial wage economy had for black workers' in their desire to acquire either primary or supplemental income, and provide further insight into the black social network that existed within the area.

Individually and collectively, during the late nineteenth century black workers' labor and agency were critical to the construction of the Chesapeake and Ohio Railroad, the industrialization of southern West Virginia, and the rise of Huntington. Notably, not unlike the web of relations initiated by the C&O's development in Appalachia, black workers' labor helped link various economic sectors within the town to each other and the broader economy. Operating in the streets as hod carriers, draymen, porters, hostlers, drivers, and teamsters, black labor proved crucial to Huntington's industrial growth via the transportation of goods and services.[130]

Given this reality, four key developments emerged by the mid-1890s. First is the continuing critical nature of unskilled and semi-skilled black labor to the city. In the late 1890s the C&O initiated special trains to bring workers to the shops from other areas in the city. As one white city resident recalls, "Every morning a shop train was run from 16th Street, where a community of black people live, to the shops at 27th Street. The men would climb in, sit down, and ride to the shops and be brought back home after work."[131] Second, some measure of occupational mobility existed as workers departed old jobs to acquire new ones, albeit overwhelmingly within the same class. Though constrained to the bottom of the occupational ladder, greater opportunities afforded many men lateral and, some, upward mobility. Third, the first skilled black workers appeared, represented by the city's first black contractors, the aforementioned William O. James and Dan Hill, and in 1895 by carpenter William Thomas and plasterers William Byrd and George Phipps. Last, as embodied by William T. McKinney, principal of Douglass High School, and Mattie Mitchell, the city's first black nurse, the city's first black professionals arrived.

As suggested by Mitchell's vocation, occupational diversity for the city's black women increased during the period from 1880 to 1891, from two to eight fields. While most were confined to some type of domestic service—in the case of laundress Mary Carter, for example, one of the earliest black migrants—there were washerwomen, an ironer, a chambermaid, and a boardinghouse proprietress and land owner, Caroline Holley. Notably absent are black female laborers, suggesting social and occupational gender proscriptions. However, the expanded range of job options suggests some increasing affluence and economic stability among many of Huntington's black migrant families. For instance, in comparison to the 15 percent of black women who cited their occupations as "at home" in 1880, fully 67 percent of black women in the 1891 directory cited theirs as the same. Such a development can be explained by three possible scenarios: the departure of greater numbers of black women from white households due to their own increased household financial stability, the greater importance of their at-home labor to their own household maintenance, and greater scrutiny on the part of the enumerator. Still, black women's options were severely limited. In general, locked out of higher-level positions—perfectly illustrated by an ad placed by Marshall College (now Marshall University) in 1896 for a white "general work" girl—black women made the best of it and advertised their services as domestics, laundresses, or washerwomen.[132]

Undoubtedly, many of Huntington's black women also contributed to the household income in ways hidden from the public record. For instance, mindful that her husband could neither read nor write, Mrs. W. O. James assisted him in running his cement contracting business. Edna Duckworth states, "Each pay day his wife turned her washtub upside down. Then she dealt the procedes [sic] for the pay period out on the tub until they were exhausted—somewhat like dealing playing cards to each of the workers."[133] Edna's sister, Mrs. Almedia Duckworth Shelby of Covington, Kentucky,

> did everything humanly possible to provide her family with some necessities of life. When she was first married she and her husband did not even have a

bed on which to sleep. Their first child was born on the ground floor. From this humble beginning, she and her husband with a mind to attain something of their own, bought and paid for 240 acres of land. This was partly accomplished by Mrs. Shelby driving to town in an ox wagon to pick up clothes to wash, iron and deliver. Bad weather and bad roads were no obstacle. In later years by being thrifty, they were able to buy a car, a T-Model Ford which helped out greatly with the washing and iron[ing].[134]

Remarkably, Mrs. Shelby accomplished these tasks across a period during which she also gave birth to 16 children, ten of whom, along with her husband, Caesar Shelby, preceded her in death.[135] Mrs. James's and Mrs. Shelby's hard work and industriousness, like that of millions of black women nationwide, was integral to household stability and material gain through the continued viability of varied and, frequently, multiple endeavors. Black women were also crucial in less tangible yet no less important ways. Sometimes their work in the homes of whites and in assisting their husbands afforded them opportunities to gain social knowledge and skills, which they used to inform and navigate their new cultural surroundings.

Evidence indicates that most of Huntington's black laboring class, male and female, like black workers nationwide, found gainful employment in Huntington's emergent industrial capitalist economy. As the city grew, black residents benefited in important ways from increasing occupational diversity. In the process of performing the most arduous and dangerous jobs, they acquired new skills, autonomy, and authority. In their striving, their success provides a compelling historical counterpoint to the tragic tale of John Henry. In the intervening years of Big Bend's construction, blacks had achieved, albeit with difficulty, social and spiritual progress and the concomitant development of manhood. Yet, largely unskilled, untrained, and illiterate, Huntington's first generation of black workers remained locked at the bottom of the occupational ladder and beholden to the dictates of industry, racism, and capitalism. Their failure and/or inability to engage in concerted working-class activism or to forge interracial alliances with whites to better their position is significant and illuminates the enduring power of racial identification and class standing as inhibiting factors in the development of a black working-class consciousness. As well, it could also reveal that the town's first generation of black laborers consciously decided to pursue other tactics in the quest to combat their dehumanization and oppression. Both dynamics would fuel the development of Huntington's black institutions and complicate black political aspiration, subjects addressed in chapter 4.

As the nineteenth century closed, black workers' circumstance left many overwhelmed and frustrated. In Huntington, with employment came a racist, color-caste occupational system that stymied black advancement. What progress they made came through occupational filtering which allowed whites to move up the occupational ladder and many African Americans to come in at the bottom. Organized black working-class response to these developments was non-existent in the late-nineteenth century. There was neither a formal voice, organ, or organizational structure to publicize the value of the African American worker to Huntington, or to whites, nor any context to offer strategies to interrogate and possibly improve the situation.[136] Yet, for the vast majority, the transition to urban-industrial employment entailed some "progress": flawed, ugly, but ultimately life affirming.

CHAPTER 4

Community, Race, and Class

Black Settlement Patterns, 1871–Early 1900s

Long before the city's founding and African American settlement within it, slavery bound black people together from both sides of the Ohio River. Though not physically reconstructed after the Civil War, like so much of the South, the region underwent profound economic, psychological, and social upheaval in the postbellum period. Reconstruction transformed the lives and aspirations of black Southerners "in ways unmeasurable by statistics and in realms far beyond the reach of the law."[1] The transcendent nature of this transformation presented numerous and varied challenges for millions. Too many unanswered questions remained for black migrants to revel in their freedom for too long, to be completely oblivious to their circumstance. They, like tens of thousands of black migrants to other destinations, used various strategies and tactics to overcome economic upheaval, persistent racism, and discrimination. Thus, the decision by Huntington's black settlers to relocate to the town rested on their evaluating multiple criteria and must have caused some uneasiness among many of them. As J. W. Scott noted,

> What was the character of our first settlers? They came without money, without training, without skill, without leadership. They were mostly farm hands brought from the rural parts of Virginia by railroad contractors. They were housed in shanties, fed from commissaries, worked like horses all the week and turned out to frolic on Sundays. They had less than nothing to build on for in addition to being loaded down with all the wrongs of slavery, they were forced to accept conditions not at all conductive to morals and home getting. A dollar was regarded simply as an equivalent for so much indulgence.[2]

Thus, forging a new life in a new town required for most a tempered agenda and enlightened assessment, and was probably the black migrant's most important exercise of free will.

Within this larger context, Huntington's African American migrants lived their lives. Their historical metamorphosis coincided with the transformation of the nation, the region, and the town's rise as an industrial, economic, social, and political hub. Like black people residing in cities throughout the nation, the city's black residents surely differed on what constituted the distinguishing characteristics of community and to what extent they subscribed to it. Yet as increasing numbers settled into the city, most operated within its tentative and fluid confines, bound by a sense of moral duty, social status, and shared history.

When construction on the Chesapeake and Ohio railroad got underway, Huntington began to take on definitive shape, and businesses and industries settled in. During 1870–71, while Huntington finalized his plans, Rufus Cook, a renowned engineer from Boston, designed a city of wide streets, large blocks dissected by convenient alleys, and with large lots for dwellings and business houses of all kinds. On the eastern edge of the town, fronting Eighth Avenue on Twenty-Eighth Street, Huntington's Central Land Company built two rows of houses, one of frame, one of brick, for the use of employees during the construction of the railroad and the C&O buildings and repair shops. Ensconced within the city limits, Huntington figured that an instant population was assured for this development. Later, these houses were rented to railroad employees.

In his design, Cook envisioned the town's commercial and industrial core stretching along the southern shore of the Ohio River. Its industrial core would extend south from the docks of Holderby's Landing, adjacent to the river, continuing some three blocks, from Second Avenue to Fourth Avenue, and 16 blocks west to east from First Street to Sixteenth Street (see map 4.1). Three subdivisions formed the residential core. The largest, contiguous to the industrial section, followed the same east–west pattern as the industrial section until Eighth Avenue. Third Avenue became the primary residential section in town, and beyond it was mostly farmland. Between Seventh and Eighth Avenues the Chesapeake and Ohio Railway line passed east to west. East of this district was a second, smaller residential pocket. Stretching north to south from First Avenue to Twelfth Avenue and west to east from Twentieth Street to Twenty-Fourth Street, this area, in contrast to the first, enlarged at Eighth Avenue, extending two blocks west to Eighteenth Street. A third subdivision, undeveloped but demarcated, adjoined the second but

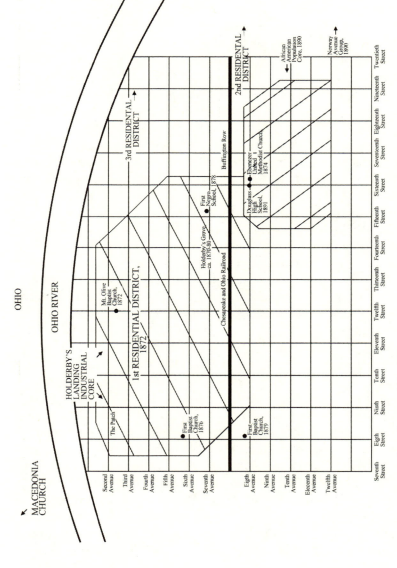

Map 4.1. Historical rendering of black Huntington, ca. 1872. Source: *Map of Huntington, West Virginia, Cabell County, 1871*, Cabell County Department of Records, Huntington, W.V., Cabell County Court House.

covered only five blocks from First Avenue to Fifth Avenue. Extending from Twenty-Fourth to Thirtieth Street, its residential contours indicated that Huntington's future population growth, at least in its early years, would follow a west-to-east direction along the banks of the Ohio River.[3]

As construction commenced, Huntington was more farmland than city, with extensive acreage of the rich river bottom flatland stretching along the Ohio owned by long-time white residents or C. P. Huntington's Land Improvement Corporation. Thus, early black migrants arrived into a makeshift village characterized by crudity and unsanitary conditions. Given this scenario, it is not surprising that many black migrants during the 1870s and 1880s settled in the embryonic commercial district, close to the water wells kept by the city (water works were not installed by the water company until 1887).

The linkages and connections binding Huntington's black community were affiliated with and a product of Cabell County's and Huntington's growth. After its incorporation in 1871, Huntington's industrial economy served as the catalyst, linking it by river to Pittsburgh and Cincinnati, and by rail to the southern West Virginia coalfields and Richmond, Virginia. In 1870 only 123 blacks, representing 1.9 percent, resided in the whole county. By 1880, the county's population more than doubled from 6,429 residents in 1870 to 13,744 in 1880. Within the city, 3,174 individuals lived with 487 black residents (a threefold increase from 1870), including 97 mulattoes, making up slightly more than half (54 percent) of the county's 902 total. That year, black residents represented 6.5 percent of the general population and 55 percent of the county's black population. The district of Guyandotte Township comprised the second-largest African American concentration with 180 (20 percent of county total), followed by the districts of Guyandotte and Barboursville, respectively.[4] By 1880 Huntington was home to more black residents than Wayne, Lincoln, and Logan (Mingo) Counties combined.

In many respects, Huntington's black population resembled that of Ironton and Portsmouth, Ohio, or Ashland, Kentucky, where historical and cultural commonalities linked black residents with those of other towns throughout the Ohio Valley. For instance, in 1880, 41 percent of Lawrence County's 1,746 black residents (located across from Cabell County) cited West Virginia as their birthplace.[5]

The growth in Huntington's black migrant influx also coincided with increases in the black populations of both Lawrence and Gallia Counties. Linked to its location on the north shore of the Ohio River, across from Huntington and Cabell County, Lawrence County saw its black population nearly double between 1860 and 1870, increasing from 685 to 1,241. By 1880, it had blossomed to 1,746 individuals, a mere twelve short of its 1890 total, the highest of the nineteenth century. Likewise, from 1860 to 1870, the black population in Gallia increased from 1,590 to 2,802, and then again during the next decade, to reach 2,945 individuals, its highest total of the century.[6]

The Barnetts, Woodsons, and thousands of other black migrants who arrived in Huntington in its early years embodied a sense of community, even as they arrived with few economic assets other than their labor. Although spatial proximity did not necessarily denote commonality or affect-laden linkages, it is impossible to separate black Huntington's social circumstance from the city's evolving physical geography and the social cohesion that existed in the "sentimental boundaries." It is within the churches, bars, parks, barber shops, and neighborhoods that black residents found fellowship, recreation, and social interaction.[7] In effect, within and around Huntington, radiating back and forth, there existed communities within communities, linking, binding, enriching, and complicating the collective aspirations of its black citizens.

Reflecting prevailing racial and political fears by the state's whites to the prospect of black equality, black migrants arriving into the town faced challenges in their quest for citizenship. As one authority notes, "From 1872 to 1882, the state's Blacks were politically unorganized. Yet, they held a certain balance of power because they were committed to neither the Democratic nor the Republican party."[8]

On the heels of the 1870 Flick Amendment (which granted suffrage to adult males), white voters demanded a state Constitutional Convention. In 1872 the Convention met, inflaming African American passions across the state because the state legislature, which had no black members, attempted to disenfranchise them. So strong was lingering Confederate sentiment among some legislators that delegate John J. Thompson of Putnam County declared that West Virginia "Negroes were less capable of self-government than the buffalo on the plains."[9]

Yet, despite Thompson's sentiments, the convention eventually settled, once and for all, the question of black enfranchisement. By six votes, the right of voting and the privilege of office holding was permanently granted to the state's black population.[10] While critical to black influx into the state, this development led to little political gain throughout the late nineteenth and early twentieth centuries. The primary impetus compelling black migration during this era was the prospect of economic gain linked to the penetration of the Chesapeake and Ohio Railroad through the state.

Settlement patterns within Cabell County and Huntington reveal the draw of urbanization, jobs, and the affiliated sociocultural benefits to black migrants:

Table 4.1 African American Population by District, Cabell County, Virginia, 1880

	District							
	Barboursville	Grant	South Grant	McComas #1 & #2	Huntington	Guyandotte	Guyandotte Township	Union #1 & #2
Black	80	2	5	3	390	39	166	11
Mulatto	17	0	2	2	97	61	14	0
Total	97	2	7	5	487	100	180	11
Percent of Total Population	11 %	0.2 %	0.7%	0.6 %	55 %	11.2 %	20 %	1.2 %

Source: William Marsh, comp., *1880 Census of West Virginia, Cabell, Wayne, Lincoln, Logan (Mingo)*, vol. 2. (Baltimore, Md.: Gateway, 1990), 3.

Table 4.2 Native Origins of Afro-Migrant Population In Huntington, West Virginia, 1880

Virginia	West Virginia	Ohio	Kentucky	Maryland	North Carolina	South Carolina
335	117	20	7	3	3	2

Source; William Marsh, comp., *1880 Census of West Virginia, Cabell, Wayne, Lincoln, Logan (Mingo)*, vol. 2. (Baltimore, Md.: Gateway, 1990), 2.

In 1880 the county's three main commercial-industrial districts of Huntington, Guyandotte Township, and Barboursville comprised 86 percent of the county's black population. Only the district of Guyandotte, with its history of a black presence, contained a sizable number of black residents (ninety-seven, or 11 percent) that could be categorized as predominantly rural. In contrast to the near equal number of blacks and mulattoes in 1870 Barboursville and Guyandotte, the three districts of Huntington, Guyandotte Township, and Barboursville contained overwhelmingly black residential populations in 1880. Owing to their proximity to C&O way stations within the county, blacks comprised 80 percent, 92 percent, and 82 percent, respectively, of each district's total African American population. Of the four districts cited, only Guyandotte possessed more mulattoes (61) than blacks (39).

Due to the embryonic nature of formal institutions in the city and county throughout the 1870s, many blacks relied on the informal networks offered by family, kin, and social contacts to assist and support in times of need. County-level census data for 1880 reveals many black households "clustered" around each other, indicating the probable existence of kin and social networks. Of the county's 90 black households, fully 79 (88 percent) lived proximally within four dwellings of another black household.[11]

The 1880 census also helps illuminate the status of Huntington's early black female population. In contrast to the greater numbers prior to the Civil War that had historically existed within the county, a changing demographic composition followed Huntington's industrialization. From 1850 to 1870, black females within the county outnumbered black males. In 1880, black men ages twenty-one and older accounted for 62 percent of the city's black population. Examination of the female population reveals that of the 137 black females ages thirteen and older, 34 (25 percent) were listed as single; 23 (17 percent) were servants and 16 (12 percent) remained "at home," either as boarders, family, or extended-family members. The 34 single females were scattered through thirty households. Notably, five black households possessed a servant. These numbers suggest that black female labor was valued in Huntington's emergent urban-industrial milieu.

Formal racial residential segregation did not exist during the city's formative years, when whites and African Americans lived in close proximity to each other, with many being neighbors.[12] Although the nature of urban living forced an integrated circumstance, many of the city's blacks, like African Americans nationwide, sought out and relished life in a segregated environment. Throughout the 1870s and 1880s, Huntington enjoyed a lively sociocultural scene beyond church attendance, revealing some class stratification. For locals and outsiders alike, and verified by coverage in local newspapers, Ingham's Hall, Burdick's Hall, and Johnston's Hall (on Second Avenue) were regular gathering places throughout the 1870s and 80s.[13] The availability of these venues offered cultural space that allowed psychic and physical distance from whites.

Speaking on black Cincinnati, Henry Louis Taylor provides important perspective: "It would be a mistake to conclude that the pervasiveness of racism meant that blacks were consumed with white machinations. . . . African Americans lived in a social universe apart from whites. The sights, sounds, smells, rhythms, melodies, and improvisations of black life existed independent of the white world and gave shape, form, texture and vibrancy

Table 4.3 Population by Race in Huntington, West Virginia, 1870–1900

Census Year	1870	1880	1890	1900
Total Population	6,429	3,174	10,108	11,923
White	6,306 (98.1%)	2,684 (84.6%)	8,876 (87.8%)	10,709 (89.8%)
Negro	123 (1.9%)	487 (15.3%)	1,231 (12.2%)	1,212 (10.2%)
Other	NT	NT	1	12

Source: U.S. Census Bureau, Tenth Census (1880), Eleventh Census (1890), Twelfth Census (1900).
Figures for 1870 comprise county totals, prior to Huntington's incorporation.
NT: not tabulated

Table 4.4 African American Population in Ohio Valley Cities, 1870–1900

	\multicolumn{8}{c}{(Total Population of African Americans / Percent of Total Population)}							
	\multicolumn{2}{c}{1870}	\multicolumn{2}{c}{1880}	\multicolumn{2}{c}{1890}	\multicolumn{2}{c}{1900}
	No.	%	No.	%	No.	%	No.	%
Pittsburgh*	3,205	2.5	6,136	3.9	10,357	3.3	20,355	4.5
Cincinnati	5,900	2.7	8,179	3.2	11,655	3.9	14,482	4.4
Louisville	14,956	14.8	20,905	16.9	28,651	18.0[†]	39,139	18.1
Evansville	1,480	6.5	2,686	9.2	5,553	10.9	74,05	12.5

* Includes Allegany city, annexed in 1906.
[†] Figure cited by Trotter is 1.8, an obvious typo given continued population growth.
Source: U.S. Census Bureau, Ninth Census (1870), Tenth Census (1880), Eleventh Census (1890), Twelfth Census, (1900); and Trotter, *River Jordan*.

to black Cincinnati."[14] For most Huntington residents and migrants, life in segregated environments provided the "distance" and space necessary to combat the indignities and start life anew.

For many who weathered the crisis of 1873 and the transition, the beginning of the new decade promised change for the better. Prior to 1880 no black property holders existed in the town.[15] From 1880 to 1885 valuation of real estate increased by 25 percent for the county, while the increase in Huntington was nearly 50 percent. For that same period the valuation of personal property for the county increased 72 percent, while within Huntington it was over 100 percent.[16] Significant numbers of Huntington's black residents contributed to and benefited from this rise. From 1880 to 1890, 23 purchased property within the city, of which 22 were men, including migrants Reverend Nelson Barnett and (now) contractor W. O. James, railroad brakeman J. A. Mangrum, hotel porter Si Manson, Caroline Holley, and former Cabell County slave and "roustabout" William Black, a notable achievement in any light.[17] Most purchased property in the residential districts south of the railroad. In addition, James farmed a large tract of land south of the C&O tracks.[18]

In the absence of a moneyed elite or petite bourgeoisie, or formal benevolent or fraternal organizations, which might have provided models to emulate as well as strategic and/or financial support (or conversely, might have constricted and constrained their ambitions), these 23 property holders symbolize the power of African American economic aspiration. Moreover, J. W. Scott noted that 18 still held their properties 20 years later.[19] Emblematic of efforts by black laborers nationally to improve their economic status, these accomplishments represent an important step in the economic development of black Huntington. From 1890 to 1900, 33 more blacks bought homes, worth an aggregate $80,000, double the value purchased the previous decade. While the primary purchasers of real estate were members of the working class, several members of the embryonic professional class bought property, some descendants of Huntington's first black migrants.[20] Some may have been assisted by the Afro-American Improvement Company, launched in 1895, which possibly provided organized efforts at land acquisition.[21]

Early industrial Huntington's inchoate yet expanding nature, the tenuous financial status of many black migrants, and the preponderance of black laborers, compels examination of early black residential patterns. However, such analysis is made difficult by three facts: first, as already noted, no black property owners existed prior to 1880; second, the "Great Flood of 1884" devastated the city, especially the commercial district; and third, no complete extant city directories could be found for any years prior to 1891–92, a possible consequence of the flood. What is known is that during the first years of the town, a number of black laborers lived adjacent to the gates of the Chesapeake and Ohio Shops (outside of the commercial core) situated on part of the land purchased by C. P. Huntington under the auspices of his Central Land Company. In the same end of town quite a number of black and white individuals and families resided on the south side of the Chesapeake and Ohio railroad near the entrance to the shops. This neighborhood was known as "the Patch." Some migrants lived in railroad housing near the banks of the Ohio near Second Avenue and in some of the emerging streets and alleyways of the downtown section.[22] In 1896, one newspaper article describes the neighborhood: "What is known as the C. & O. Patch is quite a little village of itself. Neat white houses and good gardens are the rule. The residents are mechanics and working men, thrifty and economical and belong to the law and order class."[23] Eventually, by the early twentieth century, the Patch stretched east and west along Eighth Avenue from Twenty-Fifth to Twenty-Ninth Streets, and north and south from the railroad to Ninth Avenue along Twenty-Seventh and Twenty-Eighth Streets.[24]

The influx of black laborers into southern West Virginia coincided with the movement of tens of thousands of black migrants north and west and must be viewed against the other to understand fully the historical reality and motivations behind the mass black migration into the region.[25] Continuing migrant influx from varied cultural backgrounds, improving material conditions for some and the lack of it for others, and economic disparities between white and black people created tensions and opportunities. Like municipal authorities nationwide, Huntington's white leaders, seeking to distance themselves from both the poor and the black, developed laws to protect their power and property while simultaneously perpetuating the subordinate status of those on the bottom. Moreover, lacking any incentive to examine the nature of inequities attendant to Huntington's blossoming industrial economy, the city's white civilians (like those nationwide) also sought distance, and thus lacked any overriding impulse to distinguish the poor from the criminal.

For the majority of black migrants, the exploits and enterprises into the town and area were purposeful and grounded in the twin pillars of church and community. In the quest for self-actualization, many black migrants relied on and manifested both callings, sometimes traveling far and wide. Along the way, many acquired knowledge, skills, and alliances that would benefit their lives, their community, and their race for many years afterward. For example, Virginia migrants and eventual Huntington residents Reverends R. J. Perkins and A. D. Lewis first served as pastors of Hinton's Second Baptist Church before becoming pastors of the Sixteenth Street Baptist Church in Huntington. Their respective years of residency in Hinton, and their respective arrivals in Huntington in the mid-1890s, as well as their eventual tenures at Sixteenth Street Baptist, suggests the potential of an ongoing personal and professional relationship tied to their histories as migrants.[26] Likewise, the published excerpts in the West Virginia edition of the *History of the American Negro* make clear that black migrants John Lewis Griffith and Andrew Baker utilized friendships and contacts acquired in the black enclaves affiliated with the railroad lines to facilitate social, intellectual, and professional growth before their settlement into Huntington in the mid-1880s.[27]

The Woodson family history offers a more detailed examination of the mechanics of postbellum migration. After departing in 1874, the Woodson family returned to the state in 1893, with Robert Woodson, the elder brother of Carter, the future "Father of Negro History," the first to arrive. However, prior to their arrival both brothers spent time working in Fayette County, West Virginia, first building the railroad along Loup Creek from Thurmond before working as coal miners in Nutallburg. Dr. Woodson remembered this period as an important experience in his life, for in Nutallburg he met fellow miner Oliver Jones, who, in the evenings, opened his home to other miners as a tearoom. Woodson garnered the basics of education from two uncles, John Morton Riddle and James Buchanan Riddle, in a rural school in which they taught in Virginia; his ability to read was an important factor in his relationship with Jones. After learning that Woodson could read, Jones offered him food from the tearoom in exchange for Woodson reading aloud to him and his friends. Jones subscribed to several newspapers, by both black and white publishers, some based West Virginia and some from out of state. To this group of miners, Woodson read material about the government and politics as well as matters on contemporary and historical interest, including books about black people. Of this experience, Woodson frequently credited his early backroom discussions and readings among black miners in southern West Virginia as the inspiration for his pioneering movement to recognize African American history. He noted, "In this circle the history of the race was discussed frequently, and my interest in penetrating the past was deepened and intensified."[28]

It is interesting to note that after graduating from Douglass High and prior to embarking upon his singular academic and professional career, Dr. Woodson, accompanied by Robert, taught for a time in Winona in Fayette County, where both brothers were active in various capacities with the First Baptist Church of Winona.[29] Certainly, the qualities exhibited by the two brothers help illuminate how the family (and countless other migrants) survived the rigors of slavery, relocation, and separation, and provides testament to the untold numbers of blacks throughout the South who similarly recognized the importance of advancing the race and who worked to achieve it.

The first generation of migrants entering the town after its incorporation arrived at a propitious time. In 1870, Huntington possessed no black churches or schools, no black stores or restaurants, and no black elected officials in the town or county.[30] But their foresight, initiative, perseverance, and good fortune positioned them to benefit from four important, interrelated, and overlapping historical forces.

First, while a part of the great drama of a larger intraregional movement initiated with the emancipation of millions of slaves, the initial wave of migrants into the town preceded the tens of thousands of blacks, Anglos, and European immigrants arriving into Central Appalachia and the southern West Virginia coalfields during the late nineteenth and early twentieth centuries.[31] By foregoing the rural South and rural-industrial southern West Virginia, Huntington's black migrants embarked on a social and cultural trajectory distinct from the masses who settled farther south. In 1880 the

Table 4.5. African American Population in West Virginia (by decade)

Total Population	African American Population	Percent African American	Percent increase by decade
442,014	17,980	4.0	1870 to 1880—45%
618,457	25,896	4.1	1880 to 1890—22%
762,794	32, 690	4.3	1890 to 1900—33%
958,800	43,499	4.6	1900 to 1910—34%

Source: *Statistical Abstract of the United States*, 1931, 12–13; "Negro Population in West Virginia," *Bureau of Negro Welfare and Statistics of the State of West Virginia, 1923-24*, Special Collections, James E. Morrow Library, Marshall University, Huntington, W.V., 99.

percentage of Virginia-born migrants into Huntington (29 percent) was largely consistent with that into the county the previous decade. Marriage records help to reveal the integral role the railroad played in facilitating western migration from Virginia. From 1877 to 1880, the Cabell County Marriage Register lists a total of 46 "colored" marriages (26 conducted by Nelson Barnett), of which 42 (91 percent) contained at least one individual born in a Virginia county to which or through which the C&O Railroad lines ran.[32] Assessing black influx into the state, James T. Laing notes that 92.6 percent of the Virginia natives came into West Virginia directly from Virginia.[33] These circumstances surely assisted the acculturation of thousands into their new social milieu. Thus, the first generation of Afro-Huntingtonians were linked geographically as well as geo-culturally. While not dismissing the fractures and fissures attendant to diversified black influx or the individualism inherent in human nature, a shared history and sense of duty guided the efforts of many black migrants in their attempts to establish needed black institutions. Carter G. Woodson referred to the quest as embodying "manhood." He continued, "The indisposition to labor was overcome in a healthy nature by instinct and motives of superior forces, such as love of life, the desire to be clothed and fed, the sense of security derived from provision for the future, the feeling of self-respect, the love of family and children and the convictions of duty."[34] Certainly, a testament to the optimism felt by many recent arrivals in their new surroundings is the fact that many decided to marry and settle in the city.

Second, the migrants arrived during the initial stages of the industrial revolution of the Central Appalachia plateau, a transformation led by the spread of the railroad. Thus, black migrants entered the region at the very time their labor was needed. In truth, the necessity of black labor to the economic growth of the state and region during the late-nineteenth century is incalculable. Black labor felled timber, mined coal, and built the railroad. In 1871 the Chesapeake and Ohio employed some 5,000 black laborers yet was merely one of many railroads to crisscross the region, assisting in the extraction of salt, timber, and especially coal. Thirteen separate railroads were incorporated in Huntington between 1873 and 1887.[35] Although most remained stillborn or mere spurs or branches to be acquired by the Chesapeake and Ohio, both the C&O and the Norfolk & Western Railroad (formed in 1889) survived to remake southern West Virginia and Central Appalachia.[36] In the process, they brought thousands of laborers, supplied hundreds of thousands of investment dollars, extracted millions of tons of coal, and produced tens of millions of dollars in profit. From 1870 to 1880 the state's population increased 40 percent and per-capita wealth grew from $430 to

$550.[37] So influential was Collis P. Huntington's larger-than-life imprint upon the area's black people that in 1880, Texas migrant and timber worker Isaac Reynolds and his West Virginia–born wife, Mary Ann, named their son C. P. Huntington Reynolds.[38]

Third, Huntington's burgeoning economy provided some peace of mind to many of the town's first generation of ambitious black migrants via the promise of stable wages and the prospect of long-term financial stability. After only two years of working, James Woodson "had earned enough money to purchase twenty-one acres near his father's farm in New Canton."[39] Further, Huntington's broadening economy afforded opportunities, albeit limited, for upward mobility and/or job change, a circumstance that enabled many of the first generation to avoid (or perhaps delay) the pattern of step-migration (which involved continual migration) necessitated by job competition, economic downturns, or a nondiversified economy. As an anniversary program of the First Baptist Church summarized, "The railroad brought a diversity of industries, opportunities and people to the area. In the midst of this splendid growth and development the 'colored population' also prospered in laborer and support service jobs."[40]

The last factor that contributed to black migrant influx was the absence of Jim Crow laws within the state and the retention of the franchise for black residents, "factors that facilitated school and social welfare desegregation, a greater measure of justice before the law, and the political power to preserve these institutions."[41] The first generation of black migrants arrived prior to the hardening of race relations precipitated by the rise of Jim Crow throughout the South during the late nineteenth and early twentieth centuries. As we have seen, while the "Negro question" produced protracted, contentious, and sectionalist debate within the West Virginia legislature during the state's formative political process, recognition of black political rights ultimately prevailed. Certainly, Huntington's early development (and to some extent its attraction to black migrants) can be traced in part to the presence of young, ambitious, and more liberal-minded white males, many of whom undoubtedly benefited from their status as members of prominent Cabell County families. Thus, even at its harshest, racial discrimination black migrants experienced within West Virginia was a markedly tempered strain compared with that found in other Central Appalachia states.

In part, the establishment of a rigid racial code in Virginia was retarded by the fluid state of Southern society from the end of the Civil War to the end of the century. Jack Temple Kirby notes inconsistency and unorthodoxy marked the era: as early as 1870, the Alexandria and Orange Railroad had a Jim Crow car, yet blacks rode the line throughout the 1880s without incident.

In fact, blacks frequently rode in first class everywhere in the state throughout the late 1800s. Kirby notes, "Only in 1900 did white Virginia legislators get around to codifying Jim Crow on the railways—thereby imposing through the majesty of law an orthodoxy that had not existed before."[42] This is not surprising given the recent *Plessy v. Ferguson* (1896) Supreme Court decision upholding racial segregation and the attendant objections by railroads to the legislation because of the additional cost of providing separate cars.[43] Huntington's growth (218.5 percent between 1880 and 1890), continuing migrant influx, and the presence of liberalism afforded opportunity for both black and white to interact in the spaces Jim Crow had yet to penetrate.[44] Thus, many migrants in both Virginia and West Virginia were able to exploit the strains of liberalism and societal and legal flux within the region.

The vast majority of black migrants demonstrated the important traits learned during slavery—sacrifice, resourcefulness, ingenuity, and self-sufficiency—to climb the economic ladder and to endure rough times.[45] One method was making the family's clothes. Besides making their own clothes, women made shawls for the males of the family, which were frequently worn instead of an overcoat; they also knitted stockings for the family, and "when calling they would take their yarn and knitting needles and talk while knitting, often finishing a sock while visiting."[46] Migrants also used their historically intimate knowledge of the land. Across the Ohio River, black farmers, like their fathers and, in some cases, grandfathers before them, worked the rich soil adjacent to the river, providing economic alternatives and resources for black people throughout the region. Many black residents, no doubt, on both sides of the river hunted, fished, and/or tilled vegetable gardens. As well, camp meetings and basket meetings offered regular social opportunities for networking and for bartering and selling crops and wares. Moreover, Huntington's rural surroundings, the vast stretches of forests nourished by the Ohio and Guyandotte Rivers and a number of creeks and streams, and the verdant valleys replete with wildlife provided abundant natural resources as wellsprings of nourishment and/or income. Walter Myers recalled his grandfather's knowledge and ability to live off the land:

> My granddaddy went out there on that hill and they have no money, they took their hands. There was plenty of food out there. And they [whites] wondered how they [blacks] could go out on that big poor, they called it poor land, and live. They were plenty out there to live of[f]. They knew how to live off the land, like the Indians. So . . . but whenever they raised anything, they always raised something that they could sell to make some extra change to put in this little, they called it a sugar jar or change jar or something. Now some of 'em had a pouch, they carried it with 'em.[47]

Nelson Barnett Jr. remembers playing, as a young boy, in a small building in his side yard "built by my enterprising great grandfather, the reverend Nelson Barnett," who had a dream "of creating a Black mercantile empire, of sorts, catering to the staple goods needs of the neighborhoods. He was the buyer, wholesaler and distributor, concurrent with his ministerial duties as a circuit rider."[48] In effect, Barnett "organized and serviced a group of country stores of the fruit-stand variety in and around the Ohio, Tug, and Kanawha River valleys. This endeavor appears to have been similar to that of the modern day Independent Grocers' Association (IGA)."[49]

The fond and insightful recollections above are representative of the ways black migrant families regularly utilized their industriousness, creative talents, and familiarity with the land to survive and prosper. These stories also demonstrate the enduring strategic importance linked to passing down such knowledge and expertise. Certainly, both Barnett's employment with the C&O and his travels as a pastor afforded opportunities to develop and nurture contacts with black farmers. To what extent his venture indicates abiding ties to the community is debatable, yet it is instructive that he chose to forego Huntington's bustling urban-industrial opportunities, largely catering to and controlled by the town's whites, and center his business in the countryside, offering the goods purchased from black farmers. In effect, the land offered solace and recreation, food and the future. Each example also illustrates how important it was that the Myers and Barnett families knew the value of money and the benefits of saving and frugality (refuting Scott's depiction) as stepping-stones to economic stability and, eventually, financial independence. Many black migrant families possessed the cultural knowledge and practical skills to ensure their continued viability, as well as a long-term vision to accomplish their financial goals.

By 1890, Huntington's general population had reached 10,108, with the city's black population increasing threefold from 1880 to 1,231 residents, 82 percent of the Cabell County's 1,493 black inhabitants. By now, Huntington's transition from a mere township to an urban-industrial enclave was well underway. Throughout the decade, regular and routine train travel to and from Richmond along with the construction of new rail lines serving southwestern West Virginia increased the flow of rural blacks into the city for shopping, fellowship, sightseeing, and recreation. Carl Barnett, son of Carter Barnett and the grandson of Reverend Barnett, recalled his trip to the city toward the end of the century: "My earliest memories are of the train ride from Romney to Huntington. I can still remember how everything would get black when we'd pass through those tunnels."[50] Surely, he was just one of many who maintained fond memories of their first trip to the "big city."

During this era, although black residential settlement was dispersed throughout the city, four pockets of greater concentration existed, two north of the C&O Railroad line running between Seventh and Eighth Avenues, and the other two south of the line. The first, found within and adjacent to the city's central business district, radiated away from the Ohio River from Second to Seventh Avenues, and from First to Fourteenth Streets. Comprising 16 categories of central business functions—wholesale, retail, manufacturing, artisan, religious, educational, professional service, financial, administrative, hotel, boardinghouse, private dwelling, warehouse, personal service, entertainment, and multipurpose (engaging in wholesale, retail, and manufacturing activities) establishments—this area housed large numbers of black laborers, domestics, and other unskilled and semi-skilled workers, as well as a number of widows.[51] They lived in this area for two primary reasons: cost and proximity. Intermingled within the commercial, service, and industrial businesses were affordable housing/rooming options that offered short walking distances to jobs and social/entertainment venues.

In 1895, 94 black residents lived within the Central Business District, with the largest concentration (40 adult black residents—more than triple the number living on any other street within the district) found along the city's oldest residential thoroughfare, Third Avenue, which also featured two black-owned businesses, barbershops owned by John P. Brown and Charles Seals. The vast majority of those residing in the district were black migrants who arrived after 1880 and whose socioeconomic status, presumably, locked them into utilizing rudimentary housing opportunities for a time before moving on. It is impossible to ascertain what factor or factors influenced the status and, thus, settlement patterns of black laborers to the greatest extent, but it is noteworthy that only a very few of the city's early black migrants resided in the district in 1895.[52]

Interestingly, while the city's general population expanded from 1890 to 1900, Huntington's black population actually dropped during the period from 1,231 to 1,212, reversing an upward trend from 1870 to 1890. No one answer accounts for this decrease, yet several factors may have contributed. First, construction of the Chesapeake and Ohio line from Barboursville to Logan and that of the Norfolk and Western from Logan to Kenova probably drew workers from Huntington, a point reinforced by the growth of the county's black population during the decade. Second, the Panic of 1893 may be a factor as it forced the temporary closing of the Chesapeake and Ohio Shops, the largest employer of black railroad laborers within the city. Third, the proportional increase of white migrant influx relative to black increase during the decade and resultant job competition in a tight labor market may have reduced available employment options for black laborers. Fourth, given the loss of jobs and increasing job competition, some black laborers might have relocated to the emergent coal-mining region of southern West Virginia.

Black and white migrants and residents too poor to afford better housing lived in alley dwellings and in undesirable areas on the fringes of development. One interracial enclave on the fringe was known as Buffington Row, and an examination of its population provides clues to the nature of migrant life. In 1895, of its 24 residents, 17 were African American. Of the nine males, seven were laborers, two were barbers. Of the eight women within "the Row," six were widows.[53] Given the relatively high income of the era's barbers and the presumably stable economic status of the widows, the presence of these two groups calls into question whether economics, race, or some other contingency defined residency. In contrast to the occupational status of white workers, all cited as laborers, "black workers" encompassed a broader occupational range of domestics, laborers, and barbers.[54]

Situated on Seventh Avenue between Sixteenth and Twentieth Streets, this parcel of land was one of several owned by prominent white businessman Peter C. Buffington. Several newspaper articles portray an area rife with crime and squalor. One newspaper declared, "Police Again Called to Disorderly Buffington Row," before continuing: "The people of the notorious Buffington row gathered together last night and, as usual, a general free for all fight took place. Knives, knucks, hatchets and almost everything, save gatling guns were brought into use and this morning when the police visited the scene that locality had the resemblance of a Chicago slaughter house."[55] Later that year, another article states, "A great nuisance is complained of by citizens of Seventh avenue and Locus avenue, on account of the accumulation, of filth, from stables, hog pens, and out houses between Sixteenth and Twentieth streets on the alley between Buffington row and Seventh avenue. The attention of the health officer is publicly called to this matter."[56] Another article relays, "The alley back of Buffington row is certainly in a very filthy condition, and should be renovated at once, or the sick list and death rate below Twentieth street will be greatly increased this summer."[57]

As of the mid-1890s, however, neither Buffington Row nor any other area within the city constituted a black ghetto resembling those of the mid-twentieth century. Within these areas, all were subject to inferior housing, higher incidence of disease, and higher mortality rates but blacks also faced the subtle additional burden of racial discrimination, a dynamic that may have reinforced the "congregational" instinct of black migrant settlement.[58] In this manner Huntington mirrored other Ohio River valley towns during the era.

Located in the west end of Huntington, adjacent to Central City (incorporated in 1893) and stretching west to east from Second to Tenth Streets along Eighth Avenue, and from Second to Eighth Streets on Ninth Avenue, lay the third locale of black residential concentration. Situated on the southern side of the C&O tracks, this area contained a smattering of black unskilled and semi-skilled workers mostly concentrated in small residential pockets around the major intersections of Second, Sixth, and Eighth Streets. While limited, there is some evidence of ongoing social/kin networks within this area. In 1891–92 laundress and early black migrant Martha Carter lived with her daughters Cora and Virginia in the alley between Seventh and Eighth Streets and Third and Fourth avenues, while her teamster son, Henry, lived at 1831 Virginia Avenue in Huntington's west end.[59] By 1895, after her daughters had relocated elsewhere, she and Henry, who was now a cook, relocated to rear of the dwelling at 213 Eighth Avenue, where they shared their home with bricklayer and probable boarder William Craney. The area also supported, at least for a time, two black-owned restaurants, one run by John Stephens at 210 Eighth Street, the other by Daniel and Moses Butler at 220 Eighth Street.[60]

In Huntington's west end, near the C&O lines, lay the fourth area of black residential concentration, stretching west to east from Sixteenth to Twentieth Streets, and north to south three blocks, comprising Railroad, Eighth, and Artisan Avenues. Considering its truncated length, three blocks long, and the fact that eighteen of its nineteen black residents were black laborers (with widower Sarah Waltz the exception), available evidence indicates that Railroad Avenue was probably constructed by the C & O Railroad to accommodate newly arrived laborers.

As the oldest residential and most critical main road in the enclave, Eighth Avenue contained a substantially larger and occupationally diverse presence than Railroad or Artisan Avenues. Living among the numbers of unskilled and semi-skilled workers were grocer W. T. Merchant, contractor W. O. James, and teacher W. T. McKinney. Containing the second largest black concentration within the city at 60 residents, this enclave would increasingly comprise black Huntington's population core throughout the length of this study. Part of this circumstance is attributable to the development of black institutions adjacent to and within the enclave, including the location of Ebenezer United Methodist Church and Douglass High School. Stretching from Sixteenth Street to Twentieth Street, Artisan Avenue contained 14 black residents, all unskilled laborers. In contrast to the overt social/kin networks on Eighth or Ninth Avenue corridors, only laborer A. Winston and helper Jude Peters resided in the same household, offering little evidence of explicit social/kin linkages found on Artisan.[61]

Examination of black residential settlement patterns in the mid-1890s reveals that, save for Buffington Row, a broad uniformity existed with the city's black working-class population. In effect, the compacted nature of occupational diversity limited upward mobility and residential opportunities for the majority of Huntington's black migrants. Although large numbers of them had obtained stable jobs and were improving their material position, with a few even purchasing property, constraints and barriers existed. However, it is important that there were choices as evidenced by the interracial composition of black enclaves. At the close of the nineteenth century, Huntington's black citizens were spread throughout the city and firmly ensconced within it, living adjacent to or in close proximity to black and white, rich and poor. Thus, settlement patterns seem to be a function of cost and proximity to jobs, family, and/or social networks, and black institutions.

One lasting ramification of capitalism and industrialization was the development of the numbers of men, women, and children, African Americans and whites, who engaged in criminal activity. Crime cut across racial and class divisions. Young black males, many of whom were either unemployed or underemployed, are frequently cited as the perpetrators of many of these acts. Common are newspaper accounts of thievery by black youths of food, livestock, wood, and coal, items that were the staples of life for the era. Reflecting the scholarly debate over the slave-era practice of "taking" versus "stealing," many black migrants seem to have committed crimes to feed themselves or their families.[62] Many wandered the streets as vagrants, some turned occasionally to crime, others exclusively so. Some found jobs. Some were saved from the worst of life by finding safe haven in homes or state-run facilities.[63]

Intertwined with the growth of crime and vagrancy was the rise of black-owned bars. By 1900, while the bulk of Huntington's black residential population radiated out from its commercial core and concentrated within three wards, a number of black-owned businesses remained in the city's center, including black-owned saloons, frequently to the consternation of city officials (see map 4.1). The local press portrayed these establishments, such as the "Loop de Loop," the "Muddy Duck," and the "Honky Tonk," as "notorious" and "infamous," homes to crime, vice, and prostitution.[64] These haunts, found in the Tenderloin district, catered to and employed black and white alike, including women of both races, a circumstance that inflamed the ire of the some city council members and white merchants intent on elevating the positive attributes of the city as well as reining in "negro saloons" and "craps joints."[65]

No one drew greater ire than Ed McDaniels (also cited as McDaniel), whose exploits help illuminate the ways in which some members of the black working class attempted to navigate and negotiate the shifting boundaries of power, class, and race within the city. Born in 1866, the West Virginia native arrived in Huntington around 1890 with his wife, Lizzie, and their two children; he obtained a job as a restaurant cook. From his arrival forward, McDaniels, referred to by one local newspaper as a "negro of unsavory fame, [who] seems to have straddled the line between the lawful and unlawful, favor and connection, with equal aplomb."[66] Over a five-year period his business ventures included the opening of a barber shop in the late 1890s and the saloons "Loop de Loop" and the "Muddy Duck," cited by one local newspaper as "veritable hot beds of all manner of crime, conducted with the full knowledge and consent of the police in the city."[67] Criminal activity in his establishments, or in close proximity, occurred regularly, including at least one incident in which two brothers attempted to shoot McDaniels in the "Honky Tonk."[68]

McDaniels's clientele included primarily those who occupied the lowest economic rungs of the occupational ladder, no matter the race or gender. As one authority notes about Atlanta (but the observation applies generally to circumstances among workers in burgeoning urban-industrial settings), "Domestic laborers and others escaped from their workaday worries through dance in 'jook joints' and settings also referred to as 'dives.' These were among the most (re)creative sites of black working-class amusements at the turn of century, where old and new cultural forms, exhibiting both African and European influences, were syncretized."[69] Patrons undoubtedly included many black laborers who shifted between periods of employment and unemployment, and those categorized as vagrants, loiterers, and transients by city authorities. While most may have survived by taking jobs as day laborers, others engaged in a sub-economy that included gambling, prostitution, and petty theft. Recalling the exploits of black Huntingtonians who spent time gambling on riverboats, Edna Duckworth states, "Sam Graves and Lee Overstreet made money gambling. If constables got after them, they would move from state to state."[70] Commenting on "the other black Cincinnati," "the shadow community" that existed on Cincinnati's riverfront area during the late 1860s, historian Nikki M. Taylor explains, "Many of the same people who occupied the lowest economic and social rungs of society also occupied the lowest moral rungs because of their involvement in illegal, illicit, or otherwise unsanctioned activity. And because many of them persisted in such activities, they were considered 'Pariahs, Sudras, outcasts' and inhabited the shadows of Cincinnati society."[71]

As long as those sites comprising the illegal and illicit remained few, self-contained, and localized, Huntington city authorities provided tacit approval.

Although there is no direct evidence of their patronage, the location of these venues in the heart of Huntington's commercial district almost certainly attracted social and perhaps political contacts, black and white. In effect, McDaniels's barber shop and clubs provided ample networking opportunities. As early as mid-1899 there is evidence that he sought to capitalize on these connections. Commenting on McDaniel's response to the "undelivered plums" from the local Republican Party for work done on behalf of the party in the black community, a local newspaper reported that "it was he who brought success to the republican ticket in Huntington last spring, and that he had been promised great things as his reward." Cited as "a valuable ally of the administration," McDaniels also seems to have curried favor with the mayor and city council. Over the public outcry of white business owners, the city's eight councilmen approved his license application to establish a saloon at 839 Second Avenue next to the white-owned Merchant's Hotel. His efforts seem to have produced positive results: less than a year later, he had purchased a small dwelling in the alley between Third and Fourth Avenues and Seventh and Eighth Streets for $400.[72]

Notwithstanding the fact that public opinion viewed a small number of white-owned establishments as notorious as well, including one resort referred to as "one of the most damnable dives in the city," located at 817 Second Avenue and run by white proprietress Dorsey Brown, the centralized presence of a few saloons under black proprietorship and their depiction as "dens of vices" prompted the *Huntington Advertiser* to admonish the local authorities for utter disregard of the law in their lack of policing the "ape yard on Eighth Street."[73] Eventually, continuing crime and violence associated with McDaniels and his establishments, as well as those operated by others, effected a concerted backlash, and in November 1904 the city council debated the revocation of McDaniels's liquor license. White city councilman John Farr, in defense of McDaniels, pointed out the hypocrisy of the city's white citizens and simultaneously proclaimed his objectivity; he "upbraided" the mayor stating, "It was a matter of persecution on the part of some citizens to not grant the negroes of the city the same privileges that are accorded to the white inhabitants."[74] One month later, S. F. Blake, the white proprietor of Merchant's Hotel, renewed his efforts to shut down the Honky Tonk. Speaking before the city council, Blake testified that "one woman was knocked by a burly negro into a tub of water, that a piano which kept going day and night rendered life hideous for himself and his guests; that there was constant cursing and brawling; that five or six women were kept there all the time; that they frequently appeared at the windows of the place lacking even the traditional fig leaf, much to the annoyance of himself and his guests [and] that robberies were often committed there."[75] Blake's testimony served as the beginning of the end for the Honky Tonk. Over the next two months, police raids generated by coalescing public opinion and council disapproval demonstrated that McDaniels and his club would no longer be tolerated. On February 21, 1905, the Honky Tonk closed its doors forever.[76]

That black migrants/residents of Huntington accomplished what they did is remarkable. Certainly, progressive sentiment did not mitigate notions of racial superiority held by the region's whites, nor did it translate to ideas of egalitarianism in early Huntington. As one local source noted, most black residents, like those throughout the state, were segregated into positions "horrendously unequal to the bulk of the white populace" in occupation, civil rights, and social position.[77] From the creation of the town, newspapers disparaged them.[78] Although in 1879 *Strauder v. West Virginia* made it illegal to exclude blacks from juries based solely on race, no blacks served for the first 60 years in the city's history.[79] And, although relatively few in number when compared with Virginia and the Deep South, ten lynchings occurred in West Virginia from 1890 to 1900.[80] During this period, there was *one* lynching in Huntington in 1876, involving a black man accused of murdering the husband of his white lover, with her help.[81] Yet there were attempted lynchings within the city. After being arrested for the 1895 drowning murders of his two young stepchildren in Huntington and escaping from jail some weeks later, former Buffalo Soldier and petty criminal Charles Ringo was recaptured in Point Pleasant, 45 miles away. Only the intervention of local authorities saved him from the violent intentions of the crowd of 2,000 that had gathered at the train station upon his return to Huntington.[82] This rebuff by Huntington's white authorities to extrajudicial actions by the city's white citizenry is important, for it was unusual for the era. While it does not mitigate the social, racial, or occupational hierarchy that existed in the city, it does lend credence to the contention that city officials recognized that the protection of black citizens was fundamental to the effective implementation of law and order, practicable racial relations, and the city's economic success. When whites (even police officers) were accused of crimes against the black community, they were regularly brought to justice.[83] And when blacks committed crimes against other blacks, white officials pursued justice as in any other case.[84]

In significant ways, Cincinnati's and Huntington's waterfront black communities, though situated in two separate periods, encompassed the same populations. Whereas Cincinnati's comprised those bound to the city's antebellum riverfront economy, Huntington's bound those tied to the city's postbellum railroad-based economy and, to a lesser extent, its nascent river-based economy. Bound largely by their class and occupational status, black and white, men and women, existed in an uneasy, sometimes violent, and often fluid collaboration—and not infrequently, cohabitation. For a time, McDaniels's purposeful navigation of the alternative spaces within Huntington's economy demonstrated that those operating within working-class constraints could achieve success and stature.

* * *

After the Civil War, thousands of people, followed by tens of thousands more, left homelands and homesteads. Relying on ingenuity, fortitude, family, and faith in themselves, bound by their cultural and historical commonalities, and using the well-worn paths of their ancestors, scores traveled across the Appalachians to find gainful employment and a home. Many settled into nascent rural-industrial coal towns located along the lines of the embryonic Chesapeake and Ohio Railroad, but some choose to relocate to the emergent urban-industrial town of Huntington. Here, they began to build their lives. Early black migrant influx into Huntington reveals that it is impossible to separate the greater historical forces of the era—racism, migration, capitalism, and industrialization—from the basic human desire for freedom, citizenship, autonomy, and self-determination. Like thousands of other black Southerners, black migrants endured hardship and deprivation either to start life anew in similar residential circumstances or to migrate across hundreds of miles to a place that they believed would offer better opportunity. In this respect, they were pioneers and trailblazers. In the process of their rebirth, they helped initiate the sociocultural and political transformation of Huntington, a topic discussed in chapter 5.

CHAPTER 5

Institutional Development, Public Space, and Political Aspiration in Early Huntington, 1870–Early 1900s

> As a slave his influence was felt in the formation of the state. As a freedman he has ably met the responsibilities and duties of citizenship. He has fought to maintain his rights and privileges and he has used them to promote the State's best interests. His efforts, moreover, have encouraged and stimulated cooperation from white citizens.
> —Thomas E. Posey, *The Negro Citizen of West Virginia*, 1934

Despite the complexities of life in Huntington, the city's black citizens established the institutional infrastructure necessary for self-improvement and black uplift. In the process they refuted what Rayford Logan, James Loewen, and others have enduringly labeled "the nadir" of Afro-American existence.[1] Key to this metamorphosis was increasing black movement into the "public space" and growing political agitation, all of which provided the "building blocks" of community formation.

As already noted, prior to 1872 no black churches existed in Cabell County or in Huntington. Across the river in Burlington, Ohio, Macedonia Baptist Church was, between 1811 and 1872, "the only Negro church" in the tri-state area and as such was singularly important to the rise of the black church in Huntington.[2] Founded as the Macedonia Missionary Baptist Church between 1811 and 1813, the "Mother of the Black Baptist Church movement in this part of the country" served a small number of former slaves and black enclaves on both sides of the river during its formative years. As one of the oldest members of the Providence Regular Missionary Baptist Association, formerly called the Providence Anti-Slavery Missionary Baptist Association, the church increasingly served as a nexus and conduit within a network of churches. As a consequence, a growing number of laymen and clergymen received their education and training as members of the church before moving on and starting their own churches.[3] In 1852, a sixteen-year-old William P. Cradic was baptized at Missionary Baptist. He received his license to preach at Macedonia in 1866 and was "set apart" in 1868, when he took charge of the Second Baptist Church of Ironton, Ohio (now known as Tridestone) with a membership of 12. He served as pastor there for 16 years, during which time church membership increased to 217. By the time he retired in 1908, Cradic had served "with Providence Association for 56 years [and] attended every session with exceptions of 5." He proudly relates, "I have occupied at times all the important positions in the gift of Providence Association [an] which honor I highly appreciate in my declining years."[4]

After the Civil War, Macedonia continued as the focal point for all social life for its many members, some of whom "traveled 20 miles or more on foot to church service" to the top of Charley Creek Hill, removed some miles from the Ohio River.[5] Huntington's blacks were sometimes among them. Despite Macedonia's historic centrality to the area, Cabell County's African Americans sought opportunities to worship closer to home after Huntington's establishment. As early as 1872 some of Huntington's black residents agitated for their own worship site and petitioned the mayor to use white Pea Ridge School (located on the outskirts of Huntington) as a place of worship and to "arrange the difficulties between white and colored citizens."[6] That same year, in a fundraiser for First Baptist Church, "the colored folks held a festival at [white-owned] Burdick's hall, and raised $60 for the benefit of a church which they propose to build at once if they can secure additional aid which we trust they will receive."[7] Naturally, there were white churches in the area where black people may have worshipped, including seven Baptist and six Methodist churches in Cabell County, containing 1,400 and 2,400 members, respectively, with a total property value of $16,000.[8]

Indicative of the importance of the blending of the Ohio and Virginia/West Virginia black populations was the founding of Huntington's first black church. The first Baptist church and the oldest black church in Huntington was originally founded as the Mt. Olive Baptist Church in 1872.[9] Its services were initially held in the log house of Jenny Tucker where Seventh Avenue is now. Rev. A. D. Lewis recalled, "Because there were few Baptists and other Christians here, a union church soon grew from this beginning and moved into the frame cottage situated where the Spring Hill Cemetery now is (on the present site of the Huntington State Hospital). No denominational scruples were entertained."[10] A First Baptist Church anniversary program published in 1966 describes the event, illustrating the abiding linkages between black citizens from both sides of the river:

> The forefathers who organized this historic church were Reverend Nelson Barnett, Sister Betty Barnett, Brother Walker Fry[e], Brother Henry Hunt, Sister Caroline King, and Brother W. O. James. The Reverend William (Uncle Billy) Bryant of Proctorville, Ohio served as advisor and aided the eight founding members in forming our church. Kate Colly, who was eight years old at the time, was present but not included in the membership.[11]

As one of the original "thirty-seven," who had come into Burlington, Ohio, in 1849, Reverend Fry brought close connections with Macedonia Baptist and the Providence Baptist Association, which originally included West Virginia churches as members, such as Booker T. Washington's home church, the African Zion Baptist Church at Malden. In 1873, West Virginia Baptist Churches withdrew from the Providence Association and formed the Mt. Olivet Association, which evolved into the West Virginia Baptist State Convention, organized in Charleston in 1878.[12]

The opening of "The Ebenezer Church" on Eighth Avenue formally established the second denominational group forming the "union."[13] First referred to as Ebenezer Methodist Episcopal Church in 1874, and later Ebenezer United Methodist Church, Ebenezer is the oldest church building serving Huntington's black community. Virginian Lewis Foes started the movement creating the church, culminating with the purchase of a site on the corner of Sixteenth Street and Eighth Avenue (now located between Seventeenth Street and Hal Greer Boulevard (formerly Sixteenth Street) and the south side of Eighth Avenue, where the first church was built. Other original trustees include William Morgan, Anderson Crafton, Robert S. B. Smith, and W. H. Saudindge.[14] Reverend Jacob Owens was the first pastor. The first Sunday School superintendent and first to receive a local pastor's license was Guyandotte resident John Shafer.[15] Farther removed from the commercial center near the river and south of the C & O tracks, this site, unlike the Spring Hill location, abutted a small but growing concentration of black residents along the Sixteenth Street corridor.

The formation of both Mt. Olive Baptist Church and Ebenezer United Methodist Church demonstrated the coalescing of action and vision among peoples on both sides of the river. In May 1875 Union Sunday School began regular service, with the first and third Sundays of the month reserved for preaching by a variety of city pastors.[16] The fundamental nature of their contributions to the growth of black institutions and the social-cultural evolution of black Huntington cannot be overstated. As suggested by A. D. Lewis's apt statement, "No denominational scruples were entertained," their efforts in the early 1870s lacked any articulated ideological or programmatic design beyond merely assembling black people in their own cultural spaces to worship.[17] For the newly arrived migrant, and for those contemplating relocation, this was a reassuring development.[18]

By the mid-1870s, Mt. Olive relocated to Twelfth Street between Second and Third Avenues (the second of four locations in its history), marking the rise of its prominence. One newspaper report announced the opening of "The African Church on 12th street," describing the structure as "a neat and commodious building" and suitable for use as a school during the winter.[19] In the process, the transition of the congregants from tenants to landowners and the church from Mt. Olive to First Baptist was formalized. With initiative and financial support from the black community, Mt. Olive acquired land from C. P. Huntington's Central Land Company at 834 Eighth Avenue (on the western edge of a growing black residential population center) for $1,500 and began construction of a new church in the years 1879–1880. By 1879, situated on Eighth Avenue, both First Baptist and Ebenezer United occupied sites on opposite ends of a growing black population center (see map 4.1). Located south of the railroad tracks, the churches demarcated the unofficial northern, western, and eastern contours of a growing black residential concentration. Only at Mt. Olive were there any women church trustees for any church during the entirety of this study.[20] The development of the black church within Huntington afforded black men, many for the first time, the rare opportunity for status and stature.[21]

The first group of Huntington's early black leaders was composed of men of the cloth. Many of these men were self-taught preachers whose efforts embodied the aspirations and articulated the hopes and concerns for a significant proportion of Huntington's black migrant community. Upon Reverend Barnett's death in 1909, the *Huntington Dispatch* wrote, "He lacked the learning of the schools because he was born a slave. But he was of a studious turn of mind, gifted in speech, could expound the scriptures with an insight truly remarkable, and his preaching was wonderfully effective in bringing men to Christ." The funeral service for Barnett, preached by educated black preacher Reverend I. V. Bryant, was even more expressive. "If by education we mean the drawing out of the latent powers and spreading them in glowing characters upon the canvas of the mind, if by education we mean the proper cultivation of all the faculties, the symmetrical development of the head, the heart, and the hand, together with those combined elements that make the entire man, I positively deny that he was uneducated. . . . he was taught by the Great God."[22] Throughout his life, Bryant articulated there were two urgent needs of black people: "A well-rounded Christian education and the ownership of property. If these things could be achieved, black people could compete with white people in a predominantly white society."[23] To varying degrees these men became emblematic of the broad influence later spoken of by Du Bois, Woodson, and Frazier.

Both Nelson Barnett and I. V. Bryant served as pastors at a number of churches on both sides of the river and as moderators of the Providence Regular Association annual meetings on multiple occasions.[24] For four years, from 1884 to 1888, Barnett presided over Macedonia Baptist, arguably the most prestigious black church in the area. Barnett's pastorate at Macedonia effectively affirmed him as the area's preeminent black pastor. One newspaper commented, "Genuine in faith he preached, and gained the sincerest respect of all citizens. White people frequently attended his services."[25] Both men served as delegates, elders, founding members, and guest pastors to a number of churches throughout the tri-state area. In 1888 Bryant began his first pastorate at First Baptist, which lasted three years before he moved on to pastor Walker Memorial Baptist Church in Washington, D.C.[26] As late as 1893, Barnett was still affiliated with Macedonia as a church elder.[27] Providing further evidence of the growing stature of churches and their pastors within the city, Rev. R. J. Perkins was elected President of the Colored Baptist Association held in St. Albans, West Virginia, in May 1895.[28] Three years later, The Mt. Olivet Baptist Association, "comprising more than half of the colored Baptist churches of the state," held their annual session in Huntington in 1898.[29]

One important but perhaps underappreciated aspect of the black pastors' influence in early post-bellum America was officiating black marriages. Denied the privilege as slaves, the religious and civil sanction of a union was a seminal, inspirational rite of passage for many black migrants and long-term residents. While many black residents choose the pastor of their church to solemnize the occasion, many black residents also sought the most influential and/or preeminent community pastor to conduct the ceremony. Between 1877 and 1880, Barnett officiated 26 of the 46 black marriages in the city, constituting 57 percent of the total.[30] Between 1882 and 1885 Barnett officiated 24 out of 34 black weddings in the city, accounting for 71 percent of the total.[31] In fact, Rev. A.D. Lewis relates, "On January 9, 1884, I marched down the aisle of the old Mt. Olive Baptist Church with Miss L. B. Davis on my arm. At the altar I was united in the bond of wedlock by Rev. Nelson Barnett. To this union was born four sons."[32] While certainly not the only clergy conducting ceremonies in the region, in addition to those performed in Huntington, both Barnett and Bryant presided over a number of weddings in Gallia County, Ohio, home to Gallipolis. Indeed, both men officiated at nearly fifty weddings in the county between 1882 and 1899, including Bryant's presiding at the nuptials of C. C. Barnett, Barnett's son, and Gallipolis resident Katherine "Kate" A. Whiting.[33]

The establishment of a church legitimized black individual and community aspiration in the eyes of white Huntington. Local newspapers regularly published articles on church accomplishments. Reports of baptisms and other church functions were more than an initiation of faith: they were advertisements to a skeptical public. Thus, a newspaper article citing the baptism of "eight, five males and three females" not only reassured a like-minded black population but also served as a recruiting tool. "The ceremony was performed by Rev. Mr. Fry [organizer of Mt. Olive Baptist and then pastor of Macedonia Church] from Ohio, who has been preaching for sometime to the colored church at this place, which has enjoyed quite an extensive revival."[34]

Black church activities also provided opportunities to educate whites, an important byproduct.[35] At least one prominent white preacher and city leader of the era sought out opportunities to meet black preachers, parishioners, and laborers of the area. Shortly after his appointment to Fifth Avenue Baptist Church in 1877, white Rev. W. P. Walker traveled to Ohio to attend the three-day annual meeting of the Providence Association and donated $10 upon his departure. The following Sunday he "heard Bro. Williams (colored) preach in our hall last night," a reference to the white Lallance Hall. Two years later Walker attended another association meeting for two days and preached at the Rome Methodist Episcopal Church that evening. In effect, Walker recognized the importance of linkages with the association and its black members. His attendance seems to have borne fruit: his program from Mt. Olive Baptist, included the notation, "Was elected Moderator!" clearly showing his excitement upon garnering the recognition.[36] Whether motivated by a belief that his ministry could help address (and mitigate) the "Negro problem" or by reflecting the Christian imperative of outreach to the broader community, Walker also made regular visits to the C&O Shops throughout his twenty-five-year tenure at Fifth Avenue Baptist. Walker maintained religious ties to Huntington's black churches and black community throughout the 1880s, serving as a visiting pastor for regular Sunday service in unnamed black churches and at least on one occasion welcoming a visiting black pastor into his own.[37]

Churches were instrumental in helping to maintain a particular social decorum. Macedonia's church minutes reveal member admonishment and reprimand for a number of social indiscretions, immoral acts, and perceived grievances committed within the broader community, including swearing, betting, slander, theft, and adultery.[38] Church arbitration attempted to circumscribe and guide black behavior. In the late 1870s and early 1880s, emblematic of church doctrine in the era, both the largest white church in the city, Fifth Avenue Baptist Church, and black Macedonia Baptist passed resolutions banning its members from engaging in certain social activities, primary among them dancing.[39] So pronounced was the issue during the era that Rev. I. V. Bryant published a book titled *Is Dancing a Sin?*[40] The importance of these mechanisms in bettering, stabilizing, and fortifying the race and the community should not be overlooked. Within Huntington, black migrants and residents encountered a new cultural landscape and different worldviews. In a racially discriminatory setting, most of Huntington's black inhabitants seemed to know the limits of societal sanction and observed them. Still, black institutions, led by the church in Huntington, calibrated the social behavior of its members in this new cultural environment.[41]

Perhaps the most contentious issue of the era was the question of integration of schools. West Virginia, as a political entity, might not have been "Southern," but it was (and is) the only Southern state completely within Appalachia. And it was not immune to the ongoing, often fractious debate over the question of desegregation. So contentious was the issue for Huntington's whites that 10 percent of the articles in Huntington newspapers between 1872 and 1874 were written about school integration.[42]

With the state's founding in 1863, no provision was made in the constitution for the education of Negro children. Further, in 1864 William R. White, the first superintendent of state public schools, wrote that the black freedmen were being denied access to education. "As the law stands," he writes, "I fear they will be compelled to remain in ignorance."[43] In 1866, strong opposition erupted in the Senate over using tax money to fund Negro schools in counties having few Negroes. So entrenched was debate over funding, appropriation, and enumeration, little progress was made on the subject of black schools, and for four years White's successors made no mention of "colored" schools.[44] The provision was eventually passed in 1872, ensuring that a Negro school should be established whenever there were 20 or more children, and to teach those between six and twenty-one years old. In those districts having fewer than twenty, a pro-rated appropriation was set, based on the number of black and white pupils.[45] Thus, West Virginia was the first state in the Union to establish a separate system of public schools for African Americans in the South.[46] In truth, the progression of the black school system in the northern, eastern, and central regions of West Virginia was accomplished through the state's assistance and the efforts of teachers, black and white. In Huntington, emblematic of similar efforts by African Americans throughout the South, evidence indicates the primacy of black-led education initiatives in the region.[47] Similar to national regional developments, the quest by Huntington's black laboring class to garner education was largely in stark contrast to that of white laborers. As W. E. B. Du Bois notes, "It was only the other part of the laboring class, the black folk, who connected knowledge with power; who believed that education was the stepping-stone to wealth and respect, and that wealth, without education, was crippled."[48]

Not surprisingly, the county's first Negro schools were in Guyandotte and Barboursville, the result of the efforts of black laborers (including Virginia migrants James Woodson, Nelson Barnett, and W. O. James) employed on the Chesapeake and Ohio Railroad.[49] Seventeen-year-old Ohioan Rev. I. V. Bryant in 1873 was the first teacher of the Guyandotte school.[50] At one time said to be "the greatest educator in the three-state area," Bryant was emblematic of a number of early black settlers who were born and/or lived just across the Ohio River yet were integral to the formation of Huntington's early black community.[51] The first school established near Huntington was opened in the log house on Cemetery Hill, just east of the town and a little west of Guyandotte. So small was the Negro school enumeration that the two towns had to cooperate in maintaining it.[52] In October of that same year, in a building "donated" by Robert Long, Huntington's first Negro "school" was approved by the city council. It was situated in a "very neat building finished, on 12th street [and Sixth Avenue], which can be used for a house of worship, or education as the occasion may require."[53] Dedicated on September 14, 1873, the building was also used for church services and at times was referenced as the Union Chapel and/or the African Church in Huntington newspapers.[54]

William O. James became the school's first teacher, earning $30 per month. In October 1874, James petitioned the city council to "teach [in] the [public] colored school" and was officially appointed teacher, garnering a raise to $35 per month, in line with white teachers' pay in the state, a unique circumstance in the South.[55] Over the course of the next 10 years the school moved several times, closed because of a lack of funds for five months from April to September 1875, and, with the departure of James, experienced a delay in reopening because no qualified teacher could be found.[56] The school eventually settled in the Holderby Grove (Landing) area, located "on the edge of a three-acre grove of beech trees" at the end of Fifteenth Street near present-day Seventh Avenue.[57] In the initial stages of community formation the school's many moves probably affected black attendance. Moreover, for those black residents not between ages six and twenty-one who wished to attend school, an advance payment of $4 per term was required.[58] Still, it remained the lone option for the county's black population, young and old.[59] In 1874, 43 students were enrolled in the school, with an average daily attendance of 35. Their attendance rates exceeded white attendance rates 81 percent to 76 percent.[60] In 1876 George Wilson's fourth son, Theodore, secured his teacher's certificate and entered the teaching profession at age nineteen, acquiring a job in Huntington. Then located at the corner of Third Avenue and Twelfth Street, the school was within four city blocks of his birthplace. In August 1880 Wilson, W. S. Peters, Samuel Eubanks, and W. T. Smith vied for the nomination to teach in the colored school, with Wilson winning out for the three-month term.[61] However, after the county's decision to employ no teachers with a Number 4 (provisional) certificate, James Liggins succeeded William James in 1880.[62]

William F. James and his wife, Susie, also had their origins in Ohio. In 1882 both became the full-time teachers in Huntington, posts William held for a truncated five years, dying in 1887, followed some years later by Susie.[63] As former teachers in Cheshire Colored School, a one-room Gallia County, Ohio, schoolhouse, the Jameses had traveled to work in Huntington sometime after 1877.[64] As Carter G. Woodson notes, the two were "products of the Ohio school system. They were for their time well-prepared teachers of foresight, who had the ability to arouse interest and inspire the people. He was an earnest worker, willing to sacrifice everything for the good of the cause. His wife continued for a number of years thereafter to render the system the same efficient service."[65] Recalling James's death, J. W. Scott, who was Douglass High School principal at the time, states, "After a brief illness he passed to 'pathetic dust,' bemoaned by the entire community and especially by his pupils, many of whom accompanied the body to its last resting place in Gallipolis, Ohio. Several of his pupils afterward graduated from other schools, yet they remember him as the chief inspiration in their lives."[66]

In 1875 black school enrollment figures fell, probably as a result of economic downturn attendant to the Depression of 1873. While average daily attendance in November of that year increased to 85 percent, school enrollment dropped from the initial 43 students to 28. In the year-end report issued on December 30th, there were thirty students enrolled—19 males and 11 females; average daily attendance was 23—16 for males and 7 for females, and daily attendance had dropped 9 percent to 72 percent—84 percent of the males but only 60 percent of the females.[67]

In 1880, only 38 black students, out of 143 school-age children, attended school, representing a gain of only eight students from the December 30, 1875, school report. That year, in contrast to the greater number of male students in those figures (and the greater number of males in the general population), female students exceeded males twenty-one to seventeen. The change in male/female figures correlates with a shift in the types of female students attending school. Whereas the 1875 figures reveal a statistically large number of employed female students, the 1880 census shows none. The twin effects of the Depression of 1873 and Huntington's narrowly focused economy may have reduced the opportunities for women to work and attend school. Instead, "at home" daughters are the primary attendees.[68]

In 1885 conflicting data complicates examination of black Huntington's education metamorphosis. Enrollment figures increased from October to December, yet average daily attendance decreased during the period. By October, black school enrollment was 118 pupils (lower than 1880 totals but significantly higher than the December 30, 1875, enrollment of 30) with an average daily attendance of ninety-five. Attendance rates, while the third-lowest of the city's four schools, was still an impressive 91.5 percent, just below the city average of 93.4 percent. Figures for November 1885 show 123 black students enrolled, an increase over October, yet average daily attendance dropped to 90. Further, average daily attendance dropped to 88 percent, a rate below the city's 92.25 percent. December totals show 128 black students enrolled but no average daily attendance numbers given for the month due to a citywide measles outbreak. Perhaps, as a consequence, average daily attendance dropped to 86 percent, the lowest in the city save for rural Hill School at 79 percent.[69]

School attendance was a statewide problem that city leaders acknowledged. While conceding that onset of colder weather, the holiday season, and a measles outbreak had an effect on attendance for all city students, one newspaper editorial expressed exasperation at the dwindling attendance numbers during the latter part of the year, observing that "the fickle-minded, infirm-of-purpose or child contributes a larger share than necessity; the careless parent and indifferent child—indifferent because of parental carelessness—furnish a full quota for the service of the sidewalks and street-corners; the indolent and indifferent complete the list of irregular pupils that burden the fall and retard the schools."[70]

There is no way to know whether, and to what extent, black students attended the sidewalks or street corners instead of the classroom, though it is not difficult to imagine that some did. What is clear is that the dwindling attendance trend escalated as winter worsened. While black enrollment increased to 133 students in January, average daily attendance dropped to 68 students as a consequence of "extreme cold for one week" and the continuing measles outbreak.[71] But one other development offers some insight into the seemingly paradoxical relationship between growing enrollment figures yet decreasing attendance rates. In October 1885, William F. James, "Principal of the colored school," received permission from the city council to establish the city's first night school for blacks, providing previously unavailable options for both black male and female day workers.[72]

Still, Huntington's black individuals and families availed themselves of educational opportunities in the city. By 1880, Nelson and Betty Barnett were the parents of four children, all in school, including their daughter Josephine Maria (known as Josie or Jo), born in 1872. In the household of farm worker Robert Holley and his housekeeper wife, Caroline, three of the four school-age daughters—Mary A., Maggie, and Lizzie, ages twelve, nine, and six—attended school. Minerva, the eldest daughter (age sixteen), took care of household domestic chores. In the household of laborer Thomas Wilson, long-time Cabell County resident, and his housekeeper wife, Jennie (Virginia, in the 1870 census), were economically stable enough to send three of five school-age children (the two elder daughters and the eldest son), a notable achievement given a household with seven children. Both school-age daughters, ages fourteen and twelve, attended school, while the two middle sons (nine and seven) did not.[73]

Arguably, the most important development of the 1890s was the establishment of the first black high school in Huntington in 1891. Led by a multigenerational group of local African Americans agitating for change, the board of education erected a building at the corner of Eighth Avenue and Sixteenth Street. For the vast majority of the state's black population, the city provided the only opportunity to acquire a high school education, in part because no compulsory-school-attendance law existed in West Virginia until 1897.[74] In 1911 Principal Scott commented on the achievement: "The little one room schoolhouse changed to a commodious six-room brick with a high school department."[75] The six-room brick edifice with a basement cost $15,000, housed grades 1 through 12, and was named for ex-slave, abolitionist, and nineteenth-century black intellectual Frederick Douglass. The faculty, consisting of only a handful of teachers (including Josie Barnett) and "only one instructor for the upper grades," taught a high school curriculum then only two years in length. Principal William T. McKinney, originally from Malden, West Virginia, the hometown of Booker T. Washington, presided until 1897, when he retired.[76]

The first graduating class of Douglass High School in 1893 consisted of three students: Mathew Colley, Belle Turner, and Boston Scott. Ten students, including four females, made up the graduating class of 1895. Before leaving to acquire a teaching certificate at Berea College in eastern Kentucky, future eminent historian Carter G. Woodson, "the first black American of slave parentage to earn a Ph.D. in history," graduated in 1896, along with Trent R.

Figure 5.1. Second-grade class, Douglass Junior and Senior High, 1896. Source: *The Douglass High School Reunion 1973 Souvenir Program Book*, 23. Author's files.

Jenkins.[77] Already having acquired the fundamentals of education from his two uncles, John and James Riddle, who ran a local school in Buckingham County, Virginia, Woodson (at age seventeen) accompanied his parents in 1893 from the county to Huntington, following the same pathways his father, James Henry Woodson, had traversed, along with the Barnetts, some 20 years earlier. In 1900, after obtaining his teaching certificate at Berea College in Kentucky, Carter Woodson returned to Huntington, serving as teacher and principal of Douglass. Under his supervision at Douglass a library was started, and three classes graduated while he was principal. In 1903 he resigned to attend the University of Chicago, where he received his bachelor's and master's degrees. Woodson attained his PhD in 1912, the second black to earn the distinction from Harvard (W. E. B. Du Bois was the first).[78]

While arguably the most illustrious graduate of Douglass High during the late nineteenth century, Woodson was merely one of many. Two more classes graduated in 1897. That year another Douglass graduate, Carter H. Barnett, returned to Huntington after marriage and employment as a teacher and principal in Keyser, West Virginia. Reverend Barnett's eldest son, having graduated from Denison University in 1892, "the first black person from Huntington to graduate college," succeeded McKinney as principal of Douglass.

Figure 5.2. Carter G. Woodson, then dean at West Virginia Collegiate Institute, later West Virginia State College. Source: *Ancella Bickley Collection*, West Virginia State Archives, West Virginia Division of Culture and History, Charleston, W.V.

Under Barnett's tutelage the curriculum was lengthened to four years and new courses implemented. Notably, Barnett arrived at the same time his sister, Josephine, was a teacher of the primary grades. Though not a graduate of Douglass, their brother, Constantine Clinton (formerly General McClinton), after graduating from the School of Medicine at Howard University, the first black person from Huntington to complete medical school, established Barnett Hospital on Seventh Avenue in the early 1900s, the first hospital for African Americans in the city.[79]

Graduates of Douglass and others were representatives of a nascent black professional class within the city during the 1890s, a significant milestone. J. W. Scott notes, "It was during this period that the professional negro appeared. It was during this period that the community witnessed its first class of graduates from the local schools and the home coming of young graduates from other schools. Better qualified leaders made their appearance."[80] In 1895 W. H. Gordon became the first African American admitted to the bar in Cabell County.[81] That same year, Josie Barnett graduated from Douglass. Although the educational progress of blacks in Huntington proceeded on a segregated and unequal basis, it still represented a vital expression of black collective agency.[82] At their 1901 commencement ceremony, held at the white-owned Davis Theater, contrary to prevailing practice in the Jim Crow era, "the parquet, boxes and dress circle were occupied by colored people, the balcony by white folks."[83]

The evolution of social circumstance for Huntington's black inhabitants proceeded in concert with the city's increasing importance as a regional cultural, social, commercial, and government hub, and, consequently, increasing black entry into the public space. The location of Douglass, a distance from the riverfront area of Holderby Grove, historic home to black railroad and common laborers, confirmed the de facto shift in black spatial community orientation that arguably began with the establishment of Huntington's first black churches 20 years earlier. By the 1890s Huntington was a regional hub offering attractions, shopping, and adventure for an increasingly diverse and affluent native population as well as for large groups of visitors. Foremost among these visitors were African Americans, who arrived, sometimes by the hundreds, to enjoy the city.[84] They, and others, could take advantage of a host of bars and illicit venues, go to the theater, and visit family and friends in the predominantly working-class African American residential enclaves, including Buffington Row, Central City, the West End, and the East End, where they might get a haircut at the barbershop of John Thomas and Rev. A. F. Tuck (pastor of Ebenezer Methodist Episcopal) near Third Avenue and Nineteenth Street.[85]

Black visitors and residents also reveled in the competition and fun of cakewalks. Popular during the nineteenth century, these contests involved contestants executing elaborate or amusing walking steps in the quest to acquire the prize of a cake. These contests were important examples of African Americans asserting their rights to use and enjoy more of Huntington's public space.[86] During the 1890s newspapers report Huntington's black inhabitants increasingly claiming civic space for public rituals. One event, held July 4, 1898, attracted 5,000 people, a "crowd so great," a newspaper reported, "that the management after two hours struggling with the throng deemed it best to adjourn matters to the Davis Theater."[87] Another scheduled "Grand Cake Walk" involved black citizens from several local cities up and down the Ohio River.[88] The entrance of Huntington's black citizens into public spaces historically claimed by whites is no small matter; that this phenomenon brought together people from several communities magnifies its importance.[89]

The dispersed and rural nature of West Virginia's black population and the dearth of organized recreational and social outlets within the coalfields also contributed to black influx into cities and the rise of Huntington's black working class.[90] Historian Joseph W. Moss's 1936 study of the recreational

Institutional Development, Public Space, and Political Aspiration 107

facilities available to blacks within the southern West Virginia coal-mining counties of Mercer, McDowell, and Mingo, an area comprising nine incorporated cities and towns and 40 small towns clustered around coal mines or coal camps, reports a black population of 33,000. Moss comments that there were

> only two playgrounds, only one public library, only three pool rooms that even attempt any standard of decency. Not a single coal operation supports anything approaching a recreational hall.... We find only one Y.M.C.A. which is not a Y.M.C.A. but a rooming house for the Norfolk and Western [railroad] employees, [and] not a single church or organization fosters a Camp Fire Girls or Girl Scout Troop for Negro girls.[91]

In contrast, Huntington offered a variety of recreational and social outlets for the area blacks, most revolving around church, school, and lodge. In addition to the regular visitors offered by the C&O and N&W, large numbers of shoppers and businessmen arrived into the city daily from Lincoln, Logan, and Boone Counties over the Guyan Valley Division rail line.[92] Thus, visitors could avail themselves of various options for entertainment and fellowship. People recalled some of the events with fondness. Walter Myers said, "When I was a kid, they had a pavilion out here on the [Hal Greer] boulevard and they had fine dances out there, late in the evening."[93] Denied participation on the C&O baseball team, black residents organized their own. In late May 1902, a baseball game between Ashland and Huntington teams was the first ever between two black teams held in the city.[94] Blacks could travel along the Camden Interstate Railway (the streetcar system) to Clyffeside Park, located in the city's west end, before connecting on to Catlettsburg and Ashland, Kentucky, and, finally, Ironton, Ohio.[95] The system reportedly brought more than "a thousand people every day of the year" to Huntington and attracted black people from throughout the region. In July 1902, attendees from a regional convention of the Colored Knights of Pythias filled "three solid cars" on the line. Also at the convention was the ladies court, an auxiliary of the body.[96] In September of the same year, the Charleston branch of the Colored Knights, accompanied by its fifteen-piece band, arrived in the city as participants in the celebration of Emancipation Day. A large number of visitors and transient workers rented rooms in private homes or stayed with friends.[97]

The development of parks as an "idealized space" for the area's black populace allowed black residents to reconnect to nature, but it also provided distance and a reprieve from whites, a development many of the city's African Americans surely welcomed. In 1909 African Americans from Huntington,

Ironton, Ashland, and Catlettsburg hosted an Emancipation Day celebration at Clyffeside in which upward of 5,000 attended.[98] In September 1911 Belleview Park opened. Noting the importance of the park's Labor Day opening, one black female resident said, "No more begging and borrowing. No more special days. Open to us every day. There was roller skating, moving pictures and all sorts of amusements, also a big barbecue lasting all day. The park was crowded with visitors from neighboring towns as well as home folks."[99] In 1913 Ritter Park, the city's largest park, opened, but black residents were restricted to a small area at the east end of the park. Although the park was segregated, Walter Myers indicates that the mandate was not always observed by local blacks: "They wanted to segregate the park, like the blacks play on the East end of the park and all the rest of the park for [whites]. [We] played basketball . . . and stuff like that, running and fishing. There was a lagoon out in there, kids would fish and swim in it."[100]

In response to the exclusion of the state's black homeless or neglected children from the funded orphanage in Elkins and concerned over the plight of his sister, who was left to raise her children alone after the death of her husband in a coal mine, Bluefield resident Rev. Charles E. McGhee set out to aid homeless black children. In early 1899 he incorporated an orphan's home for black children. After moving to west Huntington, to what was then Central City, McGhee opened his home on 20 acres of farmland on March 5, 1900, with 18 residents, installing a curriculum based on the Tuskegee model. Ignored and unsupported by the state in violation of federal law, McGhee was forced to solicit funds from the general public for upkeep.[101] Despite his best efforts, which included local white philanthropy, fundraisers, and a traveling band composed of male and female residents, the option on the land expired prior to its purchase, and McGhee moved the home to Blue Sulphur Springs, West Virginia, and then to a site five miles east of the city, near Guyandotte.[102]

In 1900 the home, headed by Byron A. Walcott, who was white, with Maggie A. W. Thompson as matron and Nannie V. Marrie as servant, housed seven children. The children's ages ranged from one to ten and included Thelmer Marrie, one, Cornellius Marrie, five, Helen Marrie, six, Edith A. Thompson, seven, Willie Chapmen, eight, Julian Massie, nine, and Hester A. Chapman, ten. In 1903 the state allocated $1,500 toward the expenses of the home and in 1910 assumed full responsibility for the facility, purchasing the building and grounds for $10,000. Children in the home were separated by gender, with a matron in charge of the girls and a superintendent in charge of the boys. In 1911 the home housed 64 orphans (42 boys and 22 girls), a number that increased the following year to 72 (45 boys and 27 girls).[103] Children

Institutional Development, Public Space, and Political Aspiration   109

Figure 5.3. Colored Orphans' Home and Industrial School Band along with the institution's founder, Charles McGhee (indicated as "10"), Huntington, W.V., ca. 1910. Source: *West Virginia History On View*, West Virginia and Regional History Center, WVU Libraries.

learned basic skills, which varied according to gender. Girls were taught general housework, cooking, laundering, and dressmaking. Boys were taught in agriculture, carpentry, masonry, shoemaking, blacksmithing, plumbing, and painting. Both sexes learned a common curriculum of reading, writing, arithmetic, spelling, geography, history, physiology, and grammar.[104] McGhee remained superintendent until 1915, when he was succeeded by James L. Hill. In 1920 the original building burned, with the children placed in private homes until a new building could be constructed. Although no longer used as the orphan's home, the replacement building lies on Route 60 east of Huntington.[105]

Mirroring the national growth of fraternal orders and mutual-aid organizations in the late nineteenth century, Huntington possessed chapters of the Grand United Order of Odd Fellows and the Household of Ruth as early as 1891.[106] Denied entrance into whites-only chapters, local blacks utilized avenues of cultural self-expression as well as venues for civic, economic, and political aspiration. Huntington newspaper articles chronicle the proliferation of these lodges, clubs, and benevolent organizations, citing the positive effects of their formation. The *Huntington Herald* remarked, "The colored people have lodges and organizations of a secret or social nature, which do much good. These are the lodges of Masons, Odd Fellows, Knights of Pythias, the order of St. Luke, etc."[107]

Black fraternal organizations in late-nineteenth-century Huntington participated in the cultural metamorphosis of Huntington's black institutions. Black people seeking fraternity among like-minded contemporaries, usually of similar social, racial, and/or occupational/class standings, sought insular societies in which they gained autonomy, authority, and community.[108] Throughout the 1890s and early 1900s, the indigenous creation, expansion, and increasing influence of these institutions in Huntington helped "to reinforce the communal and spiritual aspects of their culture." Furthermore, these fraternal and benevolent organizations linked black leaders from across the region and state.[109]

Formed in 1892 as the West Virginia Grand Lodge of the Knights of Pythias by Samuel W. Starks of Charleston, the group was one of the leading secret black fraternal orders of the day and included representatives from lodges at Raymond City, Huntington, Charleston, and Montgomery. Ancella Bickley notes of the organization, "It and other secret orders enhanced the sense of community and national connection among blacks, providing them with opportunities to share in business, social, and civil activities under the lodge's aegis."[110] By 1904, the Huntington Knights of Pythias Hall was hosting meetings of the Douglass Republican League, "composed of the leading colored voters of the city," occasionally, with the accompaniment of the Douglass orchestra, which members included a number of young men of the league.[111] In 1908 the Grand Lodge held its annual meeting in Huntington, with a number of business sessions held at First Baptist Church. A parade and picnic held at Clyffeside Park in Ashland, Kentucky, concluded the three-day event.[112] The Knights also provided financial support to its members. In 1909 the Huntington chapter of the Lodge contributed $2,800 in payments to orphans and widows of deceased members of the organization.[113] In November of that year, local actors participated in a performance of the drama "Thirty Years of Freedom" at the Knights of Pythias Hall, with one-third of the proceeds going to the Colored Orphans Home, and the remainder to the Ebenezer Methodist Episcopal Church.[114]

While white Huntingtonians approved of black progress within the sociocultural and educational arenas, efforts by local blacks to acquire greater political clout met with resistance throughout the late-nineteenth century. Early in the town's development, black residents were aware of the importance of the Convention of 1872 with regard to black aspiration. Initiated in the aftermath of a Democratic-Conservative victory in 1870, the convention called for a referendum on a new constitution to reverse the political gains and excessive punishment of the Rebels that the "Yankee" convention of 1863 had achieved. Among the political measures challenged were black enfranchisement and the right for blacks to seek public office.[115] An African American entrepreneur and leader of some standing in greater Huntington, Robert Long urged city blacks to vote against the measure. In mid-August 1872 a Huntington newspaper, the *Daily Press*, published his exhortations for blacks to protect their political rights:

> Now let every colored man in Cabell County rally to the polls next Thursday, come early, and vote for those who are now trying to make political capital by exciting prejudice against our color. Over one hundred of our race are in Huntington, we obey the laws and pay our taxes as well as whites, and we have the kindest feeling for our old masters in the south, but we cannot vote with them and will not help to elevate them into power as long as they indulge in unkind remarks against us or the glorious Yankees who shed their blood so freely for our freedom. Let every colored man rally and vote down the new Constitution and support Gov. Jacob, as Governor of all people.[116]

Long operated a barbershop, restaurant, and billiard parlor, and he owned several other properties, including the building he contributed to the city for the first African American school. "A colored man, not a member of any denomination," Long also advertised his services as a doctor and was thenceforth referred to as Doctor Long.[117] Evidence indicates that his influence within Huntington was substantial but short lived, with much about his life hidden from public record.[118] Long's visibility, eloquence, and affluence garnered local interest in several newspaper articles between 1872 and 1874, including unwanted attention from time to time.[119] Whether personal or politically motivated, in 1874 Long and Charles Ford were charged with "engaging in a fight and disturbing the peace, by using boisterous language" in front of a downtown hotel, and each fined one dollar and court costs.[120]

Long's exhortations plainly centered on his call for white Huntingtonians to recognize him and "over one hundred of our race" as Americans and to grant them the rights guaranteed in the U.S. Constitution. His call to action reveals recognition of his allegiance and obligations to the town's black population. To him, voting was a moral cause of the highest order. Moreover, his call presupposes the existence of residents not only similarly outraged and politically aware but also possessed of the means and will to disseminate and act on his directives. Speaking on black Huntington of 1872, Long demonstrates that, for him, group articulation and racial cohesion was an explicit goal, even though the inhabitants lacked many formal venues for cultural expression and political activism. His respectful tone and pointed words surely found a willing audience, black and white, linked by common interests.[121]

Because Huntington blacks possessed a high degree of interest in local and statewide political affairs, both political parties sought to exploit it. In early 1874, providing evidence of an ongoing network of social linkages within black Huntington, 50 blacks met "at their Chapel" to consider candidates in upcoming municipal elections. One month later, local Democrats, seeking the support of "the colored citizens of Huntington," reprimanded Dr. Long and the Radical Republicans in the local press. Later that year, the interestingly named Richard America, "the colored Demosthenes of Hinton," traveled to Huntington on the behalf of the Democratic Party to urge black voters to refrain from going to the polls in the October election. While belittling America and his overtures, the local Republican newspaper noted, "Dr. Long has more sense and ability than Richard, and he makes better sense of what he has, too."[122]

Despite the efforts of Long and other local blacks throughout the 1870s and 1880s, black residents made no political inroads. Even in the 1890s, Huntington's black leaders failed to rally sufficient voter support to acquire any office beyond low-level municipal positions.[123] Yet some were able to utilize their modicum of political clout to acquire status and stature. Noteworthy was William O. James, who received accolades from the *Advertiser* for "the efficiency and promptitude" with which he discharged his duties as Assistant Street Commissioner.[124] Chas. A. Wilson remarks that, along with Moses Butler, "a leader of the colored class," James was "looked upon by the race as the man who could get plums from the politicians." James assisted some black residents in acquiring jobs including postal carriers Ike Miller and George Hughes, and post office janitor Jenkins Gillard.[125] James's elaborate twenty-fifth-wedding-anniversary celebration perhaps suggests his success.[126]

There were, however, other notable black secular voices: migrant-turned-entrepreneur Dan Hill, once referred to by the white president of the organization of Early Settlers as "very independent and a man . . . whom the colored race respected for his intellect," mounted regular verbal attacks against the tactics of the Republican Party to disenfranchise black candidates.[127] Other black leaders also expressed their frustration with the historical apathy exhibited by the Republican Party. "The colored brother is very much in evidence this time," one local paper noted in early 1898, "and is beginning to manifest an independent spirit toward 'the gang,' that is so characteristic of that race just before election."[128] Shortly afterward, Negro Republicans met to denounce the agenda of the local ticket as well as the national party, specifically "condemning Secretary Alger for his incompetency in the management of the Spanish-American war."[129] One year later, in an explicit rebuff to the ongoing state of political affairs at the local level, African Americans established an independent Republican slate in the quest for municipal offices. Led by Moses Butler, and slating barbers Isaac Miller and Charles Seals, as well as a group of unskilled laborers from across the city, the ticket, seeking to fill the positions of mayor, clerk, treasurer, assessor, and two council seats each for the first, second, and third wards, respectively, mounted an impressive challenge—even more so when, one month later, twelve black candidates ran for seats in the various wards of the city.[130]

The formation of the "Colored Independent Republican Ticket" signaled a heightened level of activism by black working-class leaders in their quest to acquire municipal offices. It generated "a vast amount of heated discussion . . . among republican leaders on the subject of Moses and the colored voter generally" and seems to have forced the local party to respond.[131] One local newspaper, noting the arrival of former McDowell County Republican legislator and (now) pastor Christopher Payne into Huntington related, "He may be here for gospel purposes but the gospel is only an incident. He will labor faithfully to prevent Moses Butler's ticket from getting any votes."[132] Interestingly, later that month and for no apparent reason, Butler exhibited doubts over his actions and sued to have his name removed from the Independent Republican ticket. His indecision created backlash from white Republicans and seems to have contributed to fracturing the black vote.[133] In 1900 the city possessed 362 black males of voting age out of a total voting population of 3,385.[134] Perhaps illuminating the way class and race hindered working-class political aspirations, their efforts failed to garner sufficient support to win one seat, with four of the candidates failing to receive even one vote.[135] Thus, as Huntington's black residents entered the twentieth century, their political aspirations remained unmet and at the behest of white benevolence. To what extent this failure contributed to and fueled ongoing hostilities within the black community and between black aspirants is unknown. However, a local newspaper article recounting a public altercation between W. O. James and Butler suggests an explanation.[136]

Locked out of the political arena, Afro-Huntingtonians created other mechanisms to achieve their aspirations. In the spring of 1900, Huntington's first black newspaper, the *West Virginia Spokesman*, was founded and edited by C. H. Barnett (son of Reverend Barnett, brother of Dr. C. C. Barnett, and principal of Douglass High School at the time); J. W. Scott, vice principal of the school, served as editor. The paper's "political" purpose, "to promote the cause of the colored people politically by urging them to divide their vote among the two leading parties," advocated political independence as an avenue to address continuing marginalization by the state's political parties.

The *Huntington Advertiser*, which regularly covered news of the black community, proclaimed the *Spokesman* "a creditable newspaper."[137]

The involvement of two of the town's most prominent black educators and the overt political stance of the paper compelled the local board of education to respond to the threat to the status quo. "Over the recommendation of the teachers' committee," the board fired Barnett and Scott and agreed to reinstate both men only after they agreed to quit politics and cease editing the paper.[138] Barnett issued a vigorous response that ultimately led to his permanent dismissal. Responding to the charge that his paper was an arm of the Democratic Party (and perhaps distancing himself from Afro-Huntingtonians seeking or engaging in political bargaining), Barnett stated in an editorial in the paper: "No, I have never had a political pull, a religious pull, or a society pull to help me in securing or retaining a public school position and when the time comes that any of these are necessary, I am out of the business."[139]

There is some evidence that Barnett was indeed a Democrat. Barnett's grandson, Nelson Barnett Jr., believes that an anonymous letter to a local newspaper dated February 8, 1898, and signed "Negro with a Thinking Apparatus" was written by C. H. Barnett. In it, the writer speaks, as he says, for "myself and 999 other negroes in West Virginia who are tired of being dupes and cat's paws for the republican party." "In short," the writer continued, "the sooner the negro divorces himself from the republican party the better for him . . . If janitorships and third class clerks, porters, etc. is the kind of recognition we want, I assert that for 35 years service the democratic party would in my opinion have given the negro 16 to 1."[140] If the grandson's contention is true, Barnett's affiliation with the Democrat Party did not last. In 1908 Barnett served as chairman of the aforementioned four-year-old Douglass Republican League.[141]

Inarguably, the development of a professional class was crucial to black Huntington's development; however, it is important to recognize that not all professionals were leaders and not all leaders were professionals. Certainly, Huntington's earliest black leaders were men of the cloth; yet members of the working class without explicit church affiliation or record of their contribution were also important. Given the inchoate nature of early black Huntington and the dearth of available primary source material, location and definition of black leaders is problematic. Still, some discussion of the defining characteristics of black leadership must be attempted if we are to gain greater access into the nature of community and those deemed best suited to lead.

First and foremost, while they might have been advantaged educationally or financially, black leaders lived among and interacted with black Huntingtonians and, frequently, Ohio valley African Americans. Thus they were not an isolated elite. In this capacity, they knew the concerns of the other members of their community and set out to address them. Given that the African American population nearly tripled from 1880 to 1890, the absence of the 1890 federal manuscript census and extant city directories prior to 1891–92 is regrettable. Thus, establishing firm longevity parameters (10-year versus 15-year residency, for instance) is nearly impossible. It is possible, however, that the details would create an artificial barometer by which to judge an individual's contribution. Certainly, evidence of tenure is important, yet establishing a fixed time span is problematic as well. Given the fluid and embryonic state of Huntington's industry, infrastructure, and society, as well as the migratory patterns tied to the precariousness of black working-class formation, such a standard may place too great a burden of proof on those whose contributions, while noteworthy, were short lived. For instance, Robert Long's short stay in the city does not reduce his contribution. Further, surely many migrants followed the pattern of James Woodson and traveled back and forth to Virginia.

Last, logic dictates the inclusion of those who assisted in the formation or maintenance of an early black institution, headed a group, or were selected for an organizational position or office. Admittedly, this definition is problematic as well, primarily because it elevates those holding middle-class status (for which available source material exists) and diminishes the role of those within the working class (as well as women) who sought to fight injustice and inequality in their own ways. Again, Robert Long is absent from the membership rolls of various organizations and groups. Ultimately, to gain a better measure of black leadership within Huntington's formative years, we need to stretch the definition of leadership beyond the recognized networks and borders of spatial proximity, fixed tenure parameters, and formal membership to include those who imprinted and influenced aspects of the black community, whose progressive aspirations embraced and attempted to lift others within it, and whose efforts were recognized and respected by members of it.

The first generation of black Southern migrants had not let the scars of slavery incapacitate them or the rise of Negrophobia impede them. Transitioning from slavery to stability, significant numbers of Huntington's black migrants and residents passed through what Elizabeth Clark-Lewis described as "opportunity screens," based on firm religious beliefs, strong kin or augmented family support networks, and education.[142] Critical to this metamorphosis was the history of place and circumstance linking and binding black people on both sides of the Ohio River. Through the efforts and visions of both long-term antebellum settlers and postbellum migrants, the sociocultural foundation necessary to continued progression in the twentieth century was laid. In effect, each assisted Huntington's black residents to carve out a place to call their own.

Like black people across the nation, Huntington's black residents seized upon opportunity as best as they could to better their lives by establishing necessary institutions. It is important that this metamorphosis began with the efforts of Huntington's black working class. Within this class, a cadre of indigenous black community leaders assisted and in some instances initiated the construction and maintenance of churches, a school, and the conduits for political action. The development of black institutions provided the foundation for a people to acquire an education, "to rise," and to broaden their horizons. By the time a contingent of black professionals appeared in the mid-1890s, the necessary "building blocks" were firmly in place and recognized by African Americans throughout the region as the bedrock of individual aspiration, social advancement, and community formation.

Encompassing the political and social strivings of a people, the rise of these institutions coincided with African Americans' increasing political self-activity and entry into the public space as an attempt to carve out their own spaces and create their own "moral geography." This dynamic was not simplistic, linear, or unified; it was ensconced within and the result of contradictory and complementary forces, aspirations, and mentalities. Throughout Huntington's formative years, black migrants' pragmatic adaptations to their circumstance illustrated their nonconsent to their subjugation, denigration, and oppression. At the dawn of a new century, the utilization of these characteristics would be further needed as the city's commercial, manufacturing, and cultural expansion continued and Jim Crow strengthened.

CHAPTER 6

Spreading Our Wings

Afro-Huntingtonian Progress during the Era of "Benevolent Segregation"

> We have gotten out of the cellar, so to speak, and that means much. Our eyes are beginning to open. The proverbial short-sightedness of the first Negro settlers who refused to buy real estate when land was cheap was a racial blunder from which we suffer today. Yet a few who brought their families or who married out here were wise enough to buy homes.
> —Professor J. W. Scott, *Progress of the Huntington Negro*, 1911.[1]

Walter Brown was in excruciating pain. Covered in blood, he was cold and weak. He could not stop shivering and could only slightly lift his head. His breathing was labored and pained. Alone and scared, he could not feel his mangled and nearly severed legs. He was also distraught: after enduring the shock and trauma of the fall and the cold steel of the train and what seemed like an eternity on the hard ground in "the yards," and then after finally being discovered and transported, he had been denied admittance to the hospital. "No Negroes allowed," the sign read. Now, drifting in and out of consciousness, he was vaguely aware of his transport to a second hospital. But even if they admitted him there, he knew it would be too late to save him. He knew he was too near death. He could discern loud, agitated, perhaps even angry voices but could not identify any. He surmised they belonged to people trying to help him, but when he opened his eyes their faces remained hazy, their ethnicity unclear. By the time he was admitted to Kessler Hospital, he was unconscious. And, despite the best efforts of the hospital's staff, Brown would die on the operating table, having endured an ignominious, unnecessary, and lonely death. Upon hearing the circumstances of Brown's death, C. C. Barnett pledged "never again."[2]

Huntington experienced a phenomenal population explosion during the early twentieth century. Between 1900 and 1910 the city's population grew by an exceptional 161 percent, soaring from 11,923 to 31,161 inhabitants. White residential population grew by a remarkable 171 percent. Black residential population rebounded from the dip experienced during the previous decade, nearly doubling to 2,140, an increase of 77 percent. By 1900, black residents hailed from thirteen states, including significant increases in the population of Kentuckians, North Carolinians, and Tennesseans.[3] That year, illustrative of the continuing influx of families, black male and female populations were nearly equal at 605 and 607 persons, respectively, a dramatic shift from 1880, when black males represented 62 percent of the black population.[4] Even more dramatic, in 1910, nearly 80 percent of Huntington's blacks had migrated to West Virginia.[5] Mirroring national developments, Huntington city leaders implemented various measures to contain and constrain black aspirations, to varying degrees of success. One of the most enduring was the construction of "colored" Huntington. Over time, with the tacit agreement of city officials and the general population, white realtors designated both whites-only neighborhoods augmented by racially "restrictive covenants," and a blacks-only residential subdivision. In this manner, they mirrored and implemented segregationist practices present throughout the nation during the nadir of Jim Crow.[6] Within the next decade, spurred by urban growth and continuing migrant influx throughout southern West Virginia, Huntington solidified its place as the second-largest city in the state.[7]

So extensive was black migration into the southern West Virginia coalfields and urban-industrial centers that between 1890 and 1910 West Virginia was the only Southern state to increase in total population. An infusion of northern black migrants also contributed to the population increase in the region. In his study of African Americans in West Virginia, historian Joe W. Trotter found that only about 21 percent of the state's blacks lived in the southern counties in 1880. By 1910 that figure had climbed to 63 percent.[8] In conjunction with black migration into southern West Virginia, thousands of European immigrants also settled in this region. Southern West Virginia's population increased dramatically throughout the region from approximately 80,000 in 1880 to nearly 300,000 in 1910. The immigrant population from southern, central, and eastern Europe grew from 1,400 in 1880 to 18,000 (6 percent of the total) in 1910. African American growth outpaced foreign growth, expanding from 4,800 in 1880 (6 percent of the total) to more than

40,000 (14 percent of the total) in 1910.[9] These numbers represented more than twice the proportion of European immigrants in the southern part of the state and transformed the region into a "contested zone" of social tension and labor strife as native West Virginians, European immigrants, and African Americans competed for jobs, housing, and hegemony.

Notwithstanding the increasing numbers of blacks and immigrants into the region during the late nineteenth and early twentieth centuries, West Virginia remained overwhelmingly "white" in its racial composition and mentality. A Huntington newspaper article trumpeted in 1904 that, out of all the states in the Union, West Virginia "has the largest proportion of native white inhabitants," and that "out of every 1000 persons . . . 955 are white and only 45 are colored."[10] While the implementation and observance of Jim Crow–era practices did not remain static, undoubtedly white political power and notions of racial superiority remained a source of pride and unity for many whites in southern West Virginia. Former Confederate Henry Clay Ragland, editor of the influential *Logan County Banner* newspaper, no doubt articulated the thoughts of many when he congratulated an Ohio mob in 1897 for lynching an African American who had attacked a white women: "It is always very well to prate about the majesty of the law and the viciousness of mobs, but when a lady is criminally assaulted by a brute, the people who are the creators of the law become superior to the enactments of their legislatures and the machinery which they have established for their execution."[11] For Ragland and other racist whites, the primary failing of the Negro was moral. As one writer contended, "the real basis of the ideology of white supremacy was moral: blacks were innately inferior morally. This meant, simply, that nonwhites lacked a super ego, a set of built-in restraints, guilt, or other curbs on the libido."[12] For Ragland, the only black men worthy of recognition were those who were deferential, a point he reiterated in a eulogy for long-time Logan County resident "Uncle Dan" Howard, a black man who "was always polite and knew his place."[13]

During the late nineteenth and early twentieth centuries African American migrants were frequently forced to acclimate, negotiate, and navigate a kaleidoscope of racialized interactions. While state and city officials and urban industrial employers actively recruited African Americans, touting the benefits of settlement, employment, and cordial race relations, the state's white residents sought ways to constrict black entry, constrain black aspiration, circumscribe black autonomy, and, occasionally, engage in physical violence.[14] White West Virginian state and municipal authorities characterized race relations in their state as "benevolent segregation."[15] In this manner, racial relations in West Virginia and Huntington mirrored what historian George

C. Wright, in his study of Louisville between 1865 and 1930, characterized as "polite racism."[16] Like Huntington, Louisville whites controlled the racial environment by providing selective backing of black interests, helping to perpetuate an image of racial progressiveness. Thus, "polite racism," according to Wright, "proved to be effective, for it tended to lull both Afro-Americans and whites into believing that conditions in Louisville were not as bad as they were elsewhere."[17]

However, in his book on racial violence outside of Louisville and Lexington, Wright reached a very different conclusion. Stunned by the number of blacks lynched in small towns across the state at the turn of the century, Wright concluded that "racial violence, the reverse of polite racism, also existed in Kentucky and was probably more prevalent than the polite racism found in Louisville."[18] Evidence shows that urban-rural dichotomy of racial violence in Kentucky also existed within the state of benevolent segregation.

As early as the late nineteenth century the deteriorating state of race relations in southern West Virginia captured the attention of state officials. After the 1898 murder of an unarmed black woman in the Mercer County town of Bramwell and the unwillingness to local authorities to apprehend the perpetrators, State Attorney General Edgar P. Rucker expressed not only his concern over the incidence of lynching in the state in a letter to Hugh O. Woods, assistant prosecuting attorney of Princeton, West Virginia, but also the complicity of local officers in the acts, those who "connive at it and sympathize with it."[19]

Rucker's sentiments were well founded. While evidence shows that intervention by local authorities to thwart lynching efforts did occur, in the state's history West Virginians lynched 28 blacks, the vast majority from the southern region of the state and after the turn of the twentieth century.[20] In addition to public lynching, an unknown (and unknowable) number of near-lynchings occurred across the state. In response to the escalating threat of racial violence in southern West Virginia, black delegates from that region twice introduced antilynching legislation in the state legislature in the early part of the century before an antilynching law eventually passed in 1921.[21]

Local newspapers that covered lynchings or near-lynchings conducted in adjacent states illustrated the potentially corrosive power of the white-controlled press in the era of Jim Crow. In their quest to illuminate incidents of white mob action and their right to extralegal action, West Virginia's newspaper facilitated an implicit threat against incidents of local black assertiveness. This point is especially important in light of Charles S. Johnson's observation that increased frequency of lynchings in the Deep South did not dissuade black migrants from a particular area where employment opportunities existed.[22] Thus, it should come as no surprise that the rise of the state's coal industry and the attendant influx of black migrants and European immigrants helped make West Virginia's southern coalfields the state's most racially contentious region.

In addition to extralegal actions by whites, African Americans also suffered disproportionately within the state's criminal justice system. In 1900 blacks totaled just 4.7 percent of West Virginia's population yet represented 53 percent of the prison population in the West Virginia Penitentiary.[23] From 1899 to 1928 the black population totaled no more than 5.7 percent of the general population, yet it accounted for nearly 61 percent of the total persons hanged by the state, the vast majority of whom resided in the southern coalfields. In fact, both of the first two black men executed by the state arrived in West Virginia as migrant laborers from the South.[24] Certainly, for many of the state's black residents, segregation in the coalfields was more malevolent than benevolent.

Huntington was not immune from the threat of mob violence against black residents during the early twentieth century. The most serious incident occurred in August 1911, when, after the alleged murder of Harry Withrow, a "well-regarded" white assistant C&O section foreman, by section hand Charley Clyburn, reportedly "a brutal, ignorant negro," area whites attempted on consecutive nights to retrieve him from his jail cell to lynch him. Forced to respond, city authorities declared martial law and dispatched a militia, complete with riot guns, and a fire company. After using streams of water to disperse the crowd, a number of arrests were made, ending the threat.[25] Another incident ended more tragically when the "Patch men" formed a posse with guns and killed a "foreign or black man" who had shot a C&O detective, dragging his body behind a horse for blocks.[26]

One related but more subversive aspect of white coercion during the Jim Crow era was the existence of "sundown towns," where whites mandated, through the threatened or actual use of violence, that blacks vacate a town by sundown. Wheelersburg, Ohio, located to the north of Huntington, was one. Within Cabell County, Milton was not only a sundown town, but its residents clearly intended it to be an all-white one.[27]

As the industrialization of West Virginia compelled increasing numbers of native whites, European immigrants, and African Americans into the region, the fluidity of this process regularly produced fractures within the hegemony. This dynamic operated within working-class relationships, sometimes mitigating the strict adherence to and enforcement of Jim Crow. Frequently, within the "intimate spaces" of interracial contact that existed across southern West Virginia in railroad camp, mining towns, and urban-industrial cities, cordial cultural exchanges between the races informed and educated each group, despite the presence of Jim Crow. Indeed, one white Huntington resident of the interracial working-class enclave "the Patch" recalled, "There was never any trouble between colored people and white people in the Patch. Us kids would fight one day and play the next just like any kids anywhere."[28] While this might indeed have been an accurate portrayal of race relations in the neighborhood, it is difficult to believe that some neighborhood blacks did not react strongly to the lynching described above by "Patch men." Yet, even if angered and compelled to action, the low numbers of black residents in the Patch compelled a level of assessment and perhaps self-censorship. The fact that black students, unable to attend the neighborhood white school, walked a mile to Douglass Elementary and Douglass High School also reduced the opportunities for the development of racial animus and calibrated black response.

Yet the fact that the intervention of city authorities thwarted mob action illuminates the differing perspectives maintained by white authorities attempting to uphold the law against that of white residents seeking extralegal measures to subvert it (recall the near-lynching of Charles Ringo). Moreover, although the state's black residential population never reached a number or proportion that threatened the prevailing power structure, it did possess sufficient concentration in certain areas to threaten the economic status and belief systems of localized white populations.[29] Though, notably, no black Huntingtonian held any city council seat during any of the years of this study, in truth, as long as the city's black residents recognized and operated within the racial status quo (especially regarding restrictions against miscegenation), life in Huntington offered a great deal. "Keeping one's place," however, failed to stem the tide of Jim Crow–era racism, and the city's black residents sought out ways to re-calibrate race relations for greater social and/ or political equality.

One avenue to address their continuing marginalization was for black women to embrace the fellowship and agendas of female-centered endeavors. Although there is evidence of working-class black female activism in the Ohio valley, most efforts were grounded in the middle-class philosophy of respectability.[30] Black women's efforts extended the indigenous networks rooted in community and demonstrated that they were capable of creative responses to the economic, social, political, and racial barriers preventing their full inclusion into American society. In the process, black women, hoping their efforts would help refute the racial notion that all black women were immoral, embraced the moral tenets of the late Victorian era.[31] Although middle-class black women were affected by the Victorian-era ideal of "true womanhood," their efforts manifested a significant difference. The duty of ideal white women was grounded in the domestic sphere, where they attempted to oversee the moral development of their children and maintain the moral development of their husbands.[32] In contrast, ideal black womanhood bridged both the private and public spheres. At a time when black men throughout the South and in Huntington were denied entrance into the public political arena, black women's public and political contributions provided an important aspect of black political organization.[33] The ideal black woman was educated, race-conscious and often worked outside the home.[34]

Throughout the early twentieth century, the efforts of black women in Huntington embodied this ideology. Callie Barnett, mother of Dr. C. H. Barnett, was an active member of First Baptist, did sewing to supplement her husband's income, and was a member of the Afro-American Improvement Society and the local Temperance Society.[35] In 1900, Douglass High teacher Amanda Miller Coleman, wife of Rev. James D. Coleman, presented a talk on "'The Up-to-Date Woman' [setting] forth many qualifications essential to a well developed woman" to the Women's Missionary Society of Charleston, an auxiliary to the Woman's State Convention.[36] In 1909 the "'Hoop Drill' by twelve little girls for the benefit of the Ladies Mite Missionary Society was well received and quite a success by way of entertainment and finance."[37] In 1910 the Dunbar Sisters Literacy Society, consisting of seventh- and eighth-grade girls and those of the high school, performed school-related programs.[38] That summer a band of "young Misses of the Orphan Home" progressed nicely under the leadership of Lucy McGhee.[39] In 1911 the committee for woman's day celebration at the AME church was composed of Emma Bromley, Carrie Simmons, and Lula Johnson.[40]

The educational process initiated and maintained by these various entities not only involved inculcation of an individual achievement orientation but also instilled the centrality of moral vision embodying commitment to the community. Black Huntingtonian Revella E. Hughes's life story also informs this ethic and is suggestive of the importance of childrearing strategies to the success of black professional women. Historian Stephanie Shaw contends that these strategies "transformed individualistic notions of self-help and the so-called Protestant work ethic into an ethic of *socially responsible individualism*" in which the relatively few black women who achieved formal education were "looked to, encouraged to, and expected to 'take up the crosses' of those who were less able than they."[41]

Before achieving international fame as Carmella Dusche, the singer, musician and performer, and eventual Douglass High music teacher Revella Hughes developed her artistic talent within female-centered networks. Born in 1895 to George and Anna B. Page Hughes, Revella began playing piano under her mother's tutelage at age five. As a girl she served in the choir at the Sixteenth Street Baptist Church, traveled to Charleston and Institute, West Virginia (home of West Virginia Colored Institute), to perform in community-centered teas and socials, and entertained patrons in the homes of local black leaders. Although she attended Douglass High School, Hughes transferred to her mother's alma mater, Hartshorn Memorial College ("the world's first college to train African American females") in Richmond, Virginia. Chartered in 1884 to "to train colored women for practical work in the broad harvest of the world," Hartshorn was, at the time, an American Baptist Mission school. After receiving her diploma in music in 1909, she returned to Huntington, attended dinner parties, traveled, hosted guests from other cities in the state, and taught music. Over the next decade, Hughes graduated from Oberlin High School in Oberlin, Ohio, and Howard University, taught at the Washington Conservatory of Music for one year, and served as director of music at Orangeburg State College in South Carolina. In 1920 Hughes traveled to New York City, launching her onto a remarkable 30-year career trajectory in which she traveled around the globe.[42] In spite of her success and worldwide travels, Hughes considered herself a Huntingtonian and often returned to the city to visit family or perform. No doubt the efforts of such women, like those of black women nationwide, positively affected their self-esteem and helped to reinforce communal values and connections, while assisting black political aspirations.

In truth, black women's aspirations were constrained by white society and black men, who embraced attitudes and behavior that had changed little over the decades. Throughout the early twentieth century, as men moved up to positions of greater responsibility, women remained largely locked into the two fields of teaching and nursing. For instance, in Cabell County, all seven African Americans who took the teacher's examination of 1904 were women.[43] In 1895 Josephine Barnett began her forty-year teaching career at Douglass High; when she retired from the school, she possessed the record for the most service of any teacher in the city's school system.[44] After graduating as valedictorian from Douglass in 1911, Nellie Francisco, denied entrance into Huntington's Marshall College, attended a normal school in Bluefield, West Virginia, from which a student could receive a teaching certificate. After obtaining her college degree from West Virginia State College, Francisco returned to Douglass in 1915, teaching all subjects through the eighth grade. For the next fifteen years, she taught in Huntington as well as in the coalfields of southern West Virginia.[45]

Figure 6.1. Douglass High School Orchestra, Revella Hughes (left front), director. *Notan Studios Collection*, West Virginia State Archives, West Virginia Division of Culture and History, Charleston, W.V.

Black men suffered constraints as well in their professional aspirations. One important aspect of Douglass High, and doubtless other black high schools around the nation, was the employment of high proportion of African American male teachers. In 1903, building upon the accomplishments of the previous generations, Walter A. Smith and Lloyd G. Smith, members of the "Traveler" Smith family, acquired jobs at Douglass. For many, teaching (and preaching) was the only available profession, despite their schooling and credentials. In 1903, Huntington's public schools employed 59 teachers and principals. Of the 52 white teachers, the only males listed were a high school principal and one of his assistants. However, of the seven teachers at Douglass, three were male.[46] After graduating with an architecture degree from Ohio State University in 1918, Carl Barnett became a teacher, waiting 30 years before being able to practice his profession. "No firm was interested in me," Barnett states. "As soon as they saw the color of my skin they changed their minds."[47]

Within black high schools, one professional avenue open to black males but denied black females was coaching athletics. In 1915 the legendary Zelma

Davis assumed his post as coach and soon established football at the school. A graduate of Municipal College in Louisville, Kentucky, Davis's coaching career is remarkable for its length and level of success. During his forty-year tenure, Douglass won eleven state championships and 234 games, including 33 straight games from 1935 to 1938. Despite playing the best African American high school teams in the state, including Charleston's Garnet, Beckley's Stratton, Clarksburg's Kelly Miller, Parkersburg's Sumner, and Bluefield's Genoa Senior, his football teams failed to achieve a winning record only twice. In track, his team won its first state championship in 1919, before reeling off five consecutive state championships from 1921 to 1925. Four times his basketball teams advanced to the Negro National Championship Tournament.[48]

Black leaders reminded whites of the black historical presence in and contributions to the city's betterment. In early 1907 Marshall College (now Marshall University) invited avowed white supremacist South Carolina Senator Ben "Pitchfolk" Tillman to speak. Due to the overwhelming demand for tickets, the university changed the venue for his lecture from a campus auditorium to a local theater. Black response to Tillman's invitation arose shortly afterward. By early March growing animosity to his visit prompted one local newspaper to report that black residents were expressing "a threatening attitude" (through the promise of physical protest), toward Tillman's impending arrival.[49] In a 1907 petition reprinted in the *Huntington Advertiser*, prominent black leaders, including Douglass teachers J. W. Scott, J. B. Hatchett, Josie M. Barnett, Mina E. Stewart, George Scott, along with I. V. Bryant and S. A. Thurston, pastors of First Baptist and Sixteenth Street Baptist, respectively, called for city leaders to recognize the immorality of Senator Tillman's platform and to deny him a venue.[50] Though ultimately rebuffed in their effort to have the mayor forbid Tillman's appearance, the published response illuminates both the nature and limits of black middle-class resistance strategies.

Douglass students, however, used more confrontational methods. In February 1909 a series of conflicts between black students of Douglass and white children occurred, resulting in what was labeled a "serious clash," involving "twenty or more" and drawing a crowd of "hundreds." While the ongoing cause of the "racial difficulties" was not revealed, the protracted character of the tensions, the intensity of the scuffle, and the willingness of the students to exchange blows is instructive. The school students were not afraid to assert themselves and utilize methods they deemed best to deal with the issue(s), methods that probably conflicted with those advocated by their teachers, the black middle class, and certainly white authorities.[51]

While the methodologies utilized by students and their teachers differed, both groups were grounded in an articulated and operational consciousness of individual and collective self-worth. In May, Dr. Lewis B. Moore, dean of the Teachers College of Howard University, addressed the graduates and audience at the 1909 Douglass High commencement, advising them, "Much has been done for the Negro to lift the dark cloud which was a heritage of slavery and to save the country from the abyss yawning beneath it. But race progress can be measured not by what is done for a race but only by what the race does for itself." Moore also reminded the audience of the uniqueness, enormity, and promise of black progress: "Every other people have gone down before the white man but the negro. He is the first man in history who has looked the white man in the face." In the end, Moore reassured whites that segregation was amenable to both races.[52] His statement contains no overture to the gathering to emulate or replicate whiteness as the norm. Instead, his remarks advocate dignity, self-affirmation, and a positive black identity as the individual goal and ideological foundation of race advancement.

In 1911 long-time black Huntingtonian Professor Scott also articulated the self-help philosophy, albeit in a more conciliatory fashion than Dr. Moore. In his remarks to the members of the Huntington YMCA, he stated, "Any community is bound to move upward if it has within itself the influence of clean homes, good churches, and efficient schools. This trinity of social forces stands for industry and cleanliness, obedience and reverence, discipline and intelligence. With these agencies we must yet develop all the classes that belong to a well-organized social group."[53] In conveying their visions, both Moore and Scott offered expressions of the self-help philosophy embraced by the African American middle class.

J. W. Scott's long-term residency, professional status, and community ties provided him important insight (and biases) into the status of the city's African American population, past and present. As a young man in the early 1890s, Scott arrived in the city from Henrico County, Virginia, and settled at 620 Eighth Avenue, where he was soon joined by his brakeman father, Isham.[54] In 1905 he brought to bear his education, knowledge, and experiences to start the first black newspaper in the city, of which he was co-editor. Many of his observations of Huntington's black migrants were undoubtedly true: significant numbers arrived into the town subject to the whims and dictates of influential men and powerful political, legal, and economic forces. From the city's founding, "Negro shanties" dotted the city, and black crime and vagrancy proved troublesome to city leaders.[55] But equally undeniable is that few, if any, thought of themselves as impotent or pathological. When able, they celebrated. In fact, evidence indicates that the vast majority embodied the character, discipline, and will-power "conducive to morals and home getting."[56]

In concert with Douglass High's evolution, black churches and fraternal organizations continued to flourish. By 1911 Scott, then principal and teacher at Douglass, noted the existence of four black churches: First Baptist, Sixteenth Street, Young Chapel AME, and Ebenezer ME (relocated to Artisan Avenue and Sixteenth Street in 1909). Scott also noted seven lodges, including two units of the Pythians and a Knights of Pythias Brass Band, the Masonics, the True Reformers, the Odd Fellows, the Hod Carriers' Union, and the Elks. The three-story brick Knights of Pythias Hall was valued at $15,000. For women, there were branches of the St. Luke's and Household of Ruth.[57]

One additional response of black Huntingtonians to Jim Crowism was travel. Just as large numbers of African Americans arrived into the city to take advantage of its varied attractions, many of the city's black residents also traveled outside its borders.[58] In the mid-1900s, local newspapers, via columns alternately titled "Colored Notes," "Colored Folks," and later, "Afro-American Notes," began chronicling the sociocultural experiences of middle-class black Huntingtonians, providing greater insight into "hidden transcripts" of their daily activities.[59] Many of these journeys, as well as others chronicling black life in the city, were carried in the *Pittsburgh Courier*, part of the vanguard of "race" newspapers, along with Robert Abbott's *Chicago Defender* and W. E. B. Du Bois's magazine *The Crisis*, that sprang up during the early 1900s.

By the mid-1920s both the *Defender* and *Courier* were selling hundreds of thousands of copies, with the *Courier* providing extensive coverage of the lives of black West Virginians. Huntington's first correspondent to the *Courier* was Carrie Simmons. An 1897 graduate of Douglass, Simmons began forwarding her reports, which covered a variety of topics, including health, funerals, travels, relocation, parties, marriages, and pageants. Also included were her reports of black female organizations and groups like the Ladies Aid Society, the Ladies Sewing Circle, and the Rising Sons and Daughters. In general, these societies were composed of churchgoing members who paid dues that were distributed through activities that embraced a larger commitment to community uplift and moral reform.[60] Simmons's observations (and that of other community correspondents, including a number from the towns and cities from southern West Virginia) were printed in a column entitled "Afro-American Cullings."[61]

Many of these activities related directly to increasing physical segregation. As discussed in chapter 4, Buffington Row lay astride the southern of the C&O tracks. Just south of the Row, on the other side of the railroad tracks and along Eighth Avenue, lay an area eventually comprising three major subdivisions between Sixteenth and Twentieth Streets, forming the nexus of a growing black residential concentration (see map 4.1). Primarily an agricultural area prior to 1890, these three enclaves—Addition No. 1, Holderby Addition, and the Ceramic Subdivision—met three objectives. First, they ensured Huntington's continued expansion south. Second, they offered a boon for the area's white real-estate speculators that resulted in a record $900,000 in new real estate construction in 1904. Third, they helped mark the borders of "colored" Huntington.[62] Two recent studies by geographer Jacqueline A. Housel are crucial to examining the shifting racial contours of Huntington's residential population.

The first, completed in 1998, compares settlement patterns of Artisan and Doulton Avenues in the early 1900s. The second, completed in 2002, examines the formation of Huntington's first "black" residential enclave. These studies help illuminate the historical foundations contributing to the construction of "colored" Huntington.[63]

It is clear that a pattern of black settlement began emerging with the formation of the racially integrated subdivision of Addition No. 1 in 1880. This area, bounded by the railroad to the north, included Eighth and Ninth Avenues, Sixteenth and Twentieth Streets, as well as Artisan Avenue. By 1879 both of Huntington's first black churches, First Baptist and Ebenezer Methodist Episcopal (later Ebenezer United Methodist), occupied sites on opposite ends of Eighth Avenue, illustrating the southerly shift of Huntington's black migrant population. Located several blocks to the west of the embryonic black residential core, First Baptist rested near the western edge of a scattered black migrant population. In contrast, Ebenezer stood on the eastern corner of Sixteenth Street, much closer to Huntington's burgeoning black residential center and the increasing influx of poor black migrants who settled there.[64] The establishment of Douglass High School, on the west corner of Sixteenth Street and Eighth Avenue, provides further evidence of this developing pattern.

Commenting on the housing patterns in Addison No. 1, Jacqueline Housel notes,

> Typically shot-gun houses with a few I-frame houses were constructed on small lots (30 by 85) or half lots with little if any yard space. Its location midway between the central business district and the Chesapeake and Ohio Railroad Company shops were ideal for a household where two or more workers were needed to provide an income and where workers were often subject to inconsistent, part time employment. Working long hours for low pay, employees found convenient and cheap housing.[65]

The historical origin of Artisan Avenue in the early twentieth century reveals an interracial composition as black and white migrants sought affordable housing. Real-estate speculators subdivided land into smaller lots that were less expensive than those in adjacent subdivisions, thus providing greater opportunity for buyers to meet the negotiated monthly or quarterly payments. Smaller lots also allowed greater opportunities for agents to exploit prospective black buyers. For example, Sydney Coger purchased a lot for $250 that had been purchased three days earlier for $156 by real-estate broker J. M. Fuller.[66] The vicinity also included black churches such as the Young African Methodist Episcopal Chapel, located on the corner of Eighteenth and Artisan, and the Sixteenth Street Baptist Church. Established in 1905 by forty-one former members of First Baptist, formally organized under the leadership of Reverend Meadows, the church was erected between Eighth and Ninth Avenues. Reverend James D. Coleman served as its first pastor.[67]

Ceramic Subdivision, containing Doulton Avenue, lay south of Addison No. 1. Subdivided in 1905 from excess land owned by the Huntington China Company, the district included Ninth Avenue, Ritter Avenue to the south, and Sixteenth and Twentieth Streets, with lots that sold for $300 each. The racial composition of Artisan and Doulton Avenues reveals a sharp contrast in the racial residential patterns along the two avenues from Sixteenth Street to Twentieth Street. While Artisan was 40 percent African American and 60 percent white, Doulton included only three black households. Further, Housel shows that the black population along Artisan clustered from Sixteenth to Eighteenth Streets.[68]

South of the Ceramic Subdivision, just east of Sixteenth Street, lay the 22 acres comprising the Holderby Addition. Despite containing smaller lot sizes than Ceramic, Holderby's 125 lots, subdivided in 1903, possessed a number of selling points. Purchase in the district provided an elevated location, wide 50-foot avenues, fifteen-foot alleys, an option of buying an adjoining lot at the auction price, a short distance to the streetcar line, and inclusion into an all-white neighborhood. The advertisement for the lot sale stated, "One feature of the sale that will be met with universal approval is that the lots will be sold only to members of the Caucasian race, and no deed will under any circumstances be granted to any other."[69] This advertisement provided an explicit warning to Huntington's black residents that this area was off-limits, while reassuring white residents that purchasing a home protected them from the black-migrant onslaught. As the city struggled to adjust to the demographic changes and economic growth, the civic leadership and residents initiated "the construction of 'colored' Huntington."

Huntington's black population paid attention. By 1910 Artisan Avenue became home to an occupationally diverse black population, from clergymen, physicians, and teachers to laborers, barbers, and porters. In her study of Artisan Avenue's racial composition in 1920, Housel reports that "the ratio of black to white households stood at 40:60 in 1910, but 10 years later the ratio reversed to 60:40 with a doubling of the number of overall households. These statistics tend to hide the level of segregation. At all times, black households clustered in the interior of the street while white households faced or lived near the major boulevards."[70] Housel's study provides compelling evidence that the process of residential segregation was well underway on Artisan by 1920. The metamorphosis in black residential patterns should not overshadow the fact that significant numbers of black residents purchased property on the avenue throughout this period.

The establishment of an all-white enclave coincided with the founding of an ostensibly all-black one. Built on a marsh, originally on the western edge of the old Holderby family farmland, Washington Place was an area that newspapers advertised as being "exclusively for coloreds."[71] Located on the western side of Sixteenth Street and subdivided in 1905, its boundaries included Shelton Lane to the west and two small subdivisions that abutted the railroad tracks to the north. Housel reports,

> For whites, Washington Place functioned as both a plug and a buffer. The plug was a designated place where the "coloreds" who had accumulated assets could buy property and build their own homes. Thus, it was not necessary for blacks to buy property in ostensibly white areas. It also served as a buffer zone, strategically located between the ghetto and middle-class suburb.[72]

Owned by real-estate developer and avowed former Confederate J. H. Cammack, who, along with his partner J. H. Potts, developed much of Huntington's South Side, Washington Place served two purposes. First, it allowed Cammack to profit directly from blacks as they purchased his property. Second, it afforded indirect benefits from their inability to move into white areas and the possible resultant negative impact on property values. Not all residents were of the working class, though. In 1900 Rush Smith and Theodore "Doug" Brown were the proprietors of a restaurant on Front Street in Catlettsburg, Kentucky. In 1907 Smith, the father of Edna Duckworth, purchased a lot in Washington Place with a $50 down payment. By 1910 he and his wife, Georgia, resided in a modest house at 1415 Tenth Avenue. Two years later, they welcomed their first child, Edna, into the home, where she resided until her death in 2002.[73]

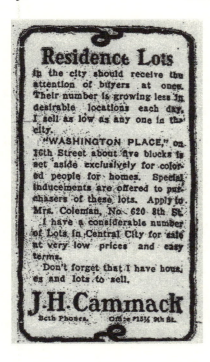

Figure 6.2. "Washington Place" advertisement, *Huntington Advertiser*, April 6, 1905.

Although "benevolent segregation" represented a potent manifestation of white racism throughout Huntington, it fails to explain two things: Why did white Huntingtonians think it necessary to implement restrictive measures? And why during this time period? Given that Huntington's black population never represented more than approximately 10 percent of the general population during the twentieth century, these questions beg consideration.

Certainly, there is no evidence that any element of black Huntington posed a direct threat to the livelihood, status, or security of white Huntington. In fact, as indicated in table 1, although Huntington's black population increased numerically from 1900 to 1910, it decreased proportionally to its white population. Moreover, in 1910 the percentage of native whites within Huntington was 87.6 percent, the highest in the nation for cities with populations of 25,000 to 100,000.[74] However, some answers are derived from the convergence of key developments. First, in 1910 Huntington's black population made up 87 percent of the county's total, forming a daily presence that could not be ignored.[75] Second, as discussed previously, along with the continuing presence of the disreputable element associated with black-owned clubs within the business district, newspapers portray an upsurge in black crime, with increasing incidents of violent crime. Along with the chronicled exploits of the more notorious, Sam Graves, Lottie McQueen, and Charles Ringo, to name a few, newspaper articles portray a city outraged over adult and juvenile crime. Both had grown especially troublesome to white authorities by the turn of the century, with juvenile crime garnering increasing attention. Increasing migrant influx contributed to rising numbers of idle youth. As early as 1898 the city council had adopted a "Curfew Ordinance, requiring children under 15 years of age to be off the streets by 8 o'clock in Winter and 9 o'clock in Summer."[76] In 1900 Huntington was home to 400 black youths between the ages of five and twenty, more than any other city in the state, save Charleston.[77] On any given day, many could be found loafing around city saloons.[78] An additional factor in juvenile crime might be attributable to industrial practices within the state. The state's industries had historically precluded the hiring of children, as was the case with women. As one authority noted, "There were 6,212 children between 10 and 15 years employed in West Virginia in 1870. They comprised 5.4% of the total working population. The same year the percentage of child workers in the United States was 20. In his report for 1904, the State Commissioner of Labor was 'proud to report' that West Virginia employed 38.6 adults to one child worker under 16 whereas corresponding figures for North Carolina and South Carolina were 5.7 and 4.6 respectively."[79] In effect, although practices within the state greatly limited the employment of children and the attendant hazards, it removed one potential solution to help address the problem of wayward youth.

By 1900, Eighth Avenue, from Eighth to Twentieth Streets, formed the artery through which the collective life force of Huntington's black community coursed. Fully 20 percent of the city's black residents lived on it.[80] Most of the petty crime was centered in (or adjacent to) the predominately black, racially mixed, working-class neighborhoods, with Eighth Avenue especially vulnerable. Thus, crime was a product of proximity and opportunity. As one article related, "The attention of the police had been directed to a gang of young hoodlums, white and black, who infest the corner of Eighth avenue and Eighteenth street, making life a burden for people who live in that neighborhood."[81] The continuing problem of vagrancy and petty crime and its locus within the increasingly black area of Eighth Avenue was surely noted by many and might have served as an incentive for those contemplating residential zoning laws and restrictive covenants as a way to bottle up the problem.

Another likely justification is the increasing acquisition of property by black Huntingtonians. Between 1890 and 1900, black residents purchased 33 properties, an indication, J. W. Scott notes, of accelerating economic maturity during the first decade of the new century:

Compared with the first 20 years of the city during which our people bought 23 pieces of real estate or about 1 piece a year we have averaged during the past ten years one piece of real estate per month. From 1900 to the present there has been a tremendous relative increase in the buying of homes.... The total value of property purchased by ... 140 Negroes during the past ten years runs up to $161,650. There are ten colored persons—eight men and two women—in the city whose combined properties will amount to $100,000. Altogether there are 190 property holders and the valuation of their real estate holdings amount to $382,650. These figures make a convincing argument that the Huntington Negro is solving the housing problem.[82]

Some real-estate transactions involved land on the periphery of Huntington's residential section in the largely undeveloped tracts located in the surrounding hills and valleys. Discussing early-twentieth-century settlement patterns, Walter Myers, a black resident of Huntington, said,

My father and aunts told me that most of the blacks could not buy property in what is known [as] the flatlands from the Guyan River to Twelve Pole. They had to buy property on the hill. The flatlands were farmlands all through this area. And they bought property along Fifth Street Hill ... Spring Hill and Walnut Hills. They lived in all of that area up until nearly the '30s. They had hundreds of acres out there. Beautiful land. It's still beautiful land.... My grandparents owned most of ... Walnut Hills area, and a lady named Mrs. Black owned from the boulevard, Hal Greer Boulevard [then Sixteenth Street], back past Eighteenth Street, she owned all that area ... [83]

The historical record largely validates Myers contentions. Denied the ability to purchase land on the rich river-bottom flatlands by the historical presence of whites, many of the city's black residents increasingly purchased land in the hills and outlying sections surrounding the city. For many of Huntington's black residents, the purchase of residential property on the outskirts proved to be a sound investment strategy.[84] As the population increased and the city spread, land values increased. Moreover, the purchases demonstrated their faith in the continuing promise of the city and its black community. In addition to purchasing lots in Central City and Huntington during the late 1890s and early 1900s, C. S. and Mary E. McClain purchased two one-acre plots of land behind Spring Hill Cemetery adjacent to Norway Avenue, one in 1907, the other in 1914, on which Bethel (Crossroads) Cemetery would be established.[85]

By the middle of the first decade of the twentieth century, a small class of black professionals existed within the city.[86] The formation of an articulate, competent, and educated professional class represented a slight but important shift in the development of black Huntington away from the historical predominance of the black worker. The development of a black professional class was inextricably linked to the foundation of intergenerational wealth acquisition attendant to family stability and access to broadening educational opportunities. It marked the beginning of the second generation of black Huntingtonians whose increasing initiative, affluence, and influence challenged perceived threats to their well-being, culminating in a legal challenge to the use of restrictive covenants in the city and, ultimately, their abolition in 1929 in *White v. White*, discussed later in the chapter. Black professionals also found "space" to operate within the system, a development repeated throughout the South.[87]

The first black hospital within Huntington opened in 1912. The creation of the hospital by Dr. C. C. Barnett, son of Rev. Nelson and brother of C. H. Barnett, was arguably the most ambitious effort of early-twentieth-century black Huntington. Trained as a physician and surgeon, Barnett became assistant city physician in 1906. It was not until 1909 that the first black ward was added to a city hospital.[88] Moreover, black patients were consigned to white doctors because black doctors lacked hospital privileges. Such circumstances invariably impacted the health and welfare of blacks needing care, and it sometimes led to tragic consequences. In one case, miner Walter Brown, in transit through the city, fell from a train in the C&O yards and was horribly mangled. Denied entrance into the C&O hospital, Brown lay on the ground for long hours until finally admitted into the Kessler Hospital, where he died on the operating table.[89] Although an extreme example, it is hard to imagine that Barnett, "a rather imposing figure who made friends easily, and [was] politically astute," could have been unaware of this incident or similar ones in which black people suffered discrimination or worse. In 1912 he established a thirty-bed hospital on Seventh Avenue, which served the needs of the city's black residents until 1929.[90]

In 1913, a year after the hospital's establishment, the *Savannah Tribune* touted it as the most modern private hospital in Huntington.[91] Later, Carter G. Woodson, Barnett's first cousin, remarking on modern facilities, reported that the hospital had 50 beds, two operating rooms with modern equipment, and an X-ray department.[92] As a result, African Americans seeking major operations chose the Barnett Hospital as their primary care center. Professor Eph Williams, a national race leader and the entrepreneur of the Silas Green Company, sent his wife and daughter to Huntington to be treated by Dr. Barnett.[93] Barnett Hospital's accomplishments were also recognized by the Chesapeake and Ohio Railroad and the War Risk Insurance Bureau, both of which hired Dr. Barnett to treat certain employees.[94]

Figure 6.3. Constantine C. Barnett: Source: *History of the American Negro, W.Va. Edition*, West Virginia Archives, West Virginia Division of Culture and History, Charleston, W.V.

In addition to providing healthcare for African Americans throughout the region, the hospital also offered educational opportunities for women through the development of a nursing school. As Darlene Clark Hine, author of *Black Women in White*, notes, "If black women were to become trained nurses, the black community had to create the requisite institutions to provide training."[95] Emblematic of this sentiment, the marriage of Barnett to nurse Clara Matthews (his second wife) in 1912 initiated the development of a nursing school within the city, culminating with its opening in 1918 as a part of the Barnett Hospital. The Barnett Hospital and Nursing School not only provided the only extant form of higher education in Huntington for blacks, but because many nursing schools nationwide did not accept African Americans, the hospital attracted blacks from all over the country.[96]

Although women's efforts were overshadowed by the achievements of male physicians within the "black hospital movement," they played important roles in the establishment of these institutions as well.[97] Women led fundraising campaigns for the institutions as well as hospital nurse-training programs.[98] In addition to organizing the nursing school, Clara Matthews Barnett served as superintendent of the hospital.[99] Although most African-American women at this time were denied opportunities to occupy administrative positions, Clara Barnett utilized her power to provide a place for African Americans to become educated. Both Dr. and Mrs. Barnett's efforts resulted in accreditation of the Barnett Hospital's nursing school by the National Medical Association, an honor rarely awarded to African American nursing schools of the time.[100]

Excellence in medical education provided by the hospital extended beyond the training of nurses. The hospital also offered internships for African American doctors.[101] Addressing the importance of this development, one authority notes, "At this time, medical school graduates were not required to complete internships or residencies in order to become physicians; however, black physicians understood the significance hospitals played in their professions. Hospitals, like Barnett's, provided physicians the opportunity to learn emerging surgical techniques and operate modern technology, which ultimately increased the reputations of these physicians. In providing an opportunity for internships, the Barnett Hospital was more advanced than other black hospitals throughout the country."[102] Only six internship programs were available to medical school graduates out of the 202 black hospitals that were established at this time.[103] The physicians who served their internships at the Barnett Hospital became respected physicians at the Tuskegee Institute and also in Boston, Massachusetts.[104]

The Barnett Hospital also provided surgical clinics for the annual meetings of the West Virginia branch of the National Medical Society.[105] Operations were performed at the hospital during the June 1915 meeting of the West Virginia Medical Association and again six years later at the Twelfth Annual Session of the West Virginia State Medical Society.[106] The fact that these surgical clinics were held at the Barnett Hospital attests to facility's level of expertise and training, the quality of modern equipment there, and Dr. Barnett's continued dedication to provide quality healthcare to the black community.

The importance of the Barnett Hospital and Nursing School to black Huntington and to the tri-state region should not be underestimated. As a regional symbol and source of racial pride and cultural development, the hospital helped demonstrate the power of black agency, intelligence, expertise, and cooperation in combating exclusion, discrimination, and injustice. Through its nurse-training program, physician internships, and surgical clinics, the hospital provided healthcare, education, and training for scores of African American men and women who were denied such opportunities in Huntington and elsewhere. In addition, as a nexus for black social interaction and educational opportunity, the hospital and nursing school helped contribute to the growth of the black middle class in the city, state, and nation.

A fourth possible reason for the imposition of racial covenants is suggested by the rise of the Socialist Party in West Virginia generally and in Huntington specifically, and in its overtures to the black working class. During the early twentieth century the Socialist Party of America made strong inroads among the state's industrial workers, especially among its coal miners. During its short tenure from 1913 to 1915, Huntington's *Socialist and Labor Star* actively recruited black members by first reminding them of their value as workers and the precariousness of their situation at the bottom of the economic ladder, second by asserting their rights to human dignity, albeit within a segregated environment:

> Colored people are becoming conscious of their dignity, and their responsibility to develop toward the white man's plane of social value. They are raising their standards of living, and are demanding bet[t]er wages, while the trade union is slowly making its way into their confidence. These facts worry the big business interests in the South of today, which is the South turned over by the landowner to the factory owner and railroad managers. Something must be done to humble the black laborer, and to prevent his children from wanting to become anything else than laborers.[107]

Their call did not go unheeded. Emblematic of the Socialist Party's growing effectiveness to capitalize on spreading worker dissatisfaction surrounding economic insecurity and growing wage inequities, local and state membership rolls increased significantly during the early 1900s. For instance, in the two presidential elections of 1908 and 1912, votes cast by West Virginia Socialists increased from 3,679 to 15,336.[108] Locally, anxiety and anger contributed to growing influence by the Socialist Party in the city. Numerous accounts in the *Labor Star* detail frequent layoffs and shutdowns by the city's largest employers, C&O and American Car and Foundry Company (formerly Ensign Manufacturing Car Works), contributing to what the paper claimed was "an appalling list of Huntington suicides within a short period" due to, among other causes, low wages.[109] In September 1914 the "colored citizens of the East End" formed the first black Socialist local in the city. Situated at Woodson Hall on Eighth Avenue, the "new organization starts off," the paper claimed, "with quite a large membership and unbound enthusiasm." The following week, the paper reported that "over fifty colored workers have signed applications to membership in the Socialist party," enough to establish a Sixteenth Street Local, "if these can be welded into a fighting force at the meeting scheduled this week."[110] By October, seventy-five black workers had signed application cards and, when combined with white locals in the central, western, and southern ends of the city, represented a growing working-class movement.[111]

On January 1, 1915, the *Socialist and Labor Star* folded. Yet, one authority relays, it is important to realize that the Socialists of the newspaper were allies of the trade-union movement in Huntington as well as in the southern West Virginia coalfields. Thus, the party was able to draw from railroad brotherhoods that populated the towns along the C&O line, including a nucleus of workers from the C&O Shops in Huntington.[112] Yet, notwithstanding those black workers who submitted applications and formed lodges, it is difficult to believe that the Socialist Party garnered many more black members beyond the numbers cited.[113]

While it is impossible to ascertain which specific development(s) initiated the concerted white response resulting in restrictive covenants, it is clear that increasing black economic clout, cultural autonomy, and social assertiveness surely played a part. Moreover, it is no coincidence that the legalization of residential segregation coincided with the emergence of a generation of black Huntingtonians who had no direct experience with slavery and who were becoming increasingly knowledgeable of their rights. White realtors realized money could be made from the sale of property to this new class of black Huntington residents. The physical boundaries of Washington Place and its orientation, in relation to Addition No. 1 (just south, on the opposite edge of Sixteenth Street), hardly seem accidental. Here, white Huntingtonians, embodying the practices and attitudes attached to Jim Crowism, attempted to centralize Huntington's black residential population through restrictions and neighborhoods designed to contain them. The construction of Douglass Junior and Senior High School within Washington Place in 1907 further solidified this process. Furthermore, the later development of Huntington's South Side, a middle-class suburb of wide boulevards, park settings, and large brick homes to the south of Washington Place, further constrained black aspirations. By 1913 the homes in this neighborhood and those to the west carried a racial restriction on each deed.[114] Thus, in large measure, the construction of "white" enclaves was achieved not by state-mandated initiatives but instead by local real-estate developers with the complicity of Huntington's white residents.

Certainly, examination of the motivations behind black settlement into Washington Place is warranted. Historical precedence demonstrates that there is nothing particularly unique about black migration into Huntington or settlement into the subdivision or, for that matter, into any of the countless other "colored" enclaves that dotted urban America during the early twentieth century. African Americans remained transitory and aspirational, availing themselves of economic, political, and/or sociocultural opportunities to better themselves. Yet, continued progress remained a difficult challenge for the race. Scott notes, "The business world of the other race is inaccessible. . . . Color prejudice stands with a drawn sword at every entrance to keep him out. But it is worse than useless to lament over the situation. Our only way out is Self Help."[115]

Significantly, although white realtors attempted to persuade local black leaders to have Washington Place certified as a black neighborhood, a tactic successfully accomplished in Bluefield, West Virginia, local blacks resisted their efforts. If implemented, such a racial zoning plan, emblematic of those initiated nationwide, would have served as a mechanism of social and racial control by formally creating what one historian called a "racially bifurcated social geography" in the city.[116] In effect, by agreeing to such a designation, local blacks would have agreed to self-segregation, allowing white realtors and, by extension, white residents to benefit socially and financially from their acquiescence. At one meeting, Walter Myers and other members of the black Young Men's Business Club rebuffed the efforts of a group of realtors by making explicit their position that agreeing to such a designation restricted not only their rights as citizens to live where they wanted but also those of their children. As Myers recounts, "I said no" and others "fell in line with me. . . . I have two children; they might want to live somewhere else in this town. . . . He [the realtor] was angry with me when we didn't sign it, so it was never certified as a black neighborhood."[117]

For those who could afford it, Washington Place offered an expression of the self-help philosophy embraced by the black middle class.[118] Examination of the Barnetts and Woodsons, migrant families who arrived together from Buckingham County, Virginia, into Huntington shortly after its founding in early 1871, offers insight into this process. Acquiring employment with the Chesapeake and Ohio Railroad shortly after their arrival, Nelson Barnett, who at the time was an itinerant preacher, and his brother-in-law James Woodson raised their families and built lives in the growing town. By the late 1890s, the children of these two families represented the first members of Huntington's black professional class. It is noteworthy that members of the Barnett and Woodson families purchased seventeen residential and investment properties in Washington Place between 1906 and 1914, surely benefiting the material well-being and aspirations of their families.[119] In fact, in 1906 Walter Myers's father, Walter Myers Sr., purchased a residential lot from Nelson Barnett. Five years later he purchased a second lot in Washington Place from the Huntington Land Company.[120]

Washington Place signaled increased self-esteem, prosperity, and security while also providing proximity to schools, churches, and businesses—and community, for those who sought it. It also offered the most explicit expression of class stratification within black Huntington. Property acquisition within the subdivision offered "distance" from whites and the black working poor, not an inconsequential consideration for many buyers.

Ultimately, property acquisition became the most important manifestation of progress for those with middle-class aspirations. As Scott observed, "There is no other feeling like the feeling that comes to a man when he can point to a piece of property and say, 'That belongs to me.'"[121] However, home ownership constituted only one of many steps toward the goal of good citizenship. Many blacks in Huntington recognized that their livelihood and status depended also on cordial relations between the races.

To ensure ongoing genial relations, Huntington's black leaders, like those across the nation, embraced two-pronged approach—one that uplifted the race, another that reassured the city's whites. To the city's black residents they espoused a prescriptive vision ensconced within the "self-help" philosophy of black responsibility and Christian education. Scott's maxims of "good citizenship" included: Have an object in view. Be systematic. Always pay cash. Be honest. Never borrow for small things. Don't gamble. Leave liquor and tobacco severely alone. Live the simple life. Work as hard to save as to make. Trust in God and keep busy. By abiding by these rules, Scott contended that "when you quit the shores of time your influence will still remain and your memory will rest like a benediction over the community in which you lived."[122] Undoubtedly, many—perhaps most—black Huntingtonians endeavored to embody such principles.

The mutual construction of race and place encapsulated by the utilization of restrictive covenants and the establishment of Washington Place illustrates the ways white Huntingtonians utilized strategies and techniques to inscribe race onto space during the first part of the twentieth century. This process was twofold. First, during the transitional period of the early 1900s, "residential segregation shifted from being driven by social practices to a legally enforced practice maintained by the use of restrictive deeds and covenants."[123] Second, the city's phenomenal growth led to the growing concentration of blue-collar workers in the suburban areas, people seeking proximity to industrial jobs and a white urban middle-class seeking proximity to the city's business center. Improvements in Huntington's infrastructure—transportation, communication, electricity, water and sewage, the continuing growth and diversity of Huntington's manufacturing and textile industries, and the mechanization of agriculture helped shift factories away from the central business district to un- and underdeveloped areas on the periphery.[124] In effect, as blacks and whites in Huntington settled into social behaviors and residential settlement patterns mandated by legal constraints, residential segregation realigned the city's urban space into racialized enclaves.[125]

In significant ways, David Delaney's historical study of Louisville is instructive, for he revealed how the attitudes of whites toward the city's blacks served not only to distinguish the relationship as patriarchal but also to define the expected behavior of the two groups. Just as in Huntington, it was "understood that Louisville was a better than average town where ugly, brutal, open racial friction was not an accepted thing."[126] Both cities prided themselves on their benevolent approach to segregation, in which spatial boundaries were clearly established and a local black elite established and maintained a black institutional framework with good schools and churches, the hallmarks of middle-class values. Yet, important to note for our purposes here, Louisville's black residents agitated in a variety of ways to shift the nature of power relations. One significant victory occurred in the decision rendered in 1917 in *Buchanan v. Warley*. In the case brought by the NAACP to challenge segregation, the U.S. Supreme Court ruled that race-restrictive zoning laws that prohibited blacks from moving into white neighborhoods, and vice versa, were unconstitutional on due process grounds. Although it was the most far-reaching decision of the era, Huntington's whites paid it no heed.

Despite the covenants (and maybe because of them), Huntington's black residents continued to believe in the power of property acquisition as a means to long-term financial stability. In 1920, among a growing number of black-owned businesses, a black-owned real-estate firm opened, drawing praise from one local paper for the continuing economic success of the city's black residents, the soundness of their real-estate purchases, and how these purchases showed that blacks sought to "greatly improve an already high order of colored citizenship."[127]

Black-owned businesses flourished by the 1920s. By 1924, 60 percent of black Huntington residents owned their homes, a figure higher than for either the black residents of Clarksburg (54.7 percent) or Charleston (45.8 percent). The aggregate worth of black real-estate holdings was approximately $1.4 million, a significant increase from the roughly $400,000 total worth cited by Scott a decade earlier. In large part, black Huntington's success was linked to a vigorous home-ownership campaign initiated near the end of the previous decade and sponsored through the cooperation of several ministers and leaders from both races. The interracial campaign directly resulted in 67 black residents purchasing homes and lots throughout the city. The success of community efforts encouraging property acquisition was so great that the Bureau of Negro Welfare and Statistics felt no need to promote the establishment of building-and-loan associations, such as those found in Beckley and Charleston. Moreover, of the 483 black-owned homes, the average number of rooms per house was 5.5, and the average number of persons per household was 3.9, 1.2 less than the city average.[128] In 1926, *Pittsburgh Courier* reporter

Table 6.1. Black-Owned Businesses in Huntington, West Virginia, 1921

Drug Store	
Dr. B. F. White, 1607 Eighth Avenue	
Hospital	
Dr. C. C. Barnett, 1201 Seventh Avenue	
Barber Shops	
G. W. Fitzgerald, 629 Ninth Street	
J. Massey, 816 Third Avenue	
G. Foster, 820 Third Avenue	
G. W. Bell, 1626 Eighth Avenue	
C. C. Johns, 830 Third Avenue	
C. S. McClain and Sons, 311 Twentieth Street.	
Moving Picture	
Dreamland Theatre—A. C. Colvin, 1620–22 Eighth Avenue	
Pressing and Cleaning Shops	
Hubert Scott, 1636 Eighth Avenue	
Ralphe–French Dry Cleaning, 817 Seventh Street	
Williams–16th Street Pressing Club, 917 Sixteenth Street	
Capt. King–Model Cleaning and Pressing, 1624 Eighth Avenue	
Contractors	
W. T. Smith–Building, 1616 Eighth Avenue	
R. H. Woodson–Building, 1654 Tenth Avenue	
H. C. Chadwick–Building, 909 Bruce Street	
E. S. Pack–Paper Hanging, 1820 Eighth Avenue	
G. Martin–Plastering, 1023 Fourteenth Street	
J. W. Taylor–Cement, 1411 Tenth Avenue	
T. Jones–Building, 802 Eighth Avenue	
T. Hackett–Building, 802 Eighth Avenue	
Hair Dressing Emporiums	
Mdme. Hooker–Poro Beauty Parlor, 1658 Eighth Avenue	
Mdme. A. Turner–Mdme. Walker, 1628 Eighth Avenue	
Mdme. E. Woodson–Poro, K. of P. Hall, 215 Ninth Street	
Mdme. Williams–Poro, 917 Sixteenth Street	
Mdme. R. L. Geter–Mdme. Walker, 1511 Eighth Avenue	
Printing Companies	
Times American Printing Company –A. N. Johnson, 827 Court Street	
Imperial Printing Company–I. Reed, 919 Sixteenth Street	
Real Estate Agents	
C. E. McGhee, 911 Eighth Avenue	
R. E. L. Washington, 2901 Eighth Avenue	
Brown & Barnett, 1201 Seventh Avenue	
Shoe Repairing Shops	
R. W. Graves, 1624 Eighth Avenue	
W. D. Mills, 1660 Eighth Avenue	

Source: *Huntington, W.V., City Directory*, 1920–2005 directories (Livonia, Mich.: Polk, 1919–2004).

George S. Schuyler reiterated the positive portrait of black Huntington's progress: "Over sixty per cent of the colored families own the houses in which they live; most of the Negroes have steady work on the railroad or in the big shops of the Chesapeake and Ohio Railroad; many work steadily for the municipality, collecting garbage and trash, and there are close to 50 barbers who don't appear to be clasping the lean hand of want. Moreover, the relations between whites and Negroes are very cordial and Negro businesses can always count upon the patronage of whites in West Virginia, no matter how strong the spirit of the Ku Klux Klan may be otherwise."[129] Yet, given their broad success, restrictive covenants prevented Afro-Huntingtonians from exercising the full measure of their citizenship: the right to live where they wanted.

Arguably, the most significant decision rendered by the West Virginia State Supreme Court during the first third of the twentieth century was one striking down restrictive covenants in the state. In the only case of its type on record within the state, black residents of Huntington initiated a legal challenge to restrictions designed to exclude them from desirable residential locations. Unlike the previous efforts by white realtors to restrain black residential settlement, the outgrowth of the 1929 victory in *White v. White* was in response to an attempt by Kate Rau and Anna E. Jones, white owners of a tract of land, to insert into a deed a provision that the property involved "should not be conveyed to or demised to Ethiopians in the city of Huntington." In 1920 Rau and Jones divided their land into eleven lots. Despite the deed stipulation, in 1926 black residents Lewis and Cora White purchased one of the lots, drawing the ire of H. B. White, the owner of six other lots in the subdivision. In an effort to restrict the Whites from occupying the premises based on the deed restriction, H. B. White initiated a legal challenge in circuit court. The case pivoted on "the right of a person selling property to prohibit the further sale of the property by its owner to persons of color."[130]

The challenge and eventual victory of Lewis and Cora White directly stem from the strategizing and financial support of local black citizens. After losing in the Cabell County Circuit Court, which upheld the contention of H. B. White and declared the deed granting the property to the Whites null and void, the Whites were served shortly thereafter with a notice to vacate the property. The challenge might have stopped there if not for the efforts of the Huntington branch of the NAACP. Speaking on these efforts was Walter Myers:

> [T]he white man didn't want a black man to move near him. The white man was named "White," and the black man was named "White." And so, it was, it was a

bitter-fought case. We hired a constitutional lawyer. That was the year I joined the NAACP. The NAACP was just starting up.... We had the Urban League. But... that wasn't their criteria. They told us to join the NAACP, which we did. And we got a charter. And so they took over and we got a constitutional lawyer.[131]

Led by H. D. Hazelwood, principal of Douglass High and president of the Huntington branch of the NAACP, the executive committee invited Charleston attorney and state president of the NAACP, T. G. Nutter, to a public forum to discuss the next step. At least one local black attendee was aware of the potential enormity of the case to the aspirations of the state's black citizens. Myers recalls that Dave Medison called for the case to be argued before the state supreme court. "Don't fight it here. If you win here, you'd be just for Huntington. This thing has got to go for the whole entire state ... [If we win] no white person couldn't say that you couldn't live by them."[132] With the financial backing of the Huntington branch and the assistance of black Huntington attorney A. D. Meadows (who had argued the case in the lower court), Nutter appealed the decision to the Supreme Court of Appeals of West Virginia. Employing a five-pronged argument, which included provisions asserting that the Whites were Negro and not Ethiopian, and the inconsistency of the covenant with the right of full ownership, Nutter and his colleagues argued their appeal. The court largely ignored the first contention and instead based its 24-page reversal on the major point contained within the second: "Any conditional restriction which completely destroys the right of the property owner to dispose of his property in any way that he desires has always been held void by all courts as inconsistent with the rights of full ownership." The decision, hailed by the national branch of the NAACP as the "most significant since the Louisville Segregation Case" of 1917, established a legal precedent protecting the state's Negroes from restrictive covenants, insofar as residence is involved, when such covenant is a part of a deed or paper denoting ownership.[133]

In the mission to "spread their wings" and take care of their own, black Huntingtonians, it is evident, accepted the consequences of life in a segregated, constraining environment as long as economic opportunity remained manifest. Yet, the impediments to their progress were formidable and adaptive. The city's rapid growth, black population increase, development of black institutions, and growing black residential concentration prompted an intensification of Jim Crowism that constrained the aspirations of Afro-Huntingtonians. By 1930, Huntington's increasing importance as a transshipment point for the Chesapeake and Ohio Railroad, vital river port, and growing manufacturing center made it West Virginia's most populous city, with 75,752 residents. Huntington's African American population growth paralleled this increase, comprising by 1930 the second largest conglomeration in the state at 4,630 residents.[134] In large measure, whites in Huntington embraced the same racialized attitudes and mechanisms operative throughout the Deep South. Though lacking the brutality and totality of race subjugation in the Deep South (for instance, West Virginia possessed no Jim Crow law), West Virginia's state-mandated system of "benevolent segregation" and prevailing notions of white superiority coalesced to form an effective bulwark, the most potent manifestation being the implementation of restrictive covenants.

Afro-Huntingtonians used a variety of oppositional strategies to assert their rights and self-worth, with education, increasing entry into public space, and property acquisition the most far reaching. Relying on the ideological pillars of religion, education, industry, and thrift, the city's black middle-class residents, like their contemporaries across the nation during the late-nineteenth and early twentieth centuries, embodied and benefited from the "self-help" philosophy. In the process, Huntington's blacks turned segregation into what historian Earl Lewis labeled "congregation," which he observes "symbolized an act of free will, whereas segregation represented the imposition of another's will. . . . [African Americans] discovered, however, that congregation in a Jim Crow environment produced more space than power. They used this space to gather their cultural bearings, to mold the urban setting."[135]

In Huntington, as across America, African American economic and political progress during the late-nineteenth and early-twentieth centuries resulted in racial advancement and social stratification that confounded and complicated the quest to forge community. Symbolic of the "communities within communities" that existed within the city and area, black Huntington represented separate, competing, *and* overlapping visions of American life—one articulated by the city's whites, the other largely embraced by its black citizens. Yet the metamorphosis of black Huntington is noteworthy for the level of cultural, social, and economic maturity achieved attendant to life within the crucible of Jim Crow. Drawn to the city's economic vitality, burgeoning black institutions, and expanding cultural offerings, a new generation of black residents arrived to acquire education, establish sociocultural ties and linkages, and garner professional opportunities. The strategies implemented by a new generation of black residents helped move them and the race forward.

Appendix A

Virginia Slave Totals, 1860

Slaveholders and Slaves in Virginia—1860

Number of slaves	1 only	2–9	10–19	20–49	over 50	total holders	total slaves	Average
Virginia holders	11,085	26,492	8,774	4,917	860	52,128	475,528	9
Cabell County holders	25	56	2	1	0	84	305	3+

Distribution of Slaves

Virginian holders owning fewer than 10 slaves	35, 577 = 72%
Virginian holders owning 10–49 slaves	13,691 = 26%
Virginian holders owning more than 50 slaves	860 = 2%

*Source: Carrie Eldridge, *Cabell County's Empire for Freedom: The Manumission of Sampson Sanders' Slaves* (Huntington, W.V.: John Deaver Drinko Academy for American Political Institution and Civic Culture, Marshall University, 1999), xvi.

Appendix B

Occupational Statistics for Huntington's African American Population

Table B.1. Occupations of African Americans by Industry, 1870

Industry	Males employed	Females employed	Total employed	Percent of labor force
Steamboat	—	—	—	—
Service	—	14	14	19%
Skilled/Semi-skilled	6	—	6	8%
Unskilled	23	20	43	59%
Entrepreneurial	—	—	—	—
Professional	—	—	—	—
Unemployed	3	7	10	14%
Total	32	41	73	100%

Source: U.S. Census Bureau, Ninth Census

Table B.2. Occupations of African American Men, 1870

Occupation	Number employed	Percent of reported working male population
Barber	1	3.5%
Drayman	1	3.5%
Farmer	5	18%
Farm worker/Works on farm	18	61%
Laborer	2	7%
Railroad laborer/Works on railroad	2	7%
Total	29	100%

Source: U.S. Census Bureau, Ninth Census

Table B.3. Occupations of African American Women, 1870

Occupation	Number employed	Percent of reported working female population
At home*	5	15%
Domestic servant	13	38%
Housekeeper/Keeper of house	16	47%
Total	34	100%

*Figure includes females age twelve and older.
Source: U.S. Census Bureau, Ninth Census

Table B.4. Occupations of African Americans by Industry, 1880

Industry	Males Employed	Females employed	Total Employed	Percent of labor force
Steamboat	3	—	3	1%
Service	13	40	53	17%
Skilled/Semi-skilled	14	—	14	4%
Unskilled	166	76	242	77%
Entrepreneurial	—	—	—	—
Professional	2	—	2	1
Unemployed	1	—	—	0.0%
Total	199	116	314	100%

Source: U.S. Census Bureau, Tenth Census

Occupational Statistics

Table B.5. Occupations of African American Men, 1880

Occupation	Number employed	Percent of reported working male population
Barber	3	1.5%
Blacksmith	1	.5%
Boiler shop worker	1	.5%
Brickyard worker	1	.5%
Cigar maker	1	.5%
Cook (incl. on steamboat)	6	3%
Depot worker	1	.5%
Drayman	2	1%
Farmer	3	1.5%
Farm worker/Works on farm	3	1.5%
Fireman	1	.5%
Foundry worker	4	2%
Hostler	6	3%
Hotel Porter	6	3%
Laborer	131	66.5%
Pastor	2	1%
Railroad laborer/Works on railroad	21	11%
Store porter	1	.5%
Store worker	1	.5%
Steamboat worker	1	.5%
Teamster	1	.5%
Total	197	100%

Source: U.S. Census Bureau, Tenth Census

Table B.6. Occupations of African American Women, 1880

Occupation	Number employed	Percent of reported working females population
At home	14	11%
Domestic servant	40	31%
Housekeeper/Keeper of house	76	58%
Total	130	100%

Source: U. S. Census Bureau, Tenth Census

Table B.7. Occupations of African Americans by Industry, 1891–1892

Industry	Males employed	Females employed	Total employed	Percent of labor force
Steamboat	0	0	0	0%
Service	22	7	29	22%
Skilled/Semi-skilled	23	8	31	24%
Unskilled	54	8	62	48%
Entrepreneurial	2	1	3	2%
Professional	5	0	5	4%
Total	106	24	130	100%

Source: Huntington (West Virginia) City Directory, 1891–92

Table B.8. Occupations of African American Men, 1891–1892

Occupation	Number employed	Percent of reported working male population
Barber	7	6.6%
Bartender	1	.9%
Blacksmith	1	.9%
Boot black	1	.9%
Carpenter	1	.9%
Clerk	1	.9%
Contractor	2	1.9%
Cook	9	8.5%
Drayman	2	1.9%
Driver	1	.9%
Foundry man	1	.9%
Grocer	2	1.9%
Hod carrier	5	4.7%
Houseboy	1	.9%
Janitor	1	.9%
Laborer	33	31%
Machine man	1	.9%
Pastor	4	3.8%
Peddler	1	.9%
Plasterer	2	1.9%
Porter	6	5.7%
Principal	1	.9%
Railroad laborer/Works on railroad	8	7.5%
Restaurant worker	1	.9%
Servant	1	.9%
Shoemaker	1	.9%
Shooting gallery	1	.9%
Shop messenger	1	.9%
Street paver	1	.9%
Teamster	3	2.8%
Waiter	5	4.7%
Total	106	99.1%

Source: Huntington (West Virginia) City Directory 1891–92

Occupational Statistics

Table B.9. Occupations of African American Women, 1891–1892

Occupation	Number employed	Percent of reported working female population
At home	47	66.2%
Boardinghouse	1	1.4%
Chambermaid	1	1.4%
Cook	5	7%
Domestic servant	6	8.4%
House keeper/Keeper of house	3	4.2%
Ironer	1	1.4%
Laundress	6	8.4%
Washerwoman	1	1.4%
Total	71	100%

Source: Huntington (West Virginia) City Directory 1891–92

Table B.10. Occupations of African Americans by Industry, 1900

Industry	Males employed	Females employed	Total employed	Percent of labor force
Steamboat	0	0	0	0%
Service	62	59	121	29.9%
Skilled/Semi-skilled	34	2	36	8.8%
Unskilled	228	4	232	57.1%
Entrepreneurial	1	1	2	.5%
Professional	12	3	15	3.7%
Total	337	69	406	100%

Source: U.S. Census Bureau, Twelfth Census

Table B.11. Occupations of African American Men, 1900

Occupation	Number employed	Percent of reported Working male population
Attorney	1	.3%
Axel forge	1	.3%
Barber	13	3.8%
Bartender	3	.9%
Blacksmith	2	.6%
Bellboy	1	.3%
Bricklayer	1	.3%
Brickmaker	2	.6%
Cab driver	3	.9%
Carpenter	1	.3%
Cart driver/driver	4	1.2%
Clergy/pastor	7	2.1%
Cook	9	2.6%
Common/day laborer	175	52%
Drayman	2	.6%
Driver	1	.3%
Farmer	6	1.7%
Farmhand	5	1.4%
Fireman	2	.6%
Foundryman	2	.6%
Grocery clerk	2	.6%
Hod carrier	8	2.4%
Hostler	1	.3%
Janitor	4	1.2%
Latch worker	2	.6%
Lath turner	1	.3%
Manager	1	.3%
Melter	1	.3%
Mortar maker	1	.3%
Physician	2	.6%
Plasterer	2	.6%
Porter	13	3.9%
Principal	1	.3%
Railroad laborer/Works on railroad	19	5.6%
Railroad porter	6	1.8%
Restaurant	1	.3%
Salesman	1	.3%
Servant	3	.9%
Stonemason	1	.3%
Teacher	1	.3%
Teamster	3	.9%
Truck builder	1	.3%
Waiter	20	5.9%
Watchman	1	.3%
Total	337	100%

Source: U.S. Census Bureau, Twelfth Census

Table B.12. Occupations of African American Women, 1900

Occupation	Number employed	Percent of reported working female population
At home	84	55%
Boardinghouse	1	.7%
Chambermaid	2	1.3%
Cook	2	1.3%
Domestic servant	34	22%
Dressmaker	3	2%
Hairdresser	1	.7%
Laundress	21	13.7%
Teacher	3	2%
Washerwoman	2	1.3%
Total	153	100%

Source: U.S. Census Bureau, Twelfth Census

Table B.13. Industry Breakdown by Jobs as Listed in Census

Steamboat
Boat hand/Steamboat hand/
Deckhand/River hand
Boatman/Steamboat man/River man
Cabin boy
Canal boatman
Fireman/Steamboat fireman
River basher
River character
River leader
River porter
Sailor
Steamboat barber
Steamboat berthmaker
Steamboat cook
Steamboat laborer
Steamboat pantry man
Steamboat steward
Steamboat waiter

Service
Artist
Baggage master
Barkeeper
Bartender
Bootblack
Butler
Carriage driver
Cash driver
Clerk
Coachman
Coffeehouse worker
Domestic
Driver
Dry-goods clerk
Eating-house worker
Express driver
Grocer
Hack driver
Help
Hosier
Hostler
Hotel watchman
Huckster
Knife shiner
Market man
Messenger
Pantry man
Peddler
Porter
Restaurant help
Servant/Maidservant/Maid
Sexton
Hoe polisher
Stable hand
Steward
Trader
Waiter/Hotel waiter

(continued)

Table B.13. *Continued*

Skilled/Semi-skilled
Baker
Barber
Blacksmith
Bricklayer
Brickmason
Brickmoulder
Builder
Cabinetmaker
Camp roofer
Carpenter
Carriage maker
Caulker
Cigarmaker
Confectioner
Cook
Cooper
Daguerreotypist
Dressmaker
Drummer
Dyer
Engineer
Farmer
Furnituremaker
Hairdresser
Machinist
Mantuamaker
Moulder
Musician
Painter
Pastry cook
Plasterer
Picture maker
Rectifier
Seamstress
Swing shop worker
Shoemaker
Silver plater
Tailor
Tanner
Tobacconist

Turner
Wheelwright
Whitewasher
Woodcutter
Wood sawyer

Unskilled
Boiler cleaner
Car porter
Chambermaid
Office cleaner
Drayman
Hack driver
Hod carrier
Housecleaner/Housework/Housekeeper
Janitor
Laborer/Day laborer/Levee laborer
Ragpicker
Washerwoman/Washer/Scourer of clothes
Water hauler
Wood guard

Entrepreneurial
Astrologist
Bedstead manufacturer
Boardinghouse keeper
Clothes dealer
Coal dealer
Fruit dealer
Landlord
Merchant
Saloon keeper
Speculator

Professional/Semiprofessional
Attorney
Clergy
Druggist
Nurse
Physician/Doctor/Root doctor
Schoolteacher
Sister/Matron
Superintendent

Notes

Preface

1. With the 1954 decision *Brown v. the Board of Education*, many Douglass High students began attending Huntington High School. In 1959 Douglass held its last graduation before closing. Many of the sons and daughters of former Douglass students attended and graduated from the school.

Chapter 1. The African American Experience in Cabell County, Virginia / West Virginia, 1825–1870

1. Historical geographer Edward K. Muller's model of regional growth provides helpful perspective; he illuminates three distinct phases of regional development: "In the 'pioneer' phase, settlers established communities far removed from commercial markets. The absence of population and the time and energy required to establish homes and farms hindered the development of agriculture beyond subsistence needs. Transportation was confined to a few natural routes." However, with increasing settler influx and population growth, "communities passed into a second, 'specialized' phase. Intraregional and interregional connections improved," resulting in increasing settlement and "the beginnings of commercial agriculture and manufacturing." In the final "transitional" phase, "national transportation and marketing systems, especially railroads, integrated communities into the national economy." Noe, "Appalachia's Civil War Genesis," 98.

2. Kyle, "Early History," 1. Speaking of the early settlers in the eastern section of Cabell County, one authority states, "Most of them belonged to the class of comfortable livers, when they worked to that end. Not a few of them, in addition to their own families, brought a number of slaves from the older settled sections. Slavery existed in its mildest form here, and while by no means universal, it was quite general. Most of the slave groups consisted of only a few negroes, but a few farms assumed

the proportions of plantations and the number of slaves exceeded a half-hundred." See Burdette, "History of Ona." Burdette lists the following as slave owners in "the neighborhood": "John Morris, John and Nathan Everett; Charles, William, and Daniel Love; John, Henry, and Thomas Dundas and their sisters, Miss Eliza Dundas and Mrs. Sophia Peyton; Sampson Handley; William P. Yates; Jonathan Switzer; Dr. Alexander McCorkle; David Harshbarger; Thomas Chapman and Beverly Maupin; Adam and William Black; James Newman; Andrew Guinn; John Miller; William Simmons; Thomas, George and Jeremiah Killgore; and Mrs. Martha Saunders and son Sampson Saunders." Burdette refers to *Sanders*; *Saunders* and *Sanders* were used interchangeably during the era.

3. In contrast to one authority's contention that Appalachians "hated slavery," recent scholarship reveals slavery to be more tightly woven into the fabric of the region's economy than previously held. Woodson, "Freedom and Slavery"; Inscoe, *Mountain Masters*; Dew, *Bond of Iron*; Noe, *Southwest Virginia's Railroad*. Further, Wilma A. Dunaway and Richard B. Drake refute the notion that slavery was less harsh in Appalachia when compared with slave conditions in the Deep South. Dunaway, *Slavery*, 5; Drake, "Slavery and Antislavery," 17.

4. Named for William H. Cabell, Virginia governor from 1805 to 1808, and located on the western boundary of Virginia, the county in 1809 included all of what is now Lincoln and Wayne Counties, a large part of Logan, Boone, and Putnam Counties, and a small portion of Wyoming County. In subsequent years the county's political boundaries shrank as other counties were formed out of it. In 1867 five districts encompassing 282 square miles in the southwestern corner of the state comprised Cabell County.

5. The two towns, exemplary of what Wilma Dunaway argues were the "periphery" and "semi-periphery"—the first and second of three interdependent tiers of regional development—increasingly served as metropoles and conduits within an expanding web of transnational commerce, prefiguring the postbellum development of the county's and region's industrial economy. See Wilma A. Dunaway, *The First American Frontier: Transition to Capitalism in Southern Appalachia, 1700–1860* (Chapel Hill: University of North Carolina Press, 1996), 5–6, 17–19; Kenneth W. Noe, "Appalachia before Mr. Peabody: Some Recent Literature on the Southern Mountain Region," *Virginia Magazine of History and Biography* 110, no. 1 (2002): 6–36.

6. Geiger, "Tragic Fate of Guyandotte," 29. Used over the decades by travelers, surveyors, merchants, settlers, slave traders, soldiers, generals, refugees, and free and freed people who walked much of its length, this Appalachian thoroughfare, known officially as the James River and Kanawha Turnpike, originated in Richmond, Virginia. From Richmond, the road followed the James River watershed to Lexington, Virginia, just across the Alleghany Mountains from West Virginia. Constructed between 1830 and 1850 and now roughly paralleled by U.S. Route 60 and Interstate 64, it was largely composed of river trails, ridges, and horse paths that wound their way across the Allegheny Mountains before ending in Lexington, Kentucky.

7. Eldridge, *Atlas of Appalachian Trails*, 29. Also see Miller, "History of Barboursville Community."

8. After manumission by their owner Mary Garland in 1852 (over the wishes of her two slave-trading brothers—the Lumpkins), Lewis Brooks, his wife, and their ten children made their way from Richmond to Proctorville, Ohio, via Guyandotte. See "Slave Days," *Ironton (Ohio) Register*, November 12, 1896.

9. McGehee, *Black Folk at Green Bottom*, 8.

10. Davis-DeEulis, "African American Literacy," 195.

11. This dynamic in turn inculcated what Davis-DeEulis calls an "'occupational literacy'—the allocation of a literate task in history"—within the core of the resident slave population of the plantation. She notes that "acquiring rudimentary English literacy," as has been extensively documented in slave narratives, also offered an avenue for the slave to achieve a sense of identity and "psychic freedom." Moreover, as Henry Louis Gates argues, literacy was also a "cultural building block in the system of creating meaning that some critics call 'fusional accommodation'—a nonassimilatory means of acculturation that [Africans] brought with them to the New World. Learning to 'read and write' was an aesthetic, as well as pragmatic necessity," which allowed one to navigate life "with a sense of historical being and 'presence.'" Davis-DeEulis, "African American Literacy," 195. See also Thompson, *Few among the Mountains*, 13.

12. Thompson, *Few among the Mountains*, 13.

13. Ibid. 25.

14. By 1825, William A. Jenkins was a wealthy shipper whose boats carried goods along the East Coast and even to Brazil. Prior to his purchase of Greenbottom, Jenkins started a successful farm called Buffalo Forge, which was home to several dozen slaves. Davis-DeEulis, "African American Literacy," 196 (quoting also from Cabell County, Virginia, Deed Book 4: 55, 107). See also Dickinson and Dickinson, *Gentleman Soldier of Greenbottom*, 13–15.

15. Addressing the connection between capitalism and slavery, Stanley Elkins provides important perspective when he notes, "The planter was now engaged in capitalistic agriculture with a labor force entirely under his control. The personal relationship between master and slave—in any case less likely to exist on large agricultural units than on smaller ones—now became far less important than the economic necessities which had forced the slave into this 'unnatural' organization in the first place." Elkins, *Slavery*, 49.

16. *Cabell County Will Book* 2, 1826–1890, Cabell County Court House, Huntington, W.V., 344.

17. Berlin, *Many Thousands Gone*, 8.

18. Originally owned by Joshua Fry before coming under the ownership of Virginia governor Wilson Cary Nicholas, the plantation was in full operation by the mid-1810s and managed by an overseer. Governor Nicholas's absentee ownership proved especially deadly. Between 1812 and 1814, twenty-two slaves, succumbing to

lax supervision as well as harsh living and working conditions, died at Greenbottom. Thompson, *Few among the Mountains*, 12–14, 25.

19. Eldridge, *Cabell County's Empire*, xi. Perspective on the impact of this law is gained from Luther P. Jackson's contention that this act effectively demarcated the end of the "the liberality and high idealism of the Revolutionary period" within the state and was a response to both Toussaint L'Overture's revolution in Haiti and Gabriel Prosser's insurrection in Richmond in 1800, as well as the development of the cotton gin and its impact on the industrial revolution. See Jackson, "Manumission," 287–88.

20. There were no court-recorded manumissions in Cabell County from 1807 to 1816. Corresponding decisions in Richmond and Petersburg had the same effect. The Virginia Assembly of 1815–16 stated that a slave emancipated after 1806 could apply to remain in the state if he or she had demonstrated "extraordinary merit." See Jackson, "Manumission," 289–90. In 1823 the state toughened its restrictions against free blacks by mandating that any Negro failing to show cause why they should remain in an area could be jailed or "hired out" for nonpayment of debts, for being destitute, or for several other reasons.

21. Moreover, Virginia required the former owner to provide for the manumitted slave after manumission to prevent him or her from becoming a burden on the community. Eldridge, *Cabell County's Empire*, 37. Also see Henning, *Statutes at Large*.

22. See "John N. Templeton Responds to Ohio Supreme Court Ruling that Free Blacks Must Post $500 Bond (1829)," *African Americans in Southeastern Ohio*, http://www.seorf.ohiou.edu/~xx057. In 1804 the Ohio legislature legally mandated that "free blacks and mulattoes provide proof of their freedom upon entering the state." In 1807, the state strengthened such restrictions by requiring free blacks and mulattoes who settled into the state to post a $500 bond "to guarantee their ability to support themselves." A series of "harsher measures" were passed by the Indiana legislature. In 1815 Indiana passed a law requiring "a $300 annual poll tax on all adult black and mulatto men." In 1831 the state mandated that all free blacks "register and post bond to guarantee 'good behavior' and viable employment against becoming 'public charge.'" In 1851 the antiblack restrictions intensified when the state adopted a new constitution that "barred blacks from settlement altogether." Kentucky was no different. In 1818 the state forbade "the immigration of free blacks from elsewhere." Moreover, in 1834 the state passed a law "requiring free blacks to post bond in order to remain in the state." See Trotter, *River Jordan*, 25.

23. "Fugitives from Slavery" (previously "Runaway Slaves"), *Ohio History Central*, July 1, 2005, http://www.ohiohistorycentral.org/entry.php?rec=626. Trotter, *River Jordan*, 25. Also see Stephen Middleton, *The Black Laws: Race and the Legal Process in Early Ohio* (Athens: Ohio University Press, 2005).

24. A number of recent studies have explored the African American experience along the Ohio River in slavery and freedom. See Salafi, *Slavery's Borderland*; Bingham, *Jordan's Banks*; Bingham, *Towns and Villages*; Griffler, *Front Line of Freedom*; Trotter, *River Jordan*; and Buchanan, *Black Life on the Mississippi*.

25. As historian Matthew Salafi avers in his study of the Ohio River borderland of Kentucky, Indiana, and Ohio, scholars have normally defined borderlands as "contested boundaries between colonial domains," and the creation of nationally recognized state borders turned borderlands into "bordered lands," yet this definition overstates the ability of borders to divide. *Slavery's Borderland*, 1–4.

26. Eldridge, *Cabell County's Empire*, xiii, xiv.

27. Ibid., 36, 51–55. The manumitted Sanders slaves were: Ada and Zeebeedee, both age eighty-seven; Solomon, his wife, Phyllis, and their children, Eli, Levi, Solomon Jr., Woodford, Jacob, and Jason; Daniel, his wife, Dorcos, and their children, Alicia, Montesque, Zebedee, Eliza, Robert, William, Elijah, and Hamilton; Charles and his sister Mary and her children, Susan, Joseph, Harriet, Mahala, Charles, and twins Theodore and Sampson; Cynthia Sanders Radford and her son Jacob; Margaret and her son Eli; Charlotte and her daughter Jane; James Sanders; Peter Sanders; Eli Sanders; Calvin Sanders (an adult who returned to the Ironton area); Calvin Sanders (a child); John Sanders; Luke, his wife, Jane, and their children; Columbus and Mary; Moses, his wife, Caroline, and their children, Albert and Robert; Hamilton Sanders (an adult); and Isom Sanders (who remained in Cabell County).

28. Hesslink, *Black Neighbors*, 44.

29. "Old Times: The Exodus of the 37 Blacks from Va., to Burlington in 1849," *Ironton Register*, March 5, 1896.

30. Melissa Rake, "Journey to Freedom," *Huntington Herald-Dispatch*, April 4, 1994.

31. See Platt, *Promised Land*, foreword, 15, 18, and Eldridge, *Freedom Lies across the Water*, xii, 1, 2. Eldridge writes that in actuality, the "37" manumitted slaves were forty-six persons due to the fact that "under aged children were rarely identified in legal documents." In total, "forty to forty-one came to Lawrence County, not the famous 'Burlington 37.'" See also "Slaves Using Underground Hid in Campbell Mansion," *Ironton Register*, February 24, 1949.

32. Gunter, "Barboursville," 21. See also Miller, "History of Barboursville Community."

33. Jones traveled 400 miles from Richmond to the Ohio River to gain freedom. Upon reaching the bank of the Kanawha River near Point Pleasant, Virginia, "where he could see the state of Ohio," Jones, great-uncle to future West Virginia State College president J. McHenry Jones, waved to a steamboat, which the captain took as a signal for him to land. After inquiring if there was any work aboard the vessel, Jones gained employment. After docking in Cincinnati, Jones was "induced by the captain and first mate to admit his inability to read or write" and his desire to learn to do both. The captain then "secured the necessary books and a slate and gave him his first lesson before leaving Cincinnati on their return trip." Jones would remain with the crew and boat for three years. See John L. Jones, "The Story of the Jones Family," *History of the Jones Family*, edited and annotated by Nancy E. Aiken and Michel S. Perdreau (Bowie, Md.: Heritage, 2001), Local History, Athens County Library Services, Nelsonville, Ohio, 3–27.

34. Stealey, *Antebellum Kanawha Salt Business*, 146.

35. "Looking Backward Eighty Years: Reminiscences as Gleaned from Mr. Hiram H. Swallow and Others Who Remember the Past of this Locality: Article II," *History of Mason County, West Virginia* (Cincinnati: Flour, 1963), 4, James E. Casto Local History Room, Cabell County Public Library, Huntington, W.V.

36. Such a dynamic existed for black steamboat workers in antebellum Mississippi. Before gaining his freedom as a fugitive slave and notoriety for his autobiography *Narrative of William Wells Brown, A Fugitive Slave*, Brown worked as a waiter aboard a steamboat that plied the Mississippi River. Though a slave, Brown relished the moments of autonomy that travel aboard the boat afforded. Recounting his experiences, Thomas Buchanan relates that Brown remembered that he "found great difference between the work in a steamboat cabin and in a cornfield." Buchanan, *Black Life on the Mississippi*, 3.

37. Schisms began to appear in the late 1820s. One prominent issue of the era revolved around the issue of representation and suffrage. Between 1829 and 1833, Virginians engaged in a series of protracted and often divisive debates over the essential nature of law and government in a modern republic. These debates revealed the abiding class and social tensions between whites on both sides of the Alleghany Mountains. Whites in the east favored "freehold" representation based on property and taxation, while those in the west favored "manhood" representation in which all, regardless of property, income, or religion, were allowed to vote. At the time, Virginia was the only state of twenty-four to adhere to freehold suffrage. Often referred to by easterners as "peasants," who, by intimation, occupied an inferior status in the Chesapeake Bay area, white-laboring westerners quoted the Bill of Rights and Thomas Jefferson's agrarian republic ideas in their quest to acquire greater political representation within the state. In effect, the disagreements reflected diverging economic and commercial practices indicative of an emerging industrial economy. The Virginia Constitutional Convention of 1829–30 addressed the issue, and in the resulting compromise, heavily slanted to the designs of easterners, the convention agreed to reduce the conditions of a freehold and to extend the suffrage to male leaseholders and heads of households who paid taxes. In April 1830, the revised constitution was submitted to the people and ratified by a vote of 26,055 to 15,563. However, within the region that would contribute to West Virginia's formation, the vote was 1,383 for ratification and 8,365 against. Thomas L. Lees of New Jersey, president of Linsley Institute, in Wheeling, Virginia, succinctly summarized the nascent sectional fissures within the state when he wrote in 1831, "That part of Virginia which borders on the Ohio is rapidly improving in wealth and population; its inhabitants have long been dissatisfied with the selfish policy and the usurpations of the eastern slave holders, whose influence in the legislative body has ever been exerted in the perpetration of an oppressive aristocracy. The people here are very different from those of the eastern part of the state. Industry is much more encouraged and respected; slavery is unpopular, and the few who hold slaves generally treat them well. The time is not far distant when Western Virginia will either liberalize the present state government, or separate itself entirely from the Old Dominion."

"1830 Virginia Constitution," in *Semi-Centennial History of West Virginia* (Charleston: Semi-Centennial Commission of West Virginia, 1913), 130–34, West Virginia Archives and History, West Virginia Division of Culture and History, http://www.wvculture.org/HISTORY/government/182930cc.html; and Curtis, " Re-Definition of Freehold Suffrage. Disagreement over slavery and religion also impacted the county. As early as 1835, one writer cites the "discipline of the Methodist Church as being a powerful stimulus toward freeing the negro in this section." See "Slavery," Fred B. Lambert Papers (FBLP hereafter), ms 76, box 3, book 5, 48. The most popular denomination in the area in the mid-1800s was Methodist. Large Methodist congregations met in Barboursville and Guyandotte, and in the early 1840, the growing national debate between proslavery and antislavery supporters within the Methodist Episcopal Church influenced residents of the area. In 1844 at Louisville, Kentucky, a major division occurred in the national body of the church over the question of slavery. In the resulting split, those churches with proslavery sympathies formed the Methodist Episcopal Church-South, remaining a separate polity until 1939, when it reunited with the Methodist Episcopal Church. Emblematic of the nation at large, the cultural differences created a schism in the local Methodist congregation, but with an interesting development: both congregations continued to use the same building, a church built in 1835 in the bend of Water Street in Guyandotte. The deep-seated yet intimate dual-congregation "remedy" of the county's Methodists symbolized the growing divide of the county's residents over the question of slavery. Geiger, *Civil War in Cabell County*, 5. J. A. Earl relates that some years later the two congregations built separate edifices. In 1858 the Methodist Episcopal Church built a frame building, which remains the oldest church building in this section of the state and probably the only Methodist Church in use in the state that has a slave gallery. J. A. Earl, "Methodism in Guyandotte," box 20, no. 9, FBLP, no. 76, 38–39. Brief examination of Cabell County attorney and Confederate captain James H. Ferguson, who won election to the House of Delegates in 1848 from Logan and Boone Counties and who served in the Constitutional Convention of 1850–51, offers additional perspective. Although he never owned slaves and professed abolitionist leanings, Ferguson defended slavery and never sought to restrict its growth or to restrict the ability of slave owners to retrieve fugitive slaves from the North. Though he supported the Southern cause, Ferguson was an ardent Unionist who was unabashed in his belief that his primary duty was ensure the primacy of the federal government. In a speech before the House of Delegates on February 18, 1850, Ferguson vociferously sided with those who had removed George W. Thompson from his office as district attorney for "sympathizing with the Negroes in the Southampton insurrection," a reference to the Nat Turner rebellion. See Bowers, "Barboursville on the Guyandotte"; Laidley, *History of Charleston*, 467; and Bailey, *Alleged Evil Genius*, 15.

38. Eldridge, *Diaries of William F. Dusenberry*, 42, 1856 entries, Eldridge, *Diaries*. See also "Slavery," box 3, no. 5, FBLP, no. 76, 4. Notably, Tom officiated at the funeral of his master, Martin Moore. See "Old Cemetery Deeds of Barboursville and Others near," box 19, no. 3, FBLP, no. 76, 43.

39. Eldridge, *Diaries*, 1855 entries, 43; 1856 entries, 26.

40. Eldridge, *Cabell County's Empire for Freedom*, 43. Eldridge relays that several of Cabell County early churches had a balcony for slaves. See "The Gwinns," box 7, no. 15, FBLP, no. 76, 16–17.

41. Eldridge, *Diaries*, 1856 entries, 1, 7, 12, 14, 23, 27, 51.

42. Thompson, *Few among the Mountains*, 25.

43. As John Blassingame pointedly makes clear, "however oppressive or dehumanizing the plantation was, the struggle for survival was not severe enough to crush all of the slave's creative instincts." Blassingame, *Slave Community*, 105.

44. As early as 1822, local residents reported problems with escaping slaves. That year an advertisement for a "wild Negro man runaway Bob" described him as having "a proud careless walk; plays the fiddle, supposed to have made for Ohio." *Western Courier* (Charleston, VA), November 9, 1822, box 15, no. 14, FBLP, no. 76, 34. In 1827 fugitive slaves, assisted by abolitionists who stole slaves from the county's slaveholders, fled to freedom. Nance writes that Captain William A. Jenkins, father of Confederate brigadier general Albert G. Jenkins, "like other plantation owners in the Ohio Valley," had a problem with runaway slaves. In 1827 Jenkins was sued by James Shelton, a local slave catcher and owner of a county plantation, for not paying him for the return of one slave. In 1848 another slave-stealing dispute compelled Jenkins to appear once again before the court. Nance, *Significance of the Jenkins Plantation*; Eldridge, *Extracts from the Records of the County Court of Cabell County, West Virginia*, Minute Book 5, 249. In 1830, after placing "Thornton, a runaway slave," in the county jail, three of the county's citizens were directed to determine his value. See Eldridge, *Extracts from the Records*, Minute Book 3, 235.

45. Eldridge, *Diaries*, 16, 17. See also Eldridge, *Cabell County's Empire for Freedom*, 43.

46. Eldridge, *Diaries*, 1855 entries, 61.

47. Escape routes traveled some thirty miles from sites along the Ohio River in Lawrence County to black communities in Getaway and Poke Patch, located near what is now Black Fork, Ohio, in Lawrence County. Gallipolis also housed safe havens, including the Paint Creek Baptist Church, formed in 1833, and the African Methodist Episcopal (John Gee) Church, founded in 1849. See Siebert, *Underground Railroad*; Miller, "Underground Railroad"; Griffler, *Front Line of Freedom*.

48. Notably, recent works have served as a corrective to the historical overemphasis on white participation in the railroad. Instead, they have illuminated the centrality of "front-line" African American bravery, contribution, and sacrifice in its continued viability and success within the Ohio River valley. See Hagedorn, *Beyond the River*; Hudson, *Fugitive Slaves*; Griffler, *Front Line*. Fergus M. Bordewich states, "For generations, Americans thought of the Underground Railroad as a mostly monochromatic narrative of high-minded white people condescending to assist terrified and helpless blacks." Bordevich, *Bound for Canaan*, 4. In her study of antebellum Cincinnati, Nikki Taylor shifts focus from individual involvement to black community activism in the Underground Railroad. Taylor, *Frontiers of Freedom*, 138–60. Philip J. Schwarz comments, "The Underground Railroad was less organized than once thought, but

one of its most prominent characteristics was that so many of the ad hoc and regular 'conductors' were African Americans." Schwarz, *Migrants against Slavery*, 36. Discussing the difference between Underground Railroad authority Wilbur Siebert's influential work *The Underground Railroad from Slavery to Freedom* (published in 1898) and subsequent revisions and editions, one scholar writes, "Interesting, while Siebert's book tended to emphasize the role of whites in assisting fugitives, the role of African Americans looms much larger in the Siebert papers." Hudson, *Fugitive Slaves*, 10. Siebert contacted hundreds of individuals thought connected to or involved in the Underground Railroad. A great many of the letters and related documents were published in his seminal study, *The Underground Railroad from Slavery to Freedom*.

49. Jones, "Story of the Jones Family," 17.

50. Ibid., 12–13.

51. Innis, "Poke Patch Station." Corliss Miller names the following black conductors from Gallia County, Ohio: John Chavis, Joseph Cousins, Chas Crossland, William Ellison, Henry Harvey, William Hocks (Leith cites Gilliam Hocks, see p. 32), Caliph James, Howell James, Isaac Stewart, Jacob Stewart, James W. Stewart, John J. Stewart, and T. N. Stewart. See Miller, "Underground Railroad."

52. See "Jim Ditcher," *African American History of Lawrence County*, comp. by Martha Kounse and Sharon Kouns, http://lawrence.lib.oh.us/black/UGRRDitcher.html; "Jim Ditcher," *Ohio History Central*, February 3, 2008, http://www.ohiohistorycentral.org/entry.php?rec=3075; "Fugitive Slave Case," *Ironton Register*, December 13, 1860; Griffler, *Front Line of Freedom*, 93; Leith, "Follow the Furnaces," 31. The passage of the draconian Fugitive Slave Act of 1850 only served to heighten the sense of danger, anger, and desperation among Northern blacks and white abolitionists by allowing the owner of a runaway slave, with little evidence, to pursue his "property" into free territory and retrieve it. The law empowered federal marshals to arrest anyone attempting to rescue, aid, harbor, or conceal a fugitive, and mandated fines up to $1,000 and imprisonment for up to six months for anyone convicted of disobeying it. The law also provided payment to bounty hunters for the capture of runaways. Thus the law served as a corruptive force, for it provided not only protection for the bounty hunter but financial incentive as well, ensuring their impunity before state law. Not only was testimony by the accused slave disallowed, there was no right to trial by jury. The most outrageous provision to many Northerners, not only abolitionists, granted federally appointed commissioners the authority to compel any bystander, no matter his beliefs, to help seize any alleged runaway. Addressing the impact of the law upon his efforts to help his people passing through Ripley, Ohio, the remarkable John P. Parker wrote, "After the passage of the Fugitive Slave Law in [1850] we had to be more secretive than ever, for it meant confiscation of property, a fine and [a] jail sentence." Parker, *His Promised Land*, 84. Born a slave in Norfolk, Virginia, in 1827, Parker eventually purchased his own freedom and in 1850 relocated to Ripley, Ohio, where he married Miranda Boulden. His exploits as an abolitionist and conductor resulted in the freedom of hundreds of runaways. He also achieved notable success as a businessman, inventor, and industrialist. Although he largely worked indepen-

dently from white Presbyterian minister and abolitionist John Rankin in Ripley, the pair helped make the town an abolitionist center and important waystation on the Underground Railroad. For more on Rankin, see Hagedorn, *Beyond the River*; and Hudson, *Fugitive Slaves*, 11, 24, 152–53.

53. In the quest to recapture their property, owners placed fugitive-slave notices in local papers, further illustrating the dangers runaways faced. In the border county of Scioto, home to the hamlet of Portsmouth, Ohio, the first fugitive-slave notice appeared in the *Scioto Telegraph* in 1820. Over the next 35 years, a total of 13 separate advertisements appeared in the paper, with the last notice published in 1855. Evans, *History of Scioto County*, 612. Many whites were more than willing to assist hunters and garner the rewards, with Portsmouth an especially strong proslavery center historically. Addressing the nature of race relations in southern Ohio during the antebellum period, William W. Griffin points out, "The nearness of many southern Ohio counties to slave states reinforced and perpetuated southern Ohio's custom of strictly enforcing the color line. Cross-river economic and social relations fostered a common culture in the Ohio Valley that was much influenced by the South's way of life, for example, regarding the roles of free blacks." Griffin, *African Americans*, 49.

54. C. Belmont Keeney, "Abolitionism," in Sullivan, *West Virginia Encyclopedia*, 1.

55. For example, the *Kanawha Valley Star* of June 30, 1857, pronounced that the goals of Thayer and his associates were "diametrically opposed to the cherished institutions" of Virginia (qtd. in Rice, "Eli Thayer," 585). In contrast, the Ashland, Ky., *American Union* of May 28, 1857, extended "a brother's hand and brother's welcome" to those abolitionists intending to migrate from the North (qtd. in Rice, "Eli Thayer," 585–86. On at least one occasion, locals took matters into their own hands. In August 1857 prominent Cabell County slaveholder and future Confederate general Albert Gallatin Jenkins visited the Ceredo site. Like Thayer, Jenkins had recently won a congressional seat, but as a Democrat. After greeting him politely, Thayer recalled that Jenkins responded by being "a surly, sour and malevolent spectator." The next day, two Negroes, "posing as runaway slaves en route to Canada, besought assistance from the 'Neighbors,' but they were told that an attempted escape would bring hardships upon their own people and were advised to return home." Thayer believed that the incident constituted a deliberate attempt by Jenkins and others to catch Thayer violating Virginia statutes and to bring down the wrath of the community and state upon the group. *Eli Thayer: Founder of Ceredo, W.Va.* (n.p.:n.d), Ceredo Historical Society Museum, Ceredo, W.Va., 10. In truth, Thayer's primary goal was to establish colonies of free laborers in the slave states. Thus, both locally and nationally, he emphasized the free-labor aspect of his enterprise and minimized Ceredo's antislavery character. In fact, he declared that he liked "engine power, better than Negro power" and that free labor would prove detrimental to continued slavery. As evidence of his convictions, he declared that the company "had four slaves of its own," who, unlike the Africans, did not "steal hams and chickens and rob clothes lines" (p. 9). Also see

Geiger, "Tragic Fate of Guyandotte"; Rice, "Eli Thayer"; and Williams, *Appalachia*, 156.

56. Wallace, *Cabell County Annals and Families*, 43. Talbott relates that a net decline of Negro population of more than 10 percent occurred during the decade of 1850 to 1860, as compared with a 25 percent increase in the white population for the area that is now West Virginia. "Most of this decline was in the number of slaves, due both to the removal of slaves to the East, and their sale to cotton states, but also to the escape of fugitive slaves or their emancipation and removal to free states. Evidence of the lost by escape, or removal from the border to prevent it, is in fact that the sharpest decline during this decade occurred in counties near the Ohio River and the Mason and Dixon Line." Talbott, "Some Legislative and Legal Aspects," 1:9.

57. "Carry Me Back," *Huntington Advertiser*, March 4, 1875.

58. "Slavery," box 3, no. 5, FBLP, no. 76, 5. Also see "Memoirs of Sampson Sanders Family," 77.

59. Nance, *Significance of the Jenkins Plantation*, 7; Bickley, "Black People and the Huntington Experience," 130. Former Barboursville resident Ida Berkley recalls that after the war, Morris returned to the county with "the slaves" in tow. She remembers particularly Ben and his wife, Mahala; Aunt 'Manda, "who always baked the corn bread for father"; and Malinda (Anderson) E. Goode

60. Thompson, *Few among the Mountains*, 25–26.

61. "The Gwinns," box 7, no. 15, FBLP, no. 76, 18–19.

62. Ibid.

63. Ibid., 4; and "Old Cemetery Deeds of Barboursville," box 19, no. 3, FBLP, no. 76, 42.

64. "'Aunt Em' Dies after Stoke, Saw Family 'Sold Down River.'" *Huntington Herald Dispatch*, April 26, 1945.

65. For instance, Mrs. Walter Mitchell reports, "Prior to the Civil War the number of slaves had been decreasing in this section, and with the close of the Civil War that chapter in the neighborhood's history closed. A few devoted servants remained with their master as long as they lived. With few exceptions the masters were faithful and kindly protectors of their wards; and for the most part the slaves looked upon their owners as their truest friends and only refuge both during and after slavery days." Mitchell, "History of Cabell Creek Community." J. W. Miller states, "I cannot close this history without saying something about our old time colored people. In making this state we took from Virginia more than half her territory, but we only inherited four per cent of the slaves. I never witnessed any of the cruelties Harriett Beecher Stowe tells us about in Uncle Tom's Cabin. The slaves were respected and honored by all regardless of the station they occupied in life. They received their freedom with full honor; they helped to carve this country out of a wilderness and no man can say aught against them." Miller, "History of Barboursville Community."

66. A report issued by the superintendent of the 1860 census stated "that in thirty states out of thirty-four the great majority of people who moved migrated to a state immediately adjacent to the state of their birth." Shepherd, "Restless Americans," 30.

Notes to Chapter 1

67. Taylor, "Making West Virginia a Free State," 145. It should be noted that the salt industry of the Great Kanawah Valley, which, from the end of the War of 1812 forward had utilized large numbers of slaves, suffered a severe decline between 1850 and 1860. John E. Stealey notes in 1850, with 3,140 persons, Kanawha County possessed more than one-third of the region's slaves, the highest total in trans-Allegheny Virginia. During the decade, "the total slave population decreased by 30 percent, and the male and female slave populations decreased by 35 percent and 23 percent, respectively. In fact, in Kanawha County there were fewer slaves in 1860 than in 1850 in every age and sex category except for males and females over fifty-nine." Stealey, *Antebellum Kanawha Salt Business*, 137, 153.

68. Mud Bridge district held the county's third-largest number, at nine slaveholders and 29 slaves, an average of 3.2 slaves per household. An average of two slaves per household existed in the district of Thorndyke, location of the county's fourth-largest population of holders and slaves, with eight holders and sixteen slaves, respectively. The remaining districts possessed only a smattering of owners and slaves. Green Bottom and Falls Mills each possessed two slaveholders, overseeing six and two slaves, respectively. Only one slaveholder resided in each of the districts of Hamlin, Ten Mile, and Paw Paw Bottom. Both Phillip Powell and Wm. McComas held three slaves, while Archibald Reynolds held five. *Population Schedules of the Eighth Census of the United States*, 1860, *Virginia Slave Schedule*, vol.1 (Washington, D.C.: National Archives, 1967).

69. For "4,444 acres," see Eldridge, *Cabell County's Empire for Freedom*, xiii. For "the largest plantation," see Nance, *Significance of the Jenkins Plantation*, 6.

70. Williams, *Appalachia*, 119.

71. *Biography of Charles Cameron Lewis*, Mason County Library, Local History, Memorial Park, Point Pleasant, WV, (n.p.: 1961), 14.

72. Interestingly, the 1850 schedule cites only one mulatto within the Jenkins's slave population. See Nance, *Significance of the Jenkins Plantation*, 7.

73. As Alrutheus A. Taylor notes, "Slavery did not become a flourishing institution [in the region], and in the decades between 1840 and 1860, the demand for slave labor in the Gulf States caused the bulk of slaves to go there." Taylor, "Making West Virginia a Free State," 132. The slave population declined as follows: 1840, 567; 1850, 389; 1860, 305. U. S. Bureau of the Census, *Ninth Census*. Eldridge, *Diaries of William F. Dusenberry*. Examples include: "George Kilgore today set free the nigger woman he paid $1600 for last fall," 46; "nigger woman sold," for "only $382," 52, both 1856 entries.

74. Johnson, *Soul by Soul*, 19.

75. Crandall Shifflett contends that although horses were better suited for post-1830 farm machinery, oxen were more valuable than horses because they were less expensive, more powerful, more tractable, did better in the heat, weighed more, and ate less. See Shifflett, *Patronage and Poverty*, 24–26.

76. Nance, *Significance of the Jenkins Plantation*, 8–9.

77. "Fifes, Swicks, Coopers, Jordans, The Caldwells, The Schlaegels, The Lesages, The Pinkertons, The Howards, Hereford," box 3, no. 17, FBLP, no. 76, 37. D. B. Scott

died July 27, 1858, at age forty in Cabell County. See Ancestry.com, *West Virginia, Deaths Index, 1853–1973*. Evidence indicates that it was far more likely that Lewis Page's father, John Page, was the overseer who committed the rapes. In 1870 John was fifty years old and the single father of six children, ages three to twenty-two, with Lewis age nine. Ancestry.com, *1870 United States Federal Census*: Family History Library Film: 553191, Hannan, Mason, West Virginia, roll M593_1692, p. 110B, image 232.

78. On December 6, 1858, Edmund and Lilla returned to the court to have their status as free persons of color affirmed. They were joined by Samuel Wallace. Former Samuel Sanders's slave, Isom Sanders, was granted the same privilege a year later. See Eldridge, *Extracts from the Records*, Minute Book 5, 149, and Minute Book 6, 151, 192.

79. Eldridge, *Cabell County's Empire*, xiii, xiv, 44.

80. Several possible reasons could explain this: the associated relationship between old age and the acquisition of sufficient assets through years of sustained labor needed to purchase one's freedom; the associated relationship between longer service and greater intimacy within the slave/master relationship, thus engendering sufficient interpersonal capital to receive manumission; the associated relationship between older age and degenerating health, thus allowing the master to reduce capital overhead and free the slave without great financial loss; and last, the increasingly harsh political conditions newly free blacks had to live under.

81. Geiger writes, "The business section of Guyandotte was completely gutted, purportedly to prevent the Confederates from returning for supplies. The Buffington Mill was burned, as was the Forest Hotel. Even churches were not immune from the torch. The Guyandotte Baptist Church was burned after two unsuccessful attempts when Union soldiers tore off the shutters and stuffed them with straw before setting them alight in the church belfry. The Guyandotte Methodist Episcopal Church, South may also have been burned. Many houses were set ablaze, with special attention given to the town's most prominent secessionists. Women and children were forced into the streets, and some of the residents reportedly had to leap out of windows to escape the flames. Union reports later declared that no homes belonging to Union supporters were torched. One eyewitness, however, claimed that the first home to be burned belonged to a Union man, as were the majority of the residences consumed by fire." Geiger, "Tragic Fate of Guyandotte," 36.

82. Indeed, Rasmussen cites scholarship by Daniel Crofts and John C. Inscoe, both of whom contend that western Virginians failed to yield to their racial insecurities. In the 1860 presidential election many western Virginians "voted for southern fire-brand John C. Breckinridge over Abraham Lincoln or Stephen Douglass, either of whom would have been far more likely to gratify the West's need for internal improvements." Rasmussen, "Charles Ambler's *Sectionalism in Virginia*," 16. See also Crofts, *Reluctant Confederates*, 83; Inscoe, *Mountain Masters*, 110.

83. Talbott, "Legislative and Legal Aspects," 1:9. In his study of fugitive slaves in Kentucky, another border state, J. Blaine Hudson concludes, "More fugitives crossed the Ohio River near Owensboro in four months in late 1861 than had done so in the previous fifty years." Hudson, *Fugitive Slaves*, 51. Throughout the Ohio River Valley, blacks fled to northern towns and cities during the war. "In rising numbers, fugitive

slaves and free blacks left the Confederate states and moved into Union territory. Under the impact of wartime migration, Louisville's black population dramatically increased from 6,800 to nearly 15,000, Cincinnati's rose from 3,730 to 5,900, Pittsburgh's from less than 2,000 to 3,200; Evansville's from no more than 100 to 1,400." Trotter, *River Jordan*, 56.

84. Departure by free blacks and relocation of slaves by their owners also help explain the drop. Talbott, "Legislative and Legal Aspects," 1:9.

85. Inscoe, *Race, War and Remembrance*, 30. See also Curry, *House Divided*, 91–92. During the state's formative years African Americans confronted post-emancipation Appalachia's white paternalism, stereotypes, and racism, which propelled negative perceptions and attitudes of black capability and progress. As one local authority contended, "southern mountaineers were first and foremost southerners and . . . viewed slavery and race not unlike those of their yeoman or even slaveholding counterparts elsewhere in the South." Cooper, "History of Lower Creek Community; Cabell County, W.Va.," 24, *Morgantown, West Virginia: Agricultural Extension Division*, 1925, Thornton Tayloe Perry II, Collection, Virginia Historical Society, Richmond, Virginia. More pointedly, Appalachian James C. Klotter notes, "Blacks in slavery and freedom were often stereotyped by whites as a lazy but wily people who believed in spirits and witches, as an immoral race in which illegitimacy was not uncommon, as an inferior class that seemed to cower in subordination when talking with whites, and—paradoxically—as a violent, savage people who needed 'civilization' and religion's guiding hand." Klotter, "Black South and White Appalachia," 833.

86. Talbott, "Legislative and Legal Aspects," 1:15.

87. As Willie Lee Rose contends, the collision between the planters' and ex-slaves' interests angered the planter, who still sought unencumbered control of land and labor. "Many mistakes made between 1865 and 1869 were owing to psychological defensiveness of a displaced elite whose world-view was shaken not only by their conquerors but also by their erstwhile slaves." Rose, "Masters Without Slaves," 89.

88. They could leave the state and then return; they could gather together without restriction; their education was both permitted and provided, if they were under age twenty-one; they were tried and punished in the same manner as whites and could give competent testimony against whites; their marital rights were recognized, and an unmarried colored mother could force the support of her child; and they could serve in separate companies of the militia, though actively only in cases of emergency. See *Union Register* (Monroe County), November 9, 1867.

89. Ibid.

90. Proposed in 1870 by former Union soldier, W. H. H. Flick, a member of the legislature of Pendleton County, the constitutional amendment grated suffrage to adult males and was ratified the following year. See Conley, *West Virginia*, 86–87.

91. Talbott writes that "the decidedly unfriendly attitude of the white people in general, and limited economic opportunities prevented Negro immigration for a few years after the War." Talbott, "Legislative and Legal Aspects," 1:9. See also Engle, "Mountaineer Reconstruction," 140.

92. Slaveholder F. D Beuhring freed all of his slaves after the war. See "Beuhring Family History," box 20, no. 9, FBLP, no. 67, 75.

93. Sullivan and Lawrence, "Black Migration," 52. By way of comparison, Talbott notes that the state's black population declined 13.5 percent during the decade of the war, "as against another twenty-five per cent growth in the number of whites" entering the state during the same period. See Talbott, "Legislative and Legal Aspects," 1:9.

94. U.S. Bureau of the Census, Population Statistics, vol. 1, *Ninth Census*.

95. Talbott, "Legislative and Legal Aspects," 1:8–9.

96. Posey, *Negro Citizen*, 5. Posey reports the black population totaled 21,144: 18,371 slave and 2,773 free. The white population totaled 355,526.

97. Eldridge provides perspective on this development when she states, "Many of the slaves had been born and raised in Cabell County; leaving their home would have been very difficult. Everything familiar, from their favorite berry patch or fishing hole to the church down the lane, was being left behind for something called freedom. Apprehension for the unknown future had to concern all the adults." Eldridge, *Cabell County's Empire for Freedom*, 46.

98. Nance, *Significance of the Jenkins Plantation*, 10. See also "Fifes, Swicks, Coopers, Jordans, The Caldwells, The Schlaegels," box 3, no. 17, FBLP, no. 76, 37; and *Ninth Census*. Though not evidence of rape, it is suggestive that Christine's son would have the same name as her former overseer.

99. To this point, Shed and Charley, the only slaves not "implicated in the 'runaway'" initiated by Fred, and thus not sold away, remained "at home" after the war. At least in part, a rationale for Charley may have been his relationship with the housemaid of Mrs. Rolfe, whom he married shortly after the war, and who bore him several children. See box 9, no. 9, FBLP, no. 76, 77.

100. For works on West Virginia's formation see Curry, *House Divided*; Foner, *Reconstruction*; Rice and Brown, *West Virginia*; and Williams, *West Virginia*.

Chapter 2. The "Grapevine Telegraph"

1. Posey reports 18,371 were slave and 2,773 were free. See Posey, *Negro Citizen of West Virginia*, 5.

2. For more on Huntington, see Evans, *Collis Potter Huntington*, and Lavender, *Great Persuader*.

3. See Bias, *History*, 85–100. See also Lavender, *Great Persuader*; Eller, "Mountain Road"; and Nelson, *Steel Drivin' Man*.

4. Nelson, *Steel Drivin' Man*, 5.

5. Eller, "Mountain Road," 73. Interestingly, as early as 1867, Huntington's associates sought financial backing from Cabell County officials. That year, the county residents voted on a proposal to subscribe $150,000 worth of stock in the Chesapeake and Ohio Railway Company. One of the conditions stipulated by West Virginia counties west of Kanawha Falls was that the amount of their investment be spent on their end of the line. Bias, *History*, 81. Ronald D. Eller notes the quoted figure is less than the amount initially sought by the railroad from the county. He states the following

figures sought from various West Virginia counties: "Kanawha, $500,000; Greenbrier, $250,000; Cabell, $300,000; Monroe, $200,000; Mercer and Raleigh, $100,000; Fayette and Putnam, $150,000; Pocahontas, Webster, Nicholas, Wyoming, Wayne, Logan and Lincoln, $50,000." See Eller, "Mountain Road," 20. To facilitate matters, at a time when the state constitution "denied the right to vote to persons who had participated in the rebellion," former Confederate soldiers who owned property were permitted to vote on the proposal. See Wallace, *Cabell County Annals and Families*, 44. Also see Bias, *History*, 73. However, as late as September 9, 1868, Wayne County was the only county within West Virginia to sign a subscription out of the projected counties through which the railroad would pass. Eller, "Mountain Road,"15.

6. A popular story conveyed through the years by locals is that Guyandotte lost the terminal due to an incident that occurred when Huntington and his party visited the town and tied their horses to hitching posts to go explore the town on foot. According to local historians, Huntington's horse backed around onto the sidewalk, obstructing passing pedestrians and compelling the mayor to fine Huntington $5. For this outrage, Huntington moved the terminal downriver. See Bias, *History*, 105, and Casto, *Huntington*, 23. See also "The City of Huntington," *Herald Dispatch*, December 24, 1895.

7. Evans, *Collis Potter Huntington*, 517.

8. Casto reports, "The years 1830–1930 are generally considered by river historians to be the 'century of the steamboat.'" See *Huntington*, 14. C. P. Huntington did prove to be prescient. Leland R. Johnson explains that even four years after its founding, the city was already hailed as one of the most important ports on the Ohio River. The city's importance as a river port and freight transshipment point continued such that by the mid-twentieth century, Huntington was recognized as the nation's "greatest inland port." Stanford, *Illustrated History*, 77.

9. Casto, *Huntington*, 23–25; Evans, *Collis Potter Huntington*, 525–26; Lavender, *Great Persuader*, 272.

10. Eller, "Mountain Road," 43.

11. Harlan, *Booker T. Washington Papers*, 2;63–85.

12. Ibid., 13.

13. John Williams Matheus, interviewed by Bishop and Isleman in Federal Writers' Project, *Slave Narratives: Ohio*.

14. Simmons, "Augusta County's Other Pioneers."

15. Dunaway, *Slavery*, 87.

16. Williams, *Appalachia*, 132. For information on the origins and evolution of the White Sulphur Springs see "History," http://www.greenbrier.com/Top-Navigation-Pages/About-Us/History.aspx; McKinney, *Civil War in Greenbrier County*, 117–18.

17. Conte, *History of the Greenbrier*, 6–11; and "History," http://www.greenbrier.com.

18. In 1857, the construction of the spa's first large hotel, officially named the Grand Central Hotel but affectionately known as "The Old White," was completed, increasing the resort's stature. McKinney, *Civil War in Greenbrier County*, 117–18. Remarking on the splendor of the Old White, *Harper's New Monthly Magazine* noted, "The grounds

at the 'White' embrace about forty acres and are laid out with great taste. In the centre stands the main hotel, a plain building 400 feet in length, with one of the largest and finest ballrooms in America, and a dining-room 300 feet long and 140 feet wide, which seats at its round tables about 1200 guests. The sleeping accommodations in other parts of the building are sufficient for about 700 persons; and as the cottages will lodge 1200 to 1400 more, the capacity of the watering-place may be set down at about 2000." See Cook, "White Sulphur Springs," 344. For quote, see Lewis, *Ladies and Gentlemen on Display*, 40.

19. Cook, "White Sulphur Springs," 341–42; Pryor, "Colonel's Story,", 212–13; and Warner, "Their Pilgrimage," 299–300, 317–19; Semmes, *John H. Latrobe*, 256–58; Reniers, *Springs of Virginia*, 90–92; Conte, *History of the Greenbrier*, 28; Lewis, *Ladies and Gentlemen on Display*, 38–45, 52–55, 156, 196–97, 199; Chambers, *Drinking the Waters*, 24–25, 95–96; and Dunaway, *Slavery*, 82–3.

20. Matthews, "Perkins and Early Related Families," 14.

21. Dunaway, *Slavery*, 83.

22. In 1850 Greenbrier County possessed the largest number of slaves in the Greenbrier region. Inter-university Consortium, *Historical, Demographic, Economic and Social Data*.

23. Lewis, *Ladies and Gentlemen on Display*, 156.

24. Ibid., 38.

25. In this manner, I contend the slaves' actions mimic those of the "trickster," the archetypal character of mythology, folklore, and literature who uses the tools of the "master's house" in new and creative ways to dismantle the existing hierarchy. Modern African American literary criticism has elevated the trickster figure as one example of how the slave system of oppression was undermined from within. Both the Signifying Monkey and Br'er Rabbit, African American folk trickster figures, present examples of the ways in which slaves and the slave community outwitted the oppressor. See Henry Louis Gates, Jr., "The 'Blackness of Blackness': A Critique of the Sign and the Signifying Monkey," *Critical Inquiry* 9, no. 4 (June 1983): 685–723; *The Signifying Monkey: A Theory of African American Literary Criticism* (New York: Oxford University Press, 1988); and Riggins R. Earl, Jr., *Dark Symbols, Obscure Signs: God, Self, and Community in the Slave Mind* (Knoxville: University of Tennessee Press, 2003).

26. "Work of Art: *Kitchen Ball at White Sulphur Springs, Virginia*," http://artnc.org/works-of-art/kitchen-ball-white-sulphur-springs-virginia. For quote, see Lewis, *Ladies and Gentlemen on Display*, 199.

27. Blassingame, *Slave Community*, 106.

28. Warner, "Their Pilgrimage," 318.

29. Windle, *Life at the White Sulphur Springs*, 32.

30. Dunaway, *Slavery*, 223.

31. Chambers, *Drinking the Waters*, 95.

32. In 1846, Dr. William Burke noted the chaos at mealtime caused by servants seizing the best of the food for their private employers or for guests who had bribed

the establishment's servants. He proposed the banning of private servants from the dining hall and the implementation of a system to reduce incidents of bribery of White Sulphur Springs servants. See Burke, *Mineral Springs of Western Virginia*.

33. Reniers, *Springs of Virginia*, 90–92.
34. Lewis, *Ladies and Gentlemen on Display*, 196–97.
35. Genovese, *Roll, Jordan, Roll*, 91
36. Lewis, *Ladies and Gentlemen on Display*, 197–98.
37. Notably, two black residents of White Sulphur Springs, Shirley C. Tillman and Albert G. Woodson, are listed as students in Wilberforce University's 1860 yearbook. See Green, *Remember Me to Miss Louisa*, 105. Founded in 1856 by members of the Methodist Episcopal Church, Wilberforce is the nation's oldest private historically black college and university.
38. As Dunaway notes, "To remain on the offensive against their owners, Appalachian slaves developed secret communication strategies. Despite great distances to work sites, slaves managed to spread important news from one plantation to another. Religious meetings, social gatherings, contacts with free blacks and poor whites, the return of hireouts, and the arrival of new slaves all proved to be effective mechanisms for moving ideas and, thereby building community solidarity." Dunaway, *Slavery*, 234. See also Lewis, *Ladies and Gentlemen on Display*, 197.
39. Washington, *Autobiography*, 19.
40. Some idea of the scale of the kitchen operation at the "White" is evident in a 1860 letter written by Elizabeth Noel to her daughter, Julia, in which she notes, "I have been all through the kitchen saw them making cake, baking pies, roasting meat [and] toasting coffee on a large scale. They rise their loaf bread in a box as large as our [chip] box, the bowl they made the cake in was as large as a large water tub, they bake five hundred pies a day, kill two beeve, 22 sheep 300 chickens cook 40 bushels of corn make from ninety five to 115 gallons of coffee twice a day besides tea & milk." See "White Sulphur Springs: Letter from Elizabeth Noel."
41. 1860 Census, Greenbrier County, Leslie Haga, compiler.
42. Lewis, *Ladies and Gentlemen on Display*, 42.
43. Dunaway, *Slavery*, 230.
44. Lewis, *Ladies and Gentlemen on Display*, 44.
45. Bickley, "Carter G. Woodson," 60–61; and White, *Hidden and Forgotten*, 14.
46. Rebecca A. Shepherd states, "Demographer Everett S. Lee . . . argues that the urge to migrate is particularly strong in a country possessing regions of some diversity, or an unexplored frontier. In such situations the normal inertia of residential persistence is overcome by the desire to migrate to take advantage of perceived opportunities at the new location." See Shepherd, "Restless Americans," 26.
47. As British historian E. G. Ravenstein noted in his landmark 1885 study on human migration, "Migration currents flow along well-defined geographical channels. They are like mighty rivers, which flow along slowly at the outset and after depositing most of the human buildings whom they hold in suspension, sweep along more impetuously, until they enter one of the great . . . reservoirs." See Ravenstein, "The Laws of Migration," *Journal of the Royal Statistical Society*, no. 2 (June 1889): 284.

48. Duckworth, *Black History of Huntington*, 3.

49. Wade, "Black Gold and Black Folk," 38.

50. In 1875 a local newspaper argued that incorrigible black men intoxicated on their liberty populated the region. "The average roustabout, or as he is called in slang, 'rooster,' is a strong black fellow, who has probably been a slave and has lit from the country for that supposed freedom and rollicking life, which the boat hand enjoys so muchly [sic] while his last trip's wages last. Generally the property of the 'rooster' consists of what he stands and sleeps in the same comprising an old flannel shirt, a pair of tattered brogans run down at the heels, and an old ragged hat. He wears neither socks, drawers nor undershirt, and has no blanket to protect him when asleep from the cold." See "The Ideal Rouster," *Huntington Advertiser*, April 15, 1875.

51. Woodson, *Century of Negro Migration*, 117, 118.

52. Perhaps Charles S. Johnson summarized it best: "After all, it means more that the Negroes who left the South were motivated more by the desire to improve their economic status than by fear of being manhandled by unfriendly whites. The one is a symptom of wholesome and substantial life purpose; the other, the symptom of a fugitive incourageous opportunism." Johnson, "Flight from Persecution," 272. In two more contemporary studies, both Neil McMillen and James Grossman show the historical reality of black internal and external movement while refuting the notion that black migration was a product of impotency and not of practical forethought. See McMillen, *Dark Journey*, and Grossman, *Land of Hope*.

53. Statistics of the Wealth and Industry, *Ninth Census*, 2.

54. U.S. Bureau of the Census, *Eighth Census*, and U.S. Bureau of the Census, *Ninth Census*.

55. Statistics on Cabell County crop production are as follows: tobacco—1860, 65,587 lbs.; 1870, 135,410 lbs.; corn—1860, 240,210 bushels; 1870, 167,600 bushels; wheat—1860, 65,715 bushels; 1870, 42,592 bushels. See Statistics of Wealth and Industry, *Ninth Census*.

56. Wallace reports, "As early as 1873 the record discloses there was a tobacco warehouse on the hills south of the city and in 1875 the Legislature passed an act providing for the inspection of tobacco and the establishment of state tobacco warehouses at Huntington and Parkesburg." See Wallace, *Cabell County Annals and Families*, 65.

57. This composite history is drawn from Mrs. Callie Barnett, interviewed by John Cyrus and Lowell Black, Huntington, W.V., Special Collections, James E. Morrow Library, Marshall University, Huntington, W.V., November 2, 1972; *Huntington Advertiser*, July 10, 1974; Rick Baumgartner, "First Families of Huntington," *Huntington Advertiser*, October 28, 1976–March 24, 1977, James E. Morrow Library, Special Collections, Marshall University; Yancey, *Echoes from the Hill*; Miller, *Centennial History of Huntington*; Casto, *Huntington*; Jacqueline Anne Coggin, *Carter G. Woodson: A Life in Black History* (Baton Rouge: Louisiana State University Press, 1993); Edna Duckworth, *A Black History of Huntington*, ed. Lana Gillespie Boggs (n.p., [1990]), James E. Morrow Library, Special Collections, Marshall University; Barnett, "Seven Generations of Barnetts," 318–20; Trotter, "Formation of Black," 284–301; Nelson L. Barnett, Jr., interview by author, Columbus, Ohio, May 17, 2002; Barnett, *Colonel*

Riddle Genealogical Chart; Herald Dispatch, February 9, 2004; and U.S. Bureau of the Census, *Tenth Census.*

58. Using the *Compendium of the Tenth Census*, Dianne Swann-Wright notes "colored" population in 1860 Buckingham County was 9,171, then 7,711 in 1870, a decline of 1,460 over the decade. See Swann-Wright, *Way Out of No Way*, 12.

59. Maloney, *History of Buckingham County*, 72. In his contention that southern slave owners lost almost half of their capital, not just their labor, as a result of the war, Yale economist Gerald David Jaynes provides further context for the financial blow the county's slave holders experienced. See Jaynes, *Branches without Roots*, 313.

60. Report on the Productions of Agriculture, *Tenth Census*, 198.

61. Swann-Wright, *Way Out of No Way*, 94.

62. Ibid.

63. White, *Hidden and Forgotten*, 83–4.

64. Ibid., 84–85.

65. Engle, "Mountaineer Reconstruction," 165.

66. Ibid.

67. U.S. Bureau of the Census, *Ninth Census*, 1870.

68. While not conclusive of a previous master-slave relationship, it is certainly suggestive that three separate white Morris households are listed as slave owners in 1860. The three households of John, owner of 12, Charles, owner of four, and James, owner of three, totaled 19 bondpersons. See *Population Schedules of the Eighth Census*.

69. U.S. Bureau of the Census, *Ninth Census*, 1870.

70. Ibid.

71. Ibid. John Shafer is listed as John Shaver, age twenty-six. U.S. Bureau of the Census, *Tenth Census*, 1880, lists him as John Shaffer, age thirty-eight.

72. Ibid.

Chapter 3. Into the Crucible

1. Stealey, "Slavery in the Kanawha Salt Industry."

2. *The History of the Chesapeake & Ohio Railway Company* (n.p,: n.d), 29, Manuscript Collection, Virginia Historical Society, Richmond, Virginia.

3. Burchett, "Promise and Prejudice," 313.

4. Perdue, Barden, and Phillips, *Weevils in the Wheat*, 152.

5. Chappell, *John Henry*, 57. Recent scholarship has proved the veracity of John Henry's existence. However, the nature of his employment has shifted from railroadman to tunneler, a position requiring greater skill and posing greater danger. For more on John Henry, see also Johnson, *John Henry*, and Williams, *John Henry*. Scott Reynolds Nelson may have put to rest discussion on the true identity of John Henry; he convincingly argues that John Henry was John William Henry, born in 1847 in Elizabeth City, New Jersey, convicted of housebreak and larceny and sent to the Virginia State Penitentiary, and whose skeleton was unearthed at the penitentiary with those of about 300 prisoners. Further, Nelson contends Henry did not work on Big Bend but on the nearby Lewis Tunnel. See Nelson, *Steel Drivin' Man*.

Notes to Chapter 3

6. One Chesapeake and Ohio Railroad document published in 1873 by the New York banking firm Fisk & Hatch commented on the perceived physical and cultural limitations of the European immigrant as a worker within the New River valley: "To the European immigrant, unaccustomed to the use of the axe, this fine growth of timber has been deemed an objection, and he has winded his way to the prairies of the West—with their chills and fevers, which most surely destroy the general health of his family—rather than undergo the unaccustomed task of clearing, in the mountain forests, the acres he needs." Dealers in government securities, Fisk and Hatch were empowered with the fiduciary responsibility of selling $15 million in 30-year bonds to help finance capitalization and construction of the C&O after C. P. Huntington purchased it from the Virginia Central Railroad in 1869. The firm went bankrupt in 1873. See Turner, "Chesapeake and Ohio Railroad." For commentary, see *Chesapeake and Ohio Railroad: Advantages*, 37.

7. Hamilton, "Early Recollections," 1.

8. Eller, "Mountain Road," 50.

9. Ibid., 49.

10. Ibid.

11. Tabscott, "John Henry," 11.

12. These include Claiborne R. Mason, Colonel T. M. R. Talcott, General Williams C. Wickham, and Cabell County resident and one-time sheriff George McKendree. See Wallace, *Huntington through Seventy-Five Years*, 77, 79–80. Speaking on Mason, Nelson states, "Mason's connection to the railroad went back to the 1840s, when it was mostly state owned. He was a self-taught railroad contractor who had first bossed slaves and free blacks in his coal mines in Chesterfield County, just south of Richmond. As railroads first came to Virginia, he had used slaves and convicts to grade and lay track, earning himself stock in the railroad." See Nelson, *Steel Drivin' Man*, 77.

13. Nelson, "Who Was John Henry?," 51. Nelson continues, "In the last two years of the Civil War, General Robert E. Lee had given Mason broad orders to hunt deserters in Albemarle County in western Virginia near Charlottesville. Mason had dutifully captured dozens of soldiers absent without leave, as well as those who had given them aid. He then brought them to the nearest town, posted notice of their execution, and hanged them. In the mountains, bitterness toward Mason lasted for decades. A major stockholder in the C&O, Mason's resume was not a liability for the railroad."

14. Ibid., 48–49.

15. *Cabell County Press* (Guyandotte, W.V.), May 9, 1870, box 15, no. 15, FBLP, no. 76, 9.

16. Ibid., 13.

17. Chappell, *John Henry*, 67. Also see Newlin, "Cultural Evaluation of John Henry," 2–4.

18. Tabscott quotes Williams, *John Henry*, 10.

19. Tabscott quotes Chappell, *John Henry*, 11.

20. Yancey, *Echoes from the Hills*, 16. For quote see Lomax and Lomax, *Best Loved American Folk Songs*, 51.

21. Nelson, *Steel Drivin' Man*, 5, 18, 24.

22. Decatur Axtell, then vice president of the C&O, states that in 1868, the railroad's debt load was $2,418,636. See Axtell, *History of the Chesapeake and Ohio*, 1.

23. Nelson writes, "About one third were killed on the railroad, and twenty-four died a few weeks later after they returned from work. The surgeon [hired by the penitentiary] stated that scurvy, dropsy, dysentery, and consumption could mostly be attributed to construction work and tunneling on the C&O." Nelson, *Steel Drivin' Man*, 25.

24. Ibid., 26.

25. See "Colored Man Killed," *Huntington Advertiser*, July 29, 1875, and "Death on the Rail," *Huntington Advertiser*, August 26, 1875.

26. Accidental death by drowning exceeded railroad-related accidents 86 to 83. Tenth Census, *Report of the Mortality*, 260–62.

27. Turner, "Chesapeake and Ohio Railroad,"165.

28. Ibid. Historian A. A. Taylor noted, "Testimony was all but unanimous that the migrant labor was efficient." See Taylor, "Negro in the Reconstruction of Virginia," 339.

29. Eller, "Mountain Road," 43.

30. Turner, "Chesapeake and Ohio Railroad in Reconstruction," 163.

31. Ibid. Quote from *Cincinnati Enquirer*, May 4, 1872.

32. Nelson, "Who Was John Henry?," 52.

33. As Nelson relates, "Tracklining is the lowest-paid railroad work, paying less than a dollar a day after the Civil War. Most trackliners had been born slaves, and before the Civil War Southern states had not allowed the teaching of slaves and free blacks. Very few trackliners were literate." Nelson, *Steel Drivin' Man*, 26.

34. Tabscott, "John Henry," 14. Also see Johnson, *John Henry*. Evidence of this contention can be found in the 1877 Great Railroad Strike in Martinsburg, West Virginia, by the workers (including significant numbers of black laborers) of the Baltimore and Ohio Railroad. The strike crippled the nation, helped to convey a newfound sense of power to labor, foreshadowing the violent conflicts in the southern West Virginia coalfields of the late nineteenth and early twentieth centuries.

35. "Facts to Talk About," 24.

36. Discussing Henry and legendary twentieth-century boxer Joe Louis, Lawrence Levine notes, "Their morality stemmed . . . from the two characteristics that typified their lives: they never preyed upon their own people and they won their victories within the confines of the legal system in which they lived. They were moral figures, too, in the sense that their lives provided more than vehicles for momentary escape; they provided models of action and emulation for other black people." Levine, *Black Culture and Black Consciousness*, 420–21.

37. Bickley and Ewen, *Memphis T. Garrison*, 15.

38. Ibid., 213.

39. Delineating the potential benefits of the extraction of mineral wealth—iron ore, carboniferous limestone, and coal—from the New River valley, the banking firm of Fisk & Hatch noted in 1873, "Having heretofore investigated and reported upon various furnaces and having in view the cheapness of coal and charcoal, fuel, labor in Virginia (colored), and the resources of water power, I am satisfied that pig iron can be made at numerous points along the road at from $18 to $20 per ton." *Chesapeake and Ohio Railroad: Advantages*, 54.

40. Sullivan, *Coal Men and Coal Towns*, 1. Sullivan notes that smokeless coal can also be found in the coal-mining areas of Kentucky.

41. *Ironton (Ohio) Weekly Journal*, February 28, 1873.

42. Eller, "Mountain Road," 59.

43. Evans, *Collis Potter Huntington*, 2:527.

44. Lewis, *Transforming the Appalachian Countryside*, 50.

45. Miller, *Centennial History of Huntington*, 41–42.

46. Eller, "Mountain Road," 54.

47. Ibid., 56.

48. Turner, "Chesapeake and Ohio Railroad in Reconstruction,"160.

49. Ibid., 165.

50. *Democratic Banner* (Milton, W.V.), May 7, 1874.

51. Frustrated and angered over not receiving pay for three months due to the Depression, 200 black workers struck. They lost not only their jobs but also two months' back pay. See Rachleff, *Black Labor in the South*, 73.

52. One source notes, "Of the country's 364 railroads, 89 went bankrupt, over 18,000 businesses failed between 1873 and 1875, unemployment reached 14 percent, while workers who kept their jobs were employed for a mere six months out of the year and suffered a 45% cut in wages, or approximately one dollar per day." See "Economic Conditions of the 1870s," https://wn.com/great_railroad_strike_of_1877.

In 1887 West Virginia outlawed the use of scrip "in payment of miners' wages and compulsory trading at company stores." While the State Supreme Court struck down the law shortly thereafter, the legislature reenacted it in 1891. See Williams, *West Virginia and the Captains of Industry*, 198–99. Historian David Corbin, among others, argued that employers engaged in monopolistic and exploitative practices through their control of stores and housing alike. Economist Price V. Fishback challenges this belief, arguing that higher transportation costs, isolated locations, and the lack of labor-market competition determined store prices and the use of scrip. See Corbin, *Life, Work, and Rebellion*, and Fishback, "Did Coal Miners Owe Their Souls?"

53. Conley, *West Virginia*, 95. One source notes, "The effects of the downturn reached the U.S. on September 18th with the failure of the banking firm Jay Cooke and Company. As Cooke was the country's top investment banker, the principal backer of the Northern Pacific Railroad [as well as prime investor in other railroads] and handled most of the government's wartime loans, its failure was catastrophic. In response, the U.S. economy sputtered and then collapsed. Shortly after Cooke's demise, the New York Stock Exchange closed for 10 days, [credit] dried up, and

foreclosures and factory closings became common." See "Economic Conditions of the 1870s," https://wn.com/great_railroad_strike_of_1877.

54. Axtell, "Wedding Journey," 1.
55. "History of the C&O," http://www.cohs.org/history.
56. Hepler, "C&O Patch," 16, qtd. in Miller, *Centennial History of Huntington*.
57. "An Order That May Cause Trouble," *New York Times*, September 17, 1885.
58. "History of the C&O."
59. Engle, "Mountaineer Reconstruction," 145.
60. Taylor, "Negro in the Reconstruction of Virginia," 337.
61. Hall, *Slave Narratives*.
62. Rick Baumgartner, "First Families of Huntington," repr. from *Huntington (W. V.) Advertiser*, 18-part series, October 28, 1976–March 24, 1977, James E. Morrow Library, Special Collections, Marshall University.
63. See *Douglass High School Reunion 1973 Souvenir Program*, 85; Duckworth, *Black History of Huntington*, 3; and Trotter, "Black Migration," 48.
64. Hall, *Slave Narratives*. A variety of reasons compelled African American migration into the southern West Virginia coalfields. To work in Pennsylvania's older, anthracite fields, prospective black miners had to navigate a system of long-established apprenticeships, which effectively locked them out of mining jobs. Kenneth Bailey cites other push factors—droughts and bad harvests, brushes with the law, death of family members (especially spouses), desires for travel and new experiences—as well as pull factors, including higher wages, less discrimination, and better education systems for their children. See Bailey, "Judicious Mixture," 127. Charles S. Johnson argues for the primacy of economic opportunity as opposed to reaction to persecution for compelling black migration. See Johnson, "How Much?"
65. Wallace, *Huntington through Seventy-Five Years*, 85.
66. Trotter, "Formation of Black Community," 284.
67. Eller, "Mountain Road," 60.
68. U.S. Bureau of the Census, *Ninth Census*.
69. Trotter, *Coal, Class, and Color*, 10.
70. Ambler, *West Virginia*, 357. Ambler reports that "in 1888 it [Bluefield] was only a flag station. . . . By 1900 it had a population of five thousand, and the 1930 census credited it with more than twenty thousand." For a history of Bluefield, see McGehee, *Bluefield, West Virginia, 1889–1989*.
71. Whear, "Carter G. Woodson."
72. U.S. Bureau of the Census, *Ninth Census*.
73. Charles P. Anson relates that "of the 115, 229 gainfully employed over ten years of age in 1870, only 8,153 or 7% were women. West Virginia's 7% women workers was less than half the percentage of wage earners in the nation at large in that year." Anson, "History of the Labor Movement," 60.
74. Figures in this paragraph are revisions of those previously cited in Fain, "Forging of a Black Community," 77.
75. U.S. Bureau of the Census, *Tenth Census*.

76. Ibid.

77. Rev. A. D. Lewis, "Huntington Church History," *The Annual Great Harvest Home Program: A Great Spiritual and Financial Drive, October 19–30, 1936*, Sixteenth Street Baptist Church and Community Center, Huntington, W.V.

78. Duckworth, *History of Black Huntington*, 4, and Baumgartner, "First Families," 26–27. The Jaspers, while not cited in 1870, are cited in the 1880 U.S. Census.

79. Wilson, "Early Settler Looking Backward."

80. U.S. Bureau of the Census, *Tenth Census*. In 1880, Black resides with his wife, Ann M. (a housekeeper), and two step children, Elizabeth and Edmonia Jones, ages fourteen and twelve, respectively. County-level black population totaled 890, 7 percent of the total county population. For county-level population, see *1880 Census of West Virginia*.

81. U.S. Bureau of the Census, *Tenth Census*.

82. In 1880 Wayne County total population was 14,728. See Jack L. Dickinson, *Wayne County, West Virginia in the Civil War* (n.p., 2003), 129.

83. Don W. Boham, interviewed by Debra L. Hogg, Oral History of Appalachia Project and Drinko Foundation, Special Collections, Marshall University, December 9, 1973.

84. See Lewis, *Black Coal Miners in America*, 122.

85. Trotter, "Formation of Black Community," 284.

86. Howard P. Wade, "Black gold and Black folk: A case study of McDowell County, West Virginia, 1890–1940," (PhD diss., University of Miami, 1990), The Library of the University of North Carolina at Chapel Hill), 87.

87. Trotter, "The Formation of Black Community," 284.

88. Numerous scholars have examined race, labor relations, unionism, and community development within the southern West Virginia coal region. Representative works include Lee, *Bloodletting in Appalachia*; Corbin, *Life, Work, and Rebellion*; Bailey, "Judicious Mixture"; Lewis, "From Peasant to Proletarian; Lewis, *Black Coal Miners in America*; Trotter, *Coal, Class, and Color*; Trotter, "Formation of Black Community"; Skeen, "Industrial Democracy"; and Bailey, "Matewan before the Massacre."

89. "In [1880] twenty-two work stoppages were reported in West Virginia, placing the state eighth from the top in a ranking of all states. . . . West Virginia experienced 304 work stoppages in the period from 1881–1905, ranking twenty-second among all the states. The state ranked tenth from the top, however, in the number of workers involved in work stoppages." See Dix, *Analysis*, 11–12.

90. *Huntington Cabell County, West Virginia* (New York: Sanborn-Perris Map Co., March 1893), 1, map online at https://www.loc.gov/item/sanborn09409_003. Formed in 1872 by Connecticut natives William H. Barnum and Eli (Ely) Ensign, with the financial backing of Collis P. Huntington, the company became a major producer of railroad-car wheels and iron castings by the mid-1870s. Within a decade of its formation, the company began producing wooden railroad freight cars. By the early 1890s Ensign had become one of the largest railroad-car builders in the nation, selling its cars to the Chesapeake and Ohio, Southern Pacific, and Central Pacific Railroads.

See "Ensign Manufacturing Company," http://www.midcontinent.org/rollingstock/builders/ensign.htm. For the 1898 strike see *The Cabell Record* (Milton, W.V.), February 24, 1898.

91. Gutman, "Negro and the United Mine Workers," 63. For a recent monograph on Davis, see Frans H. Doppen, *Richard L. Davis and the Color Line in Ohio Coal: A Hocking Valley Mine Labor Organizer, 1862–1900*, Contributions to Southern Appalachia Studies, vol. 41 (Jefferson, N.C.: McFarland, 2016).

92. Ibid., 69.

93. Ibid., 97.

94. "Norfolk and Western," see McGeehee, *Bluefield, West Virginia*, 7; and "Locomotive Engineers," Anson, "History of the Labor Movement," 77.

95. Rachleff, *Black Labor in the South*. Rachleff chronicles Richmond membership in the Knights of Labor growing from 1,500 in 1885 to more than 10,000 before the Haymarket Square bombing and a counteroffensive by Richmond firms reduced the number to fewer than 1,400 workers by 1888. The Knights of Labor held some sway in the rural-industrial coal mines of nineteenth-century Hocking, Athens, and Perry Counties. Rachleff comments on the historic significance of the Knights: "[They] were the last and most complete embodiment of labor's struggle against emergence of a new social order, based on deskilled labor, strict hierarchy at the workplace, rigid industrial and social discipline, corporate power in politics, the separation of 'life' and 'work' between home and workplace, and the development of everyday culture as a collection of purchasable commodities rather than the creation of families, workmates, and neighbors" (192). See also Gutman, "Negro and the United Mine Workers."

96. Scott, "Progress of the Huntington Negro," 2.

97. Rachleff, *Black Labor*, 114–87.

98. As W. E. B. Du Bois noted of the era, "This union of black and white labor never got a real start. First, because black leadership still tended toward the ideals of the petty bourgeois, and white leadership tended distinctly toward strengthening capitalism . . . the white worker did not want the Negro in his unions, did not believe in him as a man, dodged the question, and when he appeared at conventions, asked him to organize separately; that is, outside the real labor movement, in spite of the fact that this was a contradiction of all sound labor policy." Du Bois, *Black Reconstruction in America*, 352, 357–58.

99. Gutman, "Negro and the United Mine Workers," 117.

100. Wilson, "Early Settler Looking Backward." Both Edna Duckworth and the 1895 city directory cite Manggrum as the correct spelling. See Duckworth, "Black History of Huntington," 3, and *Huntington (West Virginia) City Directory*, 1895–96, 80.

101. *Portsmouth City Directory*, 1881–22, 31.

102. "Chronicles," *(Cincinnati) Chronicle*, January 14, 1898, 2.

103. *Report on Transportation Business in the United States*, Eleventh Census of the United States, 1890 (Washington, D.C.: GPO, 1895), 134. In contrast, the Eastern

Division, based in Staunton, Virginia, comprised more than 5,000 employees (see p. 133). Charles Bias relates, "When contractors completed the road to Huntington, C&O officials divided it into two division[s]. E. T. Smith supervised the Eastern Division with offices in Staunton. Superintendent Joseph Mallory was in charge of the Western Division with offices in Huntington." See Bias, *History of the Chesapeake and Ohio*, 115.

104. *Engineers and Fireman's Age Roster, Huntington Division, 1927*, Chesapeake and Ohio Railroad, Personnel Records, Seniority Rosters, Huntington Division, 1, Chesapeake and Ohio Historical Society, Clifton Forge, Virginia.

105. *Conductors and Brakemen*, Chesapeake and Ohio Railroad, Personnel Records, Seniority Rosters, Huntington Division, folder I, 81–54, Chesapeake and Ohio Historical Society, Clifton, Virginia.

106. Lewis, *In Their Own Interests*, 201.

107. Meier, *Negro Thought in America*, 48.

108. Brier, "Interracial Organizing," 18–43.

109. Gutman, "The Negro and the United Mine Workers," 60–70. Although the United Mine Workers, with its 20,000 members, comprised the largest African American membership of any union in the nation in 1900, it is important to note that from 1900 to 1920, no union affiliated with the railroads, manufacturing, or teachers contained African Americans. In 1890, out of 81 organizations nationwide, only six contained blacks. In 1900, only eleven contained African Americans. In 1910, nineteen contained black members. See *Negro Membership*, 101–3.

110. Anson notes that there is a lack of extant records detailing the early years of the labor movement within the state. "No complete record of the early labor movement in West Virginia—or in any other state for that matter—is obtainable. As early local, and even national, organizations came into existence in this country they usually kept poor records. Then, as these groups passed off the scene or evolved into new groups, their meagre [sic] histories were lost. As a consequence, much of the early story in West Virginia comes from isolated incidents, some trivial and others significant, incomplete union and government reports, and news items of varying importance." See Anson, "History of the Labor Movement," 73.

111. Evelyn L. K. Harris and Frank J. Krebs, "One Hundred Years with West Virginia Labor," West Virginia Centennial Commission, 1963, West Virginia Historical Archives and Manuscripts Collections, West Virginia and Regional History Collection, Charles C. Wise, Jr., Library, West Virginia University, Morgantown, 4.

112. Javersak, "Ohio Valley Trades," 8–10, 37.

113. Ibid., see chapter "The Assembly and Arbitration," 46–101.

114. *1900 Federal Census of Cabell County, West Virginia*, vol. 2, trans., KYOWA Genealogical Society, Huntington, W.V., 1999, 360, 369.

115. Javersak, "The Ohio Valley Trades," 10. For broader examination of the labor movement in West Virginia, see Anson, "History of the Labor Movement," and Posey, "Labor Movement in West Virginia."

116. Hepler, "C&O Patch," 16.

117. Casto, *Huntington*, 37.

118. "News of the C. & O. Shops," *Huntington Advertiser*, March 14, 1900. The "yard" or railroad yard refers to an area housing a complex series of railroad tracks for storing, sorting, or loading/unloading, railroad cars and/or locomotives by manual means.

119. Douglas Imbrogno, "Nellie Remembers . . .," *Huntington Herald-Dispatch*, August 20, 1981.

120. Turner and Cabbell, *Blacks in Appalachia*, 16.

121. Brady, "Reaches 50th Year of Service."

122. Hanshaw, "Train Porter."

123. See Hart, "Actively at Work," and Hart, "Retires on Pension."

124. Lewis, "Before the Founding of Our Church," 8.

125. David Barnes, interviewed by the author, January 18, 2007, and March 13, 2007. Correspondence of Walter L. Barnes to Greg Goode Sr. and Edward Holmes, July 19, 2002, and July 23, 2002. Letters in personal collection of David Barnes, Huntington, W.V. See 1930 Federal Census, and Social Security Administration, *Social Security Death Index*, Master File.

126. Imbrogno, "Nellie Remembers. . . ." For "odds and ends," see "News of the C. & O. Shops," *Huntington Advertiser*, December 18, 1899.

127. Scott, "Progress of the Huntington Negro," 3.

128. Imbrogno, "Nellie Remembers. . . ."

129. Bickley, "Black People," 133–34; African American History of Lawrence County, Ohio, "George Wilson Story, Part One," "George Wilson Story, Part Two," and "George Wilson Story, Part Three," https://lawrencecountyohio.wordpress.com/history/people/african-american-history/george-wilson.

130. For occupational statistics of Huntington's African American population, see Appendix B.

131. Hepler, "C&O Patch," 17.

132. *Huntington Advertiser*, September 8, 1896.

133. Duckworth, *Black History of Huntington*, 7.

134. Mrs. Shelby was born December 25, 1881, in Smith County, Mississippi. "Obituary," Mrs. Almedia Duckworth Shelby, Mt. Zion Baptist Church, Covington, Kentucky, Edna Duckworth Collection, program in possession of author.

135. Ibid.

136. Ancella Bickley notes the brief publication of *The Industrial Messenger*, ca. 1911. She relays no other details about the paper. See Bickley, "Black People," 146. Former Fairmont (West Virginia) State College professor Betty Hart makes no mention of the paper in her study, "A Brief History of the Black Press in West Virginia."

Chapter 4. Community, Race, and Class

1. Foner, *Reconstruction*, 410.

2. Scott, "Progress of the Huntington Negro," 3.

3. Casto, *Huntington*, 25. Providing evidence of the east–west residency patterns is the fact that city transportation was first available in 1888 with an electric streetcar

that ran from the business district east to the Guyandotte Bridge. A second line was franchised in 1890 and ran east from the business district, eventually turning south on Sixteenth Street and east on Eighth Avenue. See Wallace, *Huntington through Seventy-Five Years*.

4. *1880 Census of WV*, 2:3.

5. U.S. Bureau of the Census, *Thirteenth Census*, Population, vol. 3.

6. Ibid., 404–5; and U.S. Bureau of the Census, *Twelfth Census*, vol. 1, 552.

7. Park, "The City."

8. Wade, "Black Gold and Black Folk", 140.

9. Engle, "Mountaineer Reconstruction," 153. Addressing the fear of black social and political equality, historian John R. Sheller writes of the convention, "Proposals were made to change the name of Grant and Lincoln counties to Davis and Lee. Legislators feel that if Negroes were to vote it would be social equality, they would soon enter the schools, enter the legislative halls and that Negroes would come into the state and gain their jobs in industry and public work. Probably the last mentioned was the root of most of the fears." See Sheller, "Negro in West Virginia," 200–201.

10. Ibid., 201.

11. U.S. Bureau of the Census, *Tenth Census*.

12. Commenting on residential spatial organization in antebellum Cincinnati, historian Henry Louis Taylor accurately summarizes the situation in early black Huntington as well: "Blacks were concentrated but did not live in homogenous, racially segregated neighborhoods. They shared the living space with whites from various ethnic groups and social classes. The houses of the rich and the hovels of the poor stood within a stone's throw of each other. Many blacks and whites huddled together in wretched neighborhoods. And almost everywhere dwelling units coexisted with stores, offices, shops, warehouses, and factories. No one group could claim the living space as its own. In such a setting, the riveting of African American behavior to 'place' could not occur." Taylor, "Introduction," 3.

13. *Huntington Independent*, October 16, 1873, and October 23, 1873.

14. Taylor, "Introduction," 4.

15. U.S. Bureau of the Census, *Tenth Census*.

16. *Huntington Advertiser*, October 3, 1885

17. William F. Dusenberry's 1869 diary entries detail travel, including riverboat trips on the Ohio River by "Black William," an employee of "Robert," who was an associate of Dusenberry's. See Eldridge, *Personal Diaries*, 13–14, 16, 18–19, 31–32, 40.

18. *Cabell County West Virginia Heritage*, 87.

19. The twenty-three are: Rev. Nelson Barnett, J. M. Jasper, Jessie Cary, William Morgan, Si Manson, Dean Johnson, William Green, William Green, Manggrum and Johnson, William Freeman, Joe Dill, W. O. James, Winston Bird, John Hider, Beverly Blake, Henry Smith, Sam Curry, J. T. Hoback, Caroline Holley, Charles Sprow, Robert Humphrey, and Obie Smith. See Scott, "Progress of the Huntington Negro," 4.

20. Ibid., 5. The thirty-three are: G. W. Lee, J. L. Thomas, J. W. Fletcher, Isham Scott, Bud Liggins, Thomas Liggins, G. W. Hughes, Susie James, Rev. R. J. Perkins, Gabriel Poindexter, James Liggins, A. D. Lewis, Dr. W. S. Kearney, Alfred Gibbs, R. A.

Woodson, James West, James Woodson, Ed Cobbs, W. O. Fountain, Jack Nellons, Guy Calloway, James A. Collins, G. W. Winston, Prof. C. H. Barnett (lawyer), W. H. Harris, Alex Winston, Samuel Anderson, Miss Josie M. Barnett, Marshall Poindexter, T. W. Winkins, A. D. Mills, "Dock" Dickinson, and Richard Taylor.

21. Bickley, "Black People," 145.

22. See Wallace, *Huntington through Seventy-Five Years*, 12, and Duckworth, *Black History of Huntington*, 2–5.

23. "East End Echoes," *Huntington Advertiser*, June 9, 1896.

24. Hepler, "C & O Patch."

25. See Du Bois, *Black Reconstruction in America*, and Painter, Exodusters.

26. *History of Summers County*, 119.

27. See "John Lewis Griffith," in Caldwell, *History of the American Negro*, available at http://www.wvculture.org/history/histamne/griffith.html; *Huntington, West Virginia Directory, 1895–1896*, 61; and *Chancery Order Book 7*, 385. For Baker, see "Andrew Minor Baker," in Caldwell, *History of American Negro*, http://www.wvculture.org/history/histamne/baker.html.

28. Bickley, "Carter G. Woodson," 61–62, and Biggers, *United States of Appalachia*, 163–64.

29. Bickley, "Carter G. Woodson," 63.

30. Fain, "Forging of a Black Community," 39.

31. Ronald L. Lewis reports, "In 1870 only 36 percent of the black population of central Appalachia resided in the sixteen major coal-producing counties of the fifty-six-county region. By 1920, however, 96 percent of the blacks living in central Appalachia resided in those sixteen coal counties." Lewis, "From Peasant to Proletarian," 81. See also Laing, "Negro Miner in West Virginia"; Simmons, Rankin, and Carter, "Negro Coal Miners"; Bailey, "Judicious Mixture"; and Lawrence, *Appalachian Metamorphosis*. Central Appalachia is recognized as containing the following counties: (Kentucky) Bell, Breathitt, Carter, Clay, Elliott, Estill, Floyd, Harlan, Jackson, Johnson, Knott, Knox, Laurel, Lawrence, Lee, Leslie, Letcher, Magoffin, Martin, Menifee, Morgan, Owsley, Perry, Pike, Powell, Rockcastle, Rowan, Wayne, Wolfe, and Whitley; (Tennessee) Anderson, Campbell, Claiborne, Morgan, and Scott; (Virginia) Buchanan, Dickenson, Lee, Russell, Tazewell, and Wise; (West Virginia) Boone, Braxton, Clay, Fayette, Kanawha, Lincoln, Logan, McDowell, Mercer, Mingo, Nicolas, Raleigh, Summers, Webster, and Wyoming.

32. *Cabell County Marriage Register 2*.

33. Laing, "Negro Miner in West Virginia," 274.

34. Woodson, *Century of Negro Migration*, 116. William H. Becker asserts "four distinguishable but interrelated aspects of manhood, as manifested in the black church tradition: 1) leadership, self-assertion, 2) independence, 3) black identity, and 4) vocation." Becker, "Black Church," 180.

35. "Railroad Incorporation," Deed Index R 18, No. 1 Grantor 1808–1922, 17. The railroads are as follows: 1873–Mud River Railroad Company, Guyandotte Railroad Company; 1875–West Virginia Railroad Company; 1878–Potomac and Ohio Railroad Company; 1879), Baltimore Cincinnati and Western Railway Company; 1881–West

Virginia and Ohio, Guyan Valley; 1882–Guyan River and Logan County, Guyandotte and Great Southern Railroad; 1883–Chesapeake and Ohio; 1886–Chesapeake and Ohio; 1887–Virginia and Ohio, Ohio River.

36. Phil Conley reports that, due to the effects of the Depression of 1873, only two railroads were developed in the state between 1873 and 1881. See Conley, *West Virginia*, 95.

37. Ibid.

38. U.S. Bureau of the Census, *Tenth Census*. The Reynoldses were residents of the county, not Huntington. Isaac was the only black migrant listed from west of the Mississippi River.

39. Goggin, *Carter G. Woodson*, 9.

40. "History of First Baptist Church," 124th Church Anniversary (n.p., 1996), Special Collections, James E. Morrow Library, Marshall University, Huntington, W.V., 1.

41. Burchett, "Promise and Prejudice," 315–16.

42. Kirby, *Darkness at the Dawning*, 23. In his study of Atlanta, Montgomery, Nashville, Raleigh, and Richmond, Howard Rabinowitz notes that travel between Southern urban cities usually resulted in blacks' relegation to second-class status on railroads. Rabinowitz, *Race Relations*.

43. In an ironic twist, the C&O Shops were instructed "to furnish separate apartments [sic] for colored people on their trains." See "News of the C. & O. Shops," *Huntington Advertiser*, February 22, 1900. It is almost a certainty that black laborers assisted in this effort and that they knew the purpose of the work on the cars. We can only speculate about the reaction of black workers in the plant to this development.

44. U.S. Bureau of the Census, *Twelfth Census*, 1900.

45. Booker T. Washington's recollections of his mother's efforts to feed her family in antebellum Virginia add perspective. "Some people blame the Negro for not being more honest; but I can recall many times when, after all was dark and still, in the late hours of the night, when her children had been without food during the day, my mother would awaken us, and we would find that she had gotten from somewhere something in the way of eggs or chickens and cooked the food during the night for us. These eggs and chickens were gotten without my master's permission or knowledge. Perhaps, by some code of ethics, this would be classed as stealing, but deep down in my heart I can never decide that my mother, under such circumstances, was guilty of theft. Had she acted thus as a free woman she would have been a thief, but not so, in my opinion, as a slave. After our freedom no one was stricter than my mother in teaching and observing the highest rules of integrity." Washington, *Autobiography*, 14–15.

46. John L. Jones, "The Story of the Jones Family," *History of the Jones Family*, ed. and ann. by Nancy E. Aiken and Michel S. Perdreau (Bowie, Md.: Heritage, 2001), Local History Collection, Athens County Library Services, Nelsonville, Ohio, 15.

47. Walter and Ida Myers, interviewed by Jackie Fourie, Oral History of Appalachia Project and Drinko Foundation, Special Collections, James E. Morrow Library, Marshall University, March 28, 1996, 32–33.

48. Barnett, "Flies in the Buttermilk," 28.

49. Barnett, "Seven Generations of Barnetts," 322.

50. Strat Douthat, "Son Had to Live in White Society's Shadow," *Huntington Herald-Dispatch*, March 13, 1977.

51. Conceptual assistance supplied by Taylor, "On Slavery's Fringe," 10. Categories found in *Huntington, West Virginia Directory, 1895–1896*.

52. Early black migrant Caroline Holley and laborer Albert Jackson resided there in 1895. U.S. Bureau of the Census, *Tenth Census*; and *Huntington, West Virginia Directory, 1895–1896*.

53. *Huntington, West Virginia Directory, 1895–1896*. The cited numbers do not include examination of pages 25 or 40, which were damaged and are indecipherable. A domestic and unknown occupation constituted the remaining two.

54. *Huntington, West Virginia Directory, 1895–1896*.

55. "Notorious People Fight," *Huntington Advertiser*, January 4, 1896.

56. *Huntington Advertiser*, June 23, 1896.

57. *Huntington Advertiser*, June 24, 1896.

58. Taylor, "On Slavery's Fringe," 26.

59. *Huntington, West Virginia Directory, 1891–1892*, 16.

60. *Huntington, West Virginia Directory, 1895–1896*, 36, 42, 46, 66, 84, 85, 94, 97, 98, 108, 109, 110, and 122.

61. *Huntington, West Virginia Directory, 1895–1896*, and *Huntington, West Virginia, March 1893*, Sanborn-Perris Map Co., 1893, Cabell County Public Library, Special Collections, Huntington, W.V. .

62. Marszalek, "Slave Resistance," 637.

63. After the death of their parents, John and Vicki Edwards, within two years of each other, brothers Harry and James, ages thirteen and nine, found themselves in the Lawrence County Children's Home in 1884. Unable or unwilling to be the guardian, their sixty-six-year-old grandmother Mary Haley, the former Cabell County freewoman and now Portsmouth, Ohio, resident, oversaw their placement in the home. In 1888, after a four-year stay, both boys found homes with adoptive parents within four months of each other. See Martha J. Kounse, *Annotated Register*, 44.

64. For "Loop de Loop" and "Muddy Duck," see *Huntington Advertiser*, April 24, 1903; for "Honky Tonk" see *Huntington Advertiser*, December 8, 1903.

65. *Huntington Advertiser*, February 12, 1903.

66. *Huntington Advertiser*, December 8, 1903.

67. *Huntington Advertiser*, April 25, 1903

68. *Huntington Advertiser*, November 9, 1904.

69. Hunter, *To 'Joy My Freedom*, 171.

70. Edna Duckworth, personal recollections written October 10, 1994, in author's possession.

71. Taylor, *Frontiers of Freedom*, 34.

72. "Nothing but a Stone," *Huntington Advertiser*, June 10, 1899; *Huntington Advertiser*, December 8, 1899; and "Building Permits," *Huntington Advertiser*, November 4, 1904.

73. "One of the most," *Huntington Advertiser*, October 8, 1900; "dens of vices" and "ape yard," *Huntington Advertiser*, August 27, 1904. Though not addressed as such in

the article, the citation may refer to the club, Ape Yard, operated by Sam Graves and Ike Miller.

74. *Huntington Advertiser*, November 22, 1904. Other articles include November 22 and 26, 1904, and December 5, 1904.

75. *Huntington Advertiser*, February 21, 1905

76. Ibid.

77. *Cabell County West Virginia Heritage*, 87.

78. See *The Huntington Advertiser*, June 11, 1874, September 24, 1874, March 11, 1875, and January 16, 1876.

79. Taylor Strauder was convicted of murdering his wife; his attorneys sought to have the decision set aside because no African Americans were on the jury that condemned him. Denied on appeal in the U.S. Circuit Court, the case was argued before the U.S. Supreme Court, which reversed the decision rendered by the Supreme Court of West Virginia and ordered that Strauder be given a new trial. See Jones, "Civil Status of Negroes," 25. For information on jury composition, see Common Pleas Law Criminal Record, Cabell County Circuit Court, book 1, April 10, 1893–July 19, 1895; Common Pleas Law Criminal Record, Cabell County Circuit Court, book 2, November 4, 1895–April 21, 1898; Common Pleas Law Criminal Record, Cabell County Circuit Court, book 3, April 21, 1898–December 31, 1900; Common Pleas Law Criminal Record, Cabell County Circuit Court, book 4, January 17, 1901–July 21, 1902. Earlier records destroyed in courthouse fire in Barboursville. See also "Negroes Serve on Phipps Jury," *Huntington Herald-Dispatch*, September 22, 1931.

80. Virginia experienced an increasing number of lynching incidents during the late nineteenth century—three in 1888, seven in 1889, nine in 1892, and twelve in 1893. See Lebsock, *Murder in Virginia*, 62. For West Virginia figures see Knohaus, "'I Thought Things Would be Different There,'" 26.

81. *Huntington Herald-Dispatch*, February 14, 1909.

82. "A Narrow Escape," *Salt Lake Herald* (Salt Lake City, Utah), May 24, 1895; and "Saved His Neck: The Officers Prevented Ringo from Being Lynched," *Point Pleasant (West Virginia) Weekly Register*, May 29, 1895. For more on Ringo, see Fain, "Buffalo Soldier, Deserter, Criminal."

83. See "Bushel of Coal for his Life," "Mead Still Lives," "His Trial Postponed," "Meads Will Recover," and "Heavy Blow for a Negro," *Huntington Advertiser*, May 21, 1897, May 22, 1897, May 24, 1897, and August 31, 1897.

84. "Will Ask for Pardon," *Huntington Advertiser*, June 9, 1897.

Chapter 5. Institutional Development, Public Space, and Political Aspiration in Early Huntington, 1870–Early 1900s

1. Logan, *Negro Life*, x; Loewen, *Sundown Towns*; and Brown and Owen, *Race in the American South*, 180.

2. "The First Baptist Church of Burlington, 1983," *150th Anniversary Souvenir Book of Providence Regular Missionary Baptist Association, April 15–19, 1984*, Gallia County Historical and Genealogical Society, Gallipolis, Ohio.

3. There is some evidence that Nelson Barnett received his training and perhaps his first job at Macedonia. In contrast, there is no doubt that he was linked to the church and its members during his life in Huntington.

4. Cradic, "Partial History."

5. See "Why We Celebrate."

6. *City of Huntington Common Council Proceedings*, January 6, 1872, 17.

7. *Daily Press* (Huntington), August 9, 1872.

8. U.S. Bureau of the Census, *Compendium of Population Statistics*, 559.

9. There is some dispute over this claim. However, city records clearly show First Baptist Church petitioning the city council for recognition first. Thus, it is the oldest recognized black denomination in the city. However, Ebenezer lays rightful claim to the oldest church edifice in the city.

10. Lewis, "Before the Founding of Our Church," 3. Lewis refers to Tucker as "Aunt" but fails to identify whether the designation is a term of endearment or family relation.

11. "History of the Church," 1.

12. Bickley, "Black People and the Huntington Experience," 135.

13. *Huntington Advertiser*, November 4, 1875.

14. *Chancery Order Book* 3, 209. Although not cited in the original petition, it is believed that Jennie Hyder, possibly a member of the Hyder family who lived in Cabell County before the influx of black migrants after the Civil War, was a founder. See Bickley, "Black People and the Huntington Experience,"135.

15. "Our History," 1. Bickley states that the congregation "began worshipping on Spring Hill in the 1880s, possibly sharing space with another congregation." See "Our Mount Vernons," 123. Both Foes and Shafer, like Barnett, were illiterate at the time of their "calling," a common occurrence for the era. In 1870 black laborer Foes was the father of two, while Shafer was a mulatto farmer and father of one. See U.S. Bureau of the Census, *Ninth Census*.

16. *Huntington Advertiser*, May 6, 1875.

17. Lewis, "Before the Founding of Our Church," 3.

18. As Trotter explains, "Rooted deeply in the religious experience of southern blacks, the church in southern West Virginia helped to sustain and reinforce the black workers' spiritual and communal beliefs and practices through sermons, revival meetings, baptismal ceremonies, and funeral rites." Trotter, "Formation of Black Community," 286.

19. *Huntington Independent*, September 11, 1873. The article states the name of the building as the "Union Chapel." See also *Huntington Advertiser*, May 6, 1875.

20. Notifications by Ebenezer Methodist Episcopal Church, Mt. Olive Baptist Church, the "Baptist Church (colored) of Huntington," and the Methodist Episcopal Church of Barboursville to the Cabell County Circuit Court list no black women as elected church trustees. See *Chancery Order Book 3*, 209; *Chancery Order Book 4*, 510; *Chancery Order Book 6*, 81, 267; *Chancery Order Book 7*, 385; and *Chancery Order Book 10*, 459–60.

21. In *The Negro Church in America*, historian E. Franklin Frazier provides valuable insight into the centrality of the church and male leadership in community formation when he states, "As a result of the elimination of Negroes from the political life of the American community, the Negro church became the arena of political activity. The church was the main area of social life in which Negroes could aspire to become leaders of men. It was the area of social life where ambitious individuals could achieve distinction and the symbols of status. The church was the arena in which the struggle for power and the thirst for power could be satisfied. This was especially important to Negro men who had never been able to assert themselves and assume the dominant male role, even in family relations, as defined by American culture." Frazier, *Negro Church in America* (Liverpool: University of Liverpool, 1963), 48–49.

22. Trotter, *Coal, Class, and Color*, 42.

23. James Sands, *Sunday Times Sentinel* (Gallipolis), February 22, 2004. As a youth Bryant attended elementary studies and normal coursework in Ironton before converting at the age of fifteen and joining Macedonia Baptist. See Caldwell, *History of the American Negro*.

24. In no particular order, Barnett served at Macedonia, Mt. Olive Baptist, First Baptist Church of Burlington, First Baptist Church of Huntington, First Baptist Church of Glouster, Ohio, and First Baptist Church of Guyandotte. Bryant served at First Baptist Church of Glouster, Ohio, Bethel Missionary Baptist in Morgan Township, Ohio, African Zion Baptist in Malden, W.Va, as well as First Baptist of Charleston, where he taught the black school at Baker's Fork in 1888. See "History of the Church," 1; "Macedonia Missionary Baptist Church." Randall and Gilmer, "Black Past," 21, 52; and "Minutes of Macedonia Church," 104–31. For a more expansive examination of the historical metamorphosis of the black church in West Virginia and the role of black pastors, see Trotter, "Formation of Black Community," 292–94, and Trotter, *Coal, Class, and Color*, 39–59.

25. *Cabell County West Virginia Heritage*, 87.

26. "Isaac Vinton Bryant," http://www.wvculture.org/history/histamne/bryant.html.

27. "Minutes of Macedonia Church," 115, 118.

28. "Colored Baptist in Convention at St. Albans a Pronounced Success," *Charleston Daily Mail*, June 1, 1895. In the early 1900s, Perkins would be the founder and president of West Virginia Seminary and College. See "Church History," in *In Memory, Mortgage Burning Program*.

29. "Colored Baptists Are Coming," *Huntington Advertiser*, August 24, 1898.

30. *Cabell County Marriage Register* vol. 2.

31. Ibid.

32. Lewis, "Story of My Life," 8.

33. Barnett performed 23, while Bryant performed 26. See *Black Marriage Records, 1851–1905*, 56, 58, and "Mrs. C.C. Barnett," *Herald Dispatch* (Huntington), November 30, 1909.

34. *Huntington Advertiser*, October 22, 1874.

35. An article citing a local church fundraiser and reprinted in a Huntington newspaper makes these points more explicit: "Rev. W. W. Foreman (colored) of the Methodist church preached in the grove on the flat to large congregations last Sunday morning and evening. Both sermons were very creditable indeed. The speaker seemed very familiar with his subject and handled it well. Quite a number of white persons also attended. A collection was taken up both in the morning and evening, and although no considerable amount was raised, all seemed to contribute something, and from this fact our white friends might draw a profitable lesson. The colored people contemplate building a church at this place soon." See *Huntington Advertiser*, September 16, 1875.

36. *Diary of Reverend William Parker Walker*, entries from August 15–18, 1877; August 13 and 14, 1879; and August 19, 1880.

37. Ibid. For entries on visits to the "Shops," see entries from February 10, March 10, April 26 and 28, and May 10, 1881; and March 20, 1883. For "visiting pastor" see entries from December 15, 1881; September 24, 1883; February 16, 1885; and June 26, 1887. For "welcoming" visiting pastor, see August 23, 1885. While few, Walker did preside over ten black weddings in Huntington between 1882 and 1899. See *Cabell County (West) Virginia Marriages, 1851–1899*.

38. In all cases, the accused were granted a meeting before a church-appointed standing committee to state their side of the story. Given the increased social linkages with blacks and whites, concentrated population pockets, and small population, social ostracism from church congregants carried weight. Meeting before the committee and confessing to the transgression resulted in forgiveness by the church. The mission of the church was one of perpetuation and standardization of community-sanctioned moral and ethical codes, not punishment. In this manner, the church attempted to propagate standards of decency and neighborliness. The church committee was not a court, and it did have a limit to its patience. A number of transgressors elected not to defend or explain themselves. Failure to show before the committee in a timely fashion resulted in the "hand of fellowship being withdrawn," and the church member was officially removed from membership rolls. See "Minutes of Macedonia Church," 1–118. In this manner, black Baptist churches mirrored white Baptist churches, which also required strict requirements from its members. In March 1892 Huntington's Fifth Avenue Baptist Church dismissed 143 members who later formed Twentieth Street Baptist Church. See Brand, "Fifth Avenue Baptist Church," 80.

39. This action by Macedonia Baptist follows those of white Baptist churches. In 1878 Fifth Avenue Baptist passed a resolution stating that "the modern dance is contrary to the spirit of Christianity, subversive of piety, offensive to God, grievous to all devoted pious people, and condemned by the outside world." See Brand, "Fifth Avenue Baptist Church," 81–82. Brown and Kimball argue, "By the 1880s, many activities, such as dancing, were barred from many church facilities, and the issue of whether it was immoral for church members to dance became a matter of serious debate." See Brown and Kimball, "Mapping the Terrain," 97–98, and Hunter, *To 'Joy My Freedom*, 168–86.

40. Sands, *Sunday Times Sentinel* (Gallipolis), February 22, 2004. Though his response is hidden from the public record, it is difficult to believe Bryant would go against prevailing church doctrine and middle-class standards. Commenting on the issue of dancing, Tera W. Hunter notes, "Controversies over dance during the period reveal the power of dancing as a cultural form and the way it embodied (literally and figuratively) racial, class, and sexual tension in the urban South." Hunter, *To 'Joy My Freedom*, 170–71.

41. Brown and Kimball elaborate on increasing black entry into the public space during the late nineteenth century, a development that also marked a concomitant shift in the primacy of the church as the lone public space "owned by African Americans." In response to this development, and in the quest to distinguish themselves from secular places, church authorities sought to limit social activities in their buildings. Brown and Kimball argue, "By the 1880s, many activities, such as dancing, were barred from many church facilities, and the issue of whether it was immoral for church members to dance became a matter of serious debate." See Brown and Kimball, "Mapping the Terrain," 97–98. For chapter, see 66–115.

42. Though few, articles representing friendly, even equal social relations between blacks and whites occurred; Johnson explains that not many discuss the interracial working environment, since blacks were seen as both inferior and necessary to the city's prosperity. Like newspapers nationwide, very little mention is made of hiring practices, promotions, or training situations. Instead, emphasis is on miscegenation, then considered a criminal offense, and on mixing of children in the classroom, an issue of considerable discord. Johnson, "Not a Story to Be Told," 118, 129. Undoubtedly, Huntington's black residents discussed and debated the question of integration, yet no sampling of Negro opinion appears publicly in the newspapers printed in Huntington from June 1872 to February 1876, or in the Macedonian Church Minutes of the era. Newspaper articles give some indication that Long was an integrationist, but print media tended to portray all blacks as integrationists rather than pro-education. See Johnson, "Not a Story to Be Told," 120. No matter black sentiment, whites remained adamantly opposed to mixed-race schools. Newspaper articles expressed distrust and hostility to the Radical Republicans over the civil rights bill proposing mixed-race schools. An 1874 article asked, "Will West Virginia consent to have mixed race schools? Suppose she does not consent, what then?" Some months later, the question was again raised in the local newspaper, "Shall the party of Civil Rights and Mixed Schools get the power in the State and destroy the public school system as it did in North Carolina?" See *Huntington Advertiser*, January 29, 1874, and September 10, 1874.

43. Wade, "Black Gold and Black Folk," 190. For a detailed examination of the evolution of West Virginia legislative and legal processes regarding primary and secondary education for the state's black citizens, see Talbott, "Some Legislative and Legal Aspects, Part II," 110–20.

44. Talbott, "Some Legislative and Legal Aspects, Part II," 116.

45. Sheller, "Negro in West Virginia," 219–20. Stephen D. Engle cites the needed class size in 1866 at 16 students, reduced to fifteen in 1867 due to the scattered nature

of black communities. In 1873 the numerical requirement was raised to 25. See Engle, "Mountaineer Reconstruction," 146.

46. Greene, "Education of Negroes," 433.

47. Wade, "Black Gold and Black Folk," 191–202. Noteworthy are the efforts of John R. Clifford, the state's first practicing lawyer and editor, who challenged racial discrimination in schools before the West Virginia Supreme Court. In *Martin v. Board of Education* (1896), Clifford asked the high court to allow an exemption for blacks living in rural school districts without black schools to attend white schools. He lost. In *Williams v. Board of Education* (1898), Clifford continued his fight against segregated schools. Representing a black teacher in Tucker County paid to teach for only five months while white teachers taught and were paid for eight months, he won a civil rights victory when the State Supreme Court ruled that school boards had to provide equal pay for black and white teachers and keep black schools open for same term as white schools. In addition to the courts, Clifford fought for civil rights through his paper, the *Pioneer Press*. When it closed in 1917, it was the longest-running black newspaper in the country. See Rice, "J. R. Clifford," and "J. R. Clifford," West Virginia Archives and History, http://www.wvculture.org/history/clifford.html.

48. Du Bois, *Black Reconstruction in America*, 641.

49. Woodson, "Early Negro Education," 51.

50. "Isaac Vinton Bryant," in Caldwell *History of the American Negro*. Sheller cites Bryant as Virginia born. See Sheller, "Negro in West Virginia," 230.

51. "Makers of Providence History."

52. Woodson, "Early Negro Education," 51. The 1870 census lists 41 Negro school age children residing in the county. Guyandotte possessed the largest number with 19, followed by Barboursville with 17.

53. *Huntington Independent*, September 4, 1873, and September 11, 1873. See also Wallace, *Cabell County Annals and Families*, 140. The building seems to have been rented, as no records have been found of a city-owned edifice during this period. See *Grantor Index to Deeds 1* and *Grantee Index to Deeds 1*, which reveal no record of any real estate transaction involving a Robert Long.

54. Bickley, "Black People,"136.

55. "Council Proceedings," *Huntington Advertiser*, October 22, 1874. Regarding historical conditions for the state's black teachers, Dr. Byrd Prillerman writes, "It must be said to the honor of the school officials that absolute fairness is shown to the colored teachers both in the matter of examinations and salaries. If a colored teacher holds a first grade certificate, he is paid the same salary as a white teacher holding the same grade of certificate. If a colored teacher has ten pupils he has as long a term as any other teacher in the district . . . When one compares these conditions with the reports of the State Superintendent of Georgia for 1902, the contrast is very marked. According to his report, the average monthly salary paid white teachers that year was $36.72, and that paid colored teachers, $26.08." See Prillerman, "Growth of the Colored Schools," 275–76.

56. *City of Huntington Common Council Proceedings*, 122, 140, 151. For "delay" see "Colored School," *Huntington Advertiser*, October 7, 1875. See also Duckworth, *His-

tory of Black Huntington, 4, and Rick Baumgartner, "First Families of Huntington," repr. from *Huntington Advertiser*, 18-part series, October 28, 1976–March 24, 1977, Special Collections, James E. Morrow Library, Marshall University, Huntington, W.Va., 26–27.

57. Plantania, "Getting Ready for Life," 22.

58. *Huntington Advertiser*, October 22, 1874.

59. In 1875 Cabell County was home to fifty-eight schools, of which fifty-seven were for white students only. See "Council Proceedings," *Huntington Advertiser*, August 26, 1875. Booker T. Washington, speaking of his educational experience in Malden, recalled, "This experience of a whole race beginning to go to school for the first time, presents one of the most interesting studies that has ever occurred in connection with the development of any race. Few people who were not right in the midst of the scenes can form any exact idea of the intense desire which the people of any race showed for education. As I have stated, it was a whole race trying to go to school. Few were too young, and none too old to make the attempt to learn. As fast as any kind of teachers could be secured, not only were day schools fill, but night schools as well. The great ambition of the older people was to learn to read the Bible before they died. With this end in view, men and women who were fifty or seventy-five years old would often be found in night school. Sunday schools were formed soon after freedom, but the principal book studied in the Sunday school was the spelling book. Day school, night school, Sunday school, were always crowded, and often many had to be turned away for want of room." Washington, *Up From Slavery*, 30.

60. *Huntington Advertiser*, December 24, 1874.

61. In total, Wilson taught in Huntington for 13 years before relocating to Proctorville, Ohio, to teach. During the course of his teaching career, Wilson attended Oberlin College in 1884 and secured teaching jobs in Guyandotte and Barboursville, and Louisa and Blaine, Kentucky, before leaving the profession and resettling in Ohio. For Wilson family history see, Martha J. Kounse and Sara M. Strohmeyer, "George Wilson Story, Part One," "George Wilson Story, Part Two," and "George Wilson Story, Part Three," *African American History of Lawrence County, Ohio*, 2004, https://lawrencecountyohio.wordpress.com/history/people/african-american-history/george-wilson/. See also *City of Huntington Common Council Proceedings*, 79, 110, and 437.

62. Wallace, *Cabell County Annals and Families*, 141. No information was found on the designation, "Number 4 Certificate." Both *The History of Education in West Virginia* and *The School Laws of West Virginia* refer to three grade levels of teaching certification. As best as author can determine, Number 4 refers to the lowest grade obtainable to teach within the county, and perhaps the state, and was a type of provisional teaching certification, lasting four years, implemented to meet the short-term needs of attracting qualified teachers. Some confirmation of this analysis is revealed by a former Cabell County superintendent comments, "The history of teachers' examinations in the State has been one of vexing variety to the teachers and school officials, but has steadily moved forward in the direction of long term certificates for high grade teachers, and frequent examinations for beginners." See Superintendent B. L. Butcher, "The Transitional Period," in Ambler, *History of Education in West Virginia*, 50. Regarding Cabell

County, Ira F. Hatfield, Cabell County superintendent, alludes to the difficulty of finding teachers when he notes, "These schools were presided over by teachers imported from Ohio, Pennsylvania and other states, who, at best, possessed only the rudiments of education." See Ira F. Hatfield, "Cabell County," in Ambler, *History of Education in West Virginia*, 108. For regulations of teaching certification, see *School Law of West Virginia*, 34.

There is some disagreement over the identities, title, and tenure of Huntington's first black teachers. Woodson relays this report, "The teacher first employed was Mrs. Julia Jones, a lady who had most of the rudiments of education. Some old citizens refer to James Liggins as the first teacher in this community. In this precarious status of stinted support the school did not undergo any striking development during the first years. Not until 1882, some years after the school had been removed to Huntington itself, was there any notable change." Woodson, "Early Negro Education," 51. Qtd. from original source, Scott, "Colored School of Huntington," 266–67. Jones was from White Sulphur Springs, W.Va. The Great Annual Harvest Program of the Sixteenth Street Baptist Church notes, "The first Negro school of Huntington was established in 1876. It was started on Spring Hill with less than ten pupils. Mrs. Chink Jones of White Sulphur Springs, W. Va., near Virginia, was its first teacher. Later, 1877, the school was moved to 12th Street, and in 1879 was moved to Holderby Grove. On account of increased enrollment, in 1881, one room was added and two teachers, Frank James and Mrs. Maude Johnson were employed. Later William McKinley was made principal." See "Huntington Schools."

63. Plantania, "Getting Ready for Life," 22. Plantania reports that after five years at his post Mr. James died, followed seven years later by Mrs. James, of an epidemic. Woodson challenges some aspects of Plantania's account.

64. Matthews, *Gallia One-Room Schools*, 77.

65. Woodson reports that Mr. James worked until 1886, by which time he had "brought the institution to the rank of that of the grammar school, beginning at the same time some advanced classes commonly taught in the high schools. He was an earnest worker, willing to sacrifice everything for the good of the cause. While thus spending his energy as a sacrifice for many, he passed away respected by his pupils and honored by the patrons of the school. His wife continued for a number of years thereafter to render the system the same efficient service as the popular primary teacher upon which the success of the work of the higher grades largely depended, until she passed away in 1899. See Woodson, "Early Negro Education," 51.

66. Scott, "Colored School of Huntington," 267.

67. Ibid. "City Schools," November 18, 1875, and December 30, 1875. The disparity between male and female daily-attendance figures is largely attributable to the greater number of male students and the greater number of males in the general population. But one cannot rule out the fluid demands of childrearing, family caretaking responsibilities, and household chores, or the rigid nature of domestic employment, all of which affected young school-age females. Perhaps some black females or their families placed less value on the regular attendance of school. Or, perhaps, the travel

distance was too great or navigation too difficult. In truth, it could have been a combination of any or all of these reasons.

68. U.S. Bureau of the Census, *Tenth Census*. It is difficult to ascertain whether black females choose not to attend school or their families' lack of financial wherewithal precluded such contemplation. What is known is that black women chose, for a time, to invest in the more viable option—namely, employment and family. In a town with ever-increasing affluence and a great influx of single males, white and black, many no doubt predatory, it is reasonable to assume that black, working-class mothers sought ways to protect their daughters' "respectability" and shield them from situations of potential ridicule, shame, harassment, and the indignities and dangers of sexual assault. In a segregated society, both the street and the workplace offered little in the way of protection. Speaking on black women in twentieth-century Detroit, Victoria W. Walcott maintains that working-class African American women often found refuge in same-sex venues that discouraged heterosociability and were thus lauded by female-uplift ideologues. See Walcott, *Remaking Respectability*, 24.

69. "Report of City Schools," December 19, 1885.

70. See "City Schools," *Huntington Advertiser*, October 24, 1885; "Public Schools," *Huntington Advertiser*, November 21, 1885; "Report of City Schools," *Huntington Advertiser*, December 19, 1885; and "Non-Attendance at the Public Schools," *Huntington Advertiser*, January 2, 1886. Unfortunately, figures detailing the gender composition are lacking, preventing further examination of this phase of Huntington's black school circumstance.

71. "The City Schools," *Huntington Advertiser*, January 30, 1886.

72. "Council Proceedings," *Huntington Advertiser*, October 10, 1885.

73. U.S. Bureau of the Census, *Tenth Census of the United States*.

74. Ambler, *History of Education in West Virginia*, 229. Edward Albert Cubby relates that in 1890, in contrast to the state average daily attendance of 63 percent, for the five southwest West Virginia counties of Boone, Lincoln, Logan, McDowell, and Wyoming, average daily attendance was 51 percent. See Cubby, "Transformation," 43–44.

75. Scott, "Progress of the Huntington Negro," 5.

76. See both Plantania, "Getting Ready for Life," 21–27, and Bickley, "Our Mount Vernons," 118–22. Biographical information on McKinney published in 1895 includes the following: "He attended the public schools of his county until he was seventeen, at which age he began his first school, teaching in Fayette county, W.Va. He has taught in the schools of his own home, in the schools of Charleston, and is now filling his seventh year as principal of the colored school of our city. He came to this city in the fall of 1889." See "The First School Building," *Huntington Herald*, December 14, 1895.

77. Goggin, *Carter G. Woodson*, 1

78. Plantania, "Getting Ready for Life," 27; *Cabell County West Virginia Heritage*, 87; Barnett, "Short History of Seven Generations," 322–23; Whear, "Carter G. Woodson"; and see *Huntington Herald*, December 14, 1895, for names of teachers and biography of Professor McKinney.

79. *Cabell County West Virginia Heritage*, 87, and Barnett, "History of Seven Generations," 322–23.

80. Scott, "Progress of the Huntington Negro," 5.

81. *Huntington Advertiser*, August 12, 1895.

82. The rise of Douglass coincided with the rise of the black education system within the state, largely linked to Byrd Prillerman. His continuing efforts and advocacy as a college professor, administrator, and one of the founding members of the West Virginia Teachers' Association, the first black teachers' organization in the state, greatly assisted black aspiration. Due in fact to denied entry into the white West Virginia Education Association, the WVST facilitated teacher professional development and educational advancement for the state's black youth. The organization functioned successfully until integration in the aftermath of *Brown v. the Board of Education*. See Wade, "Black Gold and Black Folk," 193, and Sullivan, *Encyclopedia of West Virginia*, s.v. "West Virginia State Teachers' Association," by Ancella R. Bickley, 771. James D. Anderson's study on the educational experiences of Southern blacks immediately after the Civil War, *The Education of Blacks in the South*, is instructive. For, like their brethren farther south, the city's black residents demonstrated the integral role ex-slaves played in the establishment of the public-school system in the South and the criticality of their ideological imperatives and organized efforts to develop an educational system appropriate to defend and extend their emancipation. Anderson, *Education of Blacks*, 19–25. In his study of race relations in the urban South, Howard Rabinowitz illustrated how whites increasingly accommodated themselves to black access to, rather than exclusion from, essential resources and human services. The color line was not a fixed phenomenon; it was not entirely imposed by white racism, and it was not uniformly negative in its results. Rabinowitz, *Race Relations*. Tera W. Hunter notes, "African Americans used segregated spaces to bolster their autonomy and collective power and to escape exploitation by whites." Hunter, *To 'Joy My Freedom*, 100. The establishment of Douglass did not stop black aspiration for education beyond high school. In fall 1895 the West Virginia Collegiate Institute (not to be confused with the state institution) broke ground in Central City, along the western edge of Huntington. Arrangements were conducted with B. D. Elder to secure his residence and grounds as the site. The three-man board of directors, presided over by W. O. James, C. H. Duvall from Pittsburgh as secretary, and Rev. R. E. Brown from Dayton as manager, hired Professor S. L. M. Francis of the West Indies as the institute's president. For the next year, various newspaper articles reported on the progress of the school, including the projection that fifty students were scheduled for enrollment upon its November opening. Yet the institution met an ignominious fate, for in the spring of the next year, Duvall, the general manager of what was alternately termed the West Virginia Female Collegiate Institute or the West Virginia Normal Collegate [sic] Institute, was arrested for obtaining goods under false pretenses. Moses Butler and W. O. James were among those posting bond for Duvall; newspapers discontinue mention of the institution, and no records concerning it have been found. Duvall's arrest, the institution's demise, and the lack of subsequent efforts to revitalize it suggest attempts to found it were conducted poorly at best; at worst,

the efforts encompassed little more than a scam. *Huntington Advertiser*, September 26, 1895, October 5 and 22, 1895, December 12, 1895, and January 3, 1896; and Bickley, "Black People," 139. For particulars on charges and trial, see "C. H. Duval Bound Over," *Huntington Advertiser*, February 3, 1896. Local newspapers alternatively use Duval and Duvall as last names. The author has elected to use spelling of last name presented in initial newspaper references.

83. "The Douglass High School," *Huntington Advertiser*, May 11, 1901. Davis Opera House was built by B. T. Davis on the southeast corner of Third Avenue and Eighth Street in 1885 for $36,000. In 1892, after remodeling, it was renamed the Huntington Theater. See Casto, *Huntington*, 62.

84. Two examples substantiate this claim. One newspaper article, "Blue Grass Excursionists," recounted the visit of "Eleven Hundred Colored People" to the city for the day. Another reported that in the fall of 1898, members of the Tenth United States Calvary passed through the city "in three long sections" of the C&O. It continued, "Every man below the grade of commissioned officer is of African blood and it is safe to say that a more gentlemanly soldiers have never passed through this city. For "Blue Grass," see *Huntington Advertiser*, September 2, 1895. For "U. S. Calvary," see *Huntington Advertiser*, October 10, 1898.

85. *Huntington Advertiser*, August 15, 1895.

86. Starting in the late 1890s, local newspaper articles indicate the metamorphosis in the use of public space within Huntington. I attribute this phenomenon "to a growing assertiveness, increasing cultural maturation, and growing racial solidarity" of Huntington's black community. For insight into Huntington see Fain, "Forging of a Black Community," 92–111. For a discussion on the ways blacks influenced the "'moral geography' of southern urbanization," see Brown and Kimball, "Mapping the Terrain," 97–98. For chapter, see 66–115.

87. *Huntington Advertiser*, July 5, 1898.

88. *Huntington Advertiser*, July 12, 1898.

89. The late-nineteenth-century metamorphosis in the use of public space corresponds to a growing assertiveness, increasing cultural maturation, and growing racial solidarity, albeit to varying degrees and in differing ways, of black enclaves throughout the South. It also helps to gain access to the ways public space was perhaps contested by Huntington's black residents in an urban environment, what Brown and Kimball, in their study of late-nineteenth-century Richmond, label "the 'moral geography' of southern urbanization." See "Mapping the Terrain of Black Richmond," 97–98. In contrast to the immediate post–Civil War period, when churches served as an uncontested public forum, performing a multiplicity of political and leisure purposes, and thus representing a variety of "space," the claim and use of alternative secular venues by the black residents of the Ohio Valley was an overtly political act against the prevailing status quo. While suggestive of a commonality of circumstance and purpose by its participants against proscriptions from city whites, it was also a rebuttal against the city's conservative middle-class religious elements, black and white, who attempted to circumscribe certain social activities.

90. In 1929, at the West Virginia State Education Association convention held in Huntington, the official journal of the convention trumpeted the city's economic clout: "Not only does Huntington manufacture fifty million dollars' worth of goods, but she distributes the greater part of the products of the rest of the country which comes into this territory. Within the city practically every form of iron and steel necessities can be had. Other products are chinaware, tobacco, stoves, furniture, caskets, shoes, monel [nickel alloys] metal, glass and building materials." See *The West Virginia School Journal, Huntington Convention Special 1929*, West Virginia State Education Association, 9. For information on black proletarianism, see W. E. B. Du Bois, *Black Reconstruction in America*; Lewis, "From Peasant to Proletarian; Saville, *Work of Reconstruction*; and Trotter, *Black Milwaukee*; Trotter, *Coal, Class, and Color*; and Trotter, "Formation of Black Community."

91. See Moss, "Negro and Recreation," 2. In a 1924 essay, prominent West Virginian, attorney, and activist T. G. Nutter asserts a more positive circumstance for black miners living in mining towns, contending that "social, educational, and religious activities, sanitation are superior to those found in the usual small town." See "T. Gillis Nutter, West Virginia," 289–90.

92. *Huntington Chamber of Commerce*, 8–9.

93. Walter and Ida Myers, interviewed by Jackie Fourie, *Oral History of Appalachia Project*, 12.

94. "Brevities," *Huntington Advertiser*, May 29, 1902.

95. "Big Day at Clyffside," *Huntington Advertiser*, August 19, 1902, and Bickley, "Black People," 140.

96. "Trolley Ride for Pythians," and "The Colored Pythians in Session," *Huntington Advertiser*, July 23, 1902.

97. "Brevities That Will Interest You," *Huntington Advertiser*, September 22, 1902.

98. "Afro-American Notes," *Herald-Dispatch Sunday*, September 12, 1909, and "Emancipation Day to be Celebrated," *Herald-Dispatch*, September 22, 1909.

99. Carrie Simmons, "Huntington, W.Va.," *Pittsburgh Courier*, September 9, 1911.

100. Walter and Ida Myers interview, 11.

101. Before her untimely death in 1909, Gallipolis native and teacher Katherine "Kate" A. Barnett (formerly Whiting), the first wife of Dr. C. C. Barnett, was said to be one of the home's staunchest advocates. Married in Gallipolis in 1901 by Rev. I. V. Bryant, the Barnetts were married only a brief eight years. Barnett married nurse Clara B. Matthews of Farmville, Virginia, in October 1912. In 1920, the Barnetts established the Barnett Hospital and Nurses Training School, with Clara designated as superintendent. See Karen Nance and Johnny Nance, *Draft Proposal: Rehabilitation of the Historic Barnett/City Hospital* (n.p., 2006), transcript in author's files, 3–4; Barnett, "Seven Generations of Barnetts," 325.

102. "West Virginia Colored Orphans' Home," 444–45; "At Colored Orphans Home" and "Many Visitors Were Present," *Huntington Advertiser*, September 29 and October 2, 1900, as well as May 13, 1904, and June 23 and 25, 1904, editions.

103. *Public Documents of West Virginia*, 3:327.

104. Ibid.

105. Composite history derived from Bickley, "Black People," 143. Bickley explains, "According to Rev. McGhee's daughter, Mary Laura McGhee Hairston (nicknamed 'Coonie'), the residents were taught to farm and care for the orchard that was on the place. Additionally, they learned to make bricks, taught by a craftsman that Booker T. Washington sent from Tuskegee. In the first years, Rev. McGhee supported the home through donations received from churches and individuals. In addition to money, donors sent barrels of clothing. See also "West Virginia Colored Orphans' Home," 444–45; and, "At Colored Orphans Home" and "Many Visitors were Present," *Huntington Advertiser*, September 29 and October 2, 1900, as well as May 13, 1904, and June 23 and 25, 1904, editions. Census data derived from U.S. Bureau of the Census, *Twelfth Census*, roll T623 1756, p. 20B, enumeration district 6.

106. *Huntington (West Virginia) Directory, 1891–92*, 57–58.

107. *Huntington Herald*, December 14, 1895. All cited black fraternal orders originated after rejection by white charters. For information on the growth of benevolent and fraternal organizations within the state, see Trotter, "Formation of Black Community," 289–90.

108. For example, Principal William McKinney was a member of the Odd Fellows, the Knights of Pythias, and the Freemasons. See "The First School Building," *Huntington Herald*, December 14, 1895. The nature of development of Huntington's black institutions makes important links to Kenneth L. Kusmer's examination of "the positive ways" black organizations, institutions, and leadership affected black community formation. Joe W. Trotter illuminates the importance of these organizations to southern West Virginia when he argues participation in institution-building activities by African Americans reflected and stimulated the rise of vigorous black leadership. See Kusmer, *Ghetto Takes Shape*, and Trotter, "Formation of Black Community," 285.

109. For quote, "reinforce communal and spiritual aspects . . ." see Trotter, "Formation of Black Community," 290. Reporting on the cornerstone-laying ceremony of the First Baptist Church of Huntington, one newspaper article related, "Many colored persons from Charleston, Hinton [West Virginia] and other points east on the C. and O. were present. The members of the Masonic Lodge, colored, turned out in a body." See *Huntington Advertiser*, September 28, 1896. The fact that black benevolent societies arrived in Huntington a full 25 years after the city's formation and the onset of significant black migrant influx is perplexing, especially given the urgency with which Huntington's black residents addressed its educational and religious aspirations. By 1881, Portsmouth, Ohio, was home to both a branch of the Colored Masonry, started August 21, 1872, and a branch of Colored Odd Fellows. See *Portsmouth City Directory, 1881–2*, 31, 33. A lodge of the Order of Twelve, "a colored organization exclusively, based upon the secret order formed in 1852 to operate the famous underground railroad system, and operated since the emancipation upon beneficiary principles," was formed in Ironton, Ohio, in 1888. See the *Ironton Register*, February 9, 1888.

110. "Samuel L. Starks," in Caldwell, *History of the American Negro*, http://www.wvculture.org/history/histamne/bryant.html.

111. "Douglas League Held Meeting," *Huntington Dispatch*, June 10, 1908.

112. "Negro Pythians are in Session," *Huntington Dispatch*, August 5, 1908.

113. "News of Colored Folk," *Huntington Herald-Dispatch*, February 14, 1909.

114. "Afro-American Notes," *Herald-Dispatch Sunday*, November 21, 1909.

115. In the end, the ratification of a new constitution was achieved, revising much but not nearly comprising the revolutionary agenda first envisioned. Among the key provisions left intact: the right of black citizens to vote and seek public office remained, as well as a free but segregated public school system.

116. *Huntington Daily Press*, August 20, 1872.

117. *Huntington Independent*, September 4, 1873.

118. No mention of Long is revealed in the 1860, 1870, or 1880 Cabell County censuses, the 1880 West Virginia state census, or the 1870 Lawrence County census. Marriage records include a Robert Long, age twenty-nine, son of W. and N. Long, who married Susan Titts, age twenty-three, daughter of T. and E. Titts, in July 1872. See *Cabell County (West) Virginia Marriages*, 86.

119. See *Huntington Independent*, April 24, 1873, September 4, 1873, and October 16, 1873, and *Huntington Advertiser*, September 24, 1873, for examples.

120. "Police Matters," *Huntington Advertiser*, April 16, 1874.

121. *Huntington Daily Press*, August 20, 1872.

122. See "Colored Meeting," *Huntington Advertiser*, March 26, 1874, and April 2, 1874; and "Political Speaking," *Huntington Advertiser*, September 24, 1874.

123. In marked contrast to the disenfranchisement of black citizens throughout the South, Trotter argues, "Black coal miners in southern West Virginia exercised a growing impact on state and local politics. West Virginia blacks developed a highly militant brand of racial solidarity, marked by persistent demands for full equality, albeit on a segregated basis." See Trotter, "Formation of Black Community," 291. Notably, at a time when blacks helped shift the balance of power in the state to the Republicans after two decades of Democratic rule, they largely failed to make significant inroads within the party. The notable exception was in McDowell County where the pioneering achievements of blacks there, including the 1888 election of Christopher Payne, the state's first black legislator, forced the Republican Party to respect the black vote. Wade writes, "There were several outstanding men in this pioneer group: Christopher Payne, Samuel Starks, James Hazelwood, Phil Waters, H. H. Railey, James M. Ellis, John Neal, J. McHenry Jones, J. R. Clifford, Stanley McNorton, and J. Rupert Jefferson; they were the vanguard of West Virginia's Black political leaders." See Wade, "Black Gold and Black Folk," 141. Also see Posey, *Negro Citizen*, 38. Part of this circumstance can be traced to low voter turnout. In the 1896 Cabell County municipal elections, Douglass School House registered only 32 voters. See "The Result in Cabell," *Huntington Advertiser*, November 5, 1896.

124. In 1897 W. O. James assumed a position within the city government and was cited for his expertise by a local newspaper: "The Advertiser has much pleasure in commending the efficiency and promptitude with which William O. James is dis-

charging his duties as Assistant Street Commissioner." See "Holding Up His End," *Huntington Advertiser*, June 10, 1897.

125. Wilson, "Early Settler Looking Backward."

126. A condensed summary of the "grand affair" notes, "The bride wore a beautiful albatross, black lace and natural flowers. The groom was attired in conventional black. The ladies' costumes were up to date in both style of fabric and make. We are sorry we haven't space of each lady's costume, but suffice it to say that the fashionable modiste [sic] was favorably represented. The gentlemen wore the ever fashionable cut away and Prince Albert. [After] Some excellent vocal and instrumental musical selections . . . we were invited out to take our place at tastefully prepared tables that groaned beneath the load of good things pleasing to the sight and palatable to the taste. After supper[,] games and plays were engaged in until a late hour.

"The presents were handsome and useful. A club of ladies and gentlemen gave a beautiful dinner set, consisting of one hundred and two pieces, one salad set, one celery stand, two olive dishes and a twelve piece chamber set. Other presents given ere a five piece tea set, cup saucer and plate, cup, saucer and two plates, one large meat platter, three handsome fruit dishes, olive dish and two fruit dishes and a beautiful china and silver ornament." *Huntington Herald*, February 28, 1896.

127. Newspaperman Rick Baumgartner Hill's recounted his aspirations: "A Republican by persuasion, Dan also had visions of wielding great political power. From time to time he would get out of step with his party and on more than one occasion he announced that on a given evening he would make a speech on 3rd Avenue and 9th Street to 'expose the party's inequities.'" See Rick Baumgartner, "First Families of Huntington." Reprinted from *Huntington Advertiser*, 18-part series, October 28, 1976–March 24, 1977, 27 (Huntington, W.Va.: James E. Morrow Library, Special Collections, Marshall University). Wallace relates that Hill never ran for office and states, "Dan was a character. Dan would put in his appearance well in advance of the hour set for speaking, clad in a Prince Albert coat and wearing a plug hat. In every instance but one Dan was placated and abandoned his purpose of speaking." See Wallace, *Cabell County Annals and Families*, 221.

128. *Cabell Record* (Milton), February 24, 1898, KYOWVA Genealogical Society: Huntington, W.Va.

129. *Huntington Advertiser*, October 3, 1898.

130. *Huntington Advertiser*, March 3, 1899, and April 8, 1899

131. "Editorial," *Huntington Advertiser*, April 18, 1899.

132. "Earning His Daily Bread," *Huntington Advertiser*, March 18, 1899.

133. Ibid. On white backlash, see April 18, 1899, issue. On black vote, see March 27, 1899 issue.

134. U.S. Bureau of the Census, *Thirteenth Census*, Population. Black males of voting age in the county were 499.

135. *Huntington Advertiser*, April 7, 1899.

136. "A Political Argument," *Huntington Advertiser*, April 4, 1900.

137. Hart, "Brief History," 5–7. Hart reports that "J. W. Scott's name later appears as editor and publisher of a small and briefly circulated black newspaper, *The Breeze*,

which was published in the 1920s in Huntington" (see p. 7). In her monograph on the former president of West Virginia State College, James McHenry Jones, Ancella R. Bickley also notes the firing. See Bickley, "James McHenry Jones, 1859–1909," n.p., [1989], transcript in author's files. A second black newspaper, the *Huntington Enterprise*, was initiated in Huntington in September 1913 by black entrepreneur H. Rufus White. See *Socialist and Labor Star* (Huntington), September 19, 1913, and "Negro League Expels Editor for Misconduct," *Huntington Herald-Dispatch*, January 6, 1914.

138. "The School Board in Politics," *Huntington Advertiser*, July 6, 1900.

139. "Barnett Roasted the Bosses," *Huntington Advertiser*, July 29, 1900. Carter G. Woodson succeeded Barnett as principal, with Scott retaining his position as assistant principal. See *Huntington Advertiser*, September 15, 1900.

140. "A New Era in Politics," *Huntington Advertiser*, February 8, 1898.

141. "Douglass League Held Meeting," *Huntington Dispatch*, June 10, 1908.

142. Clark-Lewis, *Living On, Living Out*, 19.

Chapter 6. Spreading our Wings

1. Scott, *Progress of the Huntington Negro*, 4.

2. This is a dramatic imagining of events. For actual commentary on incident, see "Negro Died from Neglect," *Huntington Herald Dispatch*, August 10, 1909.

3. Inclusive of states cited, black Huntington comprised residents from Alabama, Georgia, Indiana, Maryland, Mississippi, Ohio, Pennsylvania, South Carolina, Virginia, and West Virginia. See U.S. Bureau of the Census, *Twelfth Census*.

4. Ibid.

5. Housel, "Side by Side."

6. Addressing the rationale for increasing racial antipathy toward black aspirations, Leon Litwack notes of white Southerners of the era: "Between 1890 and World War I, white Southerners went to extraordinary lengths to mythologize the past, to fantasize an Old South, a Civil War, a Reconstruction, and a Negro that conformed to the images they preferred to cherish, images that both comforted and reassured them. They wanted to remind themselves of black loyalty and service in the past, to honor 'the old slavery-time Negro,' the unemancipated, unreconstructed Sambos, with their 'dignified humility' and 'unfailing devotion to duty,' who remained committed to the lessons and traits they had acquired as slaves." See Litwack, *Trouble in Mind*, 185.

7. For example, Charleston's population grew by 107 percent from 1900 to 1910, and 72 percent from 1910 to 1920, while Huntington's grew by 61 percent during the same decade. In contrast, Wheeling grew by 7 percent from 1900 to 1910 and 35 percent from 1910 to 1920. See U.S. Bureau of the Census, *Fourteenth Census*. West Virginia's urban territorial growth of 66 percent from 1900 to 1910 exceeded every eastern state except Florida. See U.S. Bureau of the Census, *Thirteenth Census*.

8. Trotter, "Formation of Black Community," 284.

9. Sullivan, *Coal Men and Coal Towns*, 1.

10. *Huntington Advertiser*, September 14, 1904.

11. *Logan County Banner* (West Virginia), June 12, 1897.

12. Kirby, *Darkness at the Dawning*, 5.

13. *Logan County Banner*, September 29, 1889. For full story see, Cubby, "Transformation," 75.

14. Labor agencies and the press regularly recruited African Americans from outside the state. In one 1907 issue of the *Advocate*, an African American Charleston-based newspaper, a full-page advertisement appeared with the following headline: "Opportunity—opportunity—2,000 colored men with or without families wanted for permanent employment and residence in West Virginia." The accompanying article displayed the advantages and virtues offered by the state. "In West Virginia there is no discrimination in the public school laws . . . colored teachers are paid the same salaries as white teachers. Men wanted as miners . . . from $2.00 to $5.00 per day can be earned. It takes only a few weeks for a man to learn the trade of mining." Indicative of state government support for the recruitment of African Americans was the signing of the statement by J. M. Hazelwood, mayor of Charleston, with West Virginia Governor W. M. Dawson, given as reference. Anson, "History of the Labor Movement," 66–67. Anson cites the April 18, 1907, issue of the *Advocate*.

15. For "benevolent segregation" see Sheller, "Negro in West Virginia," 2.

16. Wright, *Life Behind a Veil*, 4.

17. Ibid., 2.

18. Wright, *Racial Violence in Kentucky*, 1.

19. *Charleston Daily Mail*, March 13, 1898. Noteworthy is black response to the lynching. Within five years, Bramwell pastor R. H. McKoy had established the headquarters of the Golden Rule Association, "one of the most energetic of the prewar black fraternal orders. Within one decade the organization celebrated its success: fifty-four subordinate lodges, twenty-six nurseries serving young people aged three to sixteen, more than 5,280 members, and more than thirteen thousand paid out in sick and death benefits." See Trotter, "Formation of Black Community," 289–90.

20. Livers, "Greenbrier Lynching," 1. Livers (now Bickley) acknowledges some discrepancy on exact numbers in her three sources stemming from difficulty in the definition of lynching: "While most definitions seem to agree that lynchings are the result of mob action, the definitions do not always agree on how many people constitute a mob." One source recounts "54 lynchings between 1882 and 1927. Of these lynchings 21 had been of whites, 33 of blacks." A second states "from 1882 to 1968 . . . 48 lynchings in the state, 20 white, 28 black." A third, chronicling 1889 to 1918, provides "28 different lynchings." See White, *Rope and Faggot*, 235; Zangrando, *NAACP Crusade*, 5; and *Thirty Years of Lynching*, 102. Tim Konhaus argues that while incidents of lynching in the state were low numerically compared with those in Southern states, they were high proportionally. See Konhaus, "I Thought Things," 25–43.

21. Livers, "Greenbrier Lynching," 1, 3. The first was introduced by Fayette County delegate John V. Coleman in 1919, the second by McDowell County delegate Harry

J. Capehart in 1921. The bill was eventually passed in 1921 as the Capehart Anti-Lynching Law, but with a reduced restitution penalty of $20,000, down from the $25,000 stipulated in the original bill. Some evidence of the law's effectiveness can be found in the *Pittsburgh Courier*, April 3, 1926, which cited the state as one with no record of lynching within the previous five years.

22. Johnson, "How Much?," 274. Specifically, Johnson sought to refute the idea that black migrant influx was the result of a fearful, impotent populace that lacked intelligence and rational thought to recognize the benefits of economic opportunity.

23. U.S. Department of Commerce, *Negroes in the United States: 1920–1932* (Washington, D.C.: GPO, 1935), 9.

24. Some discrepancy exists in the identity of the first executed, although the exact native origins of both are cited as unknown. Stan Bumgardner and Christine Kreiser identify the first two as McDowell County residents Shep Caldwell, convicted of murdering his mistress, and Frank Broadnax, also convicted of murder. See Bumgardner and Kreiser, "Thy Brother's Blood: Capital Punishment in West Virginia," *West Virginia Historical Society Quarterly* 9, no. 4, and 5, no. 1, March 1996, www.wvculture.org/history/wvhs941.html. M. Watt Espy and John Ortiz Smykla list Fayette County resident Henry Jenkins and Raleigh County resident William Martin as the first two. Both were convicted of murder and listed with unknown origins. Caldwell and Broadnax are listed as the tenth and eleventh state executions. See Espy and Smykla, *Executions*, 3:1337–47. Part of the discrepancy may derive from the fact that West Virginia mandated state-sponsored executions in 1899, while Espy and Smykla initiate their listing from 1881. Regarding McDowell County, Trotter reports, "During the period from 1899 to 1928, ten African Americans from McDowell County were hanged by the state compared to only two whites from that county." See Trotter, *Coal, Class, and Color*, 24.

25. "Victim of Negro's Hatred Dies from Awful Wounds," *Huntington Herald Dispatch*, August 28, 1910, and "Exciting Scenes Sunday Night," and "Another Attempt to Lynch Negroes Thwarted; Many Arrests are Made for Inciting Riot," *Huntington Herald Dispatch*, August 29, 1910. The fact that Huntington city authorities succeeded in stopping the lynching reveals the differing perspectives maintained by white authorities attempting to uphold the law against those of white residents seeking extralegal measures to subvert it.

26. Lida Hepler, "C&O Patch," 20.

27. *Huntington Advertiser*, December 26, 1902. For a larger discussion of sundown towns see Loewen, *Sundown Towns*. One of Loewen's more salient points is that a town need not be void of black residents to be considered a sundown town. Many whites, in fact, tolerated long-time black residents or those individuals or families considered nonthreatening to the status quo. Elaborating on Charles S. Johnson's findings, Loewen contends the greatest acts of violence were perpetuated not against the long-time resident but against the black migrant most recently arrived.

28. Hepler, "C&O Patch," 21.

29. Despite their marginalization, manipulation, and neglect by the white-controlled Republican Party, ambitious African Americans made remarkable strides at the local

level, especially in the southern counties. For a web-based timeline of African American achievement within the state, including bibliographic information, see, "Timeline of African-American History."

30. In Gallipolis, Ohio, during the early 1900s a number of black women engaged in "trading secrets" gained from the gossip gathered while working in the homes of white families. Information gained was shared with other black women involved in church work, Lincoln School (the city's black high school), in women's clubs, and even in political organizations like the Afro-American League formed in the city in 1903. After one heard of a secret plan by the city's councilmen to divide up the Third Ward where most blacks lived, which would thereby weaken black influence in municipal politics, the women spread word of the plan, preventing its implementation. "Black Women Pioneers in Gallia County Work Force," James Sands, *Sunday Times Sentinel* (Gallipolis, Ohio), February 14, 1993.

31. Higginbotham, *Righteous Discontent*, 185–229. This belief was encapsulated by an article published in the African American newspaper the *Durham Reformer* (North Carolina), and reprinted in the *Pittsburgh Courier*, which stated, "A race is no better than its women. The progress that colored women are making in morality and feminine attractiveness is truly remarkable. When the history of the race is considered along with the unrestricted assaults, which the law permitted and public opinion sanctioned, upon the chastity of our women, one cannot but be struck by the wonderful efforts which are being put forth to counteract the ingrained traditions of centuries." See "Afro-American Cullings," *Pittsburgh Courier*, July 25, 1912.

32. Welter, "Cult of True Womanhood"; Lerner, "Lady and the Mill Girl"; Ryan, *Womanhood in America*; and Donnelly, *American Victorian Woman*.

33. Higginbotham, *Righteous Discontent*; Shaw, *What a Woman Ought to Be*; Gaines, *Uplifting the Race*; and Moore, *Leading the Race*.

34. Dolita Cathcart notes, "Middle-class respectability and gender created space for black women to contest racism. In black communities, the ideal of black womanhood did not detract from black women's femininity. Black communities utilized the talents, energy and expertise of all of their members to combat racial discrimination. Black women were politicized through the club movement, church activities, reform work and education." See Cathcart, "Gilded Cage," 14.

35. Strat Douthat, "Callie Left Sons, Cried all the Way Home," *Huntington Herald-Dispatch*, March 13, 1977.

36. National Association of Colored Women's Clubs, "National Association Notes"; see also, "James D. Coleman," *History of the American Negro*, http://www.wvculture.org/history/histamne/coleman.html.

37. "Afro-American Notes," *Huntington Herald-Dispatch*, March 28, 1909.

38. *Huntington Herald-Dispatch*, March 6, 1910.

39. *Huntington Herald-Dispatch*, June 30, 1910.

40. Carrie Simmons, "Afro-American Cullings" *Pittsburg Courier*, May 27, 1911.

41. Shaw, *What a Woman Ought*, 2. Original emphasis.

42. Before the Depression cut short the golden years of the Harlem Renaissance, Hughes performed in New York theaters and movie houses, as well as on the radio.

In 1932 she returned to Huntington to care for her widowed mother in her last illness and eventually secured the position as supervisor of public-school music in Cabell County's segregated schools. After creating the Douglass High School band she led her young musicians out into the community, where they performed at major civic events and for white civic groups. After placing first in the West Virginia High School Music Contest (Negro) for three consecutive years, her high school musicians won a permanent trophy. In less than 10 years, Hughes had transformed a non-existent music program into one of statewide recognition. She also found time to complete a master's degree in music at Northwestern. Before retiring in 1955, Hughes had traveled around the globe, from Broadway to Huntington to the Middle East, performing a variety of musical genres from classical to jazz, garnering worldwide accolades, awards, and fans, and uplifting the race through multiple endeavors, including starting an award-winning musical program at Douglass. After a 25-year hiatus, Hughes would be "re-discovered" by a new generation of fans. Throughout the early 1980s she experienced career resurgence and performed at a number of venues around the country, including an appearance at New York City's Radio City Music Hall. In 1987 Hughes passed at the age of ninety-one and was posthumously inducted into the Huntington Wall of Fame the following year. For composite history see, *In Memory, Mortgage Burning Program*; "Afro-American Notes," *Huntington Herald-Dispatch*; Revella E. Hughes Papers, ii; "Eva Roberta Coles Booth," Raymond Pierre Hylton, Virginia Union University. In 1932, Virginia Union University absorbed Hartshorn; Carrie Simmons, "Afro-American Cullings," *Pittsburgh Courier*, July 7, 1911, August 12, 1911, and September 9, 1911.

43. "Took the Exam," *Huntington Advertiser*, July 23, 1904.

44. Barnett. "Short History of Seven Generations," 326.

45. James McMiller, "Chiseled Words Hold Special Place," *Huntington Herald-Dispatch*, July 2, 1978. Francisco recalled her graduation at age eighty-eight: "There were four in my class. The graduation took place in the Huntington Theatre and at that time the girls had a dress for baccalaureate, one for the graduation, and one for the reception that followed." See Plantania, "Getting Ready for Life," 23.

46. "Increased Attendance at the School," *Huntington Advertiser*, September 18, 1903. Employment figures by Nelson L. Barnett Jr.

47. Barnett's first postgraduate job took him to Clarksburg, West Virginia, where he taught manual training at a segregated high school. Soon bored with Clarksburg, he returned to Ohio to become the manual arts teacher at Wilberforce College. Shortly thereafter, he married; two years later, he and his new bride, Carrie, settled in Charleston, where he taught shop at the Garnet High School. Notably, while residing in Charleston, Barnett met Reverend Mordecai Johnson, a local minister and eventual president of Howard University. "By this time," Barnett reveals, "I had begun to think in terms of our people." Strat Douthat, "Son Had to Live in White Society's Shadow," *Huntington Herald-Dispatch*, March 13, 1977. After the Depression, Barnett settled into Huntington and began teaching manual training at Douglass. "Callie Left Sons, Cried all the Way Home," *Huntington Herald-Dispatch*, March 13, 1977.

48. *Douglass High School Reunion, 1973*, 34, 47.

49. *Huntington Dispatch*, November 28, 1906, December 12, 1906, and March 30, 1907, editions. For more on Tillman, see Litwack, *Trouble in Mind*, 189, 206, and 227.

50. "Negroes Would Stop Tillman's Lecture Here," *Huntington Advertiser*, March 27, 1907.

51. "Racial," *Huntington Dispatch*, February 5, 1909.

52. "Douglass High School Commencement Greatest Success in its History," *Huntington Herald-Dispatch*, May 29, 1909.

53. Scott, *Progress of the Huntington Negro*, 4.

54. *Huntington, West Virginia Directory, 1891–1892*, 104.

55. *Huntington Advertiser*, November 19, 1874.

56. Scott, "Progress of the Huntington Negro," 3.

57. Scott, "Progress of the Huntington Negro [Lodge and Church Directory]," 11.

58. Not all left the city solely because of racism, however. Before embarking on a career of 70 years as a blues and gospel singer, "Diamond Teeth Mary" McClain, desperate to escape beatings from her stepmother, disguised herself as a boy at age thirteen, boarded a train, and joined a circus as a singer and acrobat. Born Mary Smith in 1902, she performed in medicine and minstrel shows throughout the 1920s and 1930s. In the 1940s she took the name "Diamond Teeth Mary" when she had diamonds from a bracelet implanted in her front teeth. Over the years, McClain shared the stage with such well-known performers as Billie Holiday, Sarah Vaughan, Big Mama Thornton, Ray Charles, Duke Ellington, and Bessie Smith, who was her half-sister. She performed at Carnegie Hall, the White House, the Apollo Theater, and the Cotton Club, and toured Europe three times. It wasn't until the 1980s and 1990s that she gained national recognition. She continued to perform, appearing at regional blues festivals until her death at age ninety-seven in 2000. At her request, her ashes were sprinkled on the railroad tracks at Huntington, where she hopped her first train. She was inducted into the West Virginia Music Hall of Fame in 2011. See Michael Lipton, "Mary McClain," *e-WV: The West Virginia Encyclopedia*, https://www.wvencyclopedia.org/articles/2366.

59. For example, "Colored Folks," *Huntington Dispatch*, March 10, 1907, and "Afro-American Notes," *Huntington Herald-Dispatch Sunday*, May 23, 1909, and May 30, 1909.

60. *Douglass High School Reunion 1973*, 85. Scott, "Most Invisible of All," and "Mutual Benefit Societies," in *Black Women in America: Religion and Community*, ed. Darlene Clark Hine (New York: Facts on File, 1997), 138–40.

61. "Afro-American Cullings," *Pittsburgh Courier*, 1911 and 1912 editions.

62. *Pittsburgh Courier*, October 15, 1904. Of the nearly 100 listings provided, the only African American cited is C. H. Barnett, listed as constructing a two-story frame dwelling at 810 Seventh Avenue.

63. See Housel, "Side by Side," and Housel, "Construction of a 'Colored' Neighborhood."

64. For a history of the establishment of the black church in Huntington, see Fain, "Forging of a Black Community," 45–47 and 72–76.

65. Housel, "Construction of a 'Colored' Neighborhood," 9.

66. African American buyers included Superintendent of the State Missions Rev. Robert D. W. Meadows, who purchased a lot in 1903 on which he resided with his wife and five daughters. Virginia-born widow Eva Edmunds purchased two lots and built a house in order to reside with her daughter and four boarders. Housel, "Side by Side." Housel reports that Fuller purchased 22 lots between 1910 and 1916, with a number of them sold in a "quick turnaround sale."

67. "History of Sixteenth Street Baptist Church." The 41 are; A. D. Brown, Alice Brown, Florence Brown, Wylie Brown, Buy Calloway, W. H. Harris, Victory Holt, A. B. Hughes, G. W. Hughes, J. W. Jackson, Mattie Jackson, Carrie Johnson, Fannie Johnson, Leota Johnson, Wm. Johnson, Rev. A. D. Lewis, A. D. Lewis Jr., L. B. Lewis, L. J. Lewis, Rev. L. O. Lewis, Chas. McPherson, Pearl McPherson, Virginia McPherson, E. M. Manggrum, M.L. Manggrum, Sallie B. Miller, A. D. Mills, M. E. Mills, W. D. Mills, Anderson Odell, Wm. Poindexter, David Watkins, John Watson, Castine Wilkins, Jane Wilkins, Sarah Wilkins, T. W. Wilkins, Florence L. Williams, Alex Winston, Belle C. Winston, and G. W. Winston. Providing evidence of the abiding ties among area religious leaders, the council meeting to establish the church included Dr. R. J. Perkins, president and founder of West Virginia Seminary and College; Rev. D. W. Meadows, state missionary; Rev. Nelson Barnett, pastor Second Baptist Church, Guyandotte; Rev. S. E. Williams, pastor of Baptist Church, Ashland, Ky.; Deacon T. R. Botts, Burlington, and a representative of the Fourth Street Baptist Church, Ironton, Ohio. See "Church History," *In Memory, Mortgage Burning Program*. By 1936 a church document maintains that the church "located in the heart of the Negro population in Huntington, is the largest church in the state" with a total membership exceeding 1,200 members. See "Huntington Schools," *Annual Great Harvest Home Program*.

68. Housel, "Side by Side."

69. *Huntington Advertiser*, April 29, 1903.

70. Housel, "Construction of a 'Colored' Neighborhood," 9.

71. *Huntington Advertiser*, April 6, 1905.

72. Housel, "Construction of a 'Colored' Neighborhood." For information pertaining to Cammack see p. 10; for quote see p. 9. Of the fifteen residents of Washington Place in 1910, thirteen were laborers. See U.S. Bureau of the Census, *Thirteenth Census*.

73. Duckworth, personal recollection; *Cabell County Deed Book* 97:7; and U.S. Bureau of the Census, *Thirteenth Census*.

74. U.S. Bureau of the Census, *Thirteenth Census*, 178–180.

75. Ibid., 246.

76. *Record of Proceedings of Council*, 9.

77. U.S. Bureau of the Census, "Statistics of Population," *Twelfth Census*, 248.

78. Suggestion of such a problem is derived from proposed city council ordinance banning minors loafing in saloons. See *Record of Proceedings of Council*, 360.

79. Anson, "History of the Labor Movement," 61.

80. U.S. Bureau of the Census, *Twelfth Census*.

81. *Huntington Advertiser*, June 18, 1904.

82. Scott, "Progress of the Huntington Negro," 5, 9. This amount is in line with the 1909 valuation of $300,000 in Negro property. See "Afro-American Notes," *Huntington Herald-Dispatch*, February 21, 1909.

83. Walter and Ida Myers interview.

84. *Grantee Index to Deeds 1, Ba-Bl*, 487.

85. *Grantee Index to Deeds 1, Ma-My & M* 61:224, 225, 331; 75:319; 78:348; 105:141; 112:287; 113:484; 134:519; 147:271; and 153:152; and U.S. Bureau of the Census, *Fourteenth Census*. Originally established as an African American cemetery, though several whites are buried there, Bethel served as the primary burial site for McClain Funeral Home between the 1920s and early 1970s, before the death of Mary McClain issued its closure. It is now in a state of disrepair. See Cassandra Griffith, "Bethel Cemetery," http://www.rootsweb.ancestry.com/~wvcabell/cemetery/bethel.html.

86. Carrie Simmons, "Afro-American Cullings," *Pittsburgh Courier*, June 8, 1911. From 1912 to 1917, Huntington's first black dentist, Dr. William G. Capel, practiced in the city. See "William G. Capel," in Caldwell, *History of the American Negro*, 299–301.

87. In her study of black professionals from 1890 to 1950, Darlene Clark Hine argues that segregation "offered black Americans . . . private space to buttress battered dignity, nurture positive self-images, sharpen skills, and demonstrate expertise." Hine, "Black Professionals." Likewise, Leon Litwack declares that "the irony of segregation is that it opened up new opportunities for enterprising blacks." Litwack, *Trouble in Mind*, 374.

88. "Colored Ward Added to City Hospital," *Huntington Herald-Dispatch*, March 27, 1909.

89. "Negro Died from Neglect," *Huntington Herald-Dispatch*, August 10, 1909.

90. Quote from Barnett, "History of Seven Generations," 325. Composite history drawn from same; see also Bickley, "Black People," 147; and Nance, "Draft Proposal," 3–5.

91. "Notes on Negro Business Progress," *Savannah Tribune*, August 23, 1913.

92. Carter G. Woodson, *Historical Reader*, 129.

93. Prof. Eph Williams "owned" and "managed" the Silas Green Company, which, according to the *Freeman*, was the "largest, best, and most prominently known of all the colored amusement enterprises that travel the Southland." See "Prof. Eph Williams' Famous Troubadours," *Freeman* (Indianapolis), September 26, 1914; "Huntington, WV: an Ideal City with a Population of 50,000 with a Colored Population," *Freeman*, August 8, 1912. See Miller, "Answering the Call."

94. Ibid.

95. Hine, *Black Women in White*, xvii.

96. Bickley, "Black People," 147.

97. Arguably, the Black Hospital Movement began when Dr. Daniel Hale Williams opened the nation's first black-operated hospital, Chicago's Provident Hospital and Nurse Training School. In 1900 he encouraged the black community to create hospitals for themselves. Ten years later, the *Journal of the National Medical Association* (JNMA) reiterated the same entreaty: "In every community where possible, a

hospital should be erected." Perhaps the urgent request by the JNMA stemmed from the report by the Committee of Medical Education on Colored Hospitals, which emphasized the lack of black hospitals in the United States, citing only 15 institutions under African American management listed by the General Secretary under Colored Hospitals. African Americans hastily responded to these proposals for the establishment of black hospitals. Between 1912 and 1919, the number of black hospitals increased from 63 to 118. See Miller, "Answering the Call."

98. Gamble, *Making a Place for Ourselves*, xiv.
99. Miller, "Answering the Call."
100. Hine, *Black Women in White*, 202.
101. Woodson, *Historical Reader*, 129.
102. Miller, "Answering the Call."
103. Gamble, *Making a Place for Ourselves*, 11, 42.
104. "Dr. Barnett Is Taken by Death," *Huntington Herald-Dispatch*, December 30, 1935.
105. "Items of Interest," 278.
106. Touting the success of these clinics, *Freeman*, an African American newspaper in Indianapolis, noted, "Not a single fatality occurred, which shows, not only the dexterity of the operators, but also the careful nursing and after treatment [of the patients]." See "Huntington, WV: an Ideal City with a Population of 50,000 with a Colored Population," *Freeman*, August 8, 1912. See also "Society and Personal," 142.
107. *Socialist and Labor Star* (Huntington), August 28, 1914. Noteworthy is electoral support for Socialist Party presidential candidates from 1904 to 1920, which peaked in 1912 with voter support in the state, achieving 5.7 percent, more than any other electoral year. See Barkey, "Socialist Party." The original name of the paper was the *Socialist and Labor Star*. In April 1914, the name was changed to the *Labor Star*.
108. Ibid., October 16, 1914.
109. *Socialist and Labor Star*, May 22, 1914. KYOWVA Genealogical Society cites the following employment numbers: "Chesapeake and Ohio Ry. Shops and cars, 2200 employees; Chesapeake and Ohio Ry. Trainmen and division men, 500; and American Car and Foundry Co. freight cars, 1500." See "Employment Figures," *KYOWVA Genealogical Society*, vol. 24, no. 2 (Summer 2001): 13.
110. *Socialist and Labor Star*, September 4, 1914.
111. *Socialist and Labor Star*, October 9, 1914.
112. Barkey, "Socialist Party," 25–26.
113. In his study of the Socialist Party in Charleston, David Corbin states, "Conspicuously absent were members living in the 'slum sections' of Charleston such as the infamous 'triangle district,' the negro section, and the centers of ethnic groups. Only two negroes were members, and they were both professors at West Virginia State College." See Corbin, "Charleston Socialist Local," 19–20. For information on the *Socialist and Labor Star*, see Corbin, *Socialist and Labor Star*. For information on the Socialist Party within the state, see Barkey, "Socialist Party."
114. Housel, "Construction of a 'Colored' Neighborhood," 10.

115. Scott, *Progress of the Huntington Negro*, 10
116. Silver, "Racial Origins of Zoning," 3.
117. Housel, "Construction of a 'Colored' Neighborhood," 20.
118. Gaines, *Uplifting the Race*, 1–3.
119. See *Cabell County Deed Books* 84:375; 84:447; 108:281; 108:284: 108:286; 108:288; 112:308; 131:503; 131:505; and, 131:561.
120. *Grantee Index to Deeds 1, Ma-M and Mc*, 14c, 14d.
121. Scott, *Progress of the Huntington Negro*, 12.
122. Ibid.
123. Housel, "Construction of a 'Colored' Neighborhood," 2.
124. Ibid., 15. As Housel relates, "Contiguous with these developments was the continuing differentiation of the city's black residents socially, economically, politically, and spatially. As Huntington thrived, subdivisions developed outside of the city. And just like those white realtors who had previously sought rewards on their investment within the city's core, land speculators once again envisioned profits through the commodification of space. Similar to factories, subdivisions were created to maximize profit through a new organization of space. In order to increase value and marketability of the land, developers targeted a specific group of buyers promoting the purchase as an 'investment' in the future. This view of home as an investment represents the shift in how housing was viewed. In this new view, housing is seen in terms of its exchange value (market value), not its use value. Once the house is commodified factors that might affect its value become of primary importance to investors—land speculators, real estate agent, investors, and homeowners. It did not take long to realize that a key factor in assessing value was adjacent properties. Consequently, controlling adjacent properties became important in maintaining value. Thus, the developed area is seen in total, not as individual parcels. This commodification of housing ensured the development of housing tracts marketed to a homogenous population of households of similar class and race that would be perceived as a safe, long-term investment."
125. In *American Apartheid*, Douglass Massey and Nancy Denton emphasize the importance of examining the structure of segregation: "Residential segregation is the institutional apparatus that supports other racially discriminatory processes and binds them together into a coherent and unique and uniquely effective system of racial subordination" (8).
126. Delaney, *Race, Place and the Law*, 109.
127. "Colored Men form Realty Company," *Huntington Herald Dispatch*, March 22, 1920. Dr. C. C. Barnett was the other member of the firm Brown and Barnett. In 1921, 33 black businesses existed in Huntington, including nine contractors, six barbers, five hair-dressing shops, three real-estate firms, three pressing and cleaning shops, two shoe-repair shops, two printing companies, one hospital, one drugstore, and one moving-picture house. See *Huntington, West Virginia, City Directory, 1921*.
128. T. Edward Hill, "The Negro in West Virginia," *Report of T. Edward Hill, Director Bureau of Negro Welfare and Statistics of the State of West Virginia to Governor Ephraim F. Morgan*, 1923–24, Special Collections, Morrow Library, Marshall University, 53–56.

129. George S. Schuyler, "Huntington, W.Va.: Close to Kentucky," *Pittsburgh Courier*, February 13, 1926. Schuyler's acknowledgement of the vitality of the Ku Klux Klan in the area helps illuminate the nature of response by some whites to continuing black progress. Additional insight on the reemergence of the KKK in the region is underlined by the fact that five years earlier, Huntington newspaperman A. N. Johnson called at city to protest the attempts by the organization to establish a Huntington branch, stating that "every colored man, woman child in Huntington would resent organization of any society that would be known by the name of Ku Klux Klan" and that "that hideous name strikes terror to the heart of every negro." See "Negroes Protest Against Ku Klux," *Huntington Herald-Dispatch*, May 27, 1921.

130. Jones, "Civil Status of Negroes," 84.

131. Walter and Ida Myers interview, 8.

132. Ibid., 9.

133. Jones, "Civil Status of Negroes," 84–89; NAACP 1940–1955: General office file. Leagues—National Public Housing Conference, 1942–1947 [microfilm], *Papers of the NAACP, Part 5, Campaign against Residential Segregation, 1914–1955*, reel 12, fr. 0544-0618; and "Residential Segregation Ruled Illegal by Court," *Pittsburgh Courier*, November 23, 1929. For biographical information on Nutter, see Caldwell, *History of the American Negro*.

134. Founded in early 1871 as the western transshipment point for the Chesapeake and Ohio Railway by railroad magnate Collis P. Huntington, Huntington contained 902 black residents in 1880. For population figures associated with this study see *1880 Census of WV*; Population of Counties, lvii; U. S. Bureau of the Census, Population Statistics, *Ninth Census*; U.S. Bureau of the Census, *Tenth Census*; U.S. Bureau of the Census, *Thirteenth Census*; U.S. Bureau of the Census, *Fourteenth Census*; and U.S. Bureau of the Census, *Fifteenth Census*. The 1930 population includes 72,612 in Cabell County and 2,960 in Wayne (Westmoreland district) County. Part of Ceredo annexed to Huntington city, Cabell County, in 1923, and part (including that part annexed to Huntington city) taken to form Westmoreland district in 1924.

135. Lewis, *In Their Own Interests*.

Bibliography

Manuscript Collections

MARSHALL UNIVERSITY

Fred B. Lambert Papers
Revella E. Hughes Papers, 1895–1984
West Virginiana Collection

VIRGINIA HISTORICAL SOCIETY

Charles Austin Goddard Papers, 1857–1942.
Thornton Taylor Perry II Collection

WEST VIRGINIA UNIVERSITY

Chesapeake and Ohio Railway Company, Records 1867–1869
Frances B. Gunter Papers
George C. McIntosh Memoirs

Newspapers

Cabell County Press (Guyandotte, W.Va.)
Cabell Record (Milton, W.Va.)
Cincinnati Chronicle
Daily Press (Huntington, W.Va.)
Democratic Banner (Milton, W.Va.)
Freeman (Indianapolis)
Huntington (W.Va.) Advertiser
Huntington (W.Va.) Dispatch
Huntington (W.Va.) Herald
Huntington (W.Va.) Herald Dispatch

Huntington (W. Va.) Independent
Ironton (Ohio) Democrat
Ironton (Ohio) Register
Ironton (Ohio) Weekly Journal
Kankakee (Ill.) Daily Gazette
Logan (W. Va.) County Banner
New York Times
Pittsburgh Courier
Point Pleasant (W. Va.) Weekly Register
Register Herald (Beckley, W.Va.)
Salt Lake Herald (Salt Lake City, Utah)
Savannah (Ga.) Tribune
Socialist and Labor Star (Huntington, W.Va.)
Sunday Times Sentinel (Gallipolis, Ohio)
Western Courier (Charleston, Va.)

Primary Sources

Axtell, Decatur. "A Wedding Journey over the Chesapeake and Ohio Railway, in February, 1873, as Described by the Bridegroom to His Mother." *History of the Chesapeake and Ohio*, chapter 7. New York: United Press Syndicate, ca. 1910. Chesapeake and Ohio Historical Society, Clifton Forge, Va.

Black Marriage Records, 1851–1905. Gallia County Historical and Genealogical Society and the John Gee Black Historical Center of Gallipolis, Ohio: Broussard Memorial Library, 2005.

Burdette, Frank Lee. "History of Ona and Surrounding Country, Past and Present." *Agricultural Extension Division Community Histories*, West Virginia Archives and History, West Virginia Division of Culture and History. http://www.wvculture.org/history/agrext/ona.html.

Cabell County Deed Index. R. 18, no. 1. Ba–Bc, 1806–1922. Cabell County Court House, Huntington, W.Va.

Cabell County Marriage Register. Vol. 2, 1853–1906. Cabell County Court House, Huntington, W.Va.

Cabell County Marriages, 1890–1899. Special Collections, Cabell County Public Library.

Cabell County (West) Virginia Marriages, 1851–1899. N.p.: 1966. KYOWVA Genealogical Society, Huntington, W.Va.

Chancery Order Book 3. December 29, 1873–April 12, 1879. Cabell County Circuit Court, W.Va.

Chancery Order Book 4. 1879–1883. Cabell County Circuit Court, W.Va.

Chancery Order Book 6. 1888. Cabell County Circuit Court, W.Va.

Chancery Order Book 7. 1891. Cabell County Circuit Court, W.Va.

Chancery Order Book 10. 1897. Cabell County Circuit Court, W.Va.

The Chesapeake and Ohio Railroad: Its Advantages as a Through Passenger and Freight between the Seaboard and the West, Together with Information Concerning the Agricultural, Mineral and Mechanical Resources, the Remarkable Coal and Iron-Ore Deposits, Medicinal Springs, Scenery and Summer Resorts and the Opportunities for Settlement, Investment, and the Active Employment of Capital and Labor in Various Industries along Its Route. New York: Fisk and Hatch, 1873.

City of Huntington Common Council Proceedings. January 6, 1872.

Common Pleas Law Criminal Record. Vol. 2. Cabell County Circuit Court, November 4, 1895–April 21, 1898.

Cradic, William P. "A Partial History of the Life of William Patrick Cradic." Edna Duckworth Personal Collection, Huntington, W.Va.

Deed Book No. 111. Cabell County, Cabell County Court House, Huntington, W.Va.

Diary of Reverend William Parker Walker. August 15–August 18, 1877, entries. Fifth Avenue Baptist Church Archives, Huntington, W.Va.

The Douglass High School Reunion Souvenir Program Book, 1973. Huntington, W.Va.: Franklin Printing Co., 1973. Author's files.

"1830 Virginia Constitution." In *Semi-Centennial History of West Virginia*, 130–34. Charleston: Semi-Centennial Commission of West Virginia, 1913. West Virginia Archives and History, West Virginia Division of Culture and History. http://www.wvculture.org/HISTORY/government/182930cc.html.

1880 Census of WV, Volume II, Cabell, Wayne, Lincoln, Logan (Mingo). Compiled by William A. Marsh. Baltimore, Md.: Gateway, 1990.

Extracts from the Records of the County Court of Cabell County, West Virginia. Minute book 6. January 2, 1809, to July 6, 1863. Compiled by R. S. Douthat, County Clerk, 1932.

Eldridge, Carrie. *Abstracts of Deed Book 1, 1808–1814, Cabell County Virginia/West Virginia.* Special Collections, Cabell County Public Library, Huntington, W.Va.

———. *Cabell County VA/WV Minute Book, 1809–1815.* N.p.: n.d. Special Collections, Cabell County Public Library, Huntington, W.Va.

———. *Will Book I, 1820–1848, Cabell County Virginia/West Virginia.* N.p.: n.d. Special Collections, Cabell County Public Library, Huntington, W.Va.

Federal Writers' Project. *Slave Narratives: A Folk History of Slavery in the United States From Interviews with Former Slaves.* Vol. 12: Ohio Narratives. United States Works Progress Administration, Manuscript Division, Library of Congress, July 8, 1937.

"The First Baptist Church of Burlington, 1983." *150th Anniversary Souvenir Book of Providence Regular Missionary Baptist Association, April 15–19, 1984.* Gallia County Historical and Genealogical Society, Gallipolis, Ohio.

Foner, Phillip S., and Ronald L. Lewis, eds. *The Black Worker: A Documentary History from Colonial Times to the Present. Volume 1: The Black Worker to 1869.* Philadelphia: Temple University: 1978.

Grantee Index to Deeds 1, A, from 1808 to Dec. 31, 1922. Cabell County Court House, Huntington, W.Va.

Grantee Index to Deeds 1, Ba–Bl, from 1808 to Dec. 31, 1922. Cabell County Court House, Huntington, W.Va.

Grantee Index to Deeds 1, L, from 1808 to Dec. 31, 1922. Cabell County Court House, Huntington, W.Va.

Grantee Index to Deeds 1, Ma–My and Mc, from 1808 to Dec. 31, 1922. Cabell County Court House, Huntington, W.Va.

Gunter, Frances G. "Barboursville." N.p.: 1986. West Virginia and Regional History Collection. Charles C. Wise Jr. Library, West Virginia University, Morgantown, W.Va.

Hall, Carl F. (Boyd Co.). *Slave Narratives—A Folk History of Slavery in the United States, from Interviews with Former Slaves.* Vol. 15: Kansas, Kentucky, and Maryland Narratives. St. Clair Shores, Mich.: Scholarly, 1936.

Hamilton, A. [Alex] W. "Early Recollections of the Beginning and Completion of the Chesapeake and Ohio Railway between White Sulphur Springs and the Ohio River as to the Vicinity in and around Hawk's Nest." Charles Austin Goddard Papers, 1857–1942, Manuscript Collection, Virginia Historical Society, Richmond, Virginia.

Henning, William Walter. *The Statutes at Large: Being a Collection of All the Laws of Virginia, from the First Session of the Legislature in the Year 1619.* Vols. 1 and 2. New York: Bartow, 1823.

Hill, T. Edward. *The Negro in West Virginia: Bureau of Negro Welfare and Statistics of the State of West Virginia to Governor Ephraim F. Morgan.* 1923–24. Charleston, W.Va.

"History of the Church." *116th Church Anniversary of First Baptist Church.* Huntington, W.Va., 1988. Author's files.

"History of Sixteenth Street Baptist Church." *100th Anniversary Celebration*, Sixteenth Street Baptist Church, 2005. Author's files.

"Huntington Schools." *The Great Harvest Annual Program.* Sixteenth Street Baptist Church and Community Center, October 19–30, 1936. Author's files.

Huntington, West Virginia, City Directory, 1921. The 1920–2005 Directories. Livonia, Mich.: Polk, 1919–2004.

Huntington (West Virginia) Directory, 1891–1892. Compiled by Potts and Cammack. Hamilton, Ohio: Hamilton Pub.

Huntington, West Virginia Directory, 1985–1896. Huntington, W.Va.: Armitage, 1895.

Hylton, Raymond Pierre. "Eva Roberta Coles Boone." In *Virginia Union University*, by Raymond Pierre Hylton, 49. Mt. Pleasant, S.C.: Arcadia, 2014.

In Memory, Mortgage Burning Program, April 23–29, 1945. Sixteenth Street Baptist Church and Community Center. Author's files.

Inter-university Consortium for Political and Social Research. *Historical, Demographic, Economic and Social Data: The United States, 1790–1970.* Ann Arbor, Mich.: Inter-university Consortium for Political and Social Research, 2005.

Law Orders 14. Cabell County Circuit Court, March 18, 1895–December 14, 1896, 7, 29.

Lawrence County Birth Records, F–HA, 1868–1938. Phyllis N. Hammer Room, Briggs-Lawrence County Library, Ironton, Ohio.

Lewis, A. D. "The Story of My Life." *Twenty-Fifth Anniversary of the Sixteenth Street Baptist Church and Community Center*. Huntington, W.Va., 1930.

Lewis, Albert D. "Before the Founding of Our Church." *Twenty-Fifth Anniversary of the Sixteenth Street Baptist Church and Community Center*. Special Collections, James E. Morrow Library, Marshall University, Huntington, W.Va., 1930.

Kyle, Mrs. John. "Early History of Little Seven Mile Community: Cabell County, W.Va." Morgantown, W.Va.: Agricultural Extension Division, (n.d.), Thornton Taylor Perry II Collection, Virginia Historical Society, Richmond.

"Macedonia Missionary Baptist Church." *150th Anniversary Souvenir Book of Providence Regular Missionary Baptist Association, April 15–19, 1984*. Gallia County Historical and Genealogical Society, Gallipolis, Ohio.

"Makers of Providence History." *150th Anniversary Souvenir Book of Providence Regular Missionary Baptist Association*, August 15–19, 1984. Gallia County Historical and Genealogical Society, Gallipolis, Ohio.

Miller, J. W. "History of Barboursville Community, Cabell County." *Morgantown, West Virginia, Agricultural Extension Division*, 1925. West Virginia Archives and History, West Virginia Division of Culture and History. http://www.wvculture.org/history/agrext/barbours.html.

"Minutes of Macedonia Church, 1884–1896." N.p.: 1996. Special Collections, James E. Morrow Library, Marshall University, Huntington, W.Va.

Mitchell, Mrs. Walter. "History of Cabell Creek Community." *Farm Bureau County Life Conference, June 1925*. Mrs. Lewis E. Caldwell, compiled by KYOWVA Genealogical Society, Huntington, W.Va.

NAACP 1940–1955. General office file. Leagues—National Public Housing Conference, 1942–1947 [microfilm]. *Papers of the NAACP, Part 5, Campaign against Residential Segregation, 1914–1955*. Reel 12, fr. 0544-0618.

National Association of Colored Women's Clubs. "National Association Notes." Vol. 7, no. 11, 1900.

Negro Membership in American Labor Unions by the Department of Research and Investigations of the National Urban League. New York: Alexander, 1930.

Oral History of Appalachia Project and Drinko Foundation. Special Collections, Morrow Library, Marshall University, Huntington, W.Va.

"Our History." *126th Church Anniversary Ebenezer United Methodist Church, 1871–1997*. Huntington, W.Va., 1997.

Perdue, Charles L. Jr., Thomas E. Barden, and Robert K. Phillips, eds. *Weevils in the Wheat: Interviews with Virginia Ex-Slaves*. Charlottesville: University Press of Virginia, 1976.

Population of Counties. *Statistics of the U. S. Population*. Vol. 1 (1900). Washington, D.C.: GPO.

Population Schedules of the Eighth Census of the United States, 1860. Roll 1387, Virginia [Slave Schedules], 1:256–520.

Portsmouth (Ohio) City Directory, 1881-2. Cincinnati: Spencer and Craig, ca.1882.
Public Documents of West Virginia, 1911-1912. Vol. 3. Charleston: Union.
Record of Proceedings of Council, City of Huntington, WV, 1898-1901. January 17, 1898.
Register of Prisoners. Ohio Penitentiary, 1894-1897 and 1896-1898. Ohio Historical Society, Columbus.
The School Law of West Virginia and Opinions of the Attorney-General and Decisions of the State Superintendent of Free Schools. Charleston: Forsyth, 1897.
Schreiner-Yantis, Netti. *1815 Tax List of Cabell County, Virginia.* N.p.: 1971. Virginia Historical Society, Richmond.
Scott, J. W. "Progress of the Huntington Negro." Compliments of the YMCA of Huntington, W.Va. (n. p., 1911). Author's files.
U.S. Army Register of Enlistments, 1798-1914, Year 1885-1890.
U.S. Army Register of Enlistment, 1798-1914, Year 1891-1892.
U.S. Bureau of the Census. *Compendium of Population Statistics, 1870. Ninth Census of the United States.* Washington, D.C.: GPO, 1870.
———. *Eighth Census of the United States.* Washington, D.C.: GPO, 1860.
———. *Eleventh Census of the United States.* Washington, D.C.: GPO, 1890.
———. *Fifteenth Census of the United States.* Washington, D.C.: GPO, 1930.
———. *Fourteenth Census of the United States.* Washington, D.C.: GPO, 1920.
———. *Fourth Census of the United States.* Washington, D.C.: GPO, 1820.
———. *Ninth Census of the United States.* Washington, D.C.: GPO, 1870.
———. *Report of the Mortality and Vital Statistics of the United States.* Table 14. *Tenth Census of the United States.* Washington, D.C: GPO, 1886.
———. *Report on the Productions of Agriculture. Tenth Census of the United States.* Washington, D.C.: GPO, 1883.
———. *Report on the Statistics of Wages in Manufacturing Industries. Tenth Census of the United States.* Washington, D.C.: GPO, 1886.
———. *Seventh Census of the United States.* Washington, D.C.: GPO, 1850.
———. *The Statistics of the Wealth and Industry. Ninth Census of the United States.* Washington, D.C.: GPO, 1870.
———. *Tenth Census of the United States.* Washington, D.C.: GPO, 1880.
———. *Third Census of the United States.* Washington, D.C.: GPO, 1810.
———. *Thirteenth Census of the United States.* Vol. 2. Washington, D.C.: GPO, 1910.
———. *Twelfth Census of the United States.* Washington, D.C.: GPO, 1900.
"White Sulphur Springs: Letter from Elizabeth Noel to Her Daughter Julia, September 1, 1860." *Taking the Waters: 19th Century Medicinal Springs of Virginia.* University of Virginia, Historical Collections, Claude Moore Health Sciences Library. http://exhibits.hsl.virginia.edu/springs/whitesulphurnoel.
"Why We Celebrate Our Culture and Church." N.p.: n.d. Transcript received from Owen Pleasant, Burlington, Ohio.
Wilson, Chas. A. "An Early Settler Looking Backward." N.p.: 1925. Special Collections, Cabell County Public Library, Huntington, W.Va.

Secondary Sources

Adkins, Oscar T. *Cabell County, Virginia (now West Virginia) Families 1820.* N.p.: 1996. Special Collections, Cabell County Public Library, Huntington, W.Va.

Alexander, J. Trent. "The Great Migration in Comparative Perspective: Interpreting the Urban Origins of Southern Black Migrants to Depression-Era Pittsburgh." *Social Science History* 22, no. 3 (Autumn 1998): 349–76.

Ambler, Charles H. *A History of Education in West Virginia.* Huntington, W.Va.: Standard, 1951.

———. *West Virginia: Stories and Biographies.* 1937. Reprint, New York: Rand McNally, 1942.

Anderson, James D. *The Education of Blacks in the South, 1860–1935.* Chapel Hill: University of North Carolina Press, 1988.

Anson, Charles P. "A History of the Labor Movement in West Virginia." Ph.D. diss., University of North Carolina, 1940.

Bailey, Kenneth R. *Alleged Evil Genius: The Life and Times of Judge James H. Ferguson.* Charleston, W.Va.: Quarrier, 2006.

———. "A Judicious Mixture: Negroes and Immigrants in the West Virginia Mines, 1880–1917." In *Blacks in Appalachia*, edited by William H. Turner and Edward J. Cabbell, 117–32. Lexington: University Press of Kentucky, 1985.

Bailey, Rebecca J. "Matewan before the Massacre: Politics, Coal, and the Roots of Conflict in Mingo County, 1793–1920." Ph.D. diss., West Virginia University, 2001.

Barkey, Fred. "The Socialist Party in West Virginia from 1891 to 1920: A Study in Working-Class Radicalism." Ph.D. diss., University of Pittsburgh, 1971.

Barnett, Nelson L., Jr. *Colonel Riddle Genealogical Chart.* N.p.: n.d. Unpublished manuscript. Author's files.

———. "The Flies in the Buttermilk." Unpublished manuscript, 1968. Author's files.

———. "A Short History of Seven Generations of Barnetts." In *Honoring Our Past: Proceedings of the First Two Conferences on West Virginia's Black History*, edited by Joe William Turner and Ancella Radford Bickley. N.p.: 1991. State Archives and History Library, Charleston, W.Va.

Becker, William H. "The Black Church: Manhood and Mission." In *African-American Religion: Interpretative Essays in History and Culture*, edited by Timothy E. Fulop and Albert J. Raboteau, 177–200. New York: Routledge, 1997.

Berlin, Ira. *Many Thousands Gone: The First Two Centuries of Slavery in North America.* Cambridge, Mass.: Harvard University Press, 1984.

Bhabha, Homi. *The Location of Culture.* New York: Routledge, 1993.

Bias, Charles V. *A History of the Chesapeake and Ohio Railroad Company and Its Predecessors, 1784–1977.* Ann Arbor, Mich.: University Microfilms International, 1979.

Bickley, Ancella. "Our Mount Vernons: Historical Register Listings of Sites Significant to the Black History of West Virginia." N.p.: 1997. West Virginiana Collection, Special Collections, James E. Morrow Library, Marshall University, Huntington.

Bickley, Ancella R. "Carter G. Woodson: The West Virginia Connection." *Appalachian Heritage: A Literary Quarterly of the Southern Appalachians* 36, no. 3 (Summer 2008): 59–69.

Bickley, Ancella R., and Lynda Ann Ewen, eds. *Memphis T. Garrison: The Remarkable Story of a Black Appalachian Woman.* Athens: Ohio University Press, 2001.

Bickley, Ancella Radford. "Black People and the Huntington Experience." *Honoring Our Past: Proceedings of the First Two Conferences of West Virginia's Black History*, edited by Joe W. Trotter Jr. and Ancella Radford Bickley. N.p.: 1991. Archives and History Library, Charleston, W.Va.

Biggers, Jeff. *The United States of Appalachia: How Southern Mountaineers Brought Independence, Culture, and Enlightenment to America* (Berkeley, CA: Counterpoint Press, 2017).

Bingham, Darrel E. *On Jordan's Banks: Emancipation and Its Aftermath in the Ohio River Valley.* Lexington: University Press of Kentucky, 2006.

———. *On Towns and Villages of the Lower Ohio.* Lexington: University Press of Kentucky, 1998.

Blassingame, John. W. *The Slave Community: Plantation Life in the Antebellum South.* New York: Oxford University Press, 1979.

Bordewich, Fergus M. *Bound for Canaan: The Underground Railroad and the War for the Soul of America.* New York: HarperCollins, 2006.

Bowers, Robert R. "Barboursville on the Guyandotte." *West Virginia Magazine*, September 1989.

Brady, Bess. "Reaches 50th Year of Service." *Chesapeake and Ohio Lines Magazine* 15, no. 12 (December 1930): 75.

Brand, Irene R. "Fifth Avenue Baptist Church, 1872–1930." Master's thesis, Marshall University, 1970.

Brier, Stephen. "Interracial Organizing in the West Virginia Coal Industry: The Participation of Black Mine Workers in the Knights of Labor and the United Mine Workers, 1880–1894." In *Essays in Southern Labor History*, edited by Gary M. Fink and Merl Elwyn Reed, 18–43. Westport, Conn.: Greenwood, 1977.

Brown, David, and Clive Owen. *Race in the American South: From Slavery to Civil Rights.* Edinburgh: Edinburgh University Press, 2007.

Brown, Elsa Barkley. "Mothers of Mind." *Sage* 6, no. 1 (Summer 1989): 4–11.

Brown, Elsa Barkley, and Gregg D. Kimball. "Mapping the Terrain of Black Richmond." In Goings and Mohl, *New African American Urban History*, 66–115.

Buchanan, Thomas C. *Black Life on the Mississippi: Slaves, Free Blacks, and the Western Steamboat World.* Chapel Hill: University of North Carolina, 2004.

Bumgardner, Stan, and Christine Kreiser. "Thy Brother's Blood: Capital Punishment in West Virginia." *West Virginia Historical Society Quarterly* 9, no. 4; 10, no. 1 (1996).

Burchett, Michael H. "Promise and Prejudice: Wise County, Virginia, and the Great Migration, 1910–1920." *Journal of Negro History* 82, no. 3 (Summer 1997): 312–27.

Burke, William. *The Mineral Springs of Western Virginia.* New York: Wiley and Putnam, 1846.

Cabell County West Virginia Heritage, 1809-1996. Huntington, W.Va.: Walsworth, 1996.

Caldwell, A. B., ed. *History of the American Negro: West Virginia Edition.* Vol.2. Atlanta: Caldwell, 1923.

Casto, James E. *Huntington: An Illustrated History.* Northridge, Calif.: Windsor, 1994.

Cathcart, Dolita. "The Gilded Cage: The Struggle to Define a New Black Identity during the Gilded Age and the Progressive Era." Paper presented at National Association of African American Studies Conference, Baton Rouge, Louisiana, February 13, 2008.

Chambers, Thomas A. *Drinking the Waters: Creating an American Leisure Class at Nineteenth-Century Mineral Springs.* Washington, D.C.: Smithsonian Institution Press, 2002.

Chappell, Louis W. *John Henry: A Folk-Lore Study.* Germany: Biedermann, 1933.

Chesapeake and Ohio Employees Magazine 1, no.1 (February 1914–January 1915). Richmond, Va.: Mitchell and Hotchkiss.

Clark-Lewis, Elizabeth. *Living On, Living Out: African American Domestics in Washington, D.C., 1910-1940.* Washington, D.C.: Smithsonian Institution Press, 1994.

Clifford, James. *The Predicament of Culture: Twentieth-Century Ethnography, Literature, and Art.* Cambridge, Mass.: Harvard University Press, 1988.

Conley, Phil. *West Virginia: A Brief History of the Mountain State.* Charleston, W.Va.: Charleston Printing, 1940.

Conte, Robert S. *The History of the Greenbrier.* Charleston, W.Va.: Pictorial Histories, 1998.

Cook, John Esten. "The White Sulphur Springs." *Harper's New Monthly Magazine,* 57 (June–November 1878): 341.

Corbin, David. *The Socialist and Labor Star: Huntington W. Va., 1912-1915.* Huntington: Appalachian Movement, 1971.

Corbin, David A. "Betrayal in the Coal Fields: Eugene V. Debs and the Socialist Party of America, 1912-1914." *Journal of American History* 64, no. 4 (March 1978): 988-89.

Corbin, David Alan. "The Charleston Socialist Local: Reflections on the Rise and Fall of a Regional Socialist Movement." Master's thesis, Marshall University, 1972.

———. *Life, Work, and Rebellion in the Coal Fields: The Southern West Virginia Miners, 1880-1922.* Chicago: University of Illinois Press, 1981.

Costa, Jim. "A John Henry Ballad." *Goldenseal* 22, no. 2 (Summer 1996): 9-12.

Crofts, Daniel W. *Reluctant Confederates: Upper South Unionists in the Secession Crisis.* Chapel Hill: University of North Carolina Press, 1989.

Cubby, Edward Albert. "The Transformation of the Tug and Guyandot Valleys: Economic Development and Social Change in West Virginia, 1888-1921." PhD diss., Syracuse University, 1962.

Curry, Richard Orr. *A House Divided: A Study of Statehood and the Copperhead Movement in West Virginia.* Pittsburgh: University of Pittsburg Press, 1964.

Curtis, C. M. "The Re-Definition of Freehold Suffrage during Virginia's Constitutional Convention of 1829-1830." Paper presented at the annual meeting of the Midwest

Political Science Association, Palmer House Hilton, Chicago, Illinois, April 2004. http://citation.allacademic.com/meta/p_mla_apa_research_citation/0/8/3/9/1/pages83912/p83912-1.php

Davis, Elsa Mae, ed. *Celebrating Our Roots: Origins of Black Families in West Virginia.* Dunbar, W.Va.: McKnight's, 1976.

Davis-DeEulis, Marilyn, "Slavery on the Margins of the Virginia Frontier: African American Literacy in Western Kanawha and Cabell Counties, 1795–1840." In Puglisi, *Diversity and Accommodation*, 194–212.

Delaney, David. *Race, Place, and the Law: 1836–1948.* Austin: University of Texas Press, 1998.

Dew, Charles B. *Bond of Iron: Master and Slave at Buffalo Forge.* New York: Norton, 1994.

Dickinson, Jack L., and Kay Stamper Dickinson. *Gentleman Soldier of Greenbottom: The Life of Brig. Gen. Albert Gallatin Jenkins, CSA.* N.p.: Author, 2011.

Dix, Keith. *An Analysis of West Virginia Work Stoppages.* Morgantown: West Virginia University, 1977.

Donnelly, Mabel. *The American Victorian Woman: The Myth and the Reality.* New York: Greenwood, 1986.

Drake, Richard B. "Slavery and Antislavery in Appalachia." In Inscoe, *Appalachians and Race*, 16–26. Lexington: University Press of Kentucky, 2001.

Drake, St. Claire, and Horace R. Cayton. *Black Metropolis: A Study of Negro Life in a Northern City.* New York: Harcourt, Brace and World, 1970.

Du Bois, W. E. B. *Black Reconstruction in America, 1860 to 1880: An Essay of the Part which Black Folk Played in the Attempt to Reconstruct Democracy in America.* 1935. Repr., New York: Meridian, 1964.

———. *The Philadelphia Negro: A Social Study.* 1899. Repr., Philadelphia: University of Pennsylvania, 1967.

Duckworth, Edna. *A Black History of Huntington.* Edited by Lana Gillespie Boggs. N.p.: 1990. Special Collections, James E. Morrow Library, Marshall University.

Dunaway, Wilma A. *Slavery in the American Mountain South.* New York: Cambridge University Press, 2003.

Eldridge, Carrie. *An Atlas of Appalachian Trails to the Ohio River.* Huntington, W.Va.: CDN, 1998.

———. *Cabell County's Empire for Freedom: The Manumission of Sampson Sanders' Slaves.* Huntington, W.Va.: John Deaver Drinko Academy for American Political Institution and Civic Culture, Marshall University, 1999.

———. *Cabell County VA/WV Minute Book, 1809–1815.* N.p.: n.d. Special Collections, Cabell County Public Library, Huntington, W.Va.

———. "Freedom Lies across the River." Unpublished manuscript, 2004. Author's files.

———. *Looking at the Personal Diaries of William F. Dusenberry of Bloomington, Virginia, 1855, 1856, 1863, 1871.* Unpublished manuscript, 1998. KYOWVA Genealogical Society, Huntington, W.Va.

Bibliography

Elkins, Stanley M. *Slavery: A Problem in American Institutional and Intellectual Life*. 1976. 3rd rev. ed. Chicago: University of Chicago Press, 2013.

Eller, Ronald D. "Mountain Road: A Study of the Construction of the Chesapeake and Ohio Railroad in Southern West Virginia, 1867–1873." Master's thesis, University of North Carolina, 1973.

Engle, Stephen D. "Mountaineer Reconstruction: Blacks in the Political Reconstruction of West Virginia." *Journal of Negro History* 78, no. 3 (Summer 1993): 137–65.

Espy, M. Watt, and John Ortiz Smykla. *Executions in the United States, 1608–1987: The Espy File*. Vol. 3 (ICPSR 8451), West Virginia. First ICPSR edition (Fall 1987). Inter-university Consortium for Political and Social Research, Ann Arbor, Michigan. State Library of Ohio, Columbus.

Evans, Cerinda W. *Collis Potter Huntington*. Vol. 2. Newport News, Va.: Mariners' Museum, 1954.

Evans, Nelson W. *A History of Scioto County Together with a Pioneer Record of Southern Ohio*. Portsmouth, Ohio: Evans, 1903.

"Facts to Talk About." *Chesapeake and Ohio Lines Magazine* 21, no. 3 (March 1939): 24.

Fain, Cicero M., III. "Buffalo Soldier, Deserter, Criminal: The Remarkably Complicated Life of Charles Ringo." *Ohio Valley History* 15, no. 4 (Winter 2015): 41–62.

———. "The Forging of a Black Community: Huntington, West Virginia, 1870–1900." Master's thesis, Ohio State University, 2003.

Fishback, Price V. "Did Coal Miners 'Owe Their Souls to the Company Store'? Theory and Evidence from the Early 1900s." *Journal of Economic History* 46, no. 4 (December 1986): 1011–29.

Foner, Eric. *Reconstruction: America's Unfinished Revolution, 1863–1877*. New York: Harper and Row, 1988.

Frazier, E. Franklin. *The Negro Family in the United States*. 1937. Revised and abridged ed. Chicago: University of Chicago Press, 1967.

Franklin, John Hope. *George Washington Williams: A Bibliography*. Chicago: University of Chicago Press, 1985.

Fredrickson, George M. *The Black Image in the White Mind: The Debate on Afro-American Character and Destiny, 1817–1914*. Hanover, N.H.: Wesleyan University Press, 1971.

Friedman, Lawrence. *Crime and Punishment in American History*. New York: Basic, 1993.

Gaines, Kevin K. *Uplifting the Race: Black Leadership, Politics, and Culture in the Twentieth Century*. Chapel Hill: University of North Carolina Press, 1996.

Gamble, Vanessa Northington. *Making a Place for Ourselves: The Black Hospital Movement, 1920–1945*. New York: Oxford University Press, 1995.

Geiger, Joe, Jr. *Civil War in Cabell County, West Virginia, 1861–1865*. Charleston, W.Va.: Pictorial Histories, 1991.

———. "The Tragic Fate of Guyandotte." *West Virginia History* 54 (1995): 28–41.

Genovese, Eugene D. *Roll, Jordan, Roll: The World the Slaves Made*. New York: Vintage, 1976.

Gilroy, Paul. *The Black Atlantic: Modernity and Double Consciousness*. Cambridge, Mass.: Harvard University Press, 1993.

Goggin, Jacqueline. *Carter G. Woodson: A Life in Black History*. Baton Rouge: Louisiana State University Press, 1987.

Goings, Kenneth W., and Raymond A. Mohl, eds. *The New African American Urban History*. Thousand Oaks, Calif.: Sage, 1996.

Goings, Kenneth W., and Gerald L. Smith. "'Unhidden' Transcripts: Memphis and African American Agency, 1862–1920." In *New African American Urban History*, 141–66.

Gottlieb, Peter. *Making Their Own Way: Southern Blacks' Migration to Pittsburgh, 1916–1930*. Urbana: University of Illinois, 1987.

Green, Sharony. *Remember Me to Miss Louisa: Hidden Black-White Intimacies in Antebellum America*. Dekalb: Northern Illinois University Press, 2015.

Greene, Harry W. "The Education of Negroes in West Virginia." *Journal of Negro Education* 16, no. 3 (Summer 1947): 433–38.

Griffin, William W. *African Americans and the Color Line in Ohio, 1915–1930*. Columbus: Ohio State University Press, 2005.

Griffler, Keith. *Front Line of Freedom: African Americans and the Forging of the Underground Railroad in the Ohio Valley*. Lexington: University Press of Kentucky, 2004.

Grossman, James R. *Land of Hope: Chicago, Black Southerners, and the Great Migration*. Chicago: University of Chicago Press, 1991.

Gutman, Herbert. *The Black Family in Slavery and Freedom, 1750–1925*. New York: Pantheon, 1976.

———. "The Negro and the United Mine Workers of America: The Career and Letters of Richard L. Davis and Something of Their Meaning, 1890–1900." In *The Negro and the American Labor Movement*, edited by Julius Jacobson. Garden City, N.Y.: Anchor/Doubleday, 1968.

Hagedorn, Ann. *Beyond the River: The Untold Story of Heroes of the Underground Railroad*. New York: Simon and Schuster, 2002.

Hanshaw, Tillie. "Train Porter Calls Work a Hobby." *Chesapeake and Ohio and Hocking Valley Magazine* 14, no. 1, (January 1929): 86.

Harlan, Louis P., ed. *The Booker T. Washington Papers, 1860–89*. Vol. 2. Urbana: University of Illinois Press, 1972.

Hart, Betty L. Powell. "A Brief History of the Black Press in West Virginia." N.p.: n.d. West Virginia Archives and History Library, Charleston, W.Va.

Hart, L. W. "Actively at Work in His 80th Year." *Chesapeake and Ohio and Hocking Valley Magazine* 14, no. 5 (May 1929): 35.

———. "Retires on Pension after 60 Years." *Chesapeake and Ohio Lines Magazine* 15, no. 5 (May 1930): 67.

Henri, Florette. *Black Migration: Movement North, 1900–1920*. Anchor/Doubleday: Garden City, N.Y.: 1975.

Hepler, Linda. "The C&O Patch: Remembering a Huntington Neighborhood." *Goldenseal* 12, no. 2 (Summer 1986): 16.
Hesslink, George K. *Black Neighbors: Negroes in a Northern Rural Community*. Indianapolis: Bobbs-Merrill, 1968.
Higginbotham, Evelyn Brooks. *Righteous Discontent: The Women's Movement in the Black Baptist Church, 1880–1920*. Cambridge, Mass.: Harvard University Press, 1993.
Hine, Darlene Clark. "Black Professionals and Race Consciousness: Origins of the Civil Rights Movement, 1890–1950." *Journal of American History* 89, no. 4 (March 2003): 1279–94.
———. *Black Women in White: Racial Conflict and Cooperation in the Nursing Profession, 1890–1950*. Bloomington: Indiana University Press, 1989.
"History." The Greenbrier. http://www.greenbrier.com/Top-Navigation-Pages/About-Us/History.aspx.
The History of Summers County West Virginia. Marceline, Mo.: Walsworth, 1984.
Housel, Jacqueline A. "The Construction of a 'Colored' Neighborhood: The Shaping of Washington Place, Huntington, WV, 1905–1925." N.p.: 2002. Special Collections, Cabell County Central Library, Huntington, W.Va.
———. "Side by Side: A 1910 Comparison of Two Avenues in Huntington, WV." N.p.: 1998. Special Collections: Cabell County Central Library, Huntington, W.Va.
Hudson, J. Blaine. *Fugitive Slaves and the Underground Railroad in the Kentucky Borderland*. Jefferson, N.C.: McFarland, 2002.
Hunter, Tera W. "Domination and Resistance: The Politics of Wage Household Labor in New South Atlanta." In Goings and Mohl, *New African American Urban History*, 167–86.
———. *To 'Joy My Freedom: Southern Black Women's Lives and Labors after the Civil War*. Cambridge, Mass.: Harvard University Press, 1997.
Huntington Chamber of Commerce. Huntington, W.Va.: Standard, c. 1910.
Innis, Darleen. "Poke Patch Station." Unpublished manuscript, 1998. Gallia County (Ohio) Historical Society, Gallipolis.
Inscoe, John C. *Appalachians and Race: The Mountain South from Slavery to Segregation*. Lexington: University of Kentucky, 2001.
———, ed. *Mountain Masters, Slavery and the Sectional Crisis in Western North Carolina*. Knoxville: University of Tennessee, 1989.
———. *Race, War, and Remembrance in the Appalachian South*. Lexington: University Press of Kentucky, 2008.
"Items of Interest." *Journal of the National Medical Association* 4, no. 3 (July–September 1912): 278.
Jackson, Luther P. "Manumission in Certain Virginia Cities." *Journal of Negro History* 15, no. 3 (July 1930): 287–88.
Javersak, David Thomas. "The Ohio Valley Trades and Labor Assembly: The Formative Years, 1882–1915." PhD diss., West Virginia University, 1977.

Jaynes, Gerald David. *Branches without Roots: Genesis of the Black Working Class in the American South, 1862–1882*. New York: Oxford University Press, 1986.

Johnson, Charles S. "How Much Is the Migration a Flight from Persecution?" *Opportunity: A Journal of Negro Life* 1, no. 9 (September 1923): 272–74.

Johnson, Delores M. "Not a Story to Be Told: Discourse, Race, and Myth in Huntington, West Virginia Newspapers, 1872–1972." PhD diss., Indiana University of Pennsylvania, 1995.

Johnson, Guy B. *John Henry: Tracking Down a Negro Legend*. New York: AMS, 1969.

Johnson, Walter. *Soul by Soul: Life inside the Antebellum Slave Market*. Cambridge, Mass.: Harvard University Press, 1999.

Jones, Jacqueline. *The Dispossessed: America's Underclass from the Civil War to the Present*. New York: Basic, 1992.

———. *Labor of Love, Labor of Sorrow: Black Women, Work, and the Family from Slavery to the Present*. New York: Basic, 1995.

Jones, Lawrence N. "The Civil Status of Negroes in West Virginia as Reflected in Legislative Acts and Judicial Decisions, 1860–1940." Master's thesis, University of Chicago, 1948.

Katzman, David M. *Before the Ghetto: Black Detroit in the Nineteenth Century*. Urbana: University of Illinois Press, 1973.

Katznelson, Ira. "Working-Class Formation: Constructing Cases and Comparisons." In *Working Class Formation: Nineteenth-Century Patterns in Western Europe and the United States*, edited by Ira Katznelson and Artistide R. Zolberg, 13–22. Princeton, N.J.: Princeton University Press, 1986.

Kelley, Robin D. G. *Race Rebels: Culture, Politics, and the Black Working Class*. New York: Free Press, 1994.

———. "'We Are Not What We Seem': Rethinking Black Working-Class Opposition in the Jim Crow South." In Goings and Mohl, *New African American Urban History*, 187–239.

Kirby, Jack Temple. *Darkness at the Dawning: Race and Reform in the Progressive South*. Philadelphia: Lippincott, 1972.

Klotter, James C. "The Black South and White Appalachia." *Journal of American History* 66, no. 4 (March 1980): 832–49.

Knohaus, Tim. "'I Thought Things Would be Different There': Lynching and the Black Community in Southern West Virginia, 1880–1933." *West Virginia History: Journal of Regional Studies* 1, no. 2 (Fall 2007): 25–43.

Kounse, Martha J. *Annotated Lawrence County, Ohio Children's Home Register, 1874–1926*. Milford, Ohio: Little Miami, 2003.

Kusmer, Kenneth A. *A Ghetto Takes Shape: Black Cleveland, 1870–1930*. Urbana: University of Illinois Press, 1976.

———. "Social Status among Migrant Negroes." *Social Forces* 16, no. 4 (May 1938): 562–68.

Laidley, W. S. *History of Charleston and Kanawha County, West Virginia and Representative Citizens*. Chicago: Arnold, 1911.

Laing, James T. "The Negro Miner in West Virginia." *Social Forces* 14, no. 3 (March 1936): 416–22.

Lavender, David. *The Great Persuader*. Garden City, N.Y.: Doubleday, 1970.

Lawrence, Randy. "Appalachian Metamorphosis: Industrializing Society on the Central Appalachian Plateau, 1860–1913 (West Virginia, Kentucky, Tennessee, Virginia)." PhD diss., Duke University, 1983.

Lebsock, Suzanne. *The Free Women of Petersburg: Status and Culture in a Southern Town, 1740–1860*. New York: Norton, 1984.

———. *A Murder in Virginia: Social Justice on Trial*. New York: Norton, 2003.

Lee, Howard B. *Bloodletting in Appalachia: The Story of West Virginia's Four Major Mine Wars and Other Thrilling Incidents*. Morgantown: West Virginia University Press, 1969.

Leith, C. Robert. "Follow the Furnaces." N.p.: 2005. Special Collections, Briggs-Lawrence County Public Library, Ironton, Ohio.

Lerner, Gerda. "The Lady and the Mill Girl: Changes in the Status of Women in the Age of Jackson." *Midcontinent American Studies Journal* (Spring 1969): 5–14.

Levine, Lawrence. *Black Culture and Black Consciousness: Afro-American Folk Thought from Slavery to Freedom*. Oxford: Oxford University Press: 1977.

Lewis, Charlene M. Boyer. *Ladies and Gentlemen on Display: Planter Society at the Virginia Springs, 1790–1860*. Charlottesville: University Press of Virginia, 2001.

Lewis, Earl. *In Their Own Interests: Race, Class, and Power in Twentieth-Century Norfolk, Virginia*. Berkeley: University of California Press, 1991.

Lewis, Ronald L. *Black Coal Miners in America: Race, Class, and Community Conflict, 1780–1980*. Lexington: University Press of Kentucky, 1987.

———. "From Peasant to Proletarian: The Migration of Southern Blacks to the Central Appalachian Coalfields." *Journal of Southern History* 55 (February 1989): 77–102.

———. *Transforming the Appalachian Countryside: Railroads, Deforestation, and Social Change in West Virginia, 1880–1920*. Chapel Hill: University Press of North Carolina, 1998.

Lewis, Stephen. *An Overview of the History of Wayne County, West Virginia*. Unpublished manuscript. Special Collections, Cabell County Public Library, Huntington, W.Va.

Litwack, Leon F. *Trouble in Mind: Black Southerners in the Age of Jim Crow*. New York: Knopf, 1998.

Livers, Ancella Bickley. "The Greenbrier Lynching: A Study of West Virginia Justice." Unpublished manuscript, 1993. Special Collections, Morrow Library, Marshall University, Huntington, W.Va.

Loewen, James W. *Sundown Towns: A Hidden Dimension of American Racism*. New York: New Press, 2005.

Logan, Rayford W. *The Negro Life in American Life and Thought: The Nadir 1877–1901*. New York: Dial, 1954.

Lomax, John A., and Alan Lomax. *Best Loved American Folk Songs*. New York: Grosset and Dunlap, 1947.

Maloney, Eugene A. *A History of Buckingham County*. Waynesboro, Va.: McClung, 1976.

Marks, Carol. *Farewell—We're Good and Gone: The Great Black Migration*. Bloomington: Indiana University Press, 1989.

Marszalek, John F. "Slave Resistance." In *Dictionary of Afro-American Slavery*, edited by Randall M. Miller and John David Smith. Westport, Conn.: Greenwood, 1988.

Massey, Douglass, and Nancy A. Denton. *American Apartheid: Segregation and the Making of the Underclass*. Cambridge, Mass.: Harvard University Press, 1993.

Matthews, Edith E. Perkins. "Perkins and Early Related Families African Americans, Part I." N.p.: 1995, 14. Greenbrier Historical Society, Lewisburg, W.Va.

Matthews, Estivaun, ed. *Gallia One-Room Schools: The Cradle Years*. Gallipolis, Ohio: Gallia County Historical Society, 1993. State Library of Ohio, Columbus, Ohio.

McGehee, C. Stuart. *Black Folk at Green Bottom: From Slavery to Freedom on the Ohio Frontier* https://tinyurl.com/BlackFolkAtGreenBottom.

———. *Bluefield, West Virginia, 1889–1989: A Centennial History*. Jostens, 1990. Bluefield State College, Bluefield, W.Va.

McKinney, Tim. *The Civil War in Greenbrier County, West Virginia*. Charleston, W.Va.: Quarrier, 2004.

McMillen, Neil. *Dark Journey: Black Mississippians in the Age of Jim Crow*. Urbana: University of Illinois Press, 1989.

Meador, Michael M. "Carving a Niche: The Blacks of Bluefield." *Goldenseal* 13, no. 4 (Winter 1987): 19–27.

Meier, August. *Negro Thought in America, 1880–1915: Racial Ideologies in the Age of Booker T. Washington*. Ann Arbor: University of Michigan Press, 1963.

Miller, Corliss. "The Underground Railroad." Unpublished manuscript, 1996. Gallia County (Ohio) Historical Society, Gallipolis.

Miller, Doris. *A Centennial History of Huntington, 1871–1971*. Huntington, W.Va.: Franklin, 1981.

Miller, Rikki. "Answering the Call: The Creation and Cultural Significance of the Barnett Hospital." Carter G. Woodson Project, Marshall University.

Moore, Jacqueline M. *Leading the Race: The Transformations of the Black Elite in the Nation's Capital, 1880–1920*. Charlottesville: University of Virginia Press, 1999.

Moore, Shirley Ann. "Getting There, Being There: African American Migration to Richmond, California, 1910–45." In *The Great Migration in Historical Perspective: New Dimensions of Race, Class, and Gender*, edited by Joe William Trotter Jr., 106–20. Bloomington: Indiana University Press, 1991.

Morgan, Philip D. *Slave Counterpoint: Black Culture in the Eighteenth Century Chesapeake and Lowcountry*. Chapel Hill: University of North Carolina Press, 1998.

Moss, Joseph W. "The Negro and Recreation in Southern West Virginia." Master's thesis, Ohio State University, 1936.

Moynihan, Daniel P. *The Negro Family: The Case for National Action*. Washington, D.C.: Office of Policy Planning and Research, United States Department of Labor, 1965.

Nance, Karen N. Cartwright. *The Significance of the Jenkins Plantation*. Unpublished manuscript, 1998. Author's files.

Nelson, Scott Reynolds. *Steel Drivin' Man: John Henry, The Untold Story of an American Legend*. New York: Oxford University Press, 2006.

———. "Who Was John Henry? Railroad Construction, Southern Folklore, and the Birth of Rock and Roll." In *Other Souths: Diversity and Difference in the U.S. South, Reconstruction to Present*, edited by Pippa Holloway, 38–66. Athens: University of Georgia Press, 2008.

Newlin, Regina A. "A Cultural Evaluation of John Henry." Unpublished manuscript, 1995. Chesapeake and Ohio Historical Society, Clifton Forge, Va.

Noe, Kenneth. "Appalachia's Civil War Genesis: Southwest Virginia as Depicted by Northern and European Writers, 1825–1865." *West Virginia History* 50 (1991): 91–108.

Noe, Kenneth W. *Southwest Virginia's Railroad: Modernization and the Sectional Crisis*. Urbana: University of Illinois Press, 1994.

"Opportunity to Honor:" *A Black History Month Exhibit, Artifacts and Documents from Greenbrier Historical Society and North House Museum*, February 1–March 8, 2013. Greenbrier Historical Society, Lewisburg, W.Va.

Osofsky, Gilbert. *Harlem: The Making of a Ghetto, 1890–1930*. New York: Harper and Row, 1966.

Painter, Nell Irvin. *The Exodusters: Black Migration to Kansas after Reconstruction*. 1976. Repr., Lawrence: University Press of Kansas, 1986.

Park, Robert. "The City: Suggestions for the Investigation of Human Behavior in the Urban Environment." In *The City*, edited by Robert E. Park, Ernest W. Burgess, and Roderick D. McKenzie. Chicago: University of Chicago Press, 1925.

Parker, John P. *His Promised Land: The Autobiography of John P. Parker, Former Slave and Conductor on the Underground Railroad*. Edited by Stuart Steely Sprague. New York: Norton, 1996.

Phillips, Kimberly. *Alabama North: African American Migrants, Community, and Working-Class Activism in Cleveland, 1915–1945*. Champaign: University of Illinois Press, 1999.

Philpott, Thomas L. *The Slum and the Ghetto: Neighborhood Deterioration and Middle-Class Reform, Chicago, 1880–1930*. New York: Oxford University Press, 1978.

Plantania, Joseph. "Getting Ready for Life: The Douglass High School Story." *Goldenseal* 19 (Fall 1993): 21–27.

Platt, J. Earl. *The Promised Land*. New York: Vantage, 1964.

Posey, Thomas E. "The Labor Movement in West Virginia, 1900–1948." PhD diss., University of Wisconsin, 1948.

———. *The Negro Citizen of West Virginia*. Institute: Press of West Virginia State College, 1934.

Prillerman, Byrd. "The Growth of the Colored Schools in West Virginia." In *The History of Education in West Virginia, 1907*, West Virginia State Department of Education, 274–76. Charleston: Tribune, 1907.

Pryor, Mrs. Roger A. "The Colonel's Story." In *The White Sulphur Springs: The Traditions, History, and Social Life of the Greenbrier White Sulphur Springs*, edited by William Alexander MacCorkle. New York: Neale, 1916.

Puglisi, Michael J., ed. *Diversity and Accommodation: Essays on the Cultural Composition of the Virginia Frontier*. Knoxville: University of Tennessee Press, 1997.

Rabinowitz, Howard N. *Race Relations in the Urban South, 1865–1890*. New York: Oxford University Press, 1978.

Rachleff, Peter J. *Black Labor in the South: Richmond, Virginia, 1865–1890*. Philadelphia: Temple University Press, 1984.

Randall, James D., and Anna E. Gilmer. "Black Past." N.p.: 1989. West Virginia Archives and History Library, Charleston.

Rasmussen, Barbara. "Charles Ambler's *Sectionalism in Virginia*: An Appreciation." *West Virginia History: A Journal of Regional Studies* 3, no. 1 (Spring 2009): 1–36.

Ravenstein, E. G. "The Laws of Migration." *Journal of the Royal Statistical Society* 2 (June 1889): 284.

Reniers, Perceval. *The Springs of Virginia: Life, Love, and Death at the Waters, 1775–1900*. Chapel Hill: University of North Carolina Press, 1941.

Rice, Connie. "J. R. Clifford and the Struggle for Equal Rights in West Virginia." *Conference Papers—Association for the Study of African American Life and History*. 2004 Annual Meeting, Pittsburgh, Penn.

Rice, Otis K. "Eli Thayer and the Friendly Invasion of Virginia." *Journal of Southern History* 37, no. 4 (November 1971): 585–86.

Rice, Otis K., and Stephen W. Brown. *West Virginia: A History*. 2nd ed. Lexington: University of Kentucky Press, 1993.

Rose, Willie Lee. "Masters without Slaves." In *Slavery and Freedom*, edited by William W. Freehling, 73–89. New York: Oxford University Press, 1982.

Ryan, Mary P. *Womanhood in America: From Colonial Times to the Present*. New York: New Viewpoint, 1975.

Salafi, Matthew. *Slavery's Borderland: Freedom and Bondage along the Ohio River*. Philadelphia: University of Pennsylvania Press, 2013.

Saville, Julie. *The Work of Reconstruction: From Slave to Wage Labor in South Carolina, 1860–1870*. New York: Cambridge University Press, 1994.

Schwarz, Philip J. *Migrants against Slavery: Virginians and the Nation*. Charlottesville: University Press of Virginia, 2001.

Scott, Anna Firor. "Most Invisible of All: Black Women's Voluntary Associations." *Journal of Southern History* 56, no. 1 (February 1990): 3–22.

Scott, J. W. "The Colored School of Huntington." *History of Education in West Virginia, 1907*. Charleston: Tribune, 1907.

Semmes, John E. *John H. Latrobe and His Times, 1803–1891*. Baltimore, Md.: Remington, 1917.

Shaw, Stephanie J. *What a Woman Ought to Be and to Do: Black Professional Women Workers during the Jim Crow Era*. Chicago: University of Chicago Press, 1996.

Sheller, John. "The Negro in West Virginia before 1900." PhD diss., West Virginia University, 1954.

Shepherd, Rebecca A. "Restless Americans: The Geographic Mobility of Farm Laborers in the Old Midwest, 1850–1870." *Ohio History* 89, no. 1 (Winter 1980): 25–45.

Shifflett, Crandall A. *Patronage and Poverty in the Tobacco South: Louisa County, Virginia, 1860–1900*. Knoxville: University of Tennessee Press, 1982.

Siebert, H. Wilbur. *The Mysteries of Ohio's Underground Railroads*. Columbus, Ohio: Long's, 1951.

———. *The Underground Railroad from Slavery to Freedom*. 1898. Repr., New York: Russell and Russell, 1967.

Silver, Christopher. "The Racial Origins of Zoning in American Cities." In *Urban Planning and the African American Community: In the Shadows*, edited by June Manning Thomas and Marsha Ritzdorf. Thousand Oaks, Calif.: Sage, 1997. https://www.asu.edu/courses/aph294/total-readings/silver%20—%20racialoriginsofzoning.pdf.

Simmons, Charles W., John R. Rankin, and U. G. Carter. "Negro Coal Miners in West Virginia, 1875–1925." *Midwest Journal* 6, no. 1 (Spring 1954): 60–69.

Simmons, J. Susanne Schramm. "Augusta County's Other Pioneers: The African American Presence in Frontier Augusta County." In Puglisi, *Diversity and Accommodation*, 159–71.

Skeen, David Overton. "Industrial Democracy, Social Equality, and Violence: The West Virginia Mine Wars, 1912–1921." Master's thesis, California State University, Dominguez Hills, 1996.

"Society and Personal." *Journal of the National Medical Association* 10, no. 3 (July–September 1918): 142.

Spear, Allen H. *Black Chicago: The Making of a Negro Ghetto, 1890–1920*. Chicago: University of Chicago Press, 1967.

Stanford, Leland R. *An Illustrated History of the Huntington District U. S. Army Corps of Engineers, 1754–1974*. Washington, D.C.: GPO, 1977.

Stealey, John E., III. *The Antebellum Kanawha Salt Business and Western Markets*. Lexington: University Press of Kentucky, 1993.

———. "Slavery in the Kanawha Salt Industry." In Inscoe, *Appalachians and Race*, 50–73.

Sullivan, Charles Kenneth. *Coal Men and Coal Towns: Development of the Smokeless Coalfields of Southern West Virginia, 1873–1923*. New York: Garland, 1989.

Sullivan, Ken, ed. *The West Virginia Encyclopedia*. Charleston: West Virginia Humanities Council, 2006.

Sullivan, Ken, and Randy Lawrence. "Black Migration to Southern West Virginia, 1870–1930." *Goldenseal* 23, no. 4 (Fall 1997): 52–53.

Swann-Wright, Dianne. *A Way Out of No Way: Claiming Family and Freedom in the New South*. Charlottesville: University of Virginia Press, 2002.

Tabscott, Robert. "John Henry: The Story of a Steel-Driving Man." *Goldenseal* 22, no. 2 (Summer 1996): 50–54.

Talbott, Forrest. "Some Legislative and Legal Aspects of the Negro Question in West Virginia during the Civil War and Reconstruction, Part I." *West Virginia History* 24, no. 1 (October 1962): 1–31.

———. "Some Legislative and Legal Aspects of the Negro Question in West Virginia during the Civil War and Reconstruction, Part II." *West Virginia History* 24, no. 2 (January 1963): 110–31.

Taylor, A. A. "The Negro in the Reconstruction of Virginia [Part 1]: The Migration." *Journal of Negro History* 11, no. 2 (April 1926): 243–415.

Taylor, Alrutheus A. "Making West Virginia a Free State," *Journal of Negro History* 6, no. 2 (April 1921): 131–73.

Taylor, Henry L. "On Slavery's Fringe: City-Building and Black Community Development in Cincinnati, 1800–1850." *Ohio History* 95 (Winter–Spring 1986).

Taylor, Henry Louis, Jr. "Introduction: Race and the City, 1820–1970." In *Race and the City: Work, Community, and Protest in Cincinnati, 1820–1970*, edited by Henry Louis Taylor Jr., 1–28. Urbana: University of Illinois Press, 1993.

Taylor, Nikki M. *Frontiers of Freedom: Cincinnati's Black Community, 1802–1868.* Athens: Ohio University Press, 2005.

"T. Gillis Nutter, West Virginia." In *These "Colored" United States: African American Essays from the 1920s*, edited by Tom Lutz and Susanna Ashton, 289–90. New Brunswick, N.J.: Rutgers University Press, 1996.

Thompson, Robert Michael. *Few among the Mountains: Slavery in Wayne County.* N.p.: 2012. Author's files.

"A Timeline of African-American History in West Virginia." West Virginia Division of Culture and History. http://www.wvculture.org/HISTORY/archivesindex.aspx.

Toll, William. "Free Men, Freedmen, and Race: Black Social Theory in the Gilded Age." *Journal of Southern History* 44, no. 4 (November 1978): 571–98.

Trotter, Joe William, Jr. "African American Workers: New Directions in U.S. Labor Historiography." *Labor History* 35, no. 4 (Fall 1994): 495–523.

———. *Black Milwaukee: The Making of an Industrial Proletariat, 1915–1945.* Urbana: University of Illinois Press, 1985.

———. *Coal, Class, and Color: Blacks in Southern West Virginia, 1915–1932.* Urbana: University of Illinois Press, 1990.

———. "The Formation of Black Community in Southern West Virginia Coalfields." In Inscoe, *Appalachians and Race*, 284–301.

———. "Race, Class, and Industrial Change: Black Migration to Southern West Virginia, 1915–1932." In *The Great Migration in Historical Perspective: New Dimensions in Race, Class, and Gender*, edited by Joe W. Trotter Jr., 46–67. Bloomington: Indiana University Press, 1991.

———. *River Jordan: African American Urban Life in the Ohio Valley.* Lexington: University Press of Kentucky, 1998.

Turner, Charles. "The Chesapeake and Ohio Railroad in Reconstruction, 1865–1873." *North Carolina Historical Review* 31, no. 1 (1954): 150–72.

Turner, William H., and Edward J. Cabbell, eds. *Blacks in Appalachia.* Lexington: University of Kentucky, 1985.

"Virginia Union University." *The History of Jim Crow.* Teacher Resources. http://www.jimcrowhistory.org/scripts/jimcrow/glossary.cgi?term=v&letter=yes.

Wade, Howard P. "Black Gold and Black Folk: A Case Study of McDowell County, West Virginia, 1890–1940." PhD diss., University of Miami, 1990.

Wagner, Thomas E., and Phillip J. Obermiller. *African American Miners and Migrants: The Eastern Kentucky Social Club*. Urbana: University of Illinois Press, 2004.

Walcott, Virginia W. *Remaking Respectability: African American Women in Interwar Detroit*. Chapel Hill: University of North Carolina Press, 2001.

Walker, Clarence. *Deromanticizing Black History*. Knoxville: University of Tennessee Press, 1991.

Wallace, George Selden. *Cabell County Annals and Families*. Richmond, Va.: Garrett and Massie, 1935.

———. *Huntington through Seventy-Five Years*. Huntington, W.Va.: 1947.

Warner, Dudley Charles. "Their Pilgrimage." In *The White Sulphur Springs: The Traditions, History, and Social Life of the Greenbrier White Sulphur Springs*, edited by William Alexander MacCorkle. New York: Neale, 1916.

Washington, Booker T. *An Autobiography: The Story of My Life and Work*. Toronto, Ont.: Nichols, 1901.

———. *Up from Slavery: An Autobiography*. New York: Doubleday, 1901.

Welter, Barbara. "The Cult of True Womanhood, 1820–1860." *American Quarterly* (Summer 1966): 151–74.

"West Virginia Colored Orphans' Home." *West Virginia Review* 2, no. 12 (September 1925): 444–45.

Whear, Nancy. "Carter G. Woodson: An Annotated Chronology of his Life." N.p.: n.d. Special Collections, Cabell County Library, Huntington, W.Va.

White, Charles H. *The Hidden and Forgotten: Contributions of Buckingham Blacks to American History*. Marceline, Mo.: Walsworth, 1985.

White, Walter. *Rope and Faggot: A Biography of Judge Lynch*. New York: Knopf, 1929.

Williams, Brett. *John Henry: A Bio-Bibliography*. Westport, Conn.: Greenwood, 1983.

Williams, John Alexander. *Appalachia: A History*. Chapel Hill: University of North Carolina Press, 2002.

———. *West Virginia: A History*. Morgantown: West Virginia University Press, 2001.

Windle, Mary Jane. *Life at the White Sulphur Springs; or, Pictures of a Pleasant Summer*. Philadelphia: Lippincott, 1857.

Woodson, Carter G. *A Century of Black Migration*. 1918. Repr., New York: Russell and Russell, 1969.

———. "Early Negro Education in West Virginia." *Journal of Negro History* 7, no. 1 (1922): 51–65.

———. "Freedom and Slavery in Appalachian America." *Journal of Negro History* 1, no. 2 (1916): 132–50.

———. *A Historical Reader*, ed. James L. Conyers. New York: Garland, 2000.

"Work of Art: *Kitchen Ball at White Sulphur Springs, Virginia*." http://artnc.org/works-of-art/kitchen-ball-white-sulphur-springs-virginia.

Wright, George C. *Life Behind a Veil: Blacks in Louisville, Kentucky, 1865–1930*. Baton Rouge: Louisiana State University Press, 1985.

———. *Racial Violence in Kentucky, 1865–1940: Lynching, Mob Rule, and "Legal Lynchings."* Baton Rouge: Louisiana State University Press, 1990.

Yancey, Bessie Woodson. *Echoes from the Hill: A Book of Poems.* Washington, D.C.: Associated, 1939.

Zangrando, Robert L. *The NAACP Crusade against Lynching, 1909–1950.* Philadelphia: Temple University Press, 1980.

Index

Abbott, Robert, 128
abolitionist movement, 10–11. *See also* Underground Railroad
Afro-American Improvement Company, 78
Alabama, 20
America, Richard, 112
Ashland, KY, 73

Baker, Andrew, 79
Banks, John Henry, 65
Barboursville, WV, 2, 73, 75; during Civil War, 17; Negro schools in, 100; Underground Railroad and, 10
Barnes, U. L. Sr., 65
Barnett, Callie, 123
Barnett, Carl, 84, 125, 208n47
Barnett, Carter H., 104–105, 113–114
Barnett, Catherine A. "Kate," 200n101
Barnett, C. C., 135–136, 213n127
Barnett, Clara Matthews, 136
Barnett, Josephine, 105, 124, 126
Barnett, Nelson, 39–40, 77, 84, 96–98, 103, 140, 190n3, 191n24
Barnett, Nelson Jr., 84, 114
Barnett Hospital, 105, 135–137, 143, 200n101
Belleview Park, 108
"benevolent segregation," 119–120, 132, 146
benevolent societies, 109–110, 128, 201nn108–109
Berea College, 104
Berkley, Ida, 167n59
Berlin, Ira, 4

Bickley, Ancella, 110
Big Bend Tunnel, 46, 49
Black, William, 58, 77
black churches, 87, 93–99, 128–130, 190n18; dancing and, 99, 192n39, 193nn40–41; Ebenezer United Methodist Church, 87, 95, 190n9, 190nn14–15; maintenance of decorum and, 98–99, 192n38; marriages and, 97–98; preachers as civic leaders, 96–97, 114, 191n21; white attendees, 98, 192n35
black coaches, 125–126
black community leaders, 114–116, 141; fraternal organizations and, 109–110, 201n108; home ownership and, 142; politicians, 202n123; preachers as, 96–97, 114, 191n21
black enfranchisement, 18, 74, 111, 202n123
black hospitals, 135–137, 211n97, 212n106
black laborers, 68–69, 81, 149–156; black female workers, 56–57, 67–68, 124, 150–151, 153, 155; children as, 133; C&O railroad and, 45–51, 54–55, 58–59, 62, 64–66, 81; enslaved (*see* slavery); in Huntington, 50, 56–58, 62, 64, 66, 68; labor activism of, 60–64; lack of occupational opportunity, 68–69, 125; occupational diversity for, 66–68, 149–151; occupational statistics, 149–156; recruitment of, 205n14; Socialist Party and, 138–139. *See also* black professional workers
black middle class, 127–128, 137, 140–142, 146; women and, 122–123, 207n34

Index

black migration, 78, 92, 118, 174nn46–47, 175nn50–52, 206n22; black enfranchisement and, 74; into Cabell County, 23, 25, 37–38, 41, 44, 74–75; C&O Railroad and, 74, 81; following emancipation, 18–19, 21, 23, 37, 39–40, 159n8, 170n91; into Huntington, 39, 70–71, 73–75, 78–83, 85, 118, 127, 139; juvenile crime and, 133; migrants' skills, 83–84; origins of migrants, 75; social cohesion and, 74; into West Virginia, 25, 37–38, 44, 59, 78, 81, 118–119, 180n64; White Sulphur Springs Resort and, 37; Woodson family, 79–80

black owned bars, 88–91

black-owned newspapers, 113–114, 128, 203n137

black political activity, 111–114, 202n123, 203n127, 206n29; anti-racist protests, 126–127; of black women, 122–123, 207n30

black professional workers, 105, 114, 116, 134–135, 140, 194n47; coaches, 125–126; doctors and nurses, 135–137; occupational statistics, 150, 151, 153, 156; professional women, 123–124; teachers, 101, 102–103, 125, 194n55, 195nn61–62, 196nn63–65, 198n82

black property ownership, xii, 77–78, 133–134, 139–142, 144, 146, 185nn19–20, 210n66

Blacks, William, 77

black schools, 99–106, 125–126, 174n37, 193n45, 198n82; attendance statistics, 101–102, 196n67; female students and, 101, 196n67, 197n68; in 19th century, 195n59, 196n62; role of ex-slaves in founding, 198n82; school integration and, 99, 157n1, 193n42, 194n47; teachers at, 101, 102–103, 125, 194n55, 195nn61–62, 196nn63–65, 198n82. *See also* Douglass High School

black womanhood, 122–123, 207n31, 207n34

black women workers, 56–57, 67–68, 123–124, 150–151, 153, 155, 180n73; as nurses, 136–137; school and, 197n68

Blake, S. F., 90

Blassingame, John, 30, 164n43

Blow, Reason and Daniel, 34

Bluefield, WV, 55, 180n70

Bowlin, James B., 20

The Breeze (newspaper), 203n137

Brier, Stephen, 63

Broadnax, Frank, 206n24

Bromley, Emma, 123

Brooks, Lewis, 159n8

Brown, Dorsey, 90
Brown, John P., 85
Brown, Theodore "Doug," 131
Brown, Walter, 117–118, 135
Brown, William Wells, 162n36
Brown v. the Board of Education (1954), 157n1
Bryant, I. V., 96–100, 126, 191n23, 193n40
Buchanan v. Warley (1917), 142
Buckingham County, 39
Buffington, Peter, 15, 86
Buffington Row, 86, 88
Burlington, OH, x, 9, 12, 93; Underground Railroad and, 10–11
Burlington 37, x, 6, 95, 161n31
Butler, Daniel, 87
Butler, Moses, 87, 112–113
Byrd, William, 67

Cabell, William, 1
Cabell County, WV, 158n4; agricultural economy of, 39, 175n55; black migration into, 23, 25, 37–38, 41, 44, 74–75; black wealth in, 41–44; during Civil War, 17, 21, 169n81; demographics of, 13, 16–17, 19–20, 41–43, 75; districts of, 41–42; effect of emancipation on, 38–39, 176nn58–59; free blacks in, 15–17; post-war black population of, 21, 41, 171n97, 171n99; schools in, 194n52, 195n59; slavery in, 2–4, 8–9, 13, 17, 19, 147, 157n2, 163n37, 168n68; "whitening" of, 19. *See also* Huntington, WV

cakewalks, 106
Caldwell, Shep, 206n24
Camden Interstate Railway, 107
Cammack, J. H., 131
Carter, Henry, 87
Carter, Martha, 87
Carter, Mary, 67
cemeteries, 134, 211n85
Ceramic Subdivision, 129–130
Ceredo, WV, 10, 166n55
Chappell, Louis, 49
Charleston, WV, 19, 133, 204n7; black property ownership in, 142; fraternal orders in, 107, 110; Socialist Party in, 212n113
Chavis, William, 10
Chesapeake and Ohio (C&O) Railroad, 23–24, 39, 44, 145, 171n5, 178n22, 182n103; black labor used in construction/operation of, 45–51, 54–55, 58, 62, 64–66, 81, 85, 178n33; black migration and, 81; commuter trains and, 66; deaths of railroad workers, 49–50, 178n23, 178n26; depres-

Index

sion of 1873 and, 52–54, 179n52; economic impact of, 52; European laborers and, 46, 177n6; Huntington as western terminus of, 24, 171n5; segregated facilities, 187n43; strikes on, 48, 178n34
Chicago Defender, 128
Cincinnati, OH, 76–77, 185n12
citizenship of former Confederates, 23, 170n90
citizenship of former slaves, 18, 23, 170n88
Civil War, 17, 169n81
Clark-Lewis, Elizabeth, 115–116
Clifford, John R., 194n47
Clinton, Constantine, 105
Clyburn, Charley, 121
coal mining, 51–52; black migration and, 80, 186n31; labor unions and, 182n95; mining towns, 200n91; racial conflict and, 60, 121; railroads and, 55; Socialist Party and, 138
Coger, Sydney, 130
Coleman, Amanda Miller, 123
Coleman, James D., 130
Colley, Mathew, 103
Colored Independent Republican Ticket, 113
Colored Masonry, 62
Colored National Labor Union, 61
Colored Orphans' Home and Industrial School, 108–109
Colored Waiters Alliance, 62
Connally, Beatrice Vinson, 66
Convention of 1872, 74, 110–111, 185n9, 202n115
Cook, Rufus, 71
Cradic, William P., 94
Crafton, Anderson, 95
criminal activity, 88, 189n79; adjudicated in churches, 192n38; disproportionate punishment for, 121, 206n24
The Crisis (magazine), 128

Davis, Richard L., 60, 63
Davis, Zelma, 125–126
Davis-DeEulis, Marilyn, 4
Dean, Patsey, 41, 44
Delaney, David, 141–142
Depression of 1873, 52–54, 101, 179nn52–53
Dicher, James, 10
D'lea (enslaved person), 3
Douglass High School, xii, 67, 87, 103–104, 106, 129, 157n1, 198n82; black coaches at, 125–126; black teachers at, 125; founding of, 103; music program of, 208n34; school desegregation and, 157n1

Douglass-Huntington High School Black Alumni Reunion, x
Douglass Republican League, 110, 114
Du Bois, W. E. B., 100, 104, 128
Duckworth, Edna, xi, 36–37, 66–67, 89, 131
Dunaway, Wilma, 26, 32
Dunbar Sisters Literacy Society, 123
Dusche, Carmella, 123
Dusenberry, William F., 9, 19
Duvall, C. H., 198n82

Ebenezer United Methodist Church, 87, 95, 190n9, 190nn14–15
election of 1860, 169n82
Eller, Ronald, 47
emancipation, 17–21, 37; in Cabell County, 38–39; migration following, 18–19, 21, 23, 37, 39–40, 167n56
Emancipation Day celebrations, 107–108
Engle, Stephen D., 41
Ensign Manufacturing, 60, 64, 181n90
Eubanks, Samuel, 101
Evansville, IL, 77
executions, 121, 206n24

Farr, John, 90
Ferguson, James H., 163n37
Fifteenth Amendment, 18, 170n90
Flick Amendment, 18, 74, 170n90
Foes, Lewis, 95
Ford, Charles, 111
Francisco, Nell Radford, 64, 124
fraternal organizations, 109–110, 128, 201nn108–109
free blacks, 5, 15–16, 35, 160n22, 169nn78–80; citizenship of, 18; re-enslavement of, 5–6, 15–16, 160nn19–20; at White Sulphur Springs resort, 34–35
Fry, Joshua, 159n18
Fry, Walker, 6
Fugitive Slave Act, 165n52
Fuller, J. M., 130
Fullerton, Lewis, 16

Gallia County, OH, 73–74, 164n47
Garrett, Billy "Doc," ix
Garrison, Memphis T., 51
Genovese, Eugene D., 33
Georgia, 20
Gillard, Jenkins, 112
Golden Rule Association, 205n19
Gordon, W. H., 105
Grand Lodge of the Knights of Pythias, 110

Grand United Order of Odd Fellows, 109
Graves, Sam, 89, 132
"Great Flood of 1884," 78
Great Kanawah valley, 26
Great Railroad Strike of 1877, 60
Greenbottom Plantation, 1–5, 7, 13–15, 159n18; slave churches at, 12; slave literacy at, 3–4, 8, 21
Greenbriar County: black migration and, 37; demographics of, 36–37; slavery in, 173n22
Griffith, John Lewis, 79
Gutman, Herbert, 60
Guyandotte, 2, 13, 24, 42–43, 73, 75; C&O railroad and, 172n6; during Civil War, 17, 169n81; effect of emancipation on, 38; Methodist Church in, 163n37; Negro schools in, 100; Underground Railroad and, 10
Guyan Valley Division rail line, 107

Haley, Mary, 16
Hamilton, A. W. (Alex), 46
Hannah, John, 4
Hartshorn Memorial College, 124
Hatchett, J. B., 126
Haymarket Riot, 60
Hazelwood, H. D., 145
Henry, John, 46, 51, 68, 176n5, 178n36
Hill, Cecil, 64
Hill, Dandridge, 57, 67, 112, 203n127
Hill, James L., 109
Hine, Darlene Clark, 135–136
Holderby, Susan, 13
Holderby Addition, 129–130
Holley, Caroline, 67, 77, 103
Holley, Robert, 103
Honky Tonk Saloon, 88–91
Hopkins, Millie, 56
Household of Ruth, 109, 128
Housel, Jacqueline A, 129–130
Howard, "Uncle Dan," 119
Hughes, George, 112
Hughes, Revella E., 123–125, 207n42
Huntington, Collis P., 24, 44, 46, 49, 171n5; depression of 1873 and, 52–54; influence of, 82; loss of C&O Railroad, 54
Huntington, WV, xi–xii, 84, 106, 118, 145–146; author's experience of, x; black cemeteries in, 134, 211n85; black churches in, 94–99, 128–130, 201n109; black community leaders in, 114–116, 134–135; black female residents of, 56–57, 76, 123–124; black hospitals in, 135–137; black laborers in, 50, 56–58, 62, 64, 66, 68, 82; black middle class in, 127–128, 137, 140–142, 146; black migration into, 39, 70–71, 73–75, 78–83, 85, 118, 127, 139; black owned bars in, 88–91; black owned businesses, listed, 143, 213n127; black-owned newspapers in, 113–114; black property ownership in, xii, 77–78, 133–134, 139–142, 185nn19–20; black residential neighborhoods of, 78, 85–88, 118, 128–131, 133, 139–140; black schools in, 100–106, 125, 196n62, 198n82 (*see also* Douglass High School); city parks in, 107–108; crime in, 88–91, 132–133; demographics of, 73, 75–76, 113, 118, 132, 145–146, 214n134; depression of 1873 and, 52–53; discrimination against black residents, 91; economy of, 52, 56–57, 73, 82, 200n90; founding of, 24–25, 44; fraternal orders in, 109–110, 201nn108–109; growth of, 83, 118, 141, 145–146, 204n7; Jim Crow attitudes in, xii, 116, 122, 139, 145–146; Jim Crow laws and, 82–83, 122, 128, 145; labor activism in, 60–62; labor unions in, 63–64; layout and construction of, 71–73; legal challenges to segregation in, 144–145; lynchings in, 91, 121–122, 206n25; public transportation in, 107, 184n3; recreational spaces in, 106–107; residential segregation in, 76–77, 118, 128–132, 134–135, 139–142, 144–145; Socialist Party in, 137–139; as steamboat port, 172n8; use of public spaces within, 106, 199n86, 199n89; as western terminus of C&O railroad, 24, 171n5, 214n134
Huntington Knights of Pythias Hall, 110
Hyder, Jennie, 190n14

Illinois, 5
Indiana, 5, 160n22
Ironton, OH, 73, 107–108

Jackson, Gerald, 63
Jackson, Pat, 65
James, Frank, 196n62
James, Mrs. William O., 67–68
James, Susie, 101, 196nn63–65
James, William F., 101, 102–103, 196nn63–65
James, William O., 57, 67, 77, 87, 112, 202n124; Butler and, 113; as school teacher, 100
James River and Kanawah Turnpike, 2, 11, 26, 158n6

Index

Jasper, "Grandpa" Jackson, 57
Jasper, James Murray, 57
Jenkins, Albert Gallatin, 2, 4, 14–15, 164n44, 166n55
Jenkins, Henry, 206n24
Jenkins, Janetta, 12
Jenkins, Thomas Jefferson, 20
Jenkins, Trent R., 103–104
Jenkins, William A., 1, 4, 12, 14–15, 20, 159n14, 164n44
Jim Crow laws, 21, 82–83, 122; Jim Crow attitudes in Huntington, xii, 116, 122, 139, 145–146; relative lack of in WV, 82, 106, 121–122, 146; residential segregation and, 118, 146; travel and, 128
John Henry myth, 51, 68, 176n5, 178n36
Johnson, Charles S., 120
Johnson, Guy, 51
Johnson, John, 47
Johnson, Lula, 123
Johnson, Maude, 196n62
Johnson, Walter, 14–15
Jones, Anna E., 144
Jones, Chink, 196n62
Jones, J. McHenry, 161n33
Jones, Joseph, 7–8, 161n33
Jones, Julia, 196n62
Jones, Oliver, 79
juvenile crime, 132–133

Kanawah and New River coalfield, 55
Kanawah Valley salt mines, 46, 168n67
Kelley, Jane, 56
Kentucky: escape of slaves to, 169n83; free blacks in, 160n22; racial composition of, 20
Kessler Hospital, 117, 135
Kirby, Jack Temple, 82–83
Kitchen Ball at White Sulphur Springs, Virginia (Mayr, 1838), 29, 31
Knights of Labor, 61, 63, 182n95
Knights of Pythias, 110, 128, 201n108
Ku Klux Klan, 214n129

labor activism, 59–61; black workers and, 60–64, 182n98, 183n109; labor unions, 61–64, 182n95, 183nn109–110; racial conflict and, 59–60; strikes, 48, 53, 60, 178n34, 179n51, 181n89
Lacy, Mary, 1–5, 15, 20–21, 43
Laing, James T., 81
Lawrence County, OH, 73–74

Layne, Emma Anderson "Auntie Em," 13
Lees, Thomas L., 162n37
Lewis, Albert D., 57, 65, 79, 94, 96–97
Lewis, Charlene M. Boyers, 33
Lewis, Charles Cameron, 14
Lewis, Earl, 62
Liggins, James, 101, 196n62
literacy, 79; of black women, 56–57; of slaves, 3–4, 8, 12, 21, 159n11
Loewen, James, 93
Logan, Rayford, 93
Long, Robert, 100, 111–112, 115
Louis, Joe, 178n36
Louisville, KY, 77, 120, 141–142
lynchings, 91, 119–122, 189n80, 205n20, 206n25; anti-lynching laws, 120, 205n21; black response to, 205n19

Macedonia Missionary Baptist Church, 93–94, 97
Mangrum, J. A., 77
Manson, Si, 77
marriages, 18, 81, 97–98, 203n126
Marrie, Nannie V., 108
Marshall College, 67, 126
Martin, William, 206n24
Maryland, 20
Mason, Clairborne R., 47, 177nn12–13
Matheus, John William, 25
Matthews, Edith E. Perkins, 28
Mayr, Christian Friedrich, 29, 31
McClain, C. S. and Mary E., 134
McClain, "Diamond Teeth Mary," 209n58
McDaniels, Ed, 88–92
McDowell County, 38, 202n123
McGhee, Charles E., 108–109
McGhee, Lucy, 123
McKinney, William T., 67, 87, 103, 196n62, 197n76, 201n108
McQueen, Lottie, 132
Meadows, A. D., 145
Medison, Dave, 145
Merchant, W. T., 87
Methodist Church, 163n37. *See also* Ebenezer United Methodist Church
Miller, Ike, 112
Miller, Isaac, 113
Mitchell, Mattie, 67
Mitchell, Mrs. Walter, 167n65
Moore, Lewis B., 127
Moore, Martin, 13
Morgan, J. P., 54

Morgan, William, 95
Morris, Benjamin and Mandalay, 41–42
Morris, Charles, 11, 167n59
Morris, George and Nancy, 43
Morris, John, 13, 15
Morris, Samuel, 41
Morton, Jeremiah, 35
Moss, Joseph W., 106
Mt. Olivet Baptist Association, 97
Mt. Olive Baptist Church, xii, 94–96
Myers, Walter, 83–84, 107–108, 134, 140, 144
Myers, Walter Sr., 140

National Association of the Advancement of Colored People (NAACP), xii; *White v. White* (1929) and, 144–145
Negro schools, 43
New River valley, 25, 179n39
Nicholas, Wilson Cary, 159n18
nitroglycerin, 48–49
Nordhoff, Charles, 47
Norfolk and Western (N&W) Railroad, 55, 61, 81
North Carolina, 20
Nutter, T. G., 145, 200n91

occupational mobility, 66–67
occupational statistics, 149–156
Ohio: black laborers in, 66; free blacks in, 5, 160n22; slave-hunting in, 166n53; slaves escaping to, 10–11, 164n47
Ohio River: as border between free and slave states, 5–6, 10, 161n25, 167n56, 169n83
Ohio Valley Trades and Labor Assembly, 63
Overstreet, Lee, 89

Page, Lewis (John), 15, 168n77
Parker, Asbury, 7, 11
Parker, John P., 165n52
Payne, Christopher, 113, 202n123
Perkins, Belle, 56
Perkins, R. J., 79, 97
Peters, W. S., 101
Phipps, George, 67
Pioneer Press, 194n47
Pittsburgh, PA, 77
Pittsburgh Courier, 128
Plessy v. Ferguson (1896), 83
Pocahontas coalfield, 55
"polite racism," 119–120, 142
political agitation, 40–41, 93, 126; Convention of 1872 and, 110–111; in Louisville, 142; Socialist Party and, 138–139
poll taxes, 160n22
Portsmouth, OH, 73
Potts. J. H., 131
Prillerman, Byrd, 198n82
property ownership. *See* black property ownership
Providence Regular Missionary Baptist Association, 93–94

Radford, James, 66
Radford, William "Anderson," 40, 65–66
Ragland, Henry Clay, 119
Rau, Kate, 144
Reconstruction era, 70
recruitment of black workers, 47, 119, 205n14
Reed, Temperance, 10
regional development, phases of, 157n1
representation, freehold *vs.* manhood, 162n37
Republican Party, 74, 112–113, 202n123, 206n29; school desegregation and, 193n42
residential segregation, 213n125; in 19th century Huntington, 76, 134; in 20th century Huntington, 118, 128–132, 139–141, 144; benefits of, 211n87; "benevolent segregation," 119–120, 132, 146; legal challenges to, 135, 142, 144–145; self-segregation, 140; subdivisions and, 213n124
Reynolds, Isaac, 82
Richardson, Lewis, 50
Riddle, Anne Eliza, 22, 36, 40
Riddle, James Buchanan, 79, 104
Riddle, John Morton, 79, 104
Riddle, Robert, 22
Riddle, Robert D., 36
Ringo, Charles, 91, 122, 132
Ritter Park, 108
Rose, Anderson, 20, 43
Rose, Mary Charlott Perkins, 28
Routh, Matilda Jane, 33
Rowe, Jim, 11
Rucker, Edgar Pl, 120

Sanders, Sampson, 6, 161n27
Saudindge, W. H., 95
Schuyler, George S., 144
Scott, Boston, 103
Scott, D. B., 15
Scott, George, 126

Index

Scott, J. W., 61, 65–66, 70, 77, 101, 105, 127–128; black newspapers and, 113–114, 127, 203n137; black property ownership and, 133–134, 141; political activity of, 126; self-help philosophy of, 141
scrip, 53, 179n52
Seals, Charles, 85, 113
self-help philosophy, 127, 140–141, 146
Shafer, John, 95, 176n71
Shaw, Stephanie, 123
Shelby, Almedia Duckworth, 67–68
Shelton, James, 164n44
Silas Green Company, 135, 211n93
Simmons, Carrie, 123, 128
Simmons, Conwelzie, 11
Sixteenth Street Baptist Church, 79, 130, 210n67
skilled black workers, 67
slavery, 147; in Appalachia, 158n3, 174n38; in Cabell County, 2–4, 8–9, 13, 17, 19, 147, 157n2, 163n37, 168n68; capitalism and, 159n15; "chattel principle" of, 14–15; during Civil War, 17; demographics of, 13–14, 19, 36, 168n67; discrimination faced by former slaves, 170n85; emancipation of slaves, 17–20; enslaved persons' resistance to, 9–11; free blacks and, 5–6, 15–16; Fugitive Slave Act, 165n52; at Greenbottom Plantation, 13–15, 159n18; in Greenbriar County, 173n22; at Kanawah Valley salt mines, 46, 168n67; labor performed by slaves, 15, 28, 174n40; literacy and, 3–4, 8, 12, 21, 159n11; manumission of slaves, 5–6, 160nn20–21, 161n27; Methodist Church and, 163n37; political representation and, 162n37; re-enslavement, 5, 160n19; religious observance of slaves, 9, 12, 174n38; runaway slaves, 10–11, 14, 164n44, 165n52, 166n53, 166n55, 167n56; selling of slaves' families, 13–15; sexual violence against enslaved women, 15, 20, 35, 168n77; slave population by county, 19, 36; steamboats and, 7–8, 161n33, 162n33; subcultures of resistance and, 32–33; transportation systems and, 26; trickster figure, 173n25; violence against slaves, 5, 15; westward migration and, 25–26, 37, 159n8; at White Sulphur Springs resort, 27–37, 173n32, 174n40
Smith, Lloyd G., 125
Smith, Robert S. B., 95
Smith, Rush, 66, 131
Smith, Walter A., 125
Smith, W. T., 101
Socialist and Labor Star, 138
Socialist Party, 137–139, 212n107, 212n113
South Carolina, 20
Spencer, Susan, x, 6
sports leagues, 107; black coaches of, 125–126
Stanford, Leland, 24
Starks, Samuel W., 110
Stealey, John E., 8
steamboats, 7–8, 161n33, 162n36, 172n8
Stephens, John, 87
Stewart, Mina E., 126
Strauder v. West Virginia, 91
strikes, 48, 53, 60, 178n34, 179n51, 181n89
subcultures of resistance, 32–33
Sullivan, Charles Kenneth, 45
"sundown towns," 121, 206n27
Swallow, Hiram H., 8
Swann-Wright, Dianne, 39

Talbott, Forrest, 17
Tarr, Edward, 25
Taylor, Henry Louis, 76, 185n12
Taylor, Nikki M., 89, 164n48
teaching certification, 195n62
Tennessee, 20
Thayer, Eli, 10–11, 166n55
Thirteenth Amendment, 18
Thomas, William, 67
Thompson, John J., 74
Thompson, Maggie A. W., 108
Thurston, S. A., 126
Tillman, Ben "Pitchfork," 126
tobacco production, 39
trickster figure, 173n25
Trotter, Joe W., 59
Tucker, Elijah and Virginia, 44
Tucker, Jenny, 94
Turner, Belle, 103
Turner, Marcellus, 65
Twyman, James "Pap," 6

Underground Railroad, 5, 10–11; African Americans' centrality in, 164n48, 165n51, 165n52; benevolent societies and, 201n109
United Mine Workers, 61, 63, 183n109

Vanderbilt, Cornelius, 54
Vinson, Frank, 66
Virginia: lynchings in, 189n80; racial composition of, 13, 20, 36; WV secession from, 23. *See also* West Virginia

Virginia Central Railroad Company, 46
Virginia Constitutional Convention, 162n37
voting, 40–41, 112, 162n37, 202n123

Wade, Howard D., 38
Walcott, Byron A., 108
Walker, W. P., 98
Washington, Booker T., 25, 34, 64, 187n45
Washington Place, 131–132, 139–140
Watson, Maggie, 56
Wayne County, 58
West Virginia: absence of Jim Crow laws in, 82–83; "benevolent segregation" in, 119, 146; black migration into, 25, 37–38, 44, 59, 78, 81, 118–119, 180n64; black schools in, 99, 198n82; coal mining in, 51–52, 55; constitution of, 110–111, 202n115; demographics of, 118–119; depression of 1873 and, 53–54; fraternal orders in, 110; labor strife in, 60; labor unions in, 63–64, 183n110; legal challenges to segregation in, 144–145; lynchings in, 91, 120–121, 205n20; political representation and, 162n37; race relations in, 120–121; racial composition of, 13, 18–20, 23, 118–119, 167n56, 171n93; railroad construction in, 45–51; secession from Virginia, 23; Socialist Party in, 137–139, 212n107, 212n113; urban growth in, 204n7; white/European immigration to, 59–60. *See also* Cabell County; Huntington, WV
West Virginia Collegiate Institute, 198n82
West Virginia Colored Orphans' Home, 108, 200n101, 201n105
West Virginia Spokesman, 113–114
West Virginia Teachers' Association, 198n82

Wheelersburg, OH, 121
Wheeling, WV, 63–64, 204n7
White, H. B., 144
White, Lewis and Cora, 144
White, William R., 99
White Sulphur Springs resort, 26–37, 172n18; black migration and, 37; during Civil War, 36–37; culture of slaves at, 27–36, 173n32; free blacks at, 34–35
white supremacy, 119
White v. White (1929), 135, 144–145
Wickham, W. C., 53
Wilberforce University, 174n37
Wiley, Waitman T., 18
Wilkins, Tom, 57
Williams, Eph, 135
Williams, William, 13
Williamson-Logan coalfield, 55
Wilson, Charles A., 112
Wilson, Charles R., 62
Wilson, George, 66, 195n61
Wilson, Theodore, 101
Wilson, Thomas, 103
Winding Gulf coalfield, 55
Witcher, Stephen, 16
Withrow, Harry, 121
Woods, Hugh O., 120
Woodson, Carter G., 40, 55, 79–80, 101, 105, 135, 204n139; education of, 103–104
Woodson, James Henry, 40, 104, 115
Woodson, Robert, 55, 79–80
work camps, 47
Wright, George C., 119–120

Yancey, James Henry, 49

CICERO M. FAIN III is a professor of history at the College of Southern Maryland.

The University of Illinois Press
is a founding member of the
Association of University Presses.

University of Illinois Press
1325 South Oak Street
Champaign, IL 61820-6903
www.press.uillinois.edu